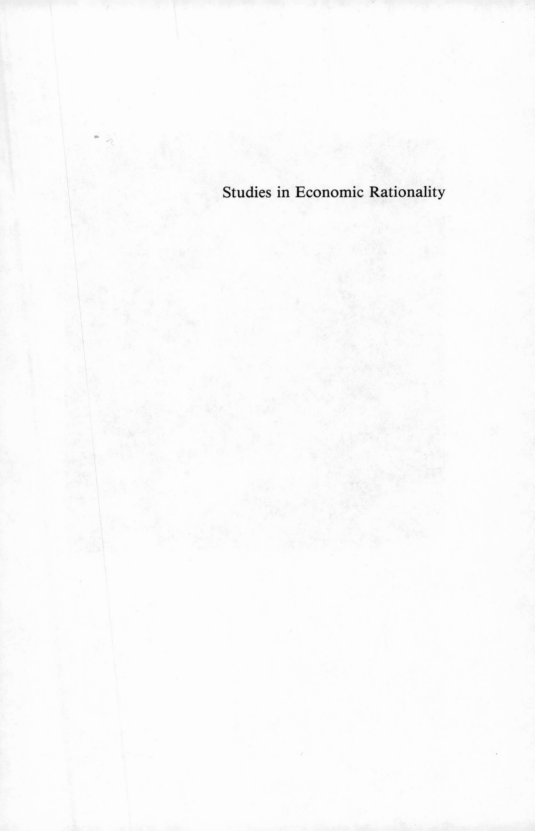

Studies in Economic Rationality

Harvey Leibenstein

Studies in
Economic Rationality
X-Efficiency Examined and Extolled

Essays written in the tradition of and to honor
HARVEY LEIBENSTEIN

Edited by
Klaus Weiermair and Mark Perlman

Ann Arbor
The University of Michigan Press

Copyright © by The University of Michigan 1990
All rights reserved
Published in the United States of America by
The University of Michigan Press
Manufactured in the United States of America

1993 1992 1991 1990   4 3 2 1

Library of Congress Cataloging-in-Publication Data

Studies in economic rationality ; X-Efficiency examined and extolled /
  edited by Klaus Weiermair and Mark Perlman.
      p.   cm.
  Includes bibliographical references.
  ISBN 0-472-10154-4 (alk. paper)
  1. Efficiency, Industrial — Congresses.   2. Microeconomics —
Congresses.   3. Comparative management — Congresses.   I. Weiermair,
Klaus, 1939-   . II. Perlman, Mark.
HC79.I52S78   1990
338.5 — dc20   89-77534
                                                                      CIP

Preface

As noted in the Introduction, this volume contains papers given at a 1988 conference on X-Efficiency.

During the planning of that conference Professor Weiermair and I anticipated that Professor Leibenstein would play an active role as a discussant, critic, and synthesizer. Our plans were overtaken by events; in August 1987 both Professor and Mrs. Leibenstein were injured in a devastating automobile accident, one that left him in a coma for the better part of several months. That he regained consciousness at all is testimony to the miraculous care provided him by trained physicians and, above all else, through the resourceful and imaginative devotion of his wife, Margaret Libnic Leibenstein. Yet, his recovery has been slow — sufficiently delayed as to warrant his retirement from the Harvard faculty.

It is appropriate for several reasons that this volume be dedicated to Harvey Leibenstein as a festschrift. First, Professor Leibenstein's roles as a creative thinker, covering work in the fields of demographic economics, macroeconomic investment policy, administrative organization, and micro-microtheory, warrant special notice being taken of his multi-faceted genius and the profound original contributions in his long career. Second, that career stretching from an undergraduate training at the Sir George Williams University in Montreal, to degrees at Northwestern and Princeton universities, with teaching appointments at Illinois Institute of Technology (where he was a junior colleague of Herbert Simon and Franco Modigliani), and then through the professorial ranks at the University of California, Berkeley, and ultimately as the first Andelot Professor of Population Economics at Harvard University, made him one of several bands of active, major scholars, first as a brilliant student and then as a cooperative colleague and as a great teacher. Third, the organization of the Bellagio conference was per se notice of the continued vitality of his ideas; a vitality that has led other scholars to work explicitly in one of the traditions created by him.

Writing as an experienced economics editor, I have long noted that the great drawback of festschriften has been their usual diffuseness of subject matter, and for that reason festschriften are usually viewed, particularly by publishers, as uneconomic honors. Yet, in the discussion with Dr. Colin Day, director of the University of Michigan Press, about using this volume as a festschrift, his immediate reaction was enthusiasm. As he noted, this is a festschrift admittedly focused on only one aspect of Professor Leibenstein's work, but, as my own essay suggests, that aspect should be seen as but part of the several that we could have used.

Years ago (1958) when Robert Frost was being given a doctorate *honoris causa* at Berkeley, he commented that he saw his individual poems, at their best, as stars, but the role of the critics and scholars who studied them was to suggest whether they formed a constellation. Leibenstein's work is, in my view, clearly a constellation; yet, his X-efficiency star is one of great magnitude; it has shone, shines, and will shine in the future very bright, indeed.

Mark Perlman

Contents

Introduction
Klaus Weiermair and Mark Perlman   1

Part 1. Micro-Microtheory Revisited

The Evolution of Leibenstein's X-Efficiency Theory
Mark Perlman   7

X-Efficiency and Contestability Theory: A Clash of
Paradigms?
John Hatch   27

Ex-Ante and Ex-Post Criticisms of X-Efficiency Theory
and Literature
Roger S. Frantz   43

Commentary
Klaus Weiermair and Marvin E. Rozen   63

Part 2. Motivational Foundations of Economic Behavior

Human Behavior: Ipsative and Objective Possibilities
Bruno S. Frey   71

X-Efficiency, Implicit Contracting, and the Theory of
the Firm
Marvin E. Rozen   95

Supply of Incentives and Demand for Motivation:
A Microanalysis
Klaus Weiermair   127

Commentary
Friedrich Fürstenberg   147

Part 3. The Design and Structuring of Organizations

Norms, Convention, and the Design of Organizations
Friedrich Fürstenberg   153

The Patterning of Work Meanings That Are Coterminus
with Work Outcome Levels for Individuals and
Organizations in Japan, West Germany, and the United
States
   George W. England   165

On the Foundations of Socio-Behavioral Economics:
X-Efficiency as Standard, Norm, and Actual Behavior
   Kurt Dopfer   181

Commentary
   Bruno S. Frey   199

Part 4. Organizational Adaptation and Change

X-Efficiency, Transaction Costs, and Organizational
Change
   Claudio U. Ciborra   205

Commentary
   R. C. O. Matthews   223

**Part 5. Normative Implications of X-Efficiency in Business
Strategy and Governmental Policies**

The Impact of the Income Tax on Work Effort and
X-Inefficiency in Enterprises
   Armin Bohnet and Martin Beck   227

The Charitable Nonprofit Sector: X-Efficiency, Resource
Allocation, and Organization
   R. C. O. Matthews   253

The Competitive Position of British Industry: Are
Nonprice Factors a Problem and Is X-Inefficiency the
Cause?
   Arthur Francis   277

Institutions, X-Efficiency, Transaction Costs, and
Socioeconomic Development
   Erik Thorbecke   295

Commentary
   Klaus Weiermair and J. H. Hatch   315

Part 6. Measurement Problems

Interfirm, Interregional, and International
Differences in Labor Productivity:
Variations in the Levels of X-Inefficiency as a Function
of Differential Labor Costs
  Morris Altman   323

On the Measurement of the Relative Efficiency of a Set
of Decision-Making Units
  Wade D. Cook, Ya'akov Roll, and Alex Kazakov   351

Commentary
  R. C. O. Matthews   369

**Part 7. Summary and the Outlook for X-Efficiency
Theory**

X-Efficiency: Past, Present, and Future
  Roger S. Frantz   373

Index   391

Introduction

Klaus Weiermair and Mark Perlman

Part of the hubris of our discipline is a belief that microeconomic theory has reached the high plateau of sophistication. "In any intellectual field of inquiry there are subjects that are mature and subjects in their infancy, and the classical theory [*sic*] of the consumer and the firm must be counted as mature subjects" (Varian 1987, 463). Yet, Varian goes on to note that principal among the failings of modern microeconomics are imperfections in the understanding of competition and information.

> What does the future hold? It seems to me that the current "infant" subject of microeconomics is the research that is examining the "micro-microeconomics" of firms, consumers and markets. By this I mean the investigations that attempt to go behind the "black box" of the neoclassical firm, consumer and market, and try to understand the internal functioning of these economic institutions. (Ibid.)

The recent and ongoing process of economic restructuring in many industrialized and industrializing countries reveals ever again the increased importance of *variations* in human effort and *discretionary* behavior on the part of both workers and management in dealing and coping with accelerated technological change, global competition, and altered social values. Thus, in a significant way, a 1988 symposium on "Efficiency, Internal Organization, and Comparative Management," based on Leibenstein's path-breaking X-efficiency paradigm, came at an opportune time. For the orthodox assumptions of "narrowly defined maximizing behavior" contained in much of neoclassical economics have rarely come under a greater attack than currently. That much of this attack comes to economics from such neighboring disciplines as management theory, industrial psychology, and organizational theory does not make it in any way less meaningful. At the same time voices within the economics discipline have regularly been calling for "more relevant, realistic, and imaginative" theorems in dealing with microeconomic behavior. In this regard X-efficiency theory is seen to hold great promise, and, for this reason, this symposium, held in Bellagio (Como), Italy, during May 1988, was organized to explore further the applicability of the X-efficiency paradigm to a number of interrelated and unanswered questions and problems in the economic theory of the firm.

The full conference proceedings, with one exception, form the content of this volume. In Part 1 the first three articles by Perlman, Hatch, and Frantz place Leibenstein and his theorizing in the context of both traditional and experimental economics. Perlman's article presents the development of Leibenstein's interests and works, the influence of his teachers who shaped much of his subsequent analyses and concerns, and the manner in which his work fits into the history of economic thought. Hatch shows the relationship between X-efficiency theory and other activities on the frontiers of economic research, notably the theory of contestable markets. And Frantz's article on ex-ante and ex-post theorizing and X-efficiency gives a general account of critical discussions of X-efficiency concepts within the post-Keynesian (really the post-Myrdalian) economics literature.

The articles of Frey, Rozen, and Weiermair in Part 2 share the common theme that traditional economics has lacked certain relevant behavioral concepts ordinarily housed in the disciplines of sociology and psychology. Frey's use of "ipsative" (i.e., subjective) as opposed to objective possibility sets and associated maximizing behavior reflects his explorations. Rozen offers relational exchanges and/or implicit contracts as additional paths to understanding. And Weiermair suggests "other-regarding" behavior as a complement to the Leibensteinian X-efficiency theory in order to develop theoretical constructs that enrich various amalgams of economic and psychological theorizing. Part 3 addresses the issue of selective behavior within the context of norms and conventions and, as such, it discusses the role of norms in the structuring and design of organizations. Scope and methodology vary considerably in this section. Fürstenberg demonstrates the role and importance of norms and conventions in the structuring and functions of organizations beyond pure economic explanations of exchange and maximizing behavior. England presents an empirical account on international variations in discretionary (X-efficiency) work effort and work values. And, finally, Dopfer offers an epistomological treatment of normative behavior, discussed in terms of both received and new economic doctrine.

The contribution in Part 4 is designed to explore X-efficiency considerations under conditions of organizational adaptation and change. Ciborra, basing his report on competing theories of transaction costs and X-efficiency, presents insights concerning the nature of organizational inertia and organizational change.

Part 5 turns the focus to applications of X-efficiency theory particularly as they relate to public policy issues. First, Bohnet and Beck use the X-efficiency theory to show the effect of changes in income taxes on the effort of workers and management. They also discuss the effect of tax changes on output and profits. Next, Matthews renders an interesting account in which he discusses the application of X-efficiency and inefficiency in a particular sector of British nonprofit organizations. Francis's article follows; he presents a general analysis of X-efficiency in British industry and its consequences for international competitiveness. Thorbecke's article explores differing institutional and organizational arrangements within and between firms in a sample of developing countries and analyzes the impact of these arrangements on X-efficiency and ultimately on the process of socioeconomic development. In so doing he provides both an additional appraisal of the position and status quo of the X-efficiency paradigm within the realm of economic theories dealing with institutional change as well as a convenient feedback loop to the general questions and concerns of X-inefficiency raised throughout the proceedings, particularly as they relate to contemporary economic theorizing.

Part 6 considers measurement questions and concludes with a discussion of the outlook with respect to the status quo and further development of X-efficiency theory. Altman attempts to demonstrate that in certain situations X-efficiency can be present even under conditions of perfect competition in the product market. He argues that relatively low wages in certain firms can shelter the relative X-inefficient firms and, thus, permit X-inefficiency. Cook, Roll, and Kazakov use a data envelopment analysis to delineate efficiency frontiers in nonprofit organizations and to detect varying levels of X-inefficiency. Finally, in Part 7, Frantz's concluding article displays a perception of the research agenda for those working in the X-efficiency theory area.

It is clear that the great part of this symposium dealt with the consequences of Leibenstein's X-efficiency theory. Yet, we cannot omit particular reference to Professor Harvey Leibenstein, the scholar. Having been all but fatally injured in an automobile accident in the late summer of 1987, he could not attend the conference at Bellagio and was unable to comment on the articles. For those there, as well as all economists alert to his magnificent contributions on several frontiers of economic theorizing, these absences are matters of personal and collective regret. Yet, his slow but steady return to health has been one of the great examples of discipline and devotion of our time. We dedicate the volume to him and to his wife, Marjorie.

We also wish to thank the Rockefeller Foundation for its generous and luxuriant hospitality at the historic Villa Serbelloni; particularly we thank Miss Susan Garfield (New York) and Mr. and Mrs. Robert Celli (Villa Serbelloni, Bellagio) for their cooperation and high standards of professional assistance. And we thank the Directors of the Earhart Foundation (Ann Arbor), Mr. Robert Kennedy (its president) and the other officers of that foundation for a substantial grant, which helped to make the whole effort (including the editing of this manuscript) a successful reality. Similarly, we would like to thank the director of the Fritz Thyssen Foundation in Cologne, West Germany, Dr. R. Kerscher, for a generous grant which helped defray a substantial portion of the travel costs.

Part 1
Micro-Microtheory Revisited

The Evolution of Leibenstein's X-Efficiency Theory

Mark Perlman

Introduction

This article has three substantive parts. In the first the theory is presented. The second offers my understanding of the evolution of Leibenstein's thinking: (1) From the time (before 1950) when he was examining methods for showing the interaction of individual consumer demand schedules; (2) through the development of his concern for relating population needs to optimal national investment policy; and (3) to the point where his attention turned to micro-microeconomic theory. The third part places X-efficiency theory in the stream of the history of economic thought.

The X-Efficiency Theory

Among the most recent efforts Professor Leibenstein has made to expound his ideas about X-efficiency theory is the description he wrote in *The New Palgrave* (1987). The "concept" of X-efficiency, he writes, is one thing; the "theory" explaining it is another.

The concept refers to a regularly observable phenomenon. It is that firms not only perform their productive functions with considerable "preventable" waste, but that if one looks only at the "molecular" unit (i.e., the firm) one misses an important area of preventable waste. It is the interactive, but somewhat constrained, economically bargained decision making among "atomistic" individuals within the firm.

X-efficiency theory is an effort to explain this phenomenon at all levels. This loss to the firm (deviation from the "optimal") is not only a result of technical (i.e., technological) incompetence (refusal to abandon outmoded equipment and systems as well as other manifestations of psychological inertia, or cultural or individual sloth); it also is a result of an inability and/or an unwillingness to achieve (or is perhaps a breakdown of) fully specified organizational (contractual) relationships and obligations, rights and responsibilities, coordination and focus.

In Leibenstein's words, as edited:

X-efficiency theory represents a line of reasoning based on postulates that differ from standard micro theory. . . . The postulates of the theory . . . [are:]
[First:] *Relaxing Maximizing Behavior*: . . . it is assumed that some forms of decision making, such as . . . habits, conventions, moral imperatives, standard procedures, or emulation, . . . can be and frequently are of a non-maximizing nature. . . . not depend-[ing] on careful calculation. . . . Other decisions attempt at maximizing utility. In order to deal with the max/non-max mixture we use . . . [the] psychological . . . Yerkes-Dodson Law, . . . at low pressure levels individuals will not put much effort into carefully calculating their decisions, but as pressure builds they move toward more maximizing behavior. At some point too much pressure can result in disorientation and a lower level of decision performance.
[Second:] *Inertia*: . . . functional relations are surrounded by inert areas, within which changes in certain values of the independent variables do not result in changes of the dependent variable.
[Third:] *Incomplete Contracts*: . . . the employment contract is incomplete in that the payment side is fairly well specified, but the effort side remains mostly unspecified.
[Fourth:] *Discretion*: . . . [the] employees have effort discretion within certain boundaries, and . . . top management has discretion with respect to working conditions and some aspects of wages.
. . . the employees on the one side and management on the other . . . both jointly determine the outcome. Thus, . . . [there is] a latent Prisoner's Dilemma problem. . . .
In general the Prisoner's Dilemma problem solution will be avoided . . . [because] a system of conventions which depends on the history of human relations within the firm is likely to lead to an outcome that is usually intermediate between the Prisoner's Dilemma outcome and the optimal solution.
. . . [F]or every effort option that employees choose the firm will want to choose the minimum wages and working conditions, . . . Similarly, for every . . . working condition level . . . the firm chooses, the employees will want [their minimum tolerated working-condition-level]. This . . . [would be] the Prisoner's Dilemma outcome, which . . . is not likely. . . . However, this adversarial-relations problem between employees and managers is compounded by another free-rider problem. Every employee has a free-rider

incentive to move to the [his tolerated] minimum level . . ., even though he or she might want others to work effectively. . . . overall effort would be reduced to the minimum if they all followed their individual self-interest. Clearly, . . . individual rationality cannot solve the Prisoner's Dilemma problem. Something akin to "group rationality" . . . is required to achieve an improved solution.

. . . [C]onventions should be viewed as solutions to multiequilibrium, coordination problems, and . . . can provide superior solutions to the Prisoner's Dilemma outcome. . . . A coordinated solution is superior to an uncoordinated outcome. However, the various [possible] coordinated solutions . . . need not be equally good.

. . . [E]ffort . . . and working-conditions conventions can bring about a non-Prisoner's Dilemma solution. . . . Thus, the effort convention is a coordinated solution . . . superior to uncoordinated individual behavior. Similar remarks hold for managerial decisions. Of course, the . . . [minimum-working condition level] has to be viable in the sense that it must represent a long-run profitable outcome, although not necessarily the maximum profit level.

There is a difference between the creation of a convention and adherence to it. . . . [C]reation may come [from] . . . leadership of some managers, . . . some employees, or . . . some initial effort levels being chosen arbitrarily. Once established, a convention reduces the flexibility of employees' behavior. Thus, new employees will adhere to the convention, and possibly support it through sanctions on others.

Although stable to small changes of its independent variables, an effort convention need not stay at its initial level indefinitely. The concept of inert areas suggests that a large enough shock can destabilize a convention. Once destabilized it is no longer clear whether the dynamics of readjustment will lead to a superior or inferior situation for both sides, or a situation under which one side gains at the expense of the other. Such considerations (and fears) help to stabilize the convention.

. . . [U]nder low-pressure conditions the postulate of nonmaximizing behavior . . . [explains] why firm members may stick with their conventions and impose supporting sanctions even in situations where they would be better off not doing so. Non-calculating, situation-response behavior helps to shore up the convention-solution to the Prisoner's Dilemma problem, and to shore up the persistence of nonoptimal conventions . . . [and] helps to explain the existence and persistence of X-inefficient behavior. (1987, 934–35)

I draw on some of his other writings to expand the foregoing material. His emphasis on micro-microanalysis, as indicated, puts the spotlight on the reaction of atomistic individual motivation to various kinds of constraints. As noted, within every economic unit there are numerous individuals, each of whom prefers to do his or her own thing. But what can be said about that "thing"? It is a compromise between what the individual accepts as something with which he or she is culturally comfortable, which he or she personally prefers, and whatever must be done if the job is to be retained and/or the firm is to survive. What is true of workers as individuals is comparably true of management as individuals and even owners as individuals. Thus, those employing the X-efficiency theory (unlike most economists) recognize the profession's basic unit, the firm, as a molecular *aggregate*, made up of individualistic atoms compressed under various kinds of pressure.

Under usual conditions these molecular aggregates operate at less than maximum efficiency because there are abounding disparate atomistic individual motivations (incomplete contractual specification permitting greater choice by the worker, inertia leading to the ignoring of rule breaking, and/or nature of the job allowing more or less personal discretion, which permits individuals to choose their levels of effort). Under certain unusual conditions, particularly those arising from changes in external pressures such as price competition from other firms, the firm is forced to reduce costs. The freedom for these disparate motivations to interact is then reduced, and the pressure to develop a lower cost system is increased. The very economic survival of the firm may require that what individuals *like* or *ought* to offer in the way of output gives way to what they feel they *must* offer. This shift to unusual conditions, whatever may precipitate it, means that management decides that neither it nor the workers can be left to follow former procedures. It could also mean that the owners (shareholders) can come to the same conclusion about management.

All of this goes beyond a mere power struggle. X-efficiency theory also states that even under pressure there are inert areas surrounding the existent levels of effort. These inert areas reflect the disutility of effort; the benefit to be gained by the change must exceed the cost of changing, or else the effort level will remain the same. Leibenstein defines "inert areas" as areas of choice that are left untouched for a variety of quite different reasons ranging from a sheer inability to penetrate to the high costs of penetration. There are, however, problems of bargaining standoff. These come under the game theoretic Prisoner's Dilemma rubric.

Under usual conditions firms produce and consume without much serious attention to leakages in the output stream.[1] Insofar as the usual output varies from the unusual or "might have been," assuming identical cost inputs are the same for the two contrasting sets of conditions, we can estimate quantitatively X-inefficiency, or the amount lost by the firm because of the impact of this aspect of worker and management individualism. That loss is X-inefficiency; or to put the matter the other way around, we can identify and estimate this "X-efficiency gain" as the product of stringent pressure.

One point of X-efficiency theory is that firms do not maximize because each firm's managers are not completely in command of the full spectrum of the decision-making process. Management must cope with each worker's motivation preferences, and in some instances the latter are so complex, even contradictory at points, that a best outcome is no more than management's collective (but no less subjective) conclusion that it has done as much as it can and (whatever that was) it was good enough to keep the firm economically afloat. Firms do not maximize because true maximization requires a level of control not consistent with free will. In Part 4, we shall return to this point since it is a differentiating aspect from the sets of reasons offered by others for firms not truly maximizing.

The Evolution of Leibenstein's Thinking

In *Who's Who in Economics*, Leibenstein describes his contribution as:

The microeconomics of human fertility, and X-efficiency theory (the non-allocative aspects of inefficiency). The latter attempts to develop a mode of analysis which relaxes the maximization assumption of conventional micro-theory, and substitutes postulates under which individuals are non-maximizers when there is little pressure on them, approaching maximizing behavior as external pressure increases. Behavior according to convention is an important aspect of this approach. Also, current research involves the application of the Prisoner's Dilemma paradigm to normal economic behavior. (Blaug 1986, 508)

---

1. I see no reason why X-efficiency theory should not be adapted to the purchasing and consuming activities of the household. Indeed, what is amazing is the number of times Mitchell's "backward art" has been republished and cited without anyone mentioning the underlying rationality conditions (cf. Mitchell 1912).

Prior to the X-Efficiency Theory

Going into and beyond any author's description of his own work to present an interpretation of the underlying thinking process, including assumptions and methodological preferences, is hazardous. One does it not only because of strong personal feelings of interest in helping to make the author more generally understood,[2] but also from a pedagogical commitment that by so interpreting an author one links his views with other similar but not identical views: "In my Father's house there are many mansions."

Leibenstein's X-efficiency theory can be seen in a variety of ways, and I would not expect that others will necessarily see either his contribution, or the way it emerged, along the precise lines I suggest. But, nonetheless, I present the theory from my vantage point first as a sequel to his earlier research programs, second as his novel approach to microeconomics, and third as reflecting a set of generally agreeable (to me) methodological preferences.

Scholars must and should go beyond their teachers, but the influence of certain teachers often remains. So it is with Leibenstein, who went well beyond what he had been given in class or otherwise. The impact of two of his Princeton professors, Oskar Morgenstern and Frank Notestein, seems to me to have been there from the beginning of his publications. I intuit that Morgenstern's influence has lasted longer — it shaped (or perhaps reinforced) Leibenstein's perception of what theory was about ("providing a framework for understanding"), the role of subjectivity in contrast to "objective rationality,"[3] and a taste for the

2. I provided a forum for Leibenstein to discuss two of the critical elements in his X-efficiency theory — his criticisms of simpleminded rationality and his judgment that those who write on the theory of the firm have focused on an inappropriate level of aggregation (Leibenstein 1974b, 1979a).

3. Part of Leibenstein's disassociation from neoclassical economics reflects the impact of Morgenstern's own brand of Austrian economics. In the flow of ideas, early Austrian economics came to stand for many things: the role of subjectivity, the importance of demand from which was derived supplies of consumer goods from which were derived supplies of higher order goods; resistance to mathematical formulations; a strong preference for free markets; and an opposition to socialism, etc. Morgenstern was intellectually very independent and differed greatly from many of his contemporary Austrians. For one thing, he was, from early on, interested in quantification and headed a private research organization studying business cycles. For another, he came to represent one type of formalism — the mathematics involved in the point theorem and game theory. What stands out about Morgenstern's brand of Austrian economics was its concern with how choices were made, particularly on the demand side. While not all of the questions on which Leibenstein has written have that as the dominant theme, his work on the interdependence of consumer choice, human fertility, and, derivatively, X-efficiency theory does.

kinds of demonstrations now associated with game theory and/or with experimental economics.

The Morgenstern influence came through clearly in Leibenstein's lengthy multifaceted 1950 essay, "Bandwagon, Snob, and Veblen Effects in the Theory of Consumers' Demand." This article established Leibenstein's reputation and reveals (in my judgment, at least) the complex intertwining of ideas and exposition that has made his contribution into a strong and original intellectual strand.

Although Leibenstein started that article with an incorrect Morgenstern assertion that the market demand curve cannot be a summation of individual curves, the point of his effort was to show how one could construct a market demand curve illustrating interdependent as well as independent consumer preferences. In the process Leibenstein differentiated goods wanted for the direct utility services they provide from goods wanted for ancillary (self-identification) reasons.

This differentiation was achieved by suggesting an experiment; different consumers were initially to be asked how much of a particular good or service each wanted at a variety of prices. Each consumer was then asked how much he or she would take if others' preference schedules were made known. Leibenstein conjectured that if an individual augmented a previously independently derived demand for any good upon learning that others shared the preference, that good had a "bandwagon" quality. If that same bit of knowledge led to a reduced desire for the good, the result was a "snob" effect. There was also the possibility of a Veblen effect, which suggested that consumption, per se, of a good might carry some form of special prestige rather than utility; as such it was slightly different from the snob effect.

One important contribution was Leibenstein's proposed ingenious method of iterative questioning so that dependence or independence of response could be assured. It anticipated much of what is now occurring in the new subfield of experimental economics.

That article presented the Leibenstein argument in two modes; one was literary, as in the Marshallian "main text" form. The other was geometrical, as in the Marshallian footnote but also as in the Joan Robinson main text style. I shall refer to this point later; it goes to the Leibenstein choice of rhetoric.

His dissertational effort was more in the Notestein tradition (Leibenstein 1951). Notestein's interest was in problems, not in analytical modes. Notestein's problem was the question of too high birthrates. His method was generalization, and he is best known to a generation of American demographers for his attachment to the Demographic Transition hypothesis (in industrialized societies increases in life expectancy [lower death rates for every cohort group] precede lower fertility [and birth] rates by about a generation).

Leibenstein's 1957 book, *Economic Backwardness and Economic Growth*, is something of an outgrowth of his dissertation (Leibenstein 1951) as well as its 1954 adaption, *A Theory of Economic Demographic Development*.[4] Once again, the Leibenstein interest in the interdependency of individual preferences, manifested in a desire for personal [household] economic improvement, holds center stage. For reasons of brevity it suffices here to add only that understanding both the role of individual motivation and the fact that there are limits to human understanding about oneself (to say nothing about others) are clearly the points of entry to his work.

During this period Leibenstein worked with Walter Galenson on topics of national production functions (considered timely during the 1950s).[5] Conventional wisdom, challenged by them, was that backward (a term then used without embarrassment) countries with high levels of disguised unemployment (that is underutilized, particularly low-wage labor) were not well-advised to introduce labor-intensive manufacturing methods (Galenson and Leibenstein 1955). Rather, if they wanted to enter international markets they were wise to look for state-of-the-art technology.[6] This conclusion was consistent with the point that individual motivation was the key to competitive economic performance; if individual motivation was a general social problem, then, of course, capital substitution for labor made great programmatic sense. What emerged was a pattern of differential national productivity increases. That was *the* phenomenon of the time.[7] But underlying their whole

---

4. Interest in the determinants of fertility choices persists. Whether it was the source of his interest in X-efficiency theory or has merely paralleled it is unimportant. But much of Leibenstein's bibliography comes under the heading of demographic economics (cf. Leibenstein 1962, 1964, 1974b, 1974c, 1975b, 1975c, 1976a, 1976b, 1977a, 1977b, 1978a, 1979c, 1980b, 1981a).

5. Macroeconomics was emerging during the post–World War II period. It turned attention to the work done on aggregate national constant-returns-to-scale production functions by Paul Douglas and Charles Cobb.

6. Part of the professional reaction they encountered was that this approach was exactly the hard-line "little-or-nothing-for-consumers" policy that Stalin had pursued. Both men had always been anti-Stalinist. Their conclusions, implying that there was a hard logic to Stalin's cruel investment policy, came as something of a surprise. Many first reactions found expression in strong (if irrelevantly derived) criticism of them. Leibenstein spent a great deal of time refuting critics (cf. Leibenstein 1958, 1960b, 1962, 1963, 1966b).

7. Note the date; it was the era of fine-tuning. In that period the concept of a U.S. annual productivity increase of about 4 percent was accepted almost as a given. Fabricant and others spoke of growth cycles having replaced business cycles.

analysis was the premise that empirical evaluations (by their nature ex post) provided a kind of knowledge that could not be expected to exist ex ante.

I see Leibenstein's 1960 book, *Economic Theory and Organizational Analysis*, as reflecting his mind in midpassage. He seems to have been organizing intellectually what others had written and what he made of it.[8]

The Development of the X-Efficiency Theory

Leibenstein's work on X-efficiency surfaced in the *American Economic Review* in 1966 under what ex post was a transitional title, "Allocative Efficiency vs. 'X'-Efficiency." It drew heavily on the work of many scholars trying to identify the losses in potential growth due to various kinds of traditional misallocations by management. These, Leibenstein concluded, were quantitatively trivial, ". . . frequently no more than 1/10 of 1 percent" (Leibenstein 1966, 397). But growth fluctuated much more than that small amount. What caused it? The answers, X-inefficiency as well as X-efficiency, are mentioned in passing without any effort at definition except the implication that they are due to "managements [not] bestirring themselves sufficiently, [unless] the environment forces them to do so. . . ."[9] His data were drawn largely from LDCs, with considerable emphasis put on episodic reports. His conclusion reflects an early formative state of the theory.

> [There are] three reasons for X-inefficiency. . . . These are (a) contracts for labor are incomplete, (b) the production function is not completely specified or known, and (c) not all inputs are marketed or, if marketed, are not available on equal terms to all buyers.
> . . . [F]or a variety of reasons people and organizations normally work neither as hard nor as effectively as they could. In situations where competitive pressure is light, many people will trade the disutility of greater effort, of search, and the control of other people's

---

8. A 1962 article, "Notes on Welfare Economics and the Theory of Democracy," seems to me to have reflected a more original and formative type of thinking. In it Leibenstein introduces the concept of "consent areas," perhaps a forerunner, albeit negatively phrased, of what later he was to term "inert areas."

9. The X-factor might well have referred to the unknown or residual factor in trying to explain the high U.S. annual productivity growth rate. In the course of my work, I have found many claims to being the first to note that unexplained residual. I am inclined to credit Professor Abramovitz with having been the last to have discovered the unexplained phenomenon; thereafter, it stayed discovered.

activities for the utility of feeling less pressure and of better interpersonal relations. But in situations where competitive pressures are high, and hence the costs of such trades are also high . . . [t]wo general types of movements are possible. One is . . . towards greater allocative efficiency and the other . . . involves greater degrees of X-efficiency. The data suggest that [often] the amount to be gained by increasing allocative efficiency is trivial while the amount to be gained by increasing X-efficiency is frequently significant." (Leibenstein 1966a, 412–13)

In the years that followed, Leibenstein expanded his X-efficiency theory, partly in response to comments on it and partly due to his desire to differentiate it from the work of others.[10] In 1975 the *Bell Journal* published a more polished rendition of the theory (Leibenstein 1975a). *Inter alia*, it also distinguished Leibenstein's theme from Herbert Simon's idea of firms maximizing within areas of bounded rationality and the Cyert-March thesis that firms found it irrational (or uneconomic) to fight currently dominant institutions (City Hall and certainly unions).

Two of Leibenstein's books (1976a and 1978a) came out in the late 1970s with the apparent intention of trying to present his whole thinking in detail. As I read them, the first was a major effort at locating his ideas within the profession's general perception of economic theorizing; I shall return to this aspect of X-efficiency theory in the next section. The second book was an application of X-efficiency theory within the stream of development economics. *De gustibus non disputandem est*, but the tightness of the applied argument found in the latter, has, for me at least, a special appeal. Whenever asked, I recommend it as the best formulation of X-efficiency theory for the nonspecialist.

In 1978, Leibenstein published two particularly sharply focused articles on his theory. One, a reply to the voice of price-theory orthodoxy by Professor George Stigler, presents in good natured (if biting) prose — almost matching Stigler's own style (Stigler 1976), Leibenstein's abhorrence of attempts to fit his theory into the Procrustean bed of the original Marshallian price systems legacy (Leibenstein 1978c).

The other is Leibenstein's assertion of the X-efficiency theory "while standing on one foot" (1978b):

. . . In a budgetary permissive environment the looser the ERC_j [effort responsibility consequence for any firm member j], for all j

10. Cf. Leibenstein 1969, 1972, 1973, 1974a, 1977c, 1980a, 1980b, 1981b, 1981c, 1981d, 1982a, 1982b, 1982c, 1983a, 1983b, 1985a, 1985b.

on the average, the greater the degree of X-inefficiency (i.e., the excess of actual over minimum cost) (331).

Leibenstein's general efforts, in my opinion, reached a more condensed, if not a new or higher, plane in his 1979 article, "A Branch of Economics is Missing: Micro-Micro Theory" (Leibenstein 1979a). There he discusses five important elements in his theory:

- Selective rationality (degree of maximization deviation). This relates to individual decisions regarding the degree to which deviation, reflecting a variety of inner and external pressures, from the firm's goals occur. These are spelled out and then diagramed.
- Individuals are basic decision-making units. Each individual joining the firm gets all sorts of signals from his peer group, from the hierarchy, and from historical influences.
- Effort discretion. Of course, in addition to all of these signals (or perhaps underlying them) is a set of economic pressures on the firm.
- Inert areas. Here habit takes over. Unless the firm's goals are dominant to the point of pure dictatorship, nothing changes.
- Organizational entropy. The management must struggle using centripetal integrative energy against the centrifugal individualistic forces. Failure can occur.

In a second article published in 1979, Leibenstein used tabular presentation, employed elsewhere, to contrast his theory (1979b, 129). This is worth reproduction (table 1).

Since 1979 Leibenstein has written several other books and essays. Some have been additions, often in response to comments in journals (1980a, 1980b, 1981b, 1981c, 1982a, 1982c, 1983a, 1985a, 1985b). Others have tied X-efficiency to such theoretical *Gestalts* as the economic theory of contracts (1982c), game theory (1981d, 1982c) and the general theory of management of organizations and management (1987a). The degree of the refinement increases, but the general outlines had been presented earlier.

X-Efficiency Theory in the History of Economic Thought

There are many ways for perceiving the Leibenstein X-efficiency contribution. I propose handling only three of them: as containing elements of the Marshallian partial equilibrium neoclassical analysis; as containing

18   Studies in Economic Rationality

TABLE 1. X-Efficiency Theory and Neoclassical Theory

Components	X-Efficiency Theory	Neoclassical Theory
Psychology	Selective rationality	Maximization or minimization[a]
Contracts	Incomplete[b]	Complete
Effort	Discretionary variable[c]	Assumed given
Units	Individuals	Households and firms
Inert areas	Important variable[d]	None
Agent principal	Differential interests	Identity of interests

a In neoclassical theory: "we [have] ended up with the unalloyed jewel known as the market in general equilibrium. In such a market the firm becomes a trivial and indeterminate entity. If prices of inputs and outputs are known and if the menu of techniques that translates inputs into outputs is known, then the firm can be presumed to behave quite mechanically" [Leibenstein 1979b, 128].

bIn x-efficiency theory — "Contracts are incomplete [and] . . . are likely to be asymmetrical. . . . The payment is . . . specified, but the work part is not" (1979b, 130).

cIn x-efficiency theory — The effort variable is "made up of . . . (A) activities chosen, (P) the pace of carrying out the activities, (Q) the quality of activities, and (T) the time sequence aspect. Assuming that A, P, Q, and T can be assigned values, we can then visualize the vector APQT as an effort point" (1979b, 130).

dIn x-efficiency theory — "We posit the existence of a psychological *inertial* cost of moving from one [effort] position to another. Thus an individual who finds himself in one effort position may not move to a superior effort position because the inertial cost is greater than the utility gain. Inertial cost should be viewed as a personality characteristic. An individual who is a maximizer would have zero inertial costs" (1979b, 130).

elements of Austrian subjectivism as modified by such later writers as Morgenstern and Hayek as well as by that unlikely intellectual "partner," the American institutionalists; and as a much hungered-for extension of the answer to *das Adam Smith Problem*.

Marshall

Although neoclassical economics is associated these days with Hicks-Samuelson-Solow, Leibenstein basically draws on Marshall. The Marshallian and Pigovian level of abstraction was intentionally lower than that employed by Hicks and, for the most part, by Samuelson and Solow.

What Marshall thought economics was all about was how men in their ordinary pursuits of livelihood made decisions; he deliberately eschewed formal exposition, noting that intangibles were critically apparent in that decision-making process. Formal exposition, as seen by

Marshall, was relegated to footnotes, where it did not interfere with the flow of his thinking but could be used as an explanatory device.

Leibenstein's thinking as well as his pedagogical preferences seem to parallel Marshall's. Moreover, his method (choice of rhetoric) has that same quality of episodic empiricism (with a historical dimension). He shies from the formalism of simple (purely rational) maximization, as found in mathematics, not only because it requires specification where specification (of intangibles) is impossible, but also because it employs a level of abstraction that negates the purpose of the analysis. Neither for Marshall nor for Leibenstein is a reasonable man necessarily logical; their man, having a mind influenced by cognition as well as imagination, lives in a dynamic and disequilibrating world and does his "level best" (which is a good measure short of perfect). Their reasonable man bases his decisions on habit, on his incomplete and otherwise imperfect subjective perceptions of his internal (cf. superego) pressures, and on what he must bend to because of the superiority of forces he cannot easily manage (or manage at all).

In the development of the history of economic thought, Marshall's preferred example of the firm in competition was supplanted by firms in some other relation to the market. It is often forgotten that his *Principles of Economics* was essentially an unfinished production and that Marshall clearly noted in its mathematical appendix that conditions of increasing returns not only vitiated his simple competitive model theoretically but also in actual fact. This point is commonly credited to Piero Sraffa and was popularized by Joan Robinson. But her method was far more abstract than Marshall's generally was. In terms of preferred rhetoric, Edward H. Chamberlin's was closer to the level of observed fact; Leibenstein's rhetoric (where he has the space) is also close to the level of observed fact. However, in deference to the mores of our profession at the time of his own graduate training, Leibenstein usually lays out his argument in the text in geometric (formal) terms—Mrs. Robinson's impact. In his *Beyond Economic Man*, Peter J. Kalman coauthored with him a formal statement of the theory, employing much of the rhetoric of symbolic logic: "Toward a Mathematical Formalization of X-Efficiency" (1976a).[11]

What makes X-efficiency theory so Marshallian neoclassical is something else as well. It is the role of attitude and how it is generated (created, manipulated, and handled by incentive systems). Leibenstein's interest in individuals' motivations is central to his perception of the

---

11. A much earlier effort at formal exposition was made by William S. Comanor and Leibenstein (1969).

whole economic process—not only of production but also of distribution. Individuals, Leibenstein concludes, do not and often cannot maximize.

Earlier economists offered other reasons for the failure to maximize: (1) Maximizing is perceived as economically too expensive (cf. Herbert Simon's costs of information and "satisficing"); (2) maximization is theoretically impossible—absent ex-ante perfect knowledge, there is no path to ex-post optimization (cf. G. L. S. Shackle's "uncertainty"); (3) the capacity to maximize is a limited resource—differential personal endowments or capacities create entrepreneurs and innovators (cf. Cantillon's and J. B. Say's "entrepreneur" and Schumpeter's "innovator"); (4) many have no taste, much less a penchant, for efficiency (cf. J. M. Clark's "an irrational passion for rationality"); and (5) the underlying contradictions within the specifications of the social contract and government contracts (cf. Thomas Hobbes 1651; Cyert and March 1963).

However, Leibenstein suggests that given sufficient market pressure, the individuals in the firm suppress some of their contrary or inconsistent motivations and are likely to get closer to the maximization process. This switch is one that seems to require the assertion of one set of priorities over all others—that is, the assertion of one set of individual preferences, cleaned up of its internal contradictions, over all the others. Survival pressures, to paraphrase Dr. Johnson, "powerfully clarify the mind." A measure of the presence of X-efficiency may be an inverse measure of personal liberty.

The Morgenstern-Austrian Tradition

There is also a neo-Austrian underpinning to X-efficiency theory. One key Austrian element is the role of subjectivity in the decision-making process. This element was perceived in the role of the consumer, whose tastes for consumer goods, according to Menger and his two "students," von Wieser and Böhm Bawerk, provided the "first cause" for all economic activity.

Professor Wesley Clair Mitchell, in his foreword to the English edition of von Wieser's *Social Economics* (1927, ix–xii) puts his finger on the exact point. If things occur in the mind, then how does the mind operate—a problem that von Wieser (and his group) eschewed, but which von Neumann and Morgenstern tried to handle as the minimax. Leibenstein's X-efficiency theory leads us back to the willfulness (i.e., subjectiveness) of each of the parties in any economic activities. Leibenstein adds that given sufficient pressure, one individual's decisions (the imposition of ordered and consistent preferences) can and often will replace the others' subjectiveness with that decision, which in operation thus becomes interpersonally "objective." That management's decision can be said to be the "entrepreneur-in-action." Otherwise, the entrepreneur, like everyone else, is quiescent, and production proceeds without much reference to the elimination of efficiency—the state of Leibenstein X-inefficiency.

It has been fashionable recently to categorize most modern economic theorists in sequential sets of pigeonholes. One early division is between those studying tendencies toward equilibrium and those focusing on disequilibrium. Clearly X-efficiency theory is in the latter category.

So much of the former category draws upon the equilibration mechanism of Walrasian *tâtonnement* that it is pertinent to mention that X-efficiency theory not only eschews *tâtonnement* as meaningful in the interactions between the various individuals making up the firm but seems to deny the simple rationality that Walras's and Pareto's general models required. Given outside pressures individuals are driven to communicate according to comparative status, not according to negotiated interactions. The metaphor is not Walras's *tâtonnement*; it is Pirandello's *Six Characters in Search of an Author* (for author read the some compelling force like Hobbes's *Leviathan*).

But, I think one can say more. The leading neo-Austrian of our time, Professor Hayek, has of recent years come to see the importance of economic conventions as signaling systems or communications devices. Communication devices are precisely what Hobbes identifies as language itself. Language is partly what Hayek calls "institutions," borrowing (knowingly or otherwise) the precise phrase John R. Commons used almost a century ago (cf. Perlman 1986). The impact of these conventions or institutions is one of the external pressures that can force firms to diminish their levels of X-inefficiency. X-efficiency theory requires communication or signaling within the firm. That is what the theory is largely about.

Morgenstern and Hayek came from the same mold. That they were different in the end merely indicates that the mold is at the starting point. But were they so different? Morgenstern was, it may be unnecessary to recall, Hayek's successor at the Vienna Research Institute, which they both left in the 1930s—one to go to the London School of Economics, the other to Princeton. The linkage of Leibenstein to Morgenstern is clear; the linkage of Morgenstern and Hayek to the Austrian subjectivist tradition is also obvious. The linkage of Leibenstein to the original Menger formulation is not clear; but there is a link to the Austrian post-Menger tradition, and that is where I would place Leibenstein.

Das "Adam Smith Problem"

During the latter part of the nineteenth century, there developed, particularly in Germany, great interest in purported contradictions between Smith's views of man as seen in his *Theory of Moral Sentiments* and in his *Wealth of Nations* (cf. Viner 1926). In the former, man was perceived as usually having a gregarious nature (a "herding" kind of "animal") and capable of continuous detached self-judgment of his actions, as planned and also with regard to likely consequence. In the *Wealth of Nations* single-minded, efficiency-conscious "economic man" emerged totally supreme.

X-efficiency theory can be presented as an effort to identify the active relationship between these two aspects of the individual. Why? Because X-efficiency theory explains the internal and the external pressures that cause the person in the production process to choose between what he or she would like or ought to do and what efficiency considerations, under certain conditions, force him or her to do.

I believe that X-efficiency theory goes beyond this important point. It also explains what efficiency considerations cannot force a person to do and why. That is the rubric of inert areas. In this sense Leibenstein goes beyond Smith and *das Adam Smith Problem*.

In sum, perhaps one of the more useful ways to classify Leibenstein's X-efficiency thesis is to say that its organic base is in the study of man in daily life, that being also the stem-root of Marshallian neoclassicism. It is not part of the Walrasian mathematical purely logical neoclassicism. And insofar as this last is the mainstream of our time (1988), X-efficiency is part of contemporary heterodoxy. But, as both claim their legitimacy from Smith (really the Abraham of our discipline), just which is the Isaac (whose people write the texts) and which is the Ishmael (whose people tend to control the territory) is in each reader's own interpretation.

REFERENCES

Comanor, William, and Harvey Leibenstein. 1969. "Allocative Efficiency, X-Efficiency, and the Measurement of Welfare Losses." *Economica* 36:304–9.
Cyert, Richard M., and J. G. March. 1963. *A Behavioral Theory of the Firm.* Englewood Cliffs, N.J.: Prentice Hall.
Galenson, Walter, and Harvey Leibenstein. 1955. "Investment Criteria, Productivity, and Economic Development." *Quarterly Journal of Economics* 69:343–70.
Hobbes, Thomas. 1651. *The Leviathan.*

Leibenstein, Harvey. 1950. "Bandwagon, Snob, and Veblen Effects in the Theory of Consumers' Demand." *Quarterly Journal of Economics* 54:183–207.

Leibenstein, Harvey. 1951. "Toward a Theory of Demographic Transition." Ph.D. diss., Princeton University.

Leibenstein, Harvey. 1954. *A Theory of Economic Demographic Development.* Princeton: Princeton University Press.

Leibenstein, Harvey. 1957. *Economic Backwardness and Economic Growth: Studies in the Theory of Economic Development.* New York: Wiley.

Leibenstein, Harvey. 1958. "Underemployment in Backward Economies: Some Additional Notes." *Journal of Political Economy* 66:256–58.

Leibenstein, Harvey. 1960a. *Economic Theory and Organizational Analysis.* New York: Harper.

Leibenstein, Harvey. 1960b. "Technical Progress, the Production Function and Dualism." *Banco Nazionale Lavoro* 13:345–60.

Leibenstein, Harvey. 1962. "Notes on Welfare Economics and the Theory of Democracy." *Economics Journal* 72:299–317.

Leibenstein, Harvey. 1963. "Investment Criteria and Empirical Evidence – A Reply to Mr. Ranis." *Quarterly Journal of Economics* 77:175–79.

Leibenstein, Harvey. 1964. "An Econometric Analysis of Population Growth: Comment." *American Economic Review* 54:134–35.

Leibenstein, Harvey. 1966a. "Allocative Efficiency vs. 'X-Efficiency.'" *American Economic Review* 56:392–415.

Leibenstein, Harvey. 1966b. "Incremental Capital-Output Ratios and Growth Rates in the Short Run." *Review of Economics and Statistics* 48:20–27.

Leibenstein, Harvey. 1969. "Organizational or Frictional Equilibria, X-Efficiency, and the Rate of Innovation." *Quarterly Journal of Economics* 83:599–623.

Leibenstein, Harvey. 1972. "Comment on the Nature of X-Efficiency." *Quarterly Journal of Economics* 86:327–31.

Leibenstein, Harvey. 1973. "Competition and X-Efficiency: Reply." *Journal of Political Economy* 81:765–77.

Leibenstein, Harvey. 1974a. "Comment on Inert Areas and the Definition of X-Efficiency." *Quarterly Journal of Economics* 88:689–91.

Leibenstein, Harvey. 1974b. "An Interpretation of the Economics Theory of Fertility: Promising Path or Blind Alley?" *Journal of Economic Literature* 12:457–79.

Leibenstein, Harvey. 1974c. "Socio-economic Fertility Theories and Their Relevance to Population Policy." *International Labour Review* 109:443–57.

Leibenstein, Harvey. 1975a. "Aspects of the X-Efficiency Theory of the Firm." *Bell Journal* 6:580–606.

Leibenstein, Harvey. 1975b. "The Economic Theory of Fertility Decline." *Quarterly Journal of Economics* 89:1–31.

Leibenstein, Harvey. 1975c. "On the Economic Theory of Utility: A Reply to Keeley." *Journal of Economic Literature* 13:469–72.

Leibenstein, Harvey. 1976a. *Beyond Economic Man*. Cambridge, Mass.: Harvard University Press.

Leibenstein, Harvey. 1976b. "The Problem of Characterizing Aspirations." *Population and Development Review* 2:427–31.

Leibenstein, Harvey. 1977a. "Beyond Economic Man: Economics, Politics, and the Population Problem." *Population and Development Review* 3:183–99.

Leibenstein, Harvey. 1977b. "Economic Theory of Fertility: Reply to Cullison." *Quarterly Journal of Economics* 91:349–50.

Leibenstein, Harvey. 1977c. "X-Efficiency, Technical Efficiency, and Incomplete Information Use: A Comment." *Economic Development and Cultural Change* 25:311–16.

Leibenstein, Harvey. 1978a. *General X-Efficiency Theory and Economic Development*. New York: Oxford University Press.

Leibenstein, Harvey. 1978b. "On the Basic Proposition of X-Efficiency Theory." *American Economic Review, Papers and Proceedings* 68:328–32.

Leibenstein, Harvey. 1978c. "X-Inefficiency Xists — Reply to an Xorcist." *American Economic Review* 68:203–11.

Leiberstein, Harvey. 1979a. "A Branch of Economics Is Missing: Micro-Micro Theory." *Journal of Economic Literature* 17:477–502.

Leibenstein, Harvey. 1979b. "The General X-Efficiency Paradigm and the Role of the Entrepreneur." In *Time, Uncertainty, and Disequilibrium: Exploration of Austrian Themes*, ed. Mario J. Rizzo, 127–39, 140–51. Lexington, Mass.: Lexington Books.

Leibenstein, Harvey. 1979c. "Comments on 'Fertility as Consumption: Theory from the Behavioral Sciences.' " *Conservation Research* 5:287–90.

Leibenstein, Harvey. 1980a. *Inflation, Income Distribution and X-Efficiency Theory*. London: Croom Helm.

Leibenstein, Harvey. 1980b. "Notes on the X-Efficiency Approach to Inflation, Productivity and Unemployment." In *Human Resources, Employment and Development. Volume 3: The Problems of Developed Countries and the International Economy*, ed. Burton Weisbrod and Helen Hughes, 84–96. Proceedings of the Sixth World Congress of the International Economic Association, Mexico City.

Leibenstein, Harvey. 1981a. "Economic Decision Theory and Human Fertility Behavior: A Speculative Essay." *Population and Development Review* 9:381–400.

Leibenstein, Harvey. 1981b. "The Inflation Process: A Micro-Behavioral Analysis." *American Economic Review* 71:368–73.

Leibenstein, Harvey. 1981c. "Microeconomics and X-Efficiency Theory." In *The Crisis in Economic Theory*, ed. Daniel Bell and Irving Kristol, 97–110. New York: Basic Books.

Leibenstein, Harvey. 1981d. "X-Efficiency Theory, Productivity and Growth." In *Towards an Explanation of Economic Growth*, ed. Herbert Giersch, 187–212. Symposium 1980. Kiel, FGR: Institut für Weltwirtschaft.

Leibenstein, Harvey. 1982a. "On Bull's-Eye-Painting Economics." *Journal of Post Keynesian Economics* 4:460–65.

Leibenstein, Harvey. 1982b. "The Prisoner's Dilemma in the Invisible Hand: An Analysis of Intrafirm Productivity." *American Economic Review Supplement* 72:92–97.

Leibenstein, Harvey. 1982c. "Worker Motivation and X-Efficiency Theory: A Comment." *Journal of Economic Issues* 72:872–73.

Leibenstein, Harvey. 1983a. "Intrafirm Productivity: Reply [to M. Shamid Alam]." *American Economic Review* 73:822–23.

Leibenstein, Harvey. 1983b. "Property Rights and X-Efficiency: Comment." *American Economic Review* 73:831–42.

Leibenstein, Harvey. 1985a. "Comment [on the *World Development Report, 1984*]." *Population and Development Review* 11:135–37.

Leibenstein, Harvey. 1985b. "On Relaxing the Maximization Postulate." *Journal of Behavioral Economics* 14:5–20.

Leibenstein, Harvey. 1987a. *Inside the Firm*. Cambridge, Mass.: Harvard University Press.

Leibenstein, Harvey. 1987b. "X-efficiency Theory." In *The New Palgrave*, ed. John Eatwell, Murray Milgate, and Peter Newman, 4:934–35. New York: Stockton Press.

Mitchell, Wesley Clair. 1912. "The Backward Art of Spending Money." *American Economic Review* 2:269–81.

Perlman, Mark. 1986. "Subjectivism and American Institutionalism." In *Subjectivism, Intelligibility, and Economic Understanding: Essays in Honor of Ludwig M. Lachmann on His Eightieth Birthday*, ed. Israel M. Kirzner. New York: New York University Press.

Stigler, George. 1976. "The Xistence of X-Efficiency." *American Economic Review* 66:213–16.

Viner, Jacob. 1926. "Adam Smith and Laissez Faire." In *Adam Smith, 1776–1926*, ed. John Maurice Clark et al. Lectures to Commemorate the Sesquicentennial of the Publication of "The Wealth of Nations." Chicago: University of Chicago Press.

X-Efficiency and Contestability Theory: A Clash of Paradigms?

John Hatch

The conference prospectus describes X-efficiency theory as a "new paradigm," and in terms of its emphasis on the internal workings of the firm, this seems to be a reasonable claim. In peering into the black box, which in economic theory is the firm, X-efficiency has broken the rules. Predictably its proponents have been variously ignored, ridiculed, and reprimanded, most notably by Professor Stigler. However, over 20 years after its birth (Leibenstein 1966) X-efficiency theory is still alive, and I personally noted with some pleasure Roger Frantz's reference to the fact that the 1966 Leibenstein article was "the fourth most frequently referenced article in the Social Science Citation Index (SSCI) between 1969–1980" (Frantz 1985). Casual observation suggests that this high level of interest continues, and this conference attests to the same.

In 1982 microeconomics was presented with a blockbuster theory, with the publication of *Contestable Markets and the Theory of Industry Structure*, by W. J. Baumol, J. C. Panzar, and R. D. Willig (hereafter Baumol et al.). Much of the substance of the book had, of course, appeared in a stream of journal articles in the 1970s. Considerable claims have been made for contestability theory. For example, Baumol (1982a, 1) in the 1981 American Economic Association presidential address said: "our new book enables us to look at industry structure and behavior in a way that is novel . . . it provides a unifying analytical structure to the subject area." Like X-efficiency theory, contestability theory has spawned a large literature and has drawn attention to many important but neglected areas of economics. However, it is questionable whether contestability theory can be seen as a new paradigm in the Kuhnian sense (1970). Its theoretical basis is firmly neoclassical, even though it reorients conventional market competition theory in at least two important ways and in doing so produces some important new results.

It really matters not whether either or both of these theories can be strictly seen as new paradigms; they are both significant contributions to economic thought and have been instrumental in the resurgence of interest in the theory of competition. It is, therefore, rather surprising to note the almost complete absence of any interface between the two theories in the literature. For example, Baumol et al., in their extensive bibliography, make no reference to any of Leibenstein's 20 or so papers on X-efficiency. Indeed, in the whole contestability literature, I can find only one reference to X-efficiency theory: Baumol (1982a) cryptically and briefly points out that in any contestable market there is an absence of any sort of inefficiency in production, and he goes on to name X-efficiency in a list of forms of inefficiency. I suppose that this could be seen as the end of the matter.

This article will attempt, however, to relate these two theories to each other to see whether they are compatible or even potentially symbiotic. After all, they are both basically cost-based theories of competition. X-efficiency theory is explicitly about costs, and contestability theory, certainly as it is formally presented, emphasizes production and costs rather than the demand side of markets. In this sense, both break with the neoclassical tradition and its strong emphasis on demand. Demand factors play a relatively passive role in both theories; rather it is an innovative view of the underlying cost structures that drive them.

X-Efficiency Theory 20 Years After

Partly because X-efficiency theory has spawned such a huge literature, it is often difficult to be precise about its main findings. To its credit and to that of its main proponents, Professor Leibenstein and others, X-efficiency theory has evolved significantly over the past 20 years. Writing in 1979, Leibenstein summarized the chief findings of his theory under four headings, all of which indicated that costs are not determinate, or if you like, that costs are very much exogenous to the firm. Most importantly, costs are seen as a function of the industry or market environment as well as of more traditional factors, such as technology, and within technology, scale. Indeed, I have argued elsewhere (Hatch 1979) that the most important and useful result from X-efficiency theory is that it makes costs partly a function of competitive pressures. This of course rather begs the question because competition has never been well defined in the economic literature. However, what we can be sure of is that the level of competition relates to factors outside the firm, such as rivals or potential rivals and their behavior, so that pressures of competition are exogenous to the individual firm. This is important because traditionally a firm's costs were almost wholly determined by its own decisions, and even in the special case of external economies, costs of the individual firm were not explicitly related to the level of competition in the market.

In his initial exposition, Leibenstein (1966) argued that the level of X-efficiency was a function of factors both internal and external to the firm. However, he does not attempt to assess the relative importance of these two distinct sources of efficiency, and later work, both theoretical and empirical, does not seem to have shed much light on this issue. There is evidence, however, that external conditions, for example, the presence of competitors, does systematically influence costs. The early work of Primeaux (1975, 1977) in the U.S. electrical utility industry showed that the costs of duopolists were lower than those of monopolists and by inference one can assume that larger numbers of rivals would, ceteris paribus, lower costs even further, though one would also assume that this numbers' effect upon X-efficiency would be subject to diminishing returns, perhaps with a relatively small number of rivals. One of the difficulties is that real world markets do not provide suitable data and the problem is not readily amenable to the use of experimental economics.

It may also be a gross oversimplification to see the number of rivals as a measure of competitive pressure, though traditionally this variable has been used both in theory and practice. Certainly it is more measurable than some other, perhaps more suitable, measure of the level of competition, and it has the advantage that it relates directly to the basic unit of competition, the firm. In addition a head count of firms, with appropriate assumptions, can be related to the average size of firms and, therefore, to economies of size. For all these reasons, the notion that costs may be partially a function of the number of firms in the industry or group is both interesting and analytically useful.

There are, of course, complications. X-efficiency remains a rather ambiguous concept. It appears to be a function of competitive pressures but is also a function of various other factors, notably the size of the organization. The relationship with the size of the organization is more complex than would at first appear. Popular intuition suggests that large organizations are inherently inefficient and that since theoretically this inefficiency is unlikely to be technical inefficiency and/or price inefficiency it is natural to classify it under the rather vague residual category of X-inefficiency. Primeaux's early work, which appeared to isolate X-efficiency in the sense that it controlled for technical and price factors, generally supported this view, though the imposed linearity of the model may have contributed to the result. In general the problem is that in the presence of economies of scale, size- or scale-dependent X-efficiency is apt to be confused with economies of scale. Almost all the normal methods of estimating economies of size will in fact pick up this component of X-efficiency. Indeed, the only method that should avoid this confusion is estimation based upon pure engineering data, a point well made by Maital and Roll (1985, 106). Employing this method will yield an estimate of what is theoretically technically possible and therefore will not include even size-dependent X-efficiency. The problem is that in all but relatively simple technologies such estimates are very difficult to make. Maybe we can view this as semantics. Size-dependent X-efficiency should perhaps be seen as a diseconomy of size, though we are still left with the problem that its source is qualitatively different from conventional economies of size; and, even worse, it appears to be a negative function of firm size, so it offsets conventional economies of large size.

In my 1979 paper, I attempted to build a simple model that took account of these conflicting factors. Thus, industry average costs (derived from individual firms' average costs) are, for any given output, a decreasing function of output fragmentation (the effect of competition-induced X-efficiency) but are an increasing function of output fragmentation because of the net effect of conventional economies of scale- and size-dependent X-efficiency. However, Leibenstein has suggested that X-efficiency may not always be monotonically related to organization size. This complicates matters if such cost effects are seen as part of X-efficiency; but if they are lumped with economies of size, then this problem disappears. Of course in practice, as we pointed out earlier, such economies or diseconomies are rarely likely to be separated from economies of size. In this context, Leibenstein (1984) has suggested that in Japan at least large organizations (firms) seem to be relatively X-efficient. This seems to be in contrast to Western firms where the degree of X-efficiency seems to be a negative and monotonic function of firm size. Leibenstein explains this seeming anomaly in terms of fundamental differences in management structures and job specification between Japan and the West.

The upshot of all this is that costs are a complex function of technology, factor prices, scale or size, and competitive pressures – an infinitely more interesting concept than the traditional rather sterile view of costs. In addition, the idea that costs are affected by external (to the firm) market conditions opens up a whole new series of possible insights into the workings of the competitive process. The appearance of costs as an active factor in explaining market behavior could be seen as a paradigm change. It certainly contrasts dramatically with the passive role of costs in much of neoclassical microeconomic theory. As Schwartzman (1973) pointed out in a perceptive article, price theory was developed to explain prices (exchange prices) and not to illustrate costs and productive efficiency. X-efficiency theory and other recent developments in economic theory have thrown the emphasis on costs again, or perhaps for the first time, in mainstream economics!

Contestability Theory in Context

Contestability theory is clearly a cost-based theory of markets. Its critical components are economies of scope, subadditivity, and sunk costs; revenues play a relatively passive role. Because it is a cost-based theory, it may well be possible and analytically useful to consider the integration of X-efficiency and related ideas into contestability theory. If X-efficiency is as universal as is claimed in theory and as appears from the limited empirical evidence, then a proper analysis of contestability theory must include it.

Fortunately for us, contestability theory is very rigorously defined. As we all know, it is a theory of markets and the attendant efficiency and welfare implications. The theory focuses almost exclusively on entry and exit conditions rather than on the number of incumbent competitors, and thus it emphasizes barriers to entry and exit, and potential competition. Put very simply, perfect contestability is a situation of completely free entry and exit. The threat of reversible entry into the market produces behavior by incumbents that in welfare terms replicates that of perfect competitors. Thus in the extreme case of natural monopoly, the discipline of potential competition will in many circumstances produce desirable, socially efficient, outcomes.

As a corollary, but nevertheless an important result, the strict cost framework of contestability theory produces an industry structure that is endogenous. Compare this to conventional market structure theory, where industry structure either is given or is an ill-defined outcome of historical, economic, and sociological factors together with a generous dose of chance. The model also allows one to consider the efficiency of market structure and to think in terms of an optimum market structure. It is probably not unreasonable to claim that the cost framework of contestability theory is the best enunciated so far in theoretical economics. Substitution of the concept of subadditivity for the more loosely defined concept of economies of scale and the incorporation of economies of scope in recognition of the multiproduct nature of most firms are both important improvements. For these reasons, it is worthwhile to consider how X-efficiency and related ideas might be integrated into this holistic framework and whether they will alter any of its major results. This is the main purpose of this article.

The Cost Basis of Contestability

Because it is rigorously presented, we will start with the cost framework of contestability theory taken from Baumol et al., (1982b, 279).

Consider a multiproduct industry, however defined, which displays declining ray average costs and economies of scope (including trans-ray convexity). Such a generalized total cost surface is illustrated in figure 1 as OAB and can be assumed to face any firm that produces or contemplates producing any quantity (Y_M) of the goods mix $\bar{Y}_1$ and $\bar{Y}_2$. In the context of contestability theory, we are primarily interested in potential entrants so that we can define a new set of cost curves, OCD, which includes entry costs. This surface will presumably lie above the basic cost surface at all contemplated nonzero outputs, but by an amount that can for the time being remain unspecified. We might note immediately that recognition of entry costs dichotomizes the market in a functional manner. Incumbent firms face one cost surface, while all potential entrants face another and higher cost surface. Indeed, in the Baumol model it is precisely this cost differential, based upon sunk costs (entry costs), that tempers the effect of perfect contestability. In the words of Baumol et al., (1982b, 482) "sunk costs, . . . are a prime impediment to contestability." However, such costs are determined exogenously to the firm and to the group of firms. We must now consider the unique role of X-efficiency, where the effect on costs is at least partially endogenous to the group. It is at this point that we must raise the vexing question of the industry or group.

Numbers and Market Structure

The essence of contestability is that it de-emphasizes structure and the number and size of firms; it stresses the process of competition and the potential rate of entry and exit. This is very much in the spirit of Schumpeter (1942) and many subsequent writers, who have seen competition as an ongoing process rather than a state of equilibrium. In traditional market analysis, the number and size of firms were critical but could be ascertained only when we had a clear definition of the relevant group, the industry. The problem of industry boundaries has always been a difficult one, and the introduction of multiproduct firms further complicates matters. It has been traditional to define the industry with vague reference to cross elasticities of both supply and/or demand, largely ignoring the fact that supply and demand criteria will rarely define a separable but coincident set of producers. Baumol et al. (1982b, 113) adopt this position when they say, "we therefore simply take the industry

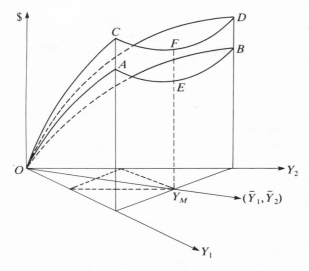

Fig. 1. Generalized total cost surface

to be composed of all suppliers of all products that are sufficiently closely related on one or the other of these criteria," (consumption and/ or production).

However, they appear to argue that the notion of the industry is relatively unimportant. The emphasis is on the firm, and following writers like Penrose (1959) and Schumpeter (1942), they see all firms as being at least potentially in competition with all other firms. The multiproduct structure of firms encourages the view that all firms are interlinked in a continuum. However, one has to admit that the notion of the group, if not the industry, may be very useful in considering the meaning and extent of potential entry. Without it, we can only really consider each and every firm as an isolate. There is no doubt that the highly unsatisfactory and ambiguous concept of the industry, like that of the genus in biology, has practical and analytical value. It is equally clear, however, that the notion of the group will be difficult to define in a genuinely multiproduct world. Firms, in a sense, are n-dimensional in product space and, although textbook expositions tend to give n the value two, clearly its real value may be very high. There is a problem of aggregation, which goes right back to the concept of a separate product. Indeed, the only way in which to group products and so perhaps to define a relevant subset of the production system would seem to be in terms of economies of scope (cost savings due to simultaneous production of different outputs). We may note that this still begs the question as to what constitutes a different output, at least on the production side.

The upshot of all this is that contestability theory is mainly about firms as individual units. Gone is the pure concept of the industry. In this sense, at least, it may have claims to being a new paradigm.

Very closely related to this issue is the notion of incumbents and potential entrants. In contestability theory this dichotomy is crucial because incumbents are disciplined by the threat of entry. If we take a firm-by-firm view of the world, then each individual firm is an incumbent and all other productive units, or some subset of them, are potential entrants. The crucial question then is: under what conditions and at what rate will entry occur or threaten to occur? If we retain some notion of the group, based logically on economies of scope, then what is the relative role of incumbents and potential entrants? Shepherd (1984) has raised this issue in the broad sense in his criticisms of contestability theory. Is it reasonable to assume that a firm, any firm, is more conscious (or as conscious) of a potential competitor than it is of an actual competitor? On the one hand, potential competitors may be almost numberless. On the other hand, the incumbent competitor presumably has a record of competitive acts and in every sense is more visible. The essence of contestability theory seems to be that in a perfectly contestable market, individual firms are at immediate, continuous risk of entry, and in a real sense, this is the equivalent of large numbers competition. This may be so, but the obverse is to ask: how many incumbents are necessary to produce the same effect? After all, it is easier to count heads than to document potential entrants, who by definition are hypothetical. The logic of contestability theory seems to be that incumbents and entrants are equal. For various perceptual and behavioral reasons this would seem to be unsustainable! It is true, however, that potential entrants may be numberless and as such may be seen to swamp incumbency. The critical issues here are the rate of entry, the elasticity of supply of entrants, and the role of the various lags in the system. Schwartz and Reynolds (1983) and Shepherd (1984) have pointed out some of the difficulties and even inconsistencies in interpreting contestability theory in a real world context.

One simplifying method would be to obtain a measure of "market structure" that incorporates both incumbents and entrants. So-called dynamic measures of concentration attempt to do this, but ex post rather than ex ante. For this reason, they never can measure contestability. The problem is that we may need to be able to measure contestability and indeed appraise it in comparison with conventional market structure in order to deduce the effect on X-efficiency. Our knowledge of numbers-related X-efficiency is imperfect. Our knowledge of the relation between contestability and incumbent numbers as factors producing X-efficiency is even more limited. Let us suppose that felt or perceived competitive pressure at the level of the individual firm does have a systematic influence on costs. Such perceived pressure can presumably come either from incumbent rivals, in the sense of sellers of the same products, or from the consciousness of potential competition, contestability. At this stage, as previously outlined, we have no basis for measuring the relative effect of these two possible influences on behavior and, therefore, costs. What we can say is that the more contestable the firm's market, the greater the pressure on the firm and presumably the lower its costs will be. In this simple model, the discipline of contestability is partly through cost effects, as well as through the more familiar price effects. Indeed, it reinforces the conclusion that monopoly in a contestable market will achieve a socially efficient, or nearly socially efficient, outcome. What we have effectively done is to internalize the numbers-dependent X-efficiency into the contestability model in the sense that contestability pressures have been assumed to influence costs in exactly the same way that actual incumbent rivalry does, and this may not be so.

An alternative view is that incumbent rivalry is either qualitatively or quantitatively different from contestability, at least in terms of its influence on costs. At this stage we need not speculate as to why this might be so. What is the evidence for these alternative suppositions? We have already pointed out that relatively little is known about the specific influence of numbers on X-efficiency. Primeaux's pioneering empirical work (1975, 1977) suggested that small numbers, in his case just two rivals, had a significant effect on costs. Work in experimental economics, though not addressed to precisely this question, lends qualified support. It is a general result in this work that the time taken to reach equilibrium prices falls rapidly as the number of market participants increases. We cannot necessarily generalize from this price result to costs, and, unfortunately, costs are difficult to model using the experimental economics methodology. However, for what it is worth, experimental results suggest that the power of "contestability" is achieved substantially with just two contestants (Coursey, Isaac, and Smith 1984). We have put contestability in quotation marks and used the word *contestants* because it appears that these experiments actually modeled incumbent markets (contested markets) rather than contestable markets, which rely solely on potential competition.

In a very recent paper, Morrison and Winston (1987) muddy the water a little by finding that the airline industry in the United States, so beloved of contestability theory, cannot be shown to be perfectly contestable, but that it is imperfectly contestable—that is, potential competition has an important positive effect upon welfare. In addition, there is some evidence that the number of potential competitors, ceteris paribus, positively influences this effect. A critical mass of potential entrants appears to be necessary before it can influence the behavior of incumbents. This is an interesting result because it may give us an insight into the relative competitive importance of potential entrants and incumbents. Unfortunately, the result is difficult to interpret precisely because the time dimension is unclear. The notion of entry has to be specified as a probability of entry within some specified time period. Herein lies the great problem with comparing entry and incumbency: one is a probability *over* time, the other a reality at *a point in* time, flow and stock!

Integrating X-Efficiency and Contestability

We must now consider the interplay of X-efficiency and contestability more formally. Both are seen as expressions of competition and both lead to a lowering of costs, though the mechanism by which this occurs differs between the two cases.

In the very simplest model, we assume that X-efficiency cost-reducing effects are confined to incumbents, members of the group. Under these circumstances, recognition of X-efficiency may alter some of the key results of contestability theory, but it requires rather special assumptions. Consider a situation where realized costs are lower for two members of a group producing a vector of outputs than they are for the single firm monopolist. Under these circumstances, and without going into details, an incumbent natural monopolist can set prices that are sustainable and, in the presence of entry and exit costs, will deter entrants. However, should numbers-dependent X-efficiency exist and should it be perceived by the potential entrants as well, then it may be sufficient to, ceteris paribus, prevent the monopolist from achieving a set of sustainable prices. Clearly, this result depends on the potential entrants' perceptions (and the monopolist's) and on the extent to which numbers-dependent X-efficiency gains offset conventional scale effects and/or net scale-dependent X-efficiency. While this model is conceived in terms of two simultaneous and equal-sized entrants, it can be generalized to a larger number of entrants, or perhaps more accurately to a greater rate of entry. It may be argued, quite reasonably, that both incumbent and potential entrants will perceive costs as defined by the underlying production function. If this is so, then it may well be that the monopolist can maintain a set of sustainable prices based upon achieved costs, even though realized costs would be substantially lower were entry to occur.

In considering these small numbers cases, it is worth remembering the added complication that the incumbent may or may not see itself as remaining in production. Should it remain in production, then presumably its post-entry costs will be subject to the same inexorable downward pressure in the presence of rivals. I say inexorable because we must recognize that numbers-dependent X-efficiency of this sort is of the nature of an externality. It is not a decision variable for the rivals, whether they be incumbents or entrants. In this sense it is exogenous. Given the essential exogeneity of the effect, it is probable that such effects will be largely outside the consciousness of firms and, thus, will in practice be unimportant. However, this is an empirical question.

If we simplify the Baumol analysis by collapsing his beautiful diagrams into two dimensions, by assuming for convenience that all incumbents and entrants produce the same multiproduct set $Y_1 \ldots Y_n$ in the same proportions, then in figure 2, OC describes the relevant total cost function. Similarly, OR is the pseudorevenue hyperplane and OD the revenue dome that defines the profitable output range, YY_M. If V, the entrants' costs inclusive of realized X-efficiency, is above OR, for example $\bar{V}$, then sustainable Ramsey prices are available for the natural monopolist. If, however, V lies below OR, for example, at $\underline{V}$, then sustainable prices are not available, and if these potential costs are foreseen, then entry will occur. Clearly, in the limiting case where $V = B$, that is, where numbers-based X-efficiency just and only just compensates for diseconomies of scale, then no entry will occur. The common sense is that sufficiently lower realized costs, consequential upon numbers and numbers alone, may preclude sustainable monopoly. We note again, however, that it all depends upon perceptions of what is after all an externality, and that by definition such externalities tend to be in the realm of the unknown!

Let us turn now to the simpler polar case, where the X-efficiency effect is in effect neutral between incumbent pressure and potential entrants pressure, the very threat of entry induces X-efficiency in the incumbent. Under these circumstances, clearly X-efficiency will not affect the results of contestability theory, which must stand or fall on other grounds. Perhaps more interesting are the multitude of possibilities where the role of incumbents and potential entrants in reducing group costs is nonzero but different.

The actual effect of X-efficiency depends very much upon perceptions of the two critical groups, the highly specified incumbent group and the basically unspecified potential entrants. One would expect, from experience and learning by doing alone, that incumbents would be more aware of the subtleties of X-efficiency than potential entrants, the more

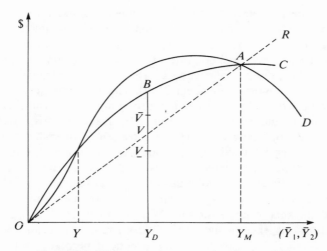

Fig. 2. X-efficiency and entry under contestability

so if X-efficiency is subject to differences related to technology, product mix, and other specific factors. Again, as yet, we have little evidence on these sorts of issues.

X-Efficiency as a Form of Externality

Contestability theory is highly self-contained. It has been able to resist criticism partly because of this. Much of its strength lies in the endogeneity of its components. As we have seen, if X-efficiency is seen as essentially endogenous, then it will have little effect on the results of contestability theory and Baumol is right in largely ignoring it and/or including it as just another cost phenomenon that can be subsumed under the general cost conditions. However, I believe that this may be an oversimplification in that at least some aspects of X-efficiency are of the nature of externalities, albeit externalities in an unfamiliar guise. Let us now consider this novel view of X-efficiency.

It has always been true that the taxonomy of efficiency in economics is somewhat ambiguous. Carlsson (1972) probably still provides one of the best attempts at sorting it out. Following his general analysis, X-efficiency appears to embrace both price and technical inefficiency within firms, whereas allocative inefficiency relates to relations among firms or any other units among which there are market relations. If we view externalities as the result of untraded interdependencies between economic agents, then immediately we can see the potential for externality-like inefficiencies within economic units (firms), where by definition decisions are made without the explicit formation of prices. In the simplest case of a group of coworkers, clearly the pace of work, one of Leibenstein's (APQ) variables, depends in a complex fashion on all members of the team. Yet individuals on the team have no direct method of bargaining with their coworkers. Thus, we have the potential for an uncorrected externality-like situation in which one worker is inhibited in his or her performance by the decision of another worker within the same group. I believe that many aspects of X-inefficiency can be traced to this as-if externality situation. If we go back to early X-efficiency theory (Leibenstein 1969, 1974), then we are in a world of effort positions chosen individually by team members but without explicit reference to their effect on other members of the organization. Clearly, much of management effort is directed at solving these problems, but many remain at least partially uncorrected. Certainly, they are not all internalized, and thus, we find disparity in the performance of firms. Note here that we do not deny the presence of generalized market pressure whether it stems from contestability or more traditional numbers-based competition, which eliminates at least some of these effects. However, even these pressures are essentially external to the firm and no mechanism exists to ensure that overall efficiency is maximized, so long as such uncorrected effects exist.

One cannot but be reminded of Coase (1937), who pointed out so cogently the essential dichotomy between what goes on inside the firm and what goes on between firms (and by inference between larger units). It does not seem surprising that analogous to uncorrected market externalities there is uncorrected nonmarket interdependence and that this has the potential to produce disparities in performance.

Interestingly, early analysis of X-efficiency, for example, Comanor and Leibenstein (1969) and Parish and Ng (1972), agonized over the social costs of X-efficiency. Our view almost turns this problem on its head in the sense that externalities are the *result* of social cost not the *cause*.

Conclusions

Both contestability theory and X-efficiency theory may have valid claims to being new paradigms in the Kuhnian sense. In the case of contestability theory, its claim is fairly explicit, though critics will say with some validity that there is little new in the theory or at least in its components. What is new is the synthesis of the components and rigor of the analysis. In the case of X-efficiency, the claim is more subtle. X-efficiency involves a different way of thinking about microeconomic questions. In a sense it raises more questions than it answers, but the questions that it raises are very fundamental and many of them have been avoided in traditional theory.

The two theories are not inimical to each other. X-efficiency can be integrated into contestability theory, though it raises many of the difficult behavioral questions that are not really fully addressed by Baumol and his coworkers. In this sense contestability theory is narrower and more conventional than X-efficiency theory and, therefore, has less claim to being a genuine paradigm change. Nevertheless, both theories have stimulated vigorous debate and have in their own way revitalized microeconomic theory. Without contributions of this sort, much of microeconomics might have become very mundane and in the new computer age may have degenerated into mindless data crunching.

REFERENCES

Baumol, W. J. 1982a. "Contestable Markets: An Uprising in the Theory of Industry Structure." *American Economic Review* 72:1–15.

Baumol, W. J., J. C. Panzar, and R. D. Willig. 1982b. *Contestable Markets and the Theory of Industry Structure*. San Diego: Harcourt Brace Jovanovich.

Carlsson, B. 1972. "The Measurement of Efficiency in Production: An Application to Swedish Manufacturing Industries 1968." *Swedish Journal of Economics* 74:468–85.

Coase, R. 1937. "The Nature of the Firm." *Economica* 4:386–405.

Comanor, W. S., and H. Leibenstein. 1969. "Allocative Efficiency, X-Efficiency and the Measurement of Welfare Losses." *Economica* 36:304–9.

Coursey, D., R. M. Isaac, and V. L. Smith. 1984. "Natural Monopoly and Contested Markets: Some Experimental Results." *Journal of Law and Economics* 27:91–113.

Frantz, R. 1985. "X-efficiency Theory and Its Critics." *Quarterly Review of Economics and Business* 25:38–58.

Hatch, J. H. 1979. "The Cost Minimizing Number of Firms and the Discipline of Competition." *Economics Letters*, no. 4:379–85.

Kuhn, T. S. 1970. *The Structure of Scientific Revolutions*. Chicago: University of Chicago Press.

Leibenstein, H. 1966. "Allocative Efficiency vs. 'X-efficiency.' " *American Economic Review* 56:392–415.

Leibenstein, H. 1969. "Organizational or Frictional Equilibria, X-Efficiency, and the Rate of Innovation." *Quarterly Journal of Economics* 83:600–23.

Leibenstein, H. 1974. "Comment on Inert Areas and the Definition of X-Efficiency." *Quarterly Journal of Economics* 88:689–91.

Leibenstein, H. 1979. "X-Efficiency: From Concept to Theory." *Challenge* 21:13–22.

Leibenstein, H. 1984. "The Japanese Management System: An X-Efficiency–Game Theory Analysis." In *The Economic Analysis of the Japanese Firm*, ed. M. Aoki, 331–57. Amsterdam and New York: Elsevier Science Publishers B.V.

Maital, S., and Y. Roll. 1985. "Solving for 'X': Theory and Measurement of Allocative and X-Efficiency at the Plant Level." *Journal of Behavioral Economics* 14:99–116.

Morrison, S. A., and C. Winston. 1987. "Empirical Implications and Tests of the Contestability Hypothesis." *Journal of Law and Economics* 30:53–66.

Parish, R., and Y. K. Ng. 1972. "Monopoly, X-Efficiency and the Measurement of Welfare Loss." *Economica* 39:301–8.

Penrose, E. 1959. *The Theory of the Growth of the Firm*. New York: Wiley.

Primeaux, W. J. 1975. "A Reexamination of the Monopoly Market Structure for Electric Utilities." In *Promoting Competition in Regulated Markets*, ed. A. Phillips, 175–200. Washington, D.C.: Brookings.

Primeaux, W. J. 1977. "An Assessment of X-Efficiency Gained Through Competition." *Review of Economics and Statistics* 59:105–8.

Schumpeter, J. A. 1942. *Capitalism, Socialism and Democracy*. New York: Harper.

Schwartz, M., and R. J. Reynolds. 1983. "Contestable Markets: An Uprising in the Theory of Industry Structure: Comment." *American Economic Review* 73:488–90.

Schwartzman, D. 1973. "Competition and Efficiency: Comment." *Journal of Political Economy* 81:756–64.

Shepherd, W. G. 1984. " 'Contestability' vs. Competition." *American Economic Review* 74:572–87.

Ex-Ante and Ex-Post Criticisms of X-Efficiency Theory and Literature

Roger S. Frantz

Introduction

In writing about X-efficiency, I have frequently asked myself how a particular statement in support of the theory could be written that would not be subject to an alternative — neoclassical — explanation. I have now come to realize that writing about X-efficiency by looking over one's shoulder in this way was the best way either never to complete a project or to wish that I had never started. Specifically, it is now apparent to me that whatever statement one could make could quickly be, and often is, countered by another, alternative explanation.

Is there a need within microeconomics for a concept such as X-efficiency? The X, in X-inefficiency stands for a nonallocative inefficiency whose source is unknown. Harberger (1954) estimated the welfare loss due to monopoly power — what I refer to as "allocative-market inefficiency" — as being 0.1 percent of the gross national product of the United States. Other estimates that followed reported similarly small welfare losses from monopoly power and tariffs. As Leibenstein pointed out, these estimates take into account only the (net) output and price distortions caused by monopoly and/or tariffs. While some outputs and prices may be very distorted, on net, the distortions are not likely to be large, as the estimates by Harberger and others confirm. Leibenstein reported and concurred with Mundell's (1962) lament that such small estimates of welfare losses might lead some to believe that economics is not very important. Leibenstein, however, took the position that a significant nonallocative X-inefficiency should be added to the allocative form of inefficiency.

Leibenstein pointed out that these estimates of allocative inefficiency assumed that firms are cost minimizers, that is, they purchase and utilize all inputs efficiently. X-efficiency (XE) theory was designed to show that protection from competitive pressure produces not only allocative-market inefficiency but an additional area of inefficiency, namely, excess unit costs of production.

Leibenstein's development of the X-efficiency concept was primarily driven by various types of data. One type was the observation that his graduate research assistant at Berkeley was underutilized! This led him to wonder whether the underutilization of inputs was a more generalized phenomenon.

Another observation was the differences between formal models of economic development and his own experiences and the experiences of several colleagues working in less developed countries. Finally, data were available that seemed inconsistent with neoclassical theory: (1) data showing that firms were able to increase their output by making relatively simple changes in the internal organization of the plant; (2) data showing that firms were not operating according to the principles of marginal analysis; and (3) macrodata showing that something other than physical labor and physical capital played an important role in the growth rates of several industrialized nations.

All three types of data seemed to warrant an investigation into alternative theories of the firm in order to fill a lacuna in economic theory that placed reliance exclusively on the concept of allocative-market inefficiency.

Another reason for believing that there is a need for the XE concept in microeconomics is that neoclassical theory assumes that firms are producing on both their production and cost functions. That is, firms are assumed to be maximizing output from given inputs including technology, and, therefore, they are minimizing unit costs. If this is the case, then the textbook presentation is accurate about the technological nature of both production and costs. If, however, the relationship between the production and cost processes is not primarily technological, then the textbook presentation needs to be modified. XE theory is one such modification: XE theory assumes that neoclassical theory is accurate but only when firms are, in fact, producing on their production and cost functions.[1] For this reason XE theory considers neoclassical theory to be a

---

1. Recent papers have shown that firms may not be producing on their production function. Fay and Medoff (1985), using microdata derived from the authors' survey of 168 U.S. manufacturing plants, report that during business downturns firms pay for approximately 8 percent more labor than is technologically warranted. Using aggregate data, Fair estimated this figure to be in the range of 4 to 4.5 percent. Fair comments that the results are important for the production function and investment literature that assumes that "firms are always 'on' their production functions. If they are not . . . it is not clear that estimates of production parameters and investment behavior that are based on the assumption of no hoarding are trustworthy" (1985, 245).

limiting case. Conversely, neoclassical arguments against XE theory become redundant: there is simply no place in neoclassical micro-economic theory for X-(in)efficiency.

Ex-Post Criticisms of XE Theory

The literature on X-efficiency, in both its theoretical and empirical aspects, has been voluminous since Leibenstein's 1966 article. As work on X-efficiency has developed and grown, it has evoked different identifiable schools of criticisms. These I shall refer to as: (1) rent-seeking, (2) leisure as output, (3) management utility under competition, and (4) property rights. I shall explore these criticisms and provide a response.

Rent-Seeking

There are two variants to the rent-seeking argument. The first variant is represented by Tullock (1967) and Schap (1985). Tullock, writing one year after Leibenstein's seminal (1966) article on XE theory, cited Leibenstein's article as an example of inefficiencies not captured by the welfare triangle. Unlike Leibenstein, however, Tullock preferred concepts more consistent with neoclassical theory. In figure 1, Tullock simply assumes that the higher costs represented by the entire area $P_m ABP_c$ are due to a firm's rational "investment," such as rent-seeking expenditures. In other words, Tullock, who did not sharply criticize XE theory as such, does not allow for the existence of X-inefficiency.

Tullock's departure from the then-neoclassical orthodoxy was similar in spirit to Leibenstein's; however, this similar departure led to different concerns and theories. Leibenstein explored nonmaximization as a source for the cost and productivity changes observed and reported in his original treatment of X-efficiency. Tullock cited some of this same data yet went on to discuss rent-seeking as a source of welfare losses. Leibenstein looked at costs above minimum levels and called them X-inefficiency. Tullock found nothing inefficient about these higher costs. He surmised that they represented a rational response to an incentive created by government; hence, these higher costs are a welfare cost of government.

David Schap's (1985) argument, far more complex than what we can fully treat in this article, contains more elements than the Tullock argument and represents an explicit criticism of XE. Schap's argument involves distinguishing a perfectly competitive X-efficient firm from both an X-efficient monopolist and an X-inefficient monopolist. Schap assumes that the excess costs of the monopolist are: (1) intrinsic to the

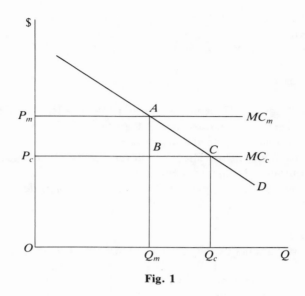

Fig. 1

firm and hence unavoidable, and (2) due to rent-seeking expenditures. Basing his argument on these two assumptions, Schap concludes that X-inefficiency is insignificant. However, if you begin with the assertion that X-inefficiency does not exist, as Schap did, then you can always conclude that X-inefficiency does not exist!

The second variant is represented by Crain and Zardkoohi (1980). Their argument is shown with the aid of figure 2.[2] In figure 2 the competitive firm produces Q_c, charges price P_c, and has long-run costs MC_c. The monopolist would produce output Q_m, charge price P_m, and have costs MC_m. The allocative-market loss due to monopoly power is thus the area ABC. Area $P_m ABP_c$ has four components to it. Area 1 represents profits; area 2 represents higher wages and salaries; and area 3 represents job perks but would also include higher costs due to factors, such as suboptimal and/or excess capacity. Finally, area 4 represents pure X-inefficiency. (However, areas 2 and 3 may also contain X-inefficiency. Higher costs due to wages and salaries may reflect X-inefficiency if these higher costs are not the outcome of rational wage policies. Area 3 may contain X-inefficiency if, for example, the costs of perks exceed the value of these perks to the recipients. Employees may prefer cash, but tax laws encourage the firm to provide perks.)

---

2. I am grateful to Don Lecraw for suggesting fig. 2 as a way of analyzing both XE theory and its critics.

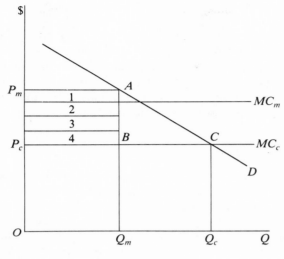

Fig. 2

Crain and Zardkoohi assume that X-inefficiency can exist and, more importantly, that it is a linear function of rent-seeking expenditures, such that an increase (decrease) in rent-seeking (which I will assume can be allocated to area 3) is offset by an equally large decrease (increase) in X-inefficiency. X-inefficiency and rent-seeking are thus substitute goods, two forms of inefficiency, both of which result in social waste. In a rent-seeking society, firms are motivated to be X-efficient so that their available rent-seeking investment funds are adequate to meet their profit goals. Since gains (reductions) in X-efficiency are offset by increases (decreases) in rent-seeking, these changes in X-(in)efficiency have no effect on net welfare. In other words, even if X-inefficiency exists, it does not result in any net changes in welfare. Society is merely facing a trade-off between two forms of inefficiency. However, similar to other critics, Crain and Zardkoohi's conclusion that X-inefficiency has no welfare impact on society is embedded in their assumption.

Two general points about rent-seeking and X-efficiency are worth noting. First, rent-seeking and XE theory are not easily comparable. Rent-seeking is a form of maximizing behavior. Rent-seeking behavior is purposeful and directed; it is a highly calculated response to a profit incentive. Furthermore, the firm is perceived to be a production function. That is, all employees are successfully directed, presumably by management, to achieve a common goal. Thus, the firm expends scarce resources on rent-seeking until the marginal benefit is equal to the marginal cost, and hence, given its rent-seeking expenditures, the firm is a cost minimizer.

Second, does a firm actually calculate its rent-seeking budget as closely as the theory of rent-seeking implies? One reason for believing that this budget is not as finely calculated as the theory implies is that some portion, perhaps a significant portion, of a firm's rent-seeking budget is allocated as dues to trade associations rather than being allocated according to the rules of marginal analysis.

Leisure as Output

Several writers, most notably George Stigler (1976), have used this approach. This approach rests on the notion that a firm produces two types of commodities. First, it produces commodities sold in the market, the common usage of the term *output*. Second, it produces nontraded commodities, such as on-the-job leisure, the quiet life, friendship, rest and relaxation, and other commodities that are similar in content. The higher unit costs that the firm might incur if it is a monopolist thus represents employees' utility and, as such, is a benefit rather than a social cost of monopoly. Assuming rational or maximizing behavior means that an individual will help produce these nontraded commodities until the marginal benefit is just equal to the marginal cost. In other words, if a firm is not minimizing its costs because employees are accepting on-the-job leisure, then it must be that the employees prefer on-the-job leisure to the profits (income) that they knowingly forego.

One response to Leibenstein's theory that higher than minimum costs are a form of inefficiency is that this is the case only if the utility gained from on-the-job leisure is heavily discounted. But, of course, if individuals choose leisure, then how can it be discounted? Therefore, according to his critics, Leibenstein must be arbitrarily defining inefficiency according to his preferred definition rather than according to the preferences of others.

Parish and Ng (1972) were among the first to use this general line of argument. They state that higher costs are a form of allocative inefficiency, not X-inefficiency. If entrepreneurs act rationally say Parish and Ng, then X-inefficiency does not produce any net social costs. This is because the leisure of the entrepreneur is part of the social product not part of social cost. Social costs arise in this context only when, for example, there is some inefficiency in the pricing of leisure. When this occurs, the person substituting leisure for income does not bear the full cost of his decision. However, because this involves a price, it is, by definition, a form of allocative inefficiency.

Martin (1978) discussed effort-leisure tradeoffs in the context of the efficiency effects of protection from international trade. Martin defined X-efficiency in terms of managerial effort. Martin, in a manner similar to that of Parish and Ng, stated that less effort means that more leisure is being produced, but that this leisure is a benefit of protection rather than a cost. Furthermore, since individual behavior is assumed to be rational, leisure is increased until its marginal benefits are equal to its cost. In other words, the producer is fully absorbing the entire rise in unit costs through a substitution of leisure for income. Higher costs — X-inefficiency if you choose — thus entail no social cost.

Martin also asserts that all welfare costs of protection are allocative. This occurs because, for example, the price of leisure is too low relative to the price of commodities while at the same time society values hard work and regards the quiet life as undesirable. In terms of figure 2, area 3 is wholly a transfer. Area 4 either does not exist or it exists but involves no welfare losses or only welfare losses that are actually allocative in nature. In other words, it follows from Martin's assumption of fully rational behavior that either X-inefficiency does not exist or it exists but is actually allocative inefficiency.

Martin's criticism, however, is based on his own model and assumptions. These assumptions, made explicit by Martin, are that the firm:

1. is a well-defined production function,
2. is perfectly competitive,
3. engages in (utility) maximizing behavior, and
4. is characterized by diminishing utility to effort.

XE theory, on the other hand, applies best to imperfect competition, assumes that production functions are not well defined, and may exhibit both maximizing and nonmaximizing characteristics. In other words, Martin uses a more traditional neoclassical model to evaluate a nontraditional, neoclassical model.

Levin (1974) argued that the production of goods and services obeys the laws of physics. Specifically, it obeys the laws of mass and energy that teach us that nothing is ever lost. Levin interprets this to mean that if the firm is producing less of its traded commodities than is possible, then it must be producing more of its nontraded commodities, such as leisure.

Peel (1974) offered the argument that a lazy work force is X-efficient if its production level maximizes the output for its own (lazy) level of effort. Furthermore, he believes that it is operationally more convenient to consider the actual output to be the maximum output. In addition, he considers noncost minimization to be consistent with X-efficiency when these costs increase the motivations of the employees. Expenditures on piped music and bonuses are two examples of such costs. (Peel confuses the importance of total costs with unit costs.)

Pasour (1982) offers a similar argument that less output and more leisure are not necessarily signs of inefficiency. And, since leisure is chosen, it obviously must be worth more than the income foregone by those individuals. Finally, Pasour defines inefficient actions as the outcome of a situation in which an opportunity for net gain has not yet been noticed. Accordingly, inefficiency creates market disequilibrium; by definition, therefore, all inefficiencies are allocative. Since unobserved opportunities are totally subjective, they cannot be observed by anyone other than the individual. The conclusion is that no one can determine when another person is being inefficient.

Pasour's definition of inefficiency is, to say the least, an unusual one. The difficulty with using it lies not in its unusualness but in its implication that individuals are always doing as well as they can: however, these individuals do not recognize all of the opportunities available to them because of a genuine lack of information, which is not caused by their unwillingness to put forth effort in searching and/or simply being aware. In other words, Pasour's definition of inefficiency implies that X-inefficiency is zero.

The leisure-effort criticism of XE theory was perhaps most forcefully presented by George Stigler (1976). When Stigler asked, "What is output?" his answer was that the product of the firm is what it sells plus commodities such as the health and leisure of its employees. Assuming rational, utility-maximizing behavior, he states that when more effort increases traded output but reduces nontraded output — leisure — then this increase represents a change in the mixture of outputs rather than an increase in efficiency. To consider this change as an increase in efficiency is to adopt a tunnel-vision definition of output and to impose one's own goals on others who have never accepted those goals. Higher costs do not involve waste; ex-post waste arises because ex-ante plans were developed in the presence of uncertainty. This type of waste is unavoidable but controllable. Ex-post waste can also arise if individuals are not maximizers. Stigler refuses to accept this possibility until a theory of errors is developed. Finally, Stigler, like the other authors writing about leisure as output, asserts that once all of the firm's inputs and outputs have been properly defined, then all firms can be shown to produce on their production functions. In terms of figure 2, area 4 represents the utility of the firm's nontraded output.

General and Concluding Remarks about Leisure as Output

The leisure-as-output argument denies the existence of X-inefficiency on the assumption that rational decision makers would never choose leisure if its value were less than its (opportunity) cost. The choice of leisure is thus a revealed preference for leisure, vis-à-vis (money) income. The higher unit costs resulting from leisure are thus absorbed by the employees. However, Crew has argued that employees are most likely to absorb these higher costs fully if they are employed in the "old neoclassical entrepreneurial firm" (1975, 158). By this he means a relatively small, competitive, owner-managed firm. Among modern firms possessing market power, this is less likely to be the case for several reasons. First, "dog-in-the-manger" type of labor-management relations leave the groups' (both sides) welfare less than it could be. Second, Crew considered X-inefficiency to be an "insidious disease" that affects behavior without announcing its presence. Third, institutional arrangements, rather than (rational) choice, often dictate the amount of leisure an employee will receive or the employee's ability to trade off leisure for income.

Crew's second argument, that all inefficiencies are allocative, rests on the assumption that every manifestation of human energy can be treated as if it were traded in a market and hence involves prices. These prices, if not explicit, must be implicit. This argument thus rests on the assertion that there is both a market for and a price of leisure and that every employee is aware of the existence of this market and also knows the current price, past prices, and expected future prices of leisure. Of course, assuming that all inefficiencies are allocative means that (implicit) prices and markets for effort must exist. These arguments are difficult either to prove or to refute, as is the argument that firms produce both traded and nontraded commodities. For these reasons I will refer to this form of allocative inefficiency as implicit price-allocative inefficiency.

These arguments put forth by the critics of XE theory are tautological. Leibenstein comments in the following way:

An example of this interpretation is the approach which argues that everyone maximizes utility, and instances that appear to falsify the theory occur because the objective function is not understood by the observer. The essence of this interpretation is bull's-eye painting. The analyst seems to be saying, "give me an observed result and I can state an objective function for which the result fits." Although this approach is frequently used by defenders of neoclassical theory, such defenders cannot really be genuine friends of the theory. In the long run such an approach must appear nothing else but foolish.

Can we say that people are ever X-inefficient? I believe we can. First, we start with the interpretation that X-inefficiency is possible. We must then state, for some specific instance, the set of procedures that an individual would have to engage in if efficiency is to result. If all the procedures are carried out, then the outcome would be efficient; but if some *necessary* procedures are not carried out, then we would view it as inefficient. (1982, 461)

Forsund, Lovell, and Schmidt have enumerated the difficulties of measuring and interpreting X-(in)efficiency estimates gained through an industry production function but have nevertheless argued that nonallocative (in)efficiencies do exist. Their response to this neoclassical critique of XE concept and to Stigler in particular is similar to Leibenstein's. They state:

Stigler basically takes the view that all perceived inefficiency is allocative inefficiency, and even this is perceived because of a failure on the part of the observer—e.g., a failure to measure all relevant inputs, or to correctly perceive what is being maximized or to account for all of the constraints on the maximization process, etc.

This kind of argument seems to be accepted by most economists. However, this is really an act of faith, since the dogma being proposed is not amenable to empirical proof or disproof. (1980, 21)

There seem to be two cases of leisure as output. The first occurs when the owners of the firm (directly or through their agents) knowingly sacrifice profits so that the workers enjoy on-the-job leisure, and the workers (in turn) prefer the leisure to the income that may also be sacrificed. This case probably does not involve any X-inefficiency. The second case includes all other cases, for example, when the employees are not aware of the trade-offs between leisure and income because of work norms, conventions, and sanctions, and/or because the owners expect a "fair day's work for a fair day's pay."

Finally, there is a literature in industrial psychology (Locke 1976) and economics (Scitovsky 1976) that demonstrates that the relationship between effort and job satisfaction is parabolic, not linear. That is, employees are often found to dislike both too little and too much effort. To treat on-the-job leisure as a desirable part of a job, per se, is thus an incorrect assumption leading to incorrect conclusions.

Management Utility under Uncertainty

Thomas DiLorenzo has argued that competitive capital markets and the fact that private-sector managers are residual claimants who must compete for jobs, make the concept of X-inefficiency a highly suspect notion (1981, 122). Furthermore, he considers his analysis applicable both to competitive and monopolistic firms, since in both environments managers' rewards are tied to profitability. It follows that the rational, utility-maximizing private-sector manager will best be able to increase his utility not by enjoying the quiet life, but by being X-efficient and increasing the firm's profits (à la Crain and Zardkoohi 1980).

Although one could argue that managers in monopolistic firms enjoy sufficient shelter from competitive pressure so as to allow them to be X-inefficient with impunity, DiLorenzo's argument is that as long as capital markets are perfect, an X-inefficient manager faces the threat of the firm being taken over with the subsequent loss of his or her own job. The key to his argument is the existence of perfect capital markets. In terms of figure 2, DiLorenzo concludes that: (1) X-inefficiency in area 3 or 4 could exist but will be forced to zero by perfect capital markets, and (2) utility-maximizing managers will increase their utility by reducing area 3 and 4 to a minimum and thus increasing profits, area 1.

The existence of perfect capital markets in the United States is a suspect notion. Elsewhere (Frantz 1984) I reviewed the evidence for perfect capital markets and showed the evidence to be inconclusive.

Property Rights

De Alessi (1983) argues against XE theory by presenting generalized neoclassical theory and showing that the assumptions, implications, and empirical evidence presented for XE theory are consistent with generalized neoclassical theory. His preference for generalized neoclassical theory is based on the fact that it is consistent with the assumptions and methodology of neoclassical theory, that is, it studies individual choices of a utility maximizer under constraints and hence can identify preference relations.

On the other hand, he discounts XE theory because it rejects the notion of maximizing behavior because: it does not consider the effects of property rights on behavior, it denies that (wealth) maximization ever occurs, and it focuses on unobservable preference relations requiring the use of the concept of the personality.

Using the concepts of property rights and transactions costs, De Alessi feels that generalized neoclassical theory is better able to explain the central postulates of XE theory and can do so using fewer assumptions. Consider, for example, the effect of positive transactions costs. Transactions costs can explain why a firm's production function is not well specified, why labor contracts are incomplete, why some inputs are not marketed, and why individuals work within an inert area or are selectively rational. Thus, inert areas exist because the benefits of change are less than the costs (transactions and adjustment costs). The existence of inert areas thus does not require an explanation that uses immensely complex notions such as personality. A simpler explanation is that the benefits are less than the costs.

Evidence presented for XE theory is also more efficiently explained by generalized neoclassical theory. For example, positive transactions costs explain why firms are not producing on their expansion path. Furthermore, noncost minimization is not necessarily inefficient since inefficiency must be defined in terms of the constraints facing that firm. What XE theory identifies as inefficiency occurs in part because it compares the performance of actual firms against an unattainable (competitive) ideal. XE theory thus commits the "nirvana fallacy." As other critics maintain, when a (rational) person chooses on-the-job leisure rather than extra income, then his or her work behavior is efficient. To quote De Alessi, "The equilibrium solution associated with a given set of constraints is efficient" (1983, 73).

Several comments are very relevant here. First, and contrary to De Alessi's statement, Leibenstein has discussed the ownership form in his book, *General X-Efficiency Theory and Economic Development.* Ownership form has also been discussed by several writers, presenting empirical results consistent with the implications of XE theory. Second, again contrary to De Alessi's statement, Leibenstein (1976, 1983, 1986) has clearly stated that he does not deny maximization. However, he allows for the possibility of both maximizing and nonmaximizing behavior and has attempted to explain under what conditions each type of behavior is most likely to be forthcoming.[3] For De Alessi, maximization is an article of faith. For Leibenstein, maximization should be the outcome of certain decision-making procedures and hence should be observable and potentially refutable. Third, it is difficult to assess De Alessi's objection to the use of the concept of personality. De Alessi's explanation for individual behavior includes the concept of utility (maximization) and hence, implicitly, the concept of the personality.

Is it really simpler to use terms such as *transactions costs* or *property*

---

3. Leibenstein (1986) has used a modern interpretation of the Yerkes-Dodson Law (1908) to discuss the relationship between pressure and the degree of rational behavior.

rights so as to make any observed behavior appear efficient? I think not. With regard to transactions costs, Oliver Williamson (1985, 20–21) has pointed out that they cannot be measured directly. As a result transactions costs are assessed by comparing various corporate forms and making ordinal judgments as to their magnitude, that is, transactions costs will be greater in organizational form A vis-à-vis organizational form B. If these costs cannot be measured directly — if they are not subject to any standard bookkeeping procedures — then it is difficult to know whether and to what extent they can explain differences in work effort and, hence, in costs among firms.

The use of property rights is also troublesome. In general, arguments about property rights have been concerned with the property rights of managers. The implication is that the firm is a production function, subject to the prevailing system of property rights. Thus, once this system is known, the managers have their incentives and the remainder of the employees fall in line to accomplish the goals that the managers design. XE theory, however, does not view the firm as a production function; to view the firm as such is to assume away X-inefficiency.

Fourth, most evidence that is consistent with the implications of XE theory is not a "nirvana fallacy." Most of the empirical work on XE theory makes comparisons between two or more real firms rather than between a real firm and a competitive ideal. In these cases the authors have attempted to compare similar firms that differ in ownership form or in market power. Is there an alternative — non-XE — explanation for these empirical results? Of course! But it cuts both ways. In a very extensive literature review on property rights, De Alessi (1980) reviewed over 100 studies. At first reading, at least 20 of these studies are consistent with the implications of XE theory.

How can we decide which explanation is preferable? Count the number of assumptions used by each theory? This would be, I believe, a pointless exercise because both theories make the same number of assumptions. For example, in not making any assumptions about the dual nature of the personality, De Alessi is assuming that the personality does not matter. Surely, we are not going to limit ourselves to explicit assumptions!

In addition, De Alessi and Leibenstein are, according to De Alessi, concerned with different questions. De Alessi states: "Leibenstein seems to be concerned with the rationality of the individual and how particular individuals might behave in particular circumstances. My concern, on the other hand, is with the rationality (logic) of the theory and its ability to explain real world phenomena" (1983, 845, fn. 2). In terms of figure 2, this fourth school of criticism denies that pure X-inefficiency, area 4, exists. Furthermore, X-inefficiency may appear to exist in area 3 because the benefit of perks to the recipients is not worth the cost. However, these perks would be produced due to factors such as positive transactions costs, uncertainty, or attenuated property rights. Regardless of the cause, these factors represent constraints on the behavior of the individual and hence represent, not X-inefficiency but constrained utility maximization. Area 3 inefficiencies are thus allocative inefficiencies.

One problem with using the concepts of utility, uncertainty, or transactions costs to explain intrafirm behavior is that none of these costs can be (or is) measured by any standard bookkeeping procedure. Each can be used in a tautological or nontautological manner. By changing the use of the term *allocative inefficiency* from allocative-market to implicit price-allocative, these critics have seemingly created a definition of inefficiency that does not allow for X-inefficiency.

Holtmann (1983), like De Alessi, maintains that both XE theory and empirical evidence are consistent with generalized neoclassical theory, which includes the concepts of uncertainty and utility maximization. For example, because uncertainty lowers expected profits, then uncertainty can explain why the owner-managed firms in the Shelton (1967) study had higher profits than did the company-managed firms. Shelton compared individual restaurants in a national restaurant chain that were identical in every respect except that at times they were managed by the company while at other times they were managed by franchise owners. Holtmann's reasoning is that owner-managers face less uncertainty about their employees' efforts than do company managers and hence will have higher profits.

Of course, the simple explanation, and the one given by the company managers themselves, is that the owner-managers watched the operation more closely than did the company managers and made higher profits. This result is not contingent upon uncertainty. The parent company may have been completely certain about the efforts of the hired managers but were profit "satisficers" rather than profit maximizers. (Why company managers would be less certain about what employees are doing several feet away is not clear, nor does Holtmann offer an explanation.) We need not assume that the owner-managers were profit maximizers. What they did was to generate higher profits, mostly by keeping costs lower than their company-manager counterparts. If Holtmann's explanation is not of the ex-post variety, it certainly seems farfetched.

Another example offered by Holtmann is with regard to Shepherd's (1972a) finding that market share and profits are not linearly related to each other; and that, that, according to Shepherd, is due to X-inefficiency among larger firms. Shepherd's explanation is that it is due to the absolute risk aversion among managers of larger firms. He offers no evidence that this is the case.

Ex-Ante Criticisms of XE Theory

By ex ante I mean that a prediction is made and tested. One example offered by Holtmann concerns Primeaux's (1977) finding that electric utility duopolists in 49 U.S. cities in the early 1960s had average costs that were (at the mean output rate) 10.75 percent lower than comparable electric utility monopolists. Furthermore, average costs were lower for the monopoly firm only in the case of the largest 10 percent of utilities. Primeaux attributes his findings to the fact that the X-inefficiency costs of monopoly power exceed the benefits of economies of scale for all but the largest firms.

Holtmann's explanation is that the lower costs among duopolists are due to greater variability in demand (maintaining a greater amount of excess capacity) among the monopolists. However, here we have a hypothesis that was tested! Here is an ex-ante criticism, a testable hypothesis/prediction made by a critic of XE theory/evidence. Primeaux (1978) tested this hypothesis on the same sample used for his cost study and found no significant difference in excess capacity between the monopolists and the duopolists. In other words, this hypothesis was not verified.

Second, a related criticism is that what is referred to as X-inefficiency is actually the results of a firm with either suboptimal capacity or excess capacity.[4] However, Weiss and Pascoe (1985), using Federal Trade Commission data for 233 U.S. manufacturing industries for the years 1974 through 1976, devised a method for distinguishing empirically among X-efficiency, suboptimal capacity, and excess capacity and reported that X-inefficiency has an independent effect on labor productivity among concentrated industries. In other words, this ex-ante criticism of XE theory and evidence is not substantiated by the Weiss and Pascoe study.

A third ex-ante criticism is that the finding that some firms within an industry are further from the industry production (cost) frontier is due not to greater X-inefficiency but to the effects of breaking in new capital. Bo Carlsson (1972) tested this view with a sample of 26 Swedish manufacturing industries for 1968. Carlsson estimated a Cobb-Douglas production function for each industry and then compared each firm's actual

---

4. A graphical exposition distinguishing among X-inefficiency, suboptimal capacity, and excess capacity is presented by Siegfried and Wheeler (1981).

(Q) and potential (Q^*) output as a measure of its X-inefficiency. In order to explain (Q/Q^*), Carlsson used measures of labor, capital, and the degree of monopoly power. His proxy for the breaking-in effects of new capital was the change in industry assets during 1968 multiplied by capital/output. In his multiple regression equation, this variable was statistically insignificant, that is, new capital did not reduce production X-efficiency. Again, an ex-ante criticism is not substantiated by the data.

Fourth, at the same time, some have argued that firms that appear to be X-inefficient are actually doing as well as they can with their older capital. This "vintage capital" model was tested by Gregory and James (1973) using a sample of 116 new factories among 46 Australian industries. For the entire sample of 46 industries, the authors reported that labor productivity in new factories was, on the average, in the range of 10 to 15 percent higher than average industry labor productivity. Salter's (1960) prediction was that this difference should be in the range of 50 to 100 percent. The authors also reported that the growth in labor productivity between 1956 and 1958 among new factories was not different from the industry average growth rate. The authors concluded that either firms are not adopting the best available technology and/or that nonvintage factors, such as X-efficiency, are significant influences on interplant, intraindustry labor productivity. In other words, this ex-ante criticism is not substantiated by data as well.

Summary and Conclusions

Most criticisms of XE theory and evidence are of the ex-post variety. That is, the critic seems satisfied to specify a utility function that can exist and is consistent with the term *rational behavior*. In other words, most critics of XE have simply assumed away its existence. In those cases where predictions were tested, the predictions were shown not to be verified. The critics have simply not proved their point.

In 1966 when Leibenstein formulated XE theory the concept of intrafirm or nonmarket behavior was relatively new to the economics profession. Leibenstein developed XE theory in order to provide an explanation for intrafirm behavior that was seemingly noncost minimizing. Because economics was mostly concerned with market behavior, the supply and demand constraints were relatively straightforward. The attempt to explain intrafirm behavior led many economists to do what they know best, that is, assert optimization under constraints. This required the specification of many more constraints.

For whatever reason, these constraints were specified both ex ante and ex post. The critics of XE theory have not proved their case because they have specified their constraints ex post. Perhaps this should lead us to rethink our belief that economic theory is an intellectual tool so powerful that it can analyze all behavior, regardless of whether this behavior is categorized as sociological, psychological, political, marital, or spiritual.

This observation is perhaps one of the major contributions of XE theory. That is, XE theory presents us with the prospect that economic theory has currently undertaken more than it can deliver. By putting forth the concept of X-efficiency — a form of inefficiency not caused by market prices deviating from marginal cost — including the concept of suboptimal behavior, Leibenstein has caused the most jealous defenders of neoclassical theory to come forth and argue their case by assertion. One can conclude that if this is what microeconomic theory now rests on, then the entry into intrafirm behavior has temporarily thrown microeconomics into a state of disequilibrium. That is, in attempting to explain intrafirm, not market, behavior, microeconomics has delved into an area that it is not equipped to handle efficiently. And there is no reason to believe that it could make the transition from market to nonmarket behavior automatically. Listening to Leibenstein's critics, one has to wonder whether perhaps Mundell was correct.

REFERENCES

Anderson, J., and R. Frantz. 1982. "The Response of Labor Effort to Falling Real Wages: The Mexican Peso Devaluation of February 1982." *World Development* 12:759–66.

Anderson, J., and R. Frantz. 1985. "Production Efficiency among Mexican Apparel Assembly Plants." *Journal of Developing Areas* 19:369–78.

Babilot, G., R. Frantz, and L. Green. 1987. "Natural Monopolies and Rent: A Georgist Remedy for X-Inefficiency among Regulated Firms." *American Journal of Sociology* 46:205–16.

Boddy, R., R. Frantz, and B. Poe-Tierney. 1986. "The Marginal Productivity Theory: Production Line and Machine Level by Work Shift and Time of Day." *Journal of Behavioral Economics* 15:1–24.

Carlsson, B. 1972. "The Measurement of Efficiency in Production: An Application to Swedish Manufacturing Industries, 1968." *Swedish Journal of Economics* 74:468–85.

Crain, M., and A. Zardkoohi. 1980. "X-Efficiency and Nonpecuniary Rewards in a Rent Seeking Society: A Neglected Issue in the Property Rights Theory of the Firm." *American Economics Review* 70:784–92.

Crew, M. 1975. *The Theory of the Firm.* New York: Longman.

Crew, M., and Paul Kleindorfer. 1985. "Governance Structures for Natural

Monopoly: A Comparative Institutional Perspective." *Journal of Behavioral Economics* 14:117–40.

De Alessi, L. 1980. "The Economics of Property Rights: A Review of the Evidence." In *Research in Law and Economics*, vol. 2, ed. R. Zerbe. Greenwich: JAI Press.

De Alessi, L. 1983. "Property Rights, Transactions Costs, and X-Efficiency: An Essay in Economic Theory." *American Economic Review* 75:64–81.

DiLorenzo, T. 1981. "Corporate Management, Property Rights, and the X-istence of X-inefficiency." *Southern Economic Journal* 48:116–23.

Fair, R. 1985. "Excess Labor and the Business Cycle." *American Economic Review* 75:239–45.

Fay, J., and J. Medoff. 1985. "Labor and Output over the Business Cycle." *American Economic Review* 75: 638–55.

Forsund, F., and P. Hjalmarsson. 1974. "On the Measurement of Productive Efficiency." *Swedish Journal of Economics* 76:141–54.

Forsund, F., C. Lovell, and P. Schmidt. 1980. "A Survey of Frontier Production Functions and of their Relationship to Efficiency Measurement." *Journal of Econometrics* 13:5–25.

Frantz, R. 1980. "On the Existence of X-Efficiency." *Journal of Post Keynesian Economics* 4:509–27.

Frantz, R. 1982. "Worker Motivation and X-Efficiency Theory: A Comment." *Journal of Economic Issues* 16:864–68.

Frantz, R. 1984. "Corporate Management, Property Rights and the Existence of X-Efficiency Once More." *Southern Economic Journal* 50:1204–8.

Frantz, R. 1985. "X-Efficiency Theory and Its Critics." *Quarterly Review of Economics and Business* 25:38–58.

Frantz, R. 1986. "X-Efficiency in Behavioral Economics." In *Handbook of Behavioral Economics*, vol. A, ed. B. Gilad and S. Kaish. Greenwich: JAI Press.

Frantz, R. 1988. *X-Efficiency: Theory, Evidence and Applications*. Boston: Kluwer Academic Press.

Frantz, R., and F. Galloway. 1985. "A Theory of Multidimensional Effort Decisions." *Journal of Behavioral Economics* 14:69–82.

Frantz, R., and L. Green. 1982. "Prejudice, Mistrust, and Labor Effort: Social Influences on Productivity." *Journal of Behavioral Economics* 11:101–31.

Gregory, R., and D. James. 1973. "Do New Factories Embody Best Practice Technology?" *Economic Journal* 83:1133–55.

Harberger, A. 1954. "Using the Resources at Hand More Effectively." *American Economic Review* 59:134–47.

Holtmann, A. 1983. "Uncertainty, Organizational Form, and X-Efficiency." *Journal of Economics and Business* 35:131–37.

Leibenstein, H. 1966. "Allocative Efficiency vs. 'X-Efficiency.' " *American Economic Review* 56: 392–415.

Leibenstein, H. 1976. *Beyond Economic Man*. Cambridge, Mass.: Harvard University Press.

Leibenstein, H. 1978a. *General X-Efficiency Theory and Economic Development*. New York: Oxford University Press.

Leibenstein, H. 1978b. "X-Inefficiency Xists: A Reply to an Xorcist." *American Economic Review* 68:203-11.

Leibenstein, H. 1982. "On Bull's-Eye-Painting Economics." *Journal of Post Keynesian Economics* 4:460-65.

Leibenstein, H. 1983. "Property Rights Theory and X-Efficiency Theory: A Comment." *American Economic Review* 73:831-42.

Leibenstein, H. 1986. "On Relaxing the Maximization Postulate." *Journal of Behavioral Economics* 15:2-16.

Levin, H. 1974. "Measuring Efficiency in Educational Production." *Public Finance Quarterly* 2:831-42.

Locke, E. 1976. "The Nature and Causes of Job Satisfaction." In *Handbook of Industrial and Organizational Psychology*, ed. M. Dunnette. Chicago: Rand McNally.

Martin, J. 1978. "X-Inefficiency, Managerial Effort and Protection." *Economica* 45:273-86.

Mundell, R. 1962. "Review of L. H. Janssen, Free Trade, Protection and Customs Union." *American Economic Review* 52:622.

Parish, R., and Y. Ng. 1972. "Monopoly, X-Efficiency, and the Measurement of Welfare Losses." *Economica* 39:301-8.

Pasour, E., Jr. 1982. "Economic Efficiency and Inefficient Economies: Another View." *Journal of Post Keynesian Economics* 4:454-59.

Peel, D. 1974. "A Note on X-Inefficiency." *Quarterly Journal of Economics* 88:687-88.

Primeaux, W. 1977. "An Assessment of X-Efficiency Gained through Competition." *Review of Economics and Statistics* 59:105-13.

Primeaux, W. 1978. "The Effect of Competition on Capacity Utilization in the Electric Utility Industry." *Economic Inquiry* 26:237-48.

Primeaux, W. 1986. *Direct Electric Utility Competition: The Natural Monopoly Myth*. New York: Praeger.

Salter, W. 1960. *Productivity and Technical Change*, Cambridge: Cambridge University Press.

Schap, D. 1985. "X-Inefficiency in a Rent-Seeking Society: A Graphical Analysis." *Quarterly Review of Economics and Business* 25:19-27.

Scitovsky, T. 1976. *The Joyless Economy*. New York: Oxford University Press.

Shelton, J. 1967. "Allocative Efficiency versus 'X-Efficiency': Comment." *American Economic Review* 57:1252-58.

Shepherd, W. 1972a. "The Elements of Market Structure." *Review of Economics and Statistics* 54:25-37.

Shepherd, W. 1972b. "Elements of Market Structure: An Inter-Industry Analysis." *Southern Economic Journal* 38:531-37.

Siegfried, J., and E. Wheeler. 1981. "Cost Efficiency and Monopoly Power: A Survey." *Quarterly Review of Economics and Business* 21:25-46.

Stigler, G. 1976. "The Xistence of X-Efficiency." *American Economic Review* 66:213–16.

Tullock, G. 1967. "The Welfare Costs of Tariffs, Monopolies, and Theft." *Western Economic Journal* 5:224–32.

Weiss, L., and G. Pascoe. 1985. "Concentration, X-Inefficiency and Mr. Peltzman's Superior Firms." Social Systems Research Institute Working Paper no. 8501. Madison: University of Wisconsin.

Williamson, O. 1985. *The Economic Institutions of Capitalism*. New York: Free Press.

Commentary

Klaus Weiermair and Marvin E. Rozen

Comments by Klaus Weiermair

The first three chapters evaluated and placed Leibenstein's contributions pertaining to X-efficiency theory in the context of:

 a. his own intellectual development and those of his peers and predecessors (Professor Perlman),
 b. vis-à-vis one major paradigm in economics dealing with cost behavior, the contestable markets hypothesis (Professor Hatch), and
 c. the contestable markets hypothesis versus mainstream (neoclassical) criticisms of the X-efficiency paradigm.

Professor Perlman, who was a colleague of Leibenstein's at Princeton, illustrates in his article the powerful influence that Morgenstern's teaching had upon Leibenstein and his subsequent work. This includes the role of subjective versus objective rationality, the notion of game theory, or more generally, experimental economics as a tool in economic analysis and the general perception of the role and importance of economic theorizing. Throughout his contribution, Professor Perlman traces the influence of Leibenstein's teachers, Morgenstern and Notestein, in conjunction with Leibenstein's concern for microeconomic phenomena spanning demographic economic development, entrepreneurship, and industrial organization.

In the second and equally interesting part of the article, Professor Perlman places the evolution of X-efficiency (rather than the evolution of Leibenstein) in the context of the history of economic thought, showing the treatment of the equivalence of X-efficiency theoretical constructs or fragments thereof in the Marshallian partial equilibrium analysis and the Austrian subjectivist school, which was followed later by the American institutionists. He also illustrates how this ties into "das Adam Smith Problem," which in North America means having read only one of the two important volumes of Smith.

Professor Hatch addresses interfirm variations in cost and productivity behavior as one of the most pressing questions of the economics profession. He considers those parts of X-efficiency theory that attempt to explain this gap and compares them with the competing contestable market hypothesis.

Both theories share the idea that competitive pressures have an effect on cost behavior; however, the contestable market hypothesis is a market-based theory of cost behavior, while X-efficiency is based on industrial behavior and interactions. Professor Hatch skillfully shows the effects that various forms of rivalry could have on cost efficiencies under either set of theoretical assumptions and draws the conclusion that to test either one successfully would be very unlikely. At the end of the article, he raises some interesting questions regarding the possibility of interpreting X-efficiency as a form of externality.

Finally, Roger Frantz's article is a thorough account of the opposition among proponents of mainstream neoclassical analysis to X-efficiency theory. Based on his earlier work, he discusses both ex-post and ex-ante theory criticisms evolving from the main arguments concerning rent-seeking, leisure as a part of the utility function, management competition, and property rights distortions.

He concludes that much of the discipline's response to X-efficiency theory has been to defend the holy shrine of profit or utility maximization under constraints by adding more constraints. Critics have not proved their point as they invariably had to build or specify their constraints ex post. He interprets the most useful portion of X-efficiency theory to be that part that explains intrafirm behavior and views the part dealing with markets and market prices as of lesser importance.

I agree with this last statement, which I would like to use in order to add some of my own comments. As a teacher in a graduate business school, where many competing theories of the firm are offered to students, I find that my teaching has been subjected to considerable competition; hence, using Leibenstein's terminology I have had to become more X-efficient. It was in this environment that I discovered Leibenstein's contributions along with other pieces of work, such as Aoki's cooperative theory of the firm. There can be no doubt, at least in my mind, that an opening of the black box of the firm, moving it from a single market-driven production function to an entity of organizations with members working toward, at times, conflicting goals, has been long overdue.

Hence, Leibenstein's greatest contribution to economic theorizing and to the economics profession has been his treatment of organizational slack. He is familiar with and well versed in other theories of firm behavior, such as organizational theory, organizational behavior, and industrial sociology/psychology.

It is interesting to note that when Leibenstein was first invited and presented to the business faculty at York University, he took great pains in his lecture to build an argument to defend the X-efficiency theory (against imaginary enemies) to a faculty that was not quibbling over the existence of X-efficiency but rather one that was saying, "We accept your priors now let's get on with the tools and show their policy relevance."

Although all three articles have pointed to the essence of Leibenstein and X-efficiency theory, they have done so from the perspective of traditional economics, defending the theory's contribution in terms of perceived and accepted market analogies. Market analogies and market theories, however, may not be an adequate way to study intrafirm behavior, and that is where micro-microtheory may enhance our understanding. This point leads to issues of human behavior that will be dealt with in following articles, hence, I will refrain from making comments.

Comments by Marvin E. Rozen

Each of these articles takes up a different aspect of X-efficiency: Perlman focuses on its relationship to the evolution of Leibenstein's thought; Hatch compares it with contestability theory; and Frantz defends its virtues against various types of criticism. My comments will follow that order.

Perlman's article is a useful and vivid reminder that context and provenance are the enriching contribution of intellectual history. We always stand on the shoulders of our predecessors. Thus, linking Leibenstein, through Morgenstern, to the Austrian school and its "Mentalist" orientation—I have always been captivated by von Weiser's (or was it Menger's?) remark expressing wonder and awe at the tremendous advantage conferred upon economists by being able to use their own minds as natural laboratories for testing their propositions—sheds new light on X-efficiency's concern with variability in human performance and its determinants. Similarly, I was not previously sufficiently aware of Leibenstein's Marshallian bent for partial equilibrium analysis within more realistic settings as opposed to more abstract and logically tight general equilibrium approaches. Likewise, organizational theory's development of the role of teams and groups and the importance of such internal arrangements become more obvious and natural features of X-efficiency. Finally, although I dare say that a majority of economists feel privately unhappy with our unidimensional economic man, it is comforting to reach back to Adam Smith's moral sentiments and Wesley C. Mitchell's backward art of spending money to justify going beyond economic man.

With regard to Leibenstein himself, two points are relevant. Stylistically, we can better appreciate Leibenstein's reliance on sophisticated reasoning rather than taking the professional fast track of mathematical precision. Surely, in the long run, the quality of our thought, and not its formal packaging, will be the determining factor. Similarly, the content of Leibenstein's thought as a process of successively redefining an original idea is clarified. The focus remains unchanged, but one gets a real sense of elaboration, enrichment, and complexity as it evolves partly from its own internal logic and partly in response to criticism from more orthodox and generally dominant approaches.

Perlman's article thus conveys a true picture of an idea in flux. It is commonsensical, appealing, slightly rough-hewn, a bit indefinite and incomplete, but for all that it conveys insights and is heuristically attractive. All in all, X-efficiency stands as a useful counter to, as Solow has recently put it, "a profession entranced by the vision of 'pure' economics [that] is likely—though not certain—to fall into the habit of modeling the economy abstractly and then forgetting that the result is an abstraction. The next thing you know, you are drawing conclusions from particular models of general competitive equilibrium and applying them to a rather different sort of real world" (*American Economic Review* 78 [1988]: 380).

In this vein, Hatch's comparison of X-efficiency and contestability as middle-level theoretical approaches is a valiant effort but perhaps raises more questions than it answers. For one thing, too many variables are being simultaneously juggled: the size and scale of firms, their number and potential entrants, strategic behavior elements, and the degree of competitive rivalry, among others. For another, these variables interact in very complicated ways, and the ability to predict specific outcomes may require the introduction of more concrete specifications relating to technology, innovation, legal structure, and historical circumstance. It is one thing to draw up a list of relevant considerations; it is a far more difficult task to model a theoretical structure encompassing their pattern of interaction and relative importance.

Perhaps a useful distinction may be made by further differentiating the aims of contestability theory and X-efficiency. The former tends to be more theoretical and ambitious in trying to devise an analytical structure capable of capturing such important elements of the modern economy as the large multiproduct firm, pervasive strategic behavior, and continuing innovation and technological change. X-efficiency's aims are more modestly and practically focused on the possibility that, whatever the external market situation, knowing more about what goes on inside the firm—the motivational and organizational factors—can lead to great improvements in firm efficiency. This difference in emphasis is implicitly revealed in Hatch's view of X-efficiency as a function solely of external market pressures, whereas I believe the inside-the-firm aspects should be accorded equal, or even greater, prominence.

Indeed, the very language heard at this conference suggests a distinction between X-inefficiency and X-efficiency. The former can more properly be viewed, à la Hatch, as largely conditioned on external factors, firms moving to their existing production frontiers under the whip of vigorous competition as they combat slack and inertia; it can be called preventing turn-off. The latter, then, would be more of an internal phenomenon, focusing on the human agent in the production process, emphasizing motivational and organizational factors, promoting turn-on and innovation, and reaching out to new production frontiers. Certainly this distinction is not absolute, and separating the externally compelled from the internally driven change is easier said than done. Yet because X-efficiency's contribution lies in introducing motivation and organization as analytically important components, it would be wrong to identify it solely with market imperfection. In the real world where competitive forces cannot always operate swiftly and surely, that would rule out important potential sources of productivity gain arising from the firm's internally generated reorganization.

Frantz's article is an admirable review of X-efficiency's ability to withstand the slings and arrows of its many critics. Partly, one has to tread very carefully through the semantic traps, language differences, and methodological quarrels that are at the root of many such critiques. As Frantz shows, assuming what is to be demonstrated, definitional sleights of hand, and ex-post rationalization loom large in many such criticisms. Partly, empirical counterdemonstrations also have generally fallen short. This is not to say that the empirical basis for X-efficiency has been overwhelmingly and definitively affirmed; much remains to be elaborated. With regard to Frantz's article, too, I believe that both the distinction between X-inefficiency and X-efficiency and the idea that middle-level theory offers solid practical ground for improving firm performance could be effectively employed in responding to critics.

In summary, although not so designed, each of these articles complements the others and affirms the validity of X-efficiency notions. Perlman places them in their historical context and establishes their antecedent links; Hatch compares them to contestability theory to illustrate implicitly their proper range and domain; and Frantz demonstrates their robustness and explanatory power in the face of vigorous criticism. What more could one ask as an introduction to this conference's themes?

Part 2
Motivational Foundations of
Economic Behavior

Human Behavior:
Ipsative and Objective Possibilities

Bruno S. Frey

Humans are Imperfect

Human beings sometimes act in a way that an outside observer may find difficult to understand. This article is concerned with two areas of paradoxical behavior. The first area is characterized by the fact that individuals regularly and systematically overestimate their possibility set: they think that they can accomplish more than is objectively possible. Examples are scholars who when writing a book or a paper tend to overestimate their work capacity, realizing as time unfolds that they need much more time to complete the scientific work.[1] Similarly, most business people regularly overcommit their time. Both scholars and business people regret overestimating their work capacity when the time to deliver arrives, but they repeatedly fall into the same trap. The foregoing examples were chosen to make it clear that such overestimation of one's possibilities is not due to inexperience, false information, or lack of intelligence.

Additional examples of overestimates of what is objectively possible are the illusion that the divorce rate does not apply to one's own marriage, or that accident rates in hazardous jobs or sports are irrelevant when a person engages in them himself or herself. Divorces and accidents are presumed to happen to others.

This work is part of an attempt to integrate economic and psychological approaches to behavior, jointly undertaken with psychologist Klaus Foppa of the University of Bern (see Foppa 1987; Frey and Foppa 1986). I am solely responsible for this particular article. Helpful comments by Charles Beat Blankart, Reiner E. Eichenberger, Beat Gygi, Beat Heggli, Gebhard Kirchgässner, Barbara Krug, Werner W. Pommerehne, Friedrich Schneider, Raphaela Schuster and Hannelore Weck-Hannemann are gratefully acknowledged. Oded Stark has made valuable comments concerning content and style. The author also benefited from the discussion at the Bellagio conference. A preliminary version of this article was presented at the *Rencontre de Kirchberg*, February 1988.
1. I also had this experience in writing this article.

The second area of paradoxical behavior is characterized by exactly the converse fact: individuals systematically underestimate the objective possibilities, i.e., they do not exhaust the possibility set available to them. An example is persons who never attend an opera performance though they can well afford to in terms of time and money, are well informed about the opportunity, and are characterized by outside observers as the type who would enjoy opera (as indeed they do if for some reason they happen to attend a performance). Another example of such underestimation of the objective possibility set is the decision not to buy a TV set (by a person who can well afford such a purchase) because one knows that one enjoys watching television. The same behavior is manifested when one decides not to start smoking, drinking, or taking drugs though one knows perfectly well that one will like it once started. Yet another example would be young people who decide against a management career though they know that once undertaken they would enjoy it.

The systematic overestimation or underestimation of one's possibility set is difficult or impossible to reconcile with the spirit of orthodox economic theory, and in particular with its central tenet, the relative price effect. This article endeavors to provide a simple and straightforward explanation of these paradoxes by differentiating between an *objective* possibility set and an *ipsative* possibility set, which is defined by the *personal* view about the possibilities. An effort is made to formulate testable propositions and to provide empirical evidence incompatible with the orthodox economic model of behavior such as that expounded by Stigler and Becker (1977). It is argued that awareness of the differences is relevant for attempts to influence human behavior through economic policy. Identifiable instances exist where an orthodox economic policy carried out by control of relative prices yields a counterproductive outcome.

The approach used here remains within the rational choice framework (and even within utility maximization), i.e., the results are not gained by assuming any kind of irrationality, or an arbitrary or unexplained shift of preferences. Rather, the economic approach to explaining human behavior is exploited more fully by differentiating between two basically different kinds of possibility sets.

Objective and Ipsative Possibility Sets

Individuals do not view the alternatives available to them as binding: some alternatives are considered that are objectively impossible, while other alternatives that are possible are disregarded.[2] The possibility set that a particular individual takes to be relevant for himself or herself — the ipsative possibility set (IPS) — differs from the objective possibility set (OPS). The difference does not lie in the fact that individuals have limited information or intelligence: these factors account for the difference between the objective and the subjective possibility set (a difference that is well known in economic theory and will therefore not be discussed here). An important feature of the difference between the ipsative and the objective possibility sets is that there is no tendency over time for the difference to narrow; rather, the difference can be maintained over long periods, and there are even circumstances in which it increases.

The two possibility sets differ in four major respects:

1. The objective possibility set is *marginal*. Small changes can be meaningfully evaluated in terms of benefits and costs. The ipsative possibility set, on the other hand, is nonmarginal or *absolute*. Alternatives are considered either in full or not at all.
2. OPS is *symmetric*. An increase or a decrease in relative prices have in principle the same effect; the sign may be positive or negative. IPS is *asymmetric*. Alternatives outside the ipsative set are beyond consideration, irrespective of how relative prices change. However, for alternatives inside the ipsative set the normal relative price effects obtain.
3. OPS is *transpersonal*. A (benevolent) outside observer who is well informed about an individual's marginal utility and marginal costs would suggest exactly those actions that the informed individual would choose. IPS is *personal*: the environment is looked at from a point of view relevant only for the particular individual. Consequently, a (benevolent) outside observer would often suggest actions different from the ones undertaken by the individual concerned.
4. OPS assumes that a *choice* between alternatives can be made, based on expected utility maximization. Accordingly, a change in relative prices has a systematic effect on behavior according to the fundamental law of demand. IPS assumes that there are cases in which no (direct) choice between alternatives is possible as autonomous processes prevent a choice being made. Individuals

---

2. In a different context, Simon has called on social scientists "to provide . . . for the limited span of attention that governs *what* considerations, out of the whole host of possible ones, will actually influence the deliberations that precede action" (1985, 302).

have *limited control* between alternatives, and a real choice can be made only by moving to the (constitutional) level where rules may be adopted.

Expected utility maximization theory, which is "the major paradigm in decision making since the Second World War" (Schoemaker 1982, 529), starts from a given set of feasible alternatives. All alternatives belong to the objective possibility set, and the theory is used to arrive at the best choice among alternatives in a risky environment. As Einhorn and Hogarth (1986, 247) state, this theory is completely in the framework of a lottery: "The study of risk has been dominated by a simple metaphor — the explicit lottery with stated probabilities and payoffs."

In economics, expected utility maximization is the standard approach when dealing with uncertainty. Examples may be found in books on public economics (e.g., Atkinson and Stiglitz 1980, or all issues of the *Journal of Public Economics*), where, for example, the decision whether to pay taxes or cheat, or whether to work in the official economy or in the shadow economy, is formulated in terms of expected utility maximization (e.g., Allingham and Sandmo 1972; Sandmo 1976). In these studies it is clear that the set of alternatives is given and fully specified, though not necessarily completely known to the individuals who are choosing. In addition to optimal taxation, the same approach is used in the neoclassical theory of public pricing (e.g., Boes 1981). Expected utility maximization is also used when the economic approach is applied to more general social problems (see Becker 1976; McKenzie and Tullock 1975).

Recently, experimental psychologists, among them Kahneman, Tversky, Slovic, and Lichtenstein (see e.g., Frey 1983; Hogarth and Reder 1987; Kahneman, Slovic and Tversky 1982) have found that a large number of paradoxical types of behavior exist that strongly argue against expected utility maximization as an explanatory model: "at the individual level most of the empirical evidence is difficult to reconcile with the principle of expected utility maximization" (Schoemaker 1982, 530). These findings also relate to real world behavior, as will be subsequently shown. Thus, for example, "Managers commonly attempt to adjust risky alternatives rather than simply choosing among them" (Mac-Crimmon and Wehrung 1986, 1988; see also March and Shapira 1987).

It might be properly concluded that the accepted approach of dealing with decision making under uncertainty fails to explain many phenomena observable at the individual level as well as at the aggregate level (see Frey and Eichenberger 1989). A new approach is needed that takes the alternatives entering into choice not as exogenously given but rather as part of an endogeneous process of choice.

Overestimation of the Ipsative Set

In the simplified case of two activities or goods X and Y, an overestimation is graphically shown in figure 1.

The objective possibility set is given by ODC, the larger ipsative possibility set by OEF. The maximum achievable utility level U_o is reached at P_o, but the individual concerned believes that utility U^d can be reached at P^d. The shaded area A indicates the overestimation area.

Two instances of overestimation will be discussed: (1) overestimation due to human nature, and (2) overestimation due to design.

Overestimation Due to Human Nature

There is a tension or conflict between point P^d that is desired but not objectively feasible, and P_o that is feasible but not the most desirable. If such an incompatibility were typical only of mentally ill persons or the result of a temporary error, the incompatibility would not have much relevance for economics. However, such an overestimation happens in many situations for perfectly normal, rational individuals, and there is no tendency for the ipsative possibility set to converge to the objective set. Nonadjustment exists because "reality" can be "constructed" in many different ways. Thus, OPS is not given but rather is the result of an interpretive process of an actor. The interpretation varies according to the context (see Tversky and Kahneman 1981) as well as according to the frame (Tversky and Kahneman 1973), i.e., psychological factors may determine the relevant problem space (Newell and Simon 1972; Schoemaker 1980).

Overestimation is particularly relevant when uncertainty is present. In this setting, an individual always finds it possible to associate himself or herself with another domain so that the experience of others becomes irrelevant from the individual's personal point of view. This ipsative probability may deviate systematically and in the long run from what in the literature is known as objective and subjective probability (see de Finetti 1968; Savage 1954): there is a tendency to underestimate negative events and to overestimate positive events. Under some circumstances, there is "a surprising . . . failure of people to infer from lifelong experience" (Kahneman, Slovic, and Tversky 1982, 18; see also Hogarth 1975). Rather, there is a "judgemental bias: people . . . [have a] predilection to view themselves as personally immune to hazards" (Fischhoff et al. 1981,

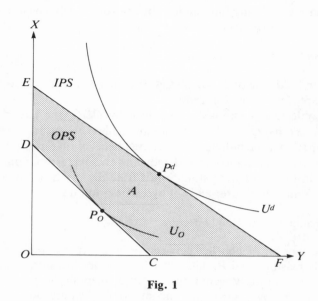

Fig. 1

29–30). According to Weinstein's findings (1980, 806) individuals are subject to "unrealistic optimism," i.e., they "tend to think they are invulnerable. They expect others to be the victims of misfortune, not themselves" (Kirscht, Haefner, Kagelas, and Rosenstock 1966).

The underestimation of negative and the overestimation of positive events have been empirically shown to hold in the following areas (to name but a few):

Cancer and other diseases. Even if people are well aware of the probability of getting cancer, they still tend to assume that it will afflict others but not themselves. More generally, most people believe that they are more likely than the average person to live beyond 80 years of age (Weinstein 1979). That this is objectively impossible does not induce individuals to think otherwise.

Car, sport, and work accidents. The great majority of individuals consider themselves to be better-than-average drivers (Svenson 1978). Each one experiences trip after trip without accident and then tends to interpret this as evidence of an exceptional driving skill. They also believe that they are less likely than the average person to be injured by the working tools they operate (Rethans 1979), and they conceive hazardous occupations to be of little risk.

Natural disasters. People are aware of the fact that floods and earthquakes may happen but assume that they will be less affected than others.

Divorce. Even if individuals are aware of the substantial risk of divorce, they tend to believe that the given risk applies to others not to their own marriage.[3]

Crime. People may know the statistical incidence of crime but still think that crime will affect the others.

Table 1 reproduces empirical evidence, based on a controlled survey, that the overextension of the ipsative set is a common feature in the areas listed above. Most of the events refer to diseases; people obviously have a very strong tendency to exclude themselves from the base of the population as a whole and to put themselves in another category ("I belong to a particularly healthy set of people"). But in all cases the underestimation of negative and the overestimation of positive events (in table 1 "living past 80") mean that the ipsative is larger than the objective possibility set:

TABLE 1.   Unrealistic Optimism for Future Life Events

Event	Mean Comparative Judgment of Own Chance versus Others' Chances (in percent)a
Having a drinking problem	−58.3***
Attempting suicide	−55.9***
Divorcing a few years after marriage	−48.7***
Having a heart attack before age 40	−38.4***
Contracting veneral disease	−37.4***
Getting lung cancer	−31.5***
Being sterile	−31.2***
Having a heart attack	−23.3***
Living past 80	12.5**
Tripping and breaking bone	− 8.3*
Having car stolen	− 7.3
Being a victim of mugging	− 5.8

Source: Weinstein (1980, 810).

aIn making a comparative judgment, students estimated the difference in percentage between the chances that an event would happen to them and the average chances for other same-sex students at their college. N = 123 to 130, depending on rating form and missing data. Student's t was used to test whether the mean is significantly different from zero.

For positive events, the response that one's own chances are greater than average is considered optimistic, and the response that one's own chances are less than average is considered pessimistic. For negative events, the definitions of optimistic and pessimistic responses are reversed.

*$p<0.05$ **$p<0.01$ ***$p<0.001$

---

3. This may be called the Elizabeth Taylor Effect: whenever she gets married, and this is often the case, she proclaims in good faith that this time it is for life — only to be divorced some time later.

the constraints in terms of monetary and nonmonetary resources are discounted by individuals when they consider their own situation. Such an overextension of the ipsative possibility set would be of little consequence for economics if it were simply in the sphere of evaluation. But it also has an important influence on behavior. For this purpose, the behavioral consequences in the five areas already listed will be sketched and empirical evidence quoted.

Diseases. Individuals tend to undergo too few tests to determine the presence of cancer (American Cancer Society 1966) and generally tend to behave as if they will live forever (as a popular saying goes), for example, a large number of people refrain from writing a last will.

Accidents. As may easily be tested by asking someone who participates in a hazardous sport whether he or she considers it to be dangerous, there is a standard reply: the accidents are attributed to insufficient training, to recklessness, or to bad equipment. This is illustrated by the following report:

> A New York graffitist who had been badly burned in an electric fire started by a spark that ignited his cans of spray paint . . . admitted that 2 weeks before his accident he read of a boy named Bernard Brown who was crushed to death while painting graffiti on trains. . . . He said "I remember laughing about it thinking he must be some kind of dude who didn't know what he was doing." (Nisbett, Borgida, Crandall, and Reed 1982, 116)

As a consequence, individuals tend to be careless, e.g., people are generally reluctant to wear seat belts in cars even while admitting that they are useful in the event of accidents (Robertson 1974), and they tend to insure too little (Robertson 1977). Those employed in hazardous occupations systematically act as if their work were not risky and tend not to use the safety equipment available voluntarily (Akerlof and Dickens 1982). People have an illusion of control: while they sometimes pay lip service to the concept of chance, they behave as if chance events can be controlled (Langer 1982; Van Raaij 1985). The same illusion is true of managers. They do not accept the idea that the risks they face are inherent in their situation (Strickland, Lewicki, and Katz 1966); rather, they make an effort to use their skills to control the risks (Adler 1980; Keyes 1985; March and Shapira 1987; Shapira 1986).

Natural disasters. There is convincing empirical evidence (Kunreuther 1976; Kunreuther et al. 1978) that even if extremely attractive flood and earthquake insurance is available (the federal government subsidizes it up to 90 percent), the large majority does not make use of it (not even those who do not speculate on help by government in the case of a disaster). The fundamental bias discussed thus induces behavior that an outside observer would have to evaluate as contrary to subjective utility maximization.

Divorce. Today more than ever, people enter into marriage with very little preparation. Few make an appropriate marriage contract or make early preparations for a possible divorce (because such acts are interpreted as evidence of lack of love). When a couple divorces, one of them often remarries, with the result that divorced persons remarrying are likely to divorce again. No learning effect takes place but rather the contrary: while first marriage rates have shown a steady decline, divorce rates and remarriage rates have climbed (Bianchi and Spain 1986, 38–39).

Crime. People living in high crime areas (and not emigrating) tend to disregard this fact, probably in order to decrease their psychic cost or cognitive dissonance (see Akerlof and Dickens 1982). As a consequence, they tend to become less careful than a (benevolent) outside observer would advise.

This discussion suggests that the extension of the ipsative set beyond the objective possibility set affects human behavior in a significant way.[4] According to this view, Becker's statement "Even irrational decision units must accept reality and could not, for example, maintain a choice that was no longer within their opportunity set" (1976, 167) turns out to be only partly true. While the second part of the sentence is obviously true (almost by definition), the first part is not; even rational individuals do not simply "accept reality" but—especially when uncertainty is involved—may maintain a cognition of reality that outside observers consider mistaken, with important consequences for behavior.

Overestimation Due to Design

The ipsative may also be extended beyond the objective possibility set as a purposeful device to induce motivation and work effort that would otherwise not be forthcoming. Similar to the Leibenstein (1976, 1978) or Hirschman (1958) view, but contrary to orthodox neoclassics, work intensity is not a given but can be influenced by appropriate personal strategies.

---

4. It should be noted that only a subset of the effects is revealed in individual behavior. Another part is evidenced by institutions created in response to the behavioral consequences of overextending the ipsative set. Thus, in all Western countries, the law requires a marriage contract because individuals tend to refrain from making one themselves.

An example of such behavior has already been given by the scholars who regularly overestimate their work capacity. While they should have the intelligence and experience to know better, they convince themselves otherwise in order to mobilize resources and to complete at least part of a task. Empirical evidence exists that this strategic bias is behaviorally relevant:

> Scientists and writers . . . are notoriously prone to underestimate the time required to complete a project, even when they have considerable experience of past failures to live up to planned schedules. A similar bias has been documented in engineers' estimates of the completion time for repairs of power stations (Kidd 1970). . . . This planning fallacy . . . occurs even when underestimation of duration or cost is actually penalized. (Kahneman and Tversky 1979, 314)

Underestimation of the Ipsative Set

In the simplified case of the two activities or goods X and Y, an underestimation is graphically shown in figure 2. The individual considered is objectively able to reach utility U^* at point P^* but does not consider the shaded area B. His or her ipsative possibility set encompasses only area OEF so that utility maximization leads to the choice of point P_o with utility U_o. To an outside observer, the individual has a utility opportunity loss of (U_o-U^*). However, the individual considered does not experience this loss because the larger objective possibility set ODC is beyond his own consideration. Empirical evidence exists (Thaler 1980) showing that opportunity costs are indeed treated quite differently from actual costs.

The underestimation of the ipsative set is again not restricted to mentally disturbed people but is a common phenomenon among perfectly rational actors. It seems that most people consider only a rather small part of what is objectively possible. To an outside observer, the life of these people appears to be rather narrow and restricted to a trodden path; obvious possibilities for improving the situation are disregarded.

There is an obvious counterargument, namely, that the people concerned do not consider area B because they would not be happy there. Such a situation is shown in figure 3 where it is assumed that the quantity $O\bar{X}$ of activity or good X is within consideration, but all quantities $X > \bar{X}$ are beyond consideration.[5] (Note that the utility curves depicted in the

---

5. For example, the individual concerned does not consider drinking more than one bottle of champagne per evening.

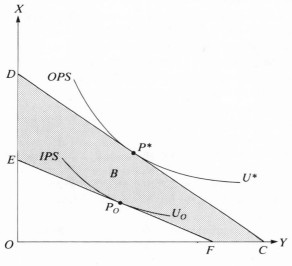

Fig. 2

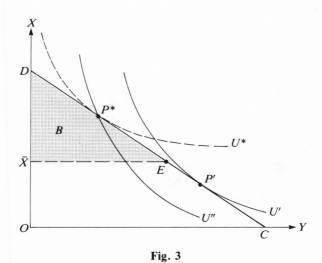

Fig. 3

area $X > \bar{X}$ are those relating to an individual not subject to an ipsative restriction).

The ipsative possibility set $O\bar{X}EC$ is a subset of the objective possibility set ODC, again area B is not considered by the individual concerned. In this case, point P' is indeed preferable to $P*$ as $U' > U''$. Such a situation is perfectly possible but different from what is discussed here. An underextension of the ipsative space means that $P*$ is a utility-maximizing equilibrium with a higher indifference curve $U*$ tangential to the objective budget line DC. It is thus argued that the individual concerned would stay at $P*$ if area B were within his or her consideration (e.g., if he or she were forced to include area B).

An underestimation of the ipsative set again may occur due to (1) human nature, or (2) design.

Underestimation Due to Human Nature

The observation that individuals sometimes disregard obvious possibilities for improving their situation is empirically well founded:

> Present research and examples drawn from everyday life show that some kinds of information that the scientists regard as highly pertinent and logically compelling are habitually ignored by people. (Nisbett et al. 1982, 116)

An important example is provided by large investment decisions of firms. The general observation that "individuals look at only a few possible outcomes rather than the whole distribution" (Alderfer and Bierman 1970) also applies to managers considering investment and divestment in multinational corporations: "The search for solutions is 'simple minded,' with the first acceptable alternative being adopted." Schmoelders (1978, 21) found that only 54 percent of industrial corporations in Northrhine-Westphalia took more than one location into consideration, 22 percent restricted the choice to two locations. A similar result is found in an extensive survey of managerial perspectives on risk and risk taking by March and Shapira (1987, 1412). Managers focus on very few aspects and sequentially consider a relatively small number of alternatives (i.e., they "satisfice" [March and Simon 1958; Simon 1955]) or sometimes only a single critical focal value. This evidence suggests that even managers acting under more or less competitive conditions consider only part of the complete objective possibility set and may therefore settle at a point judged by outside observers to be less than optimal.

Why is there not a movement away from the position of lower utility to a feasible one of higher utility, i.e., an extension of the ipsative set toward the objective possibility set? Consider figure 4, which again assumes that $X > \bar{X}$ is beyond consideration.

An author such as Becker (1962, in particular) would argue that an

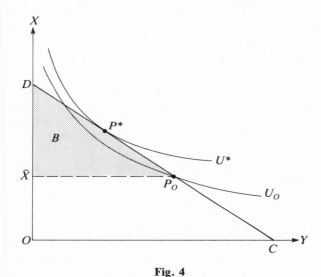

Fig. 4

individual by experiencing marginal improvements in his or her utility would be induced to move from the disequilibrium boundary solution P_o (where the highest possible utility U_o within the ipsative set $O\bar{X}P_oC$ is reached) toward P^*. However, such a possibility is simply beyond consideration: the individual concerned does not even imagine moving beyond $\bar{X}$; area B does not belong to his personal choice set. It is an instance where learning does not take place. Psychologists (e.g., Payne 1982, 397–98) have indeed stressed that learning is neither a simple nor an automatic activity; uncertainty, environmental instability, and improper assessment frameworks represent serious obstacles (e.g., Brehmer 1980; Einhorn 1980). Learning is possible only in a well-structured feedback situation and even then tends to be slow and at times incorrect, or even perverse (Einhorn and Hogarth 1978, 1986). Economists normally simply assert that learning takes place. As one psychologist, Einhorn, states:

> The area of learning [is] the focal point for considering the relative merits of psychological versus economic explanations of choice behaviour. Some economists have argued that . . . one will learn the optimal rule through interaction with the environment. Vague assertions about equilibrium, efficiency and evolutionary concepts are advanced to bolster this argument. (1982, 269)

The ipsative theory of behavior allows us to derive empirically test-able propositions that are not in line with the normal predictions of orthodox economic theory or that at least point out the great importance of limiting cases.

1. The relative price effect or the law of demand does not work in the circumstances portrayed in figure 4. When the relative price of activi-ties or goods X and Y is changed (as in fig. 5, when the relative price changes from OD/OC to OD'/OC' or to OD''/OC''), the individuals maintain their consumption at P_o (while P^* changes to P^{**} and to P^{***}).

An example is attendance at cultural events, such as the opera, concerts, or museums. Some people do not even consider attending such an activity, and, therefore, changing the price of such cultural events has no effect on their attendance. An analysis of four Rotterdam museums reveals, for example, that the rate of first visits is unaffected by price variations, while other visitors show the expected negative price elasticity of demand (Goudriaan and van't Eind 1985, 106). If pricing is used as an instrument for opening museums and other cultural institutions to new groups of visitors, one would have to expect little success. Another example is provided by tax morality that does not seem to be an issue open to marginal evaluation but rather is an issue of principle among taxpayers. Some taxpayers do not ever think of ways and means to cheat on taxes, while others with a low tax morality actively seek to evade taxes, even while taking into account the punishment to be expected if detected. In Switzerland, most citizens seem to belong to the first group, in Germany most seem to belong to the second group. A change in the relative cost of cheating on taxes versus being honest affects only the behavior of the second group. Indeed, such a relative price change may result in a perverse effect: when the government threatens citizens of high tax morality with increased punishments, this may be taken by them as an indication that the government distrusts them, which leads them to distrust the government. The game of mutual trust between citizens and government is then changed into one of opposition, with negative results for all (see also Weck-Hannemann, Pommerehne and Frey 1984). This is an illustration of the second proposition.

2. A relative price change may result in a perverse change in behav-ior. Consider figure 6. The price of activity or good X is lowered so that the objective possibility set enlarges from ODC to $OD'C$, and the (irrele-vant) equilibrium shifts from P^* to P^{**}. Actual consumption moves from P_o along $\bar{X}$ to P_1; that is, the savings due to a lower price of X are exclusively used for increasing the consumption of Y. In this case, a decrease in P_X/P_Y leads to an increase in Y/X that is contrary to the spirit

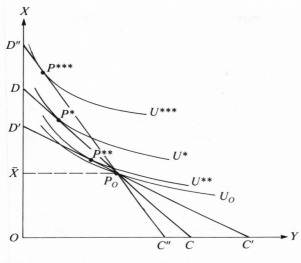

Fig. 5

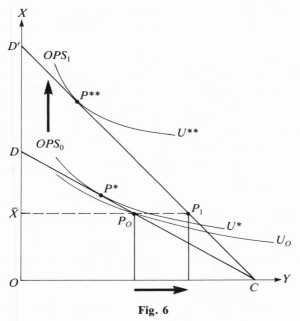

Fig. 6

of neoclassical demand theory (but does, of course, not violate it formally as the perverse reaction is due to an income effect).

Underestimation Due to Design

A rather large number of processes exist that an individual knows to be beyond his or her control.[6] Such self-coercive processes are an example of the weakness of will or *akrasia* (Sen 1974, 1979). Coercive processes or compulsory consumption (Winston 1980) where no marginal choice is possible may be of three kinds.

1. *Psychic.* Love (*l'amour fou*) and hatred (à la Michael Kolhaas or Ahab) may go so far as to lead to self-destruction of the individual. Equally, friendship and often family ties (at least in the European sense) are of an absolute nature with, at least in principle, complete trust.
2. *Physical.* Addiction on this level ranges from watching television to smoking, drinking, gambling, and drug taking and is characterized by the fact that many, or most, people find it impossible to exercise control at the margin.
3. *Social.* Many professions or careers once entered do not allow free choice to the individuals involved. This is true for prostitution and crime; an exit is difficult and sometimes not possible at all.

Coercive processes have to do with the ipsative possibility set as they are nonmarginal (absolute), asymmetric (entering is different from exiting) and beyond simple control (see sec. 2). They can indirectly be controlled only by moving to another decision-making level where an individual sets rules or constraints for himself or herself. The most famous example is of Ulysses asking his companions to bind him to the mast in order that he not fall prey to the enchanting Sirens. Such behavior is rational in a more general way:

> Man is often not rational, or rather exhibits a weakness of will. Even when not rational, man knows that he is irrational and can bind himself against the irrationality. This second-best or imperfect rationality takes care both of reason and passion. (Elster 1979, 111)

---

6. Another reason for underextending the ipsative possibility set by design is that values one cherishes would be destroyed. One does, for example, not want to consider that one may benefit at the expense of one's friends or family. This idea is not explored here.

Such behavior has been discussed in terms such as *strategic precommitment* (Elster 1977, 1982, 1986), *egonomics* (Schelling 1978, 1980), *welfare-improving constraints* (Maital 1986), as well as in other fields (economics, Hirschman 1982; philosophy, Frankfurt 1971; psychology, Ainslie 1975). Neoclassical economics has thus far dealt with this type of behavior in terms of preferences: Strotz (1955–56) envisages preferences as shifting over time; Thaler and Shefrin (1981) and Margolis (1982) distinguish two sets of preferences, one of a "doer" concerned with pursuing current utility and one of a "planner" concerned with lifetime utility who sets the constraining rules.

In the framework of ipsative theory, coercive pressures are analyzed within the two possibility sets distinguished. Consider figure 7, with X a coercive good if its consumption exceeds $\bar{X}$.

The individual knows that a choice of the utility-maximizing point P^* with utility U^* cannot be maintained but that he or she moves along the budget line to the maximum possible consumption of X at P^c (the movement is indicated by arrows). In this setting it is rational for such a knowledgeable individual not to cross $\bar{X}$ (though P^* yields higher utility than U_o) because the final consumption at P^c yields a lower utility U^c than U_o. The choice of an ipsative possibility space with $X < \bar{X}$ is preferable to the objectively possible set even though at P_o there is marginal disequilibrium.[7]

For such rule followers, two propositions may be advanced (see fig. 6):

1. An increase in the price of the activity or good subject to coercion leads to a perverse effect (a rise in P_X/P_Y decreases Y/X): the real income reduction is used only to decrease the consumption of Y and leaves X unchanged.
2. A decrease in disposable income (e.g., by an increase in taxes) reduces only Y, while orthodox theory assumes for a normal good that both X and Y are reduced.

Actions by people captured by a coercive process, on the other hand, are determined solely by the objective possibility set. A price increase of the addictive good X reduces the consumption of X because these people can no longer afford to buy quantity P_o^c but can afford only P_1^c, as shown in figure 8.

---

7. The analysis differs from Stigler and Becker's (1977) treatment of addiction because they assume that an individual may always make a marginal choice. They model the coercive process by resorting to human capital accumulated by addictive consumption.

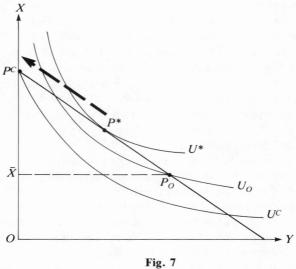

Fig. 7

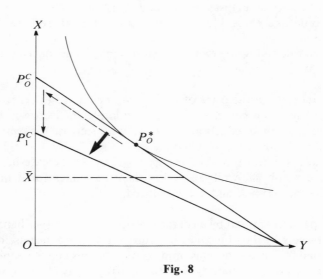

Fig. 8

There is a pure incapacitation effect that works in the same direction as the law of demand.

Society is composed of both rule followers and addicts; the aggregate effect of any policy measure such as a price increase in the addictive good X depends on both effects discussed, weighted by the respective share of individuals in the two groups and their income. The share of those following rules and that of those not doing so depends on the net benefit of limiting the ipsative possibility set. The incentive to follow the rule of not exceeding $\bar{X}$ may be derived from figure 7. The incentive is greater:

1. the lower the utility U^c of falling prey to the coercive process compared to the utility U_o of remaining within the ipsative set,
2. the smaller the maximum addictive (temporary) utility level U^*, and
3. the faster the coercive process from P^* to P^c takes place.

These propositions conform to common sense. It is, for example, reasonable that an individual is less likely to stick to a limiting rule if the expected utility from reaching the temporary maximum is large (e.g., to earn great sums of money by a criminal activity).

Concluding Remarks

Ipsative theory provides a different point of view for looking at types of human behavior that appear paradoxical at first sight. Clearly, the explanations offered do not contradict orthodox economic theory in the strict sense but only in spirit. Standard neoclassic economics, and, in particular, expected utility maximization, is flexible enough to describe "all observed human behaviour as optimal, provided it is modeled in the appropriate manner" (Schoemaker 1982, 539). In a "postdictive" sense, orthodox theory and ipsative theory are thus not mutually exclusive. The critical criteria for the differential evaluation of theories are whether one theory is more parsimonious, conforms better to common sense, and can more easily be reconciled with empirical observations (without having to add auxiliary assumptions). It is hoped that the ipsative theory of behavior, while staying within the general framework of economic theory by using utility maximization subject to constraints, meets some of these criteria.

REFERENCES

Adler, Stanley. 1980. "Risk Making Management." *Business Horizons* 23:11–14.
Ainslie, George. 1975. "Specious Reward: A Behavioural Theory of Impulsiveness and Control." *Psychological Bulletin* 82:463–96.

Akerlof, George A., and William T. Dickens. 1982. "The Economic Consequences of Cognitive Dissonance." *American Economic Review* 72:302–19.

Alderfer, Clayton P., and Harold Bierman. 1970. "Choice with Risk: Beyond the Mean and Variance." *Journal of Business* 43:341–53.

Allingham, Michael G., and Agnar Sandmo. 1972. "Income Tax Evasion: A Theoretical Analysis." *Journal of Public Economics* 1:323–38.

American Cancer Society. 1966. *A Study of Motivational and Environmental Deterrents to the Taking of Physical Examinations That Include Cancer Tests.* New York.

Atkinson, Anthony G., and Joseph E. Stiglitz. 1980. *Lectures on Public Economics.* Maidenhead: McGraw-Hill.

Becker, Gary S. 1962. "Irrational Behavior and Economic Theory." *Journal of Political Economy* 70:1–13.

Becker, Gary S. 1976. *The Economic Approach to Human Behavior.* Chicago: University of Chicago Press.

Bianchi, Suzanne M., and Daphne Spain. 1986. *American Women in Transition.* New York: Sage.

Boes, Dieter. 1981. *Economic Theory of Public Enterprise.* Berlin: Springer.

Brehmer, B. 1980. "In One Word: Not from Experience." *Acta Psychologica* 45:223–41.

Einhorn, Hillel J. 1980. "Learning from Experience and Suboptimal Rules in Decision Making." In *Cognitive Processes in Choice and Decision Behavior,* ed. Thomas S. Wallsten, 1–20. Hillsdale, N.J.: Erlbaum.

Einhorn, Hillel J. 1982. "Learning from Experience and Suboptimal Rules in Decision Making." In *Judgement under Uncertainty,* 268–83. See Kahneman, Slovic, and Tversky 1982.

Einhorn, Hillel J., and Robin M. Hogarth. 1978. "Confidence in Judgement: Persistence of the Illusion of Validity." *Psychological Review* 85: 395–416.

Einhorn, Hillel J., and Robin M. Hogarth. 1986. "Decision Making under Ambiguity." *Journal of Business* 59:225–50.

Elster, Jon. 1977. "Ulysses and the Sirens: A Theory of Imperfect Rationality." *Social Science Information* 16:469–526.

Elster, Jon. 1979. *Ulysses and the Sirens.* Cambridge: Cambridge University Press.

Elster, Jon. 1982. "Sour-Grapes-Utilitarianism and the Genesis of Wants." In *Utilitarianism and Beyond,* ed. Amartya K. Sen and Bernard Williams, 219–38. Cambridge: Cambridge University Press.

Elster, Jon, ed. 1986. *The Multiple Self.* Cambridge: Cambridge University Press.

Finetti, Bruno de. 1968. "Probability: Interpretations." In *International Encyclopedia of the Social Sciences,* vol. 12, ed. D. E. Sills, 496–504. New York: Macmillan.

Fischhoff, Baruch, Sarah Lichtenstein, Paul Slovic, Stephen L. Derby, and

Ralph L. Keeney. 1981. *Acceptable Risk*. Cambridge: Cambridge University Press.

Foppa, Klaus. 1987. "Individual Resources, Objective Constraints, and the Ipsative Theory of Behavior." Psychological Institute of the University of Bern, December. Mimeo.

Frankfurt, Harry G. 1971. "Freedom of the Will and the Concept of a Person." *Journal of Philosophy* 68:5-20.

Frey, Bruno S. 1983. "The Economic Model of Behaviour: Shortcomings and Fruitful Developments." Institute for Empirical Economic Research, University of Zurich, June. Discussion Paper.

Frey, Bruno S., and Reiner E. Eichenberger. 1989. "Should Social Scientists Care About Choice Rationalities." *Rationality and Society* 1:101-22.

Frey, Bruno S., and Klaus Foppa. 1986. "Human Behavior: Possibilities Explain Action." *Journal of Economic Psychology* 7:137-60.

Goudriaan, René, and Gerrit Jan van't Eind. 1985. "To Fee or Not to Fee: Some Effects of Introducing Admission Fees in Four Museums in Rotterdam." In *Managerial Economics of the Arts*, ed. Virginia Lee Owen and William S. Hendon, 103-9. Akron, Ohio: Association for Cultural Economics.

Hirschman, Albert O. 1958. *The Strategy of Economic Development*. New Haven: Yale University Press.

Hirschman, Albert O. 1982. *Shifting Involvements. Private Interests and Public Action*. Oxford: Martin Robertson.

Hogarth, Robin M. 1975. "Cognitive Processes and the Assessment of Subjective Probability Distributions." *Journal of the American Statistical Association* 70:271-94.

Hogarth, Robin M., and Melvin Reder, eds. 1987. *Rational Choice*. Chicago: University of Chicago Press.

Kahneman, Daniel, and Amos Tversky. 1979. "Intuitive Predictions: Biases and Corrective Procedures." In *Forecasting*, ed. S. Makridakis and S. C. Wheelwright, 313-27. TIMS, Studies in Management Science 12. New York: North Holland.

Kahneman, Daniel, Paul Slovic, and Amos Tversky, eds. 1982. *Judgement under Uncertainty: Heuristics and Biases*. Cambridge: Cambridge University Press.

Keyes, Ralph. 1985. *Changing It*. Boston: Little, Brown.

Kirscht, J. P., D. P. Haefner, S. S. Kagelas, and I. M. Rosenstock. 1966. "A National Study of Health Beliefs." *Journal of Health and Human Behavior* 7:248-54.

Kunreuther, Howard. 1976. "Limited Knowledge and Insurance Protection." *Public Policy* 24:227-61.

Kunreuther, Howard, Ralph Ginsberg, Louis Miller, et al. 1978. *Disaster Insurance Protection: Public Policy Lessons*. New York: Wiley.

Langer, Ellen J. 1982. "The Illusion of Control." In *Judgement under Uncertainty*, 231-38. See Kahneman, Slovic, and Tversky 1982.

Leibenstein, Harvey. 1976. *Beyond Economic Man*. Cambridge, Mass.: Harvard University Press.

Leibenstein, Harvey. 1978. "On the Basic Proposition of X-Efficiency Theory." *American Economic Review* 68:328–32.

MacCrimmon, Kenneth R., and Donald A. Wehrung. 1986. *Taking Risks: The Management of Uncertainty*. New York: Free Press.

McKenzie, Richard, and Gordon Tullock. 1975. *The New World of Economics*. 2d ed. Homewood, Ill.: Irwin.

Maital, Shlomo. 1986. "Prometheus Rebound: On Welfare-Improving Constraints." *Eastern Economic Journal* 12:337–43.

March, James G., and Zur Shapira. 1987. "Managerial Perspectives on Risk and Risk Taking." *Management Science* 33:1404–18.

March, James G., and Herbert A. Simon. 1958. *Organizations*. New York: Wiley.

Margolis, Howard. 1982. *Selfishness, Altruism and Rationality. A Theory of Social Choice*. Cambridge: Cambridge University Press.

Newell, A., and Herbert E. Simon. 1972. *Human Problem Solving*. Englewood Cliffs, N.J.: Prentice-Hall.

Nisbett, Richard E., Eugene Borgida, Rick Crandall, and Harvey Reed. 1982. "Popular Induction: Information Is Not Necessarily Informative." In *Judgement under Uncertainty*, 101–16. *See* Kahneman, Slovic, and Tversky 1982.

Payne, John W. 1982. "Contingent Decision Behavior." *Psychological Bulletin* 92:382–402.

Rethans, A. 1979. "An Investigation of Consumer Perceptions of Product Hazards." Ph.D. diss. University of Oregon. Quoted in *Acceptable Risk. See* Fischhoff, Lichtenstein, Slovic, Derby, and Keeney 1981.

Robertson, L. S. 1974. *Urban Area Safety Belt Use in Automobiles*. Washington, D.C.: Insurance Institute for Highway Safety.

Robertson, L. S. 1977. "Car Crashes: Perceived Vulnerability and Willingness to Pay for Crash Protection." *Journal of Community Health* 3:136–41.

Sandmo, Agnar. 1976. "Optimal Taxation – an Introduction to the Literature." *Journal of Public Economics* 6:37–54.

Savage, Leonard J. 1954. *The Foundations of Statistics*. New York: Wiley.

Schelling, Thomas C. 1978. "Egonomics, or the Art of Self-Management." *American Economic Review, Papers and Proceedings* 68:290–94.

Schelling, Thomas C. 1980. "The Intimate Contest for Self-Command." *Public Interest* 60:94–118.

Schmoelders, Guenther. 1978. *Verhaltensforschung im Wirtschaftsleben: Theorie und Wirklichkeit*. Hamburg: Rowohlt.

Schoemaker. Paul J. 1980. *Experiments on Decisions under Risk: The Expected Utility Hypothesis*. Boston: Nijhoff.

Schoemaker, Paul J. 1982. "The Expected Utility Model: Its Variants, Purposes, Evidence and Limitations." *Journal of Economic Literature* 20:529–63.

Sen, Amartya K. 1974. "Choice, Orderings and Morality." In *Practical Reason*, ed. S. Koerner, 54–67. Oxford: Oxford University Press.

Sen, Amartya K. 1979. "Rational Fools: A Critique of the Behavioural Foundations of Economic Theory." In *Philosophy and Economic Theory*, ed. Frank
Hahn and Martin Hollis, 87–109. Oxford: Oxford University Press.

Shapira, Zur. 1986. "Risk in Managerial Decision Making." Hebrew University.
Manuscript.

Simon, Herbert A. 1955. "A Behavioral Model of Rational Choice." *Quarterly
Journal of Economics* 69:99–118.

Simon, Herbert A. 1985. "Human Nature in Politics: The Dialogue of Psychology with Political Science." *American Political Science Review* 79:293–304.

Stigler, George, and Gary S. Becker. 1977. "De Gustibus Non Est Disputandum."
American Economic Review 67:76–90.

Strickland, Lloyd, Roy W. Lewicki, and Arnold M. Katz. 1966. "Temporal
Orientation and Perceived Control as Determinants of Risk Taking." *Journal of Experimental Social Psychology* 2:143–51.

Strotz, Robert H. 1955–56. "Myopia and Inconsistency in Dynamic Utility Maximization." *Review of Economic Studies* 23:165–80.

Svenson, O. 1978. "Risks of Road Transportation in a Psychological Perspective." *Accident Analysis and Prevention* 10:267–80.

Thaler, Richard H. 1980. "Toward a Positive Theory of Consumer Choice."
Journal of Economic Behavior and Organization 1:39–60.

Thaler, Richard H., and H. M. Shefrin. 1981. "An Economic Theory of Self-
Control." *Journal of Political Economy* 89:392–406.

Tversky, Amos, and Daniel Kahneman. 1973. "Availability: A Heuristic for
Judging Frequency and Probability." *Cognitive Psychology* 5:207–32.

Tversky, Amos, and Daniel Kahneman. 1981. "The Framing of Decisions and the
Psychology of Choice." *Science* 211:453–58.

Van Raaij, Fred W. 1985. "Attribution of Causality to Economic Actions and
Events." *Kyklos* 38:3–19.

Weck-Hannemann, Hannelore, Werner W. Pommerehne, and Bruno S. Frey.
1984. *Schattenwirtschaft*. Munich: Vahlen.

Weinstein, Neil D. 1979. "Seeking Reassuring or Threatening Information about
Environmental Cancer." *Journal of Behavioral Medicine* 16:220–24.

Weinstein, Neil D. 1980. "Unrealistic Optimism about Future Life Events." *Journal of Personality and Social Psychology* 39:806–20.

Winston, Gordon C. 1980. "Addiction and Backsliding: A Theory of Compulsive
Consumption." *Journal of Economic Behavior and Organization*
1:295–324.

X-Efficiency, Implicit Contracting, and the Theory of the Firm

Marvin E. Rozen

This article will explore the development of implicit contracting as an extension of X-efficiency ideas. X-efficiency implies that firms do not always perform at as high a level as they can; implicit contracting is concerned with the internal organizational arrangements best suited to elicit high-level performance. Initially, implicit contracting was based upon the relatively simple and limited idea that advantageous swaps could arise from positional differences between firms and workers relating to risk attitudes, knowledge asymmetries, and wealth portfolios, combined with the absence of other markets where workers could insure against undue income fluctuations. As the importance of effort variability, firm-specific human capital, agency-transaction costs, and organizational rent—all concepts that derive from or blend nicely with X-efficiency notions—in accounting for firm performance are better understood, implicit contracting can represent the much broader and far-reaching idea of creating an organizational structure capable of inducing workers to do their best. X-efficiency thus opened the door for a much richer and satisfactory theory of the firm and one that more closely corresponds with the ideas of managerial theorists and practitioners. Currently, however, powerful trends seem to be pushing the firm in the direction of governance modes and restructuring options distinctly antithetical to an implicit contracting approach. This article discusses these current paradoxical trends in firm organization and evaluates the ambivalent forces operating to define the firm's structure and behavior.

Development of Implicit Contract Doctrine

Contemporary discussion of the theory of the firm is increasingly recognizing the importance, if not centrality, of implicit contracting (or, alternatively, the employment relationship) as the key to greater understanding of what is happening in labor markets and on the job. From diverse points of view, the internal organization of the firm—the modalities governing interactions between workers and their employers — is being dissected and analyzed to discover more convincing explanations of recurrent stylized facts and to answer puzzling questions about differences in firm performance and behavior. In particular, recent developments in implicit contract notions are especially well suited to illustrate the characteristics and implications of this lively interest.

As with all contracts, the elements of reciprocal offer and acceptance are present: firms, in effect, offer to provide something of value to workers, say, the promise of more stable income growth, or more generally, equitable and beneficial treatment, in return for something of value to them, say, a lower wage bill, or the workers accepting the obligation to be forthcoming and put out their best effort.[1] The implicit feature of such contracts is that the behaviors and contingencies covered cannot be fully specifiable a priori since they can be neither easily described nor verified. They are subjectively perceived by all parties, and this quality leads to a self-enforcing mechanism as each party adheres to the understanding as long as its expectations concerning the other party's behavior are being broadly realized. A substantive breach by any party would trigger a like response from the other. These mutual understandings must be implicit, since a worker cannot successfully sue a firm for breaching nonspecific obligations or indefinite undertakings any more than a firm could legally compel workers invariably to do the best they possibly can. Actualizing sophisticated and complicated quid pro quos must be volitional; each party must believe that honoring implicit agreements is the best way to further its own interests.

Recognizing that the parties cannot contractually and explicitly compel each other's desired behavior implies seeking other routes to that end. Furthermore, the more subtle, intangible, and complicated the patterns of behavior sought, the greater the reliance must be on such implicit understandings. Many years ago, D. H. Robertson in characterizing the "English process of jollying along" expressed the implicit contract idea most pungently: "encouragements which are not quite promises, frowns which are not quite prohibitions, understandings which are not quite agreements" (1952, 49). As with other areas of infinitely varied human behavior, description can hardly claim the status of an existence proof, but it is nonetheless helpful in fixing the phenomena under discussion more clearly and vividly in our minds.

The earliest implicit contract ideas could be viewed as comparative

---

1. I am using the U.S. economy as the institutional referent for this article, and the labels *firm* and *workers* as the convenient and conventional terms for the relevant sets of decision makers.

advantage swaps based upon positional differences in risk attitudes of firms and workers. They were attempts to account for the stylized facts of relatively rigid money wage rates and the extensive use of layoffs rather than outright termination. As Azariadis and Stiglitz succinctly put it, "The sluggishness of money wage rates, notably in periods of relatively stable inflation, and the strong contribution of layoffs to cyclical unemployment in North America have long been two of the best-documented stylized facts in economics" (1983, 2). If workers were relatively risk averse and firms risk neutral, then this basic difference combined with the firm's superior position vis-à-vis risk absorption, information processing and forecasting, and wealth and liquidity portfolios enabled the firm to offer to smooth workers' income flows through money-wage rigidity and long-term employment guarantees. The firm was positionally well suited to make such an offer at little cost to itself. For some reason, the corresponding obligations of the worker were not so clearly defined. Presumably, the worker was made sufficiently better off by income smoothing so that, as a kind of compensating differential, the firm's overall wage bill could be lower. Or perhaps more importantly, the impact on worker morale and loyalty would presumptively yield very beneficial productivity payoffs to the firm that otherwise would not be forthcoming. In the latter instance, the implicit contract would be of the general form of "You treat me right and I will make it worth it for you,"[2] as applied to both parties. In either case, the consummation of profitable trades arose largely from the joint influence of the parties' positional differences and the absence of other markets where workers could insure against undue income fluctuations. The implicit nature of the arrangements stemmed largely from both the workers' putative lower wage bill or greater cooperation and the unwillingness of the firm, in effect, legally to feudalize its relationship to its workers.

Other versions of implicit contracts shifted the emphasis from positional differences to the consequences of associational continuity and thereby also sharply altered their underlying basis by greatly expanding the workers' role. Some stressed the inexorable buildup of firm-specific human capital, whose financing and incentives for on-the-job utilization set the stage for having to coax workers to employ their augmented capabilities fully (Becker 1975; Hall 1980). Other versions emphasized the efficiency-wage argument in which workers' effort supply was inherently (quantitatively and qualitatively) variable, and wage premiums were required to elicit higher levels of effort (Yellen 1984). For still other

---

2. In the context of an exchange relationship, this formulation is very similar to Leibenstein's "Double Golden Rule" admonition (1987, 48–54).

versions, the focus of attention became the institutional arrangements required to minimize the transaction and agency costs of gaining the workers' full cooperation (Williamson 1980). Still others argued that the shared experience and teamwork that generated organizational rent — the excess output of a going concern over what an identical collection of factors hired de novo could produce — were the critical concerns (Aoki 1980). In all of these instances, the gains inhering in associational continuity and the workers' contribution have become more important, and the process whereby potential productivity can be realized has become the focus of attention; now the possibilities for variable worker performance drive the system.[3] Workers must be bribed, coaxed, cajoled, or otherwise persuaded to do their best; bargaining is inherent in the structure of arrangements; the implicit contract takes on a different coloration. The firm must more actively seek to tap the workers' full potential by offering inducements, whose nature and magnitude might abruptly depart from traditional firm practices. Such implicit contracts are still self-enforcing since each party is free to establish its own level of compliance, but any sustained shortfall is likely to be quickly requited. The parties are locked into the fundamental swap defining their relationship: "You treat me right, and I'll put out."

These versions stressing firm-specific human capital, effort variability, transaction costs, and organizational rent can reasonably be called "implicit contracts plus" to draw attention to their more open-ended nature.[4] Two of their characteristics deserve further comment. First, they are more complicated than a straight transaction based on well-defined positional differences, since they are characterized by continuous interaction in which strategic bargaining to influence the other party's behavior will always be present. Furthermore, "treating right" and "putting out" are not simple and self-evident concepts but are laced with ambiguity and imprecision; accordingly, the parties must exercise constant vigilance, and opportunities for disagreement will be abundant. If the parties

---

3. The listing is not exhaustive. Other approaches within a broad implicit contracting framework include C. Schultze 1985, where the lagged and damped adjustment aspects are stressed; S. Grossman and O. Hart 1981, where asymmetrical knowledge between firm and worker is posited; and R. Freeman and J. Medoff 1979, where the externalities accruing from the enhancement, via collective bargaining, of the workers' voice are emphasized.

4. For a different interpretation and survey of implicit contracting, see Rosen 1985. Rosen focuses narrowly on the insurance aspects of income smoothing as a response to the risks confronting workers' firm-specific human capital and on the consequent restricted role of income effects in determining labor supply behavior. He also argues that as a practical matter, because firms face Knightian uncertainty and thus uninsurable risk, income smoothing is not very important.

wish to preserve their arrangement, they must develop means to limit the damage from real or apparent breaches of their understandings. Second, conflict in a very fundamental and basic sense will always be present. This will not simply be the ordinary higgling over terms of exchange to get the best possible deal of the moment, the ordinary economics of a little more and a little less. Rather, the pervasiveness of strategic behavior charges any action with much greater significance. As will be discussed later, questions of authority and power disposition, of legitimacy, and of basic property rights will inevitably arise as the parties struggle over the fruits of their joint activities. When such issues are joined, stakes become immeasurably higher. Once the idea of inherent variability in the workers' contribution is accepted, participatory work arrangements become a logical focus for inquiry.

Implicit contract notions, then, can powerfully illuminate what happens in labor markets and on the job; the internal arrangements affecting firm-worker interactions are center stage and will be the focus of attention. It will be most useful to explore in detail some specific areas where these interactions occur. First, wages, employment, and labor market activity, especially the job-worker matching process, will be analyzed. Second, actual behavior on the job, how work is carried out, the organizational arrangements, and the respective responsibilities of firm and workers will be reviewed. Then, inquiry will be concerned with the broad implications for the locus of authority and control and the form that property relations take. A concluding section will discuss the theoretical and policy consequences of expanded implicit contract notions for traditional theories of the firm.

What Happens in Labor Markets and On the Job

Wages

The wage, when viewed from the perspective of the employment relationship, is a much more complicated concept than standard theory's effort bargain that entails a specific money payment for a fixed and easily verified quantum of well-defined effort at the workplace. Most of all, this perspective reveals the wage's multifunctionality; it serves many purposes, seeks to achieve multiple objectives, and accordingly, at the margin, must equate a rich variety of trade-offs.

In addition to being a payment for normal effort, the wage may also perform various other functions:

1. It must properly compensate the worker-financed investment necessary to produce the general and firm-specific human capital embodied in the worker.
2. It may, in its efficiency variant, be the key for unlocking the sources of greater motivational intensity.
3. It may embody an insurance charge-off, in recognition of another party bearing the risk of income fluctuations that would otherwise fall upon the worker.
4. It can contain a lottery element as workers with imperfect mobility place their bets on future careers and levels of earnings.
5. Its level may make sense only in relation to all other conditions of work to which it may be adjusted to equalize, in equilibrium, the attractiveness with similar employments.
6. To deter shirking, it may be set so high relative to alternative job opportunities that a substantial earnings loss would be the just desserts of anyone whose termination for soldiering on the job would compel entry into that alternative labor market; conversely, it can be set initially at a low level but rise more sharply with time on the job so that the prospect of higher future earnings deters shirking today and will even encourage much diligence and striving among junior workers as the generous and glittering compensation of the senior staff is dangled before them.
7. If a firm wants to reduce costly turnover and enjoy the luxury of selecting from a large queue of high-quality applicants, a premium wage will work wonders.
8. If the firm is confronted by a strong and disciplined collective organization of workers, or the threat thereof, and with little chance for escaping such straitjacketing circumstances, the wage will have to mirror the bargaining facts of life.
9. Finally, if the wage must be responsive to the organizational rent-derived claim for a participatory share as a condition for the full utilization of worker talent and energy, some form of residual sharing will constitute part of the workers' wage.

What has thus seemed and usually been regarded as a sharply defined and exact payment for specific labor services rendered has turned into a complicated compensation package put together for a bewildering variety of reasons and seeking to achieve diverse objectives. Clearly, this functional multiplicity must leave its mark on the wage-setting process and makes it unlikely that so complex and conditional a set of circumstances can generate a simple, direct, and uniquely interpretable representation. In what proportion any given wage will be a return on capital, a lottery prize, a risk premium, an effort elicitor, a shirking deterrent, an aspirational prod, an equalizing differential, a worker-selection device, a bargained extra, and a participative residual, as well as, a payment for a standard quantum of effort, is unlikely to be an instantly available computation. Rather, any specific wage and the pattern of wages, across jobs and over time, must reflect the interplay of these various considerations, and analysis must account for a more complicated set of forces. We have, unhappily, a surfeit of potential explanations for wage behavior; and wage multifunctionality would strongly suggest a careful review of specific circumstances to discover which considerations are paramount in the particular case. Simplistic explanations, such as the wage-effort bargain, are of limited value, and wage behavior can be interpreted only in the context of the dimensional space of the employment relationship as applied in a particular circumstance.

This line of thought supports an interactionist approach between the firm and the worker because the wage now becomes an instrumentality for generating a desired outcome through a more complicated causal pattern. In other words, the wage is part of a complex and interactive strategic game; rather than necessarily being the product solely of unmitigated and overwhelming market forces, wage patterns and movements will also reflect strategic interplay. By focusing on how wages are decisively influenced by purposive interaction between firms and workers, new insights emerge and new explanations are formulated.

For instance, the concept of a unique equilibrium wage crumbles if worker productivity is dependent upon how the firm treats its workers. Likewise, an excess supply of workers does not necessarily indicate labor market disequilibrium if maintaining high applicant quality is of major importance for the firm. Similarly, if jobs are looked upon as lifetime careers, then the decision makers' perspective will be vastly different from what it would be if they were in an auction market; the current wage offers only a partial view through a very narrow window, not the total picture. General tendencies to decouple — the efforts to smooth real income change and allow for productivity trends — wage movements from the shocks of short-lasting economic transients are readily explicable from a career rather than an auction market perspective. The fact, moreover, that both high-wage and low-initial-wage schemes for deterring shirking are contradictorily argued suggests the need to proceed with caution in this area. The interactionist approach to wage behavior thus has greater richness and denser texture than traditional explanations have. There are more options, more decisions, and more strategic choice, and the usual explanatory variables are more conditionally weighted by the impact of specific circumstances; above all, unidimensional accounts must be heavily discounted. If this is to be disparagingly labeled as "ad hoccery," that is not too high a price to pay for a closer approximation to a genuine explanation for wage behavior.

Employment

Associational continuity has been the *fons et origo* of implicit contracts and the employment relationship concept. Long tenure does not, of course, characterize all jobs nor apply to all workers. Nor is its importance in any way mitigated by recognizing that the early career of many workers will be dominated by a sustained period of job shopping; jobs are experience goods, and the maxim "you don't know until you've tried it" is relevant. But when all is said and done, employment continuity stands out as a well-documented stylized fact whose rationale is easily explained. Both parties to the employment relationship benefit from sustaining the association. Workers build up their stock of firm-specific human capital, becoming more proficient and knowledgeable on the job and thereby increase their earning potential. Firms benefit directly from this potentially higher productivity and have the added sense of certainty and security from reliance on the experience-tested capabilities of their workers. For these reasons, during economic downturns, firms have traditionally hoarded their labor force, shifted workers to alternative tasks, e.g., maintenance, cleanup, repair and servicing, etc. and established clear (usually seniority-related) patterns of furlough and recall. Further, as recent collective bargaining contracts in the automobile and communications industries establish, firms are now willing to finance retraining and the teaching of new skills to workers in response to secular shifts in technology and demand. This is partly a bargaining concession, but it can also be interpreted as firms recognizing their self-interest in retaining workers with known qualities. Finally, elaborate and formal procedures relating to termination themselves testify to the importance of employment continuity; no matter what the legal status of employment-at-will doctrines, termination is not usually lightly undertaken. Fairness and equitable treatment are not abstract moral desiderata; firms know that their absence will result in a very real productivity penalty.

Although associational continuity is, thus, in the mutual self-interest of the parties, terminations of long-term employees do occur. Clearly the firm's market position overrides other considerations in the great majority of such instances; falling sales and increasing employment would indeed make an odd couple. Beyond such stiff market tests, firms will terminate highly productive senior workers for reasons other than deficient performance. For instance, Weiler states that in connection with union-organizing activity, "the current odds are about one in twenty that a union supporter will be fired for exercising rights supposedly guaranteed by federal law a half-century ago" (1983, 1781). This suggests two things: (1) Although the work force as a whole is the repository of substantial firm-specific human capital, an individual worker is not indispensable. As long as the firm's actions affect only a relatively small minority of the work force, not much of the collective and organizational skill potential will be lost; replacements can be fitted in with minimal disruption. (2) Actions by workers that challenge the firm's authority are especially serious matters; the firm will be hypersensitive to any threats to its authority and powers and will go to great lengths and expense in defense thereof.

I am not suggesting that associational continuity means employment for life because it is always a win-win situation for the parties; the employment relationship is also a struggle-struggle process, and both the potential for joint gain and the striving for a larger share at the other's expense are always present. This complex tug-of-war implies that a continuous challenge-and-response process is being played out, with many possible outcomes reflecting the shadings and gradations of players and situations. The very fact of associational continuity, moreover, by enhancing the workers' productive potential, creates the conditions for outcome variability since it widens the range of possible results, and firm-specific and organizational rent aspects insulate those outcomes from having to confront, and be kept in line by, severe market tests. If outcomes depend upon how the parties interact and experience has bestowed uniqueness upon their relationship, then what is happening in the market offers only weak oversight capabilities. In sum, associational continuity has profound implications for the nature of the employment relationship and its impact on economic variables of interest. But within the framework of continuity, the terms of association are constantly being assessed and struggled over as the parties balance the chances for mutual gain with the pursuit of self-advantage at the other's expense. Clearly, it is in society's interest to channel both parties' efforts toward the former objective of mutual gain and inhibit the latter objective from blocking that process.

Job-Worker Matching

Another area currently receiving greater recognition and discussion is the matching of jobs and workers, or more generally, the actual operation of labor markets. Both efficiency in generating correct matches and the instrumental significance of such matches are of concern. Here too, multidimensionality plays a considerable role since, *ex hypothesi*, the matchups become increasingly complex as workers and jobs must be aligned in several different dimensions rather than being indexed completely by the wage alone. Balancing the costs of search against the probability of finding a higher wage offer touches only the surface of the matching process. Moreover, as experience goods, job attributes can be known only through actual sampling, and thus preferences can be refined and reshaped. Getting to know more about the world of work and about our own work preferences and aptitudes takes time. Recent emphasis on the importance of internships, probationary periods, work-study programs, formal integration of work and schooling, and other approaches providing a structured learning period for successful job-matching provides a case in point.

Certainly one cannot very well stress the importance of implicit contracting and, at the same time, believe that the matching process can rely merely on unstructured and chance encounters. On both sides, search intensities and modalities are related to, say, career earnings prospects as a proxy for relative importance. Warm bodies might do perfectly well for casual and temporary jobs, but the more important the job and the more permanent the prospects, the more costly and extensive the search. A help-wanted sign in a window turns up acceptable dishwashers and bus-persons; the services of headhunters for technical and professional jobs, however, are not cheap. For many jobs, matching jobs and workers can involve, for all parties in varying degrees, conscious and systematic preparation, complicated signaling and screening routines, sophisticated recruiting and search strategies, and highly refined selection procedures that are all blended, figuratively speaking, into an elaborate and even highly ritualized mating dance. For lifetime career choice and sometimes even more casual selection, the matching process goes beyond searching out the highest wage offer from an imperfectly known distribution.

Nor should it be thought that matching is a once-and-for-all process. The quality of the match evolves over time as both jobs and workers naturally and inevitably change in the crucible of experience. Apart from consideration of the creation of firm-specific human capital and the implications of promotion and hierarchy, not much attention has been paid to what happens after the match. Yet that may be a critical factor. For one thing, both jobs and workers are responsive to the influence of broad social trends on work organization: the changing legal framework regarding conditions of work, the role of gender and race in defining job opportunity sets, the pervasive influence of advancing technology on job design and skill requirements, to mention a few. The world of work can never be hermetically sealed and self-contained; it is part of a larger social system and it will influence and be influenced by that system. For another, subtle changes occur as people and jobs adapt to each other. Like a new pair of shoes, jobs are remolded and reshaped as workers exercise their individuality, within the broad discretionary limits surrounding most jobs, and align the jobs more to their liking. Likewise, firms are ever alive to the possibilities for cost savings and innovative change and will find it in their interest to promote the growth of their work force's capabilities. Thus, jobs and workers undergo more or less continuous change, and firms must accordingly be concerned about maintaining the goodness of fit between jobs and workers.

The care and attention lavished on the matching process are both a testimonial to its importance and an indirect confirmation of the irrelevance of viewing labor markets in auction-market terms. If workers were perfectly homogeneous or their variation inconsequential, it would be illogical to go to great lengths to arrange good fits and to worry about maintaining them over time. Nor would we ever observe, certainly not in prosperous times, the phenomenon of immensely large numbers of job applicants for desirable job vacancies. Those long lines of qualified people or the floods of applications whenever good job openings are advertised convey significant information about the matching process. They are a very crude index of how far we can still go.

On-the-Job Behavior

Initially, implicit contracting did not have very much to say about workers' on-the-job behavior because swaps based on positional differences involved something the firm could easily supply and is of obvious value to workers; the implicit contract could accordingly take the form of greater income stability for the workers in exchange for a lower overall wage bill for the firm. Implicit contracting based solely on risk aversion could avoid the issue of worker performance. But roughly parallel to the implicit contract literature, a related and challenging line of thought was emerging that was indeed very much concerned with worker performance. Alchian and Demsetz (1972) in a seminal article argued that individual shirking was rational behavior for individual workers within a team production setup since the leisure gain was concentrated on the shirker and the consequent income loss was diffused over the team as a whole. Accordingly, that implied that workers had to be closely supervised and monitored to prevent such shirking. In this view, the problem was to enforce explicit contracts in the face of rational individual incentives to shirk rather than to elicit higher-level worker performance. More efficient monitoring and institutional structures most capable of generating it were stressed; workers must be prevented from turning off.

Development of implicit contract plus notions, however, can be viewed as a response to the Alchian-Demsetz challenge by shifting the emphasis from preventing shirking to turning workers on. Rather than stressing shirking, these doctrines instead sought to tap the inherent productive potential of a committed and cooperative work force by motivating workers to deploy their talents and energies to the fullest extent they could. As the significance of effort variability, firm-specific human capital, transaction and agency costs, and organizational rent ideas for worker productivity became increasingly apparent, and as implicit contracts moved beyond positional swaps and toward the process orientation of linking output variation to incentive structure, a new world opened up. Effort variability meant that workers could modulate their work intensity in line with their views on the adequacy of firm incentives; the firm-specific human capital embodied in these workers conferred enormous leverage on that effort variability; minimizing the exactions of transaction costs could yield great savings; and the retention of the sources of organizational rent — the teamwork and experience in working together — would likewise be very sensitive to how tangibly and generously the firm recognized such contributions. Although the specific pattern of rewards required to elicit this higher-level performance from workers is a matter of lively dispute, getting workers not to shirk seemed a niggling, narrow, and negative objective compared to unleashing the creative powers of workers to do their best.[5] In thus focusing on incentives and motivation, firms finally were directing attention toward the most pressing and practical issues they actually face; tardily, the theory of the firm was catching up with reality.

Two consequences immediately follow from this perspective. First, the issue of supervisory monitoring is relegated to secondary importance because by more directly aligning workers' self-interest with the firm's, the more powerful force of horizontal monitoring — facing the keen scrutiny of one's workmates — is brought to bear to diminish shirking. Moreover, shirking itself becomes less a matter of individual morality, of

---

5. A considerable literature has developed relating to both the underlying theory of the labor-managed firm (see Meade 1972; Stephen 1984; and Vanek 1970, 1977) and the many practical ventures involving augmented worker participation schemes (see Estrin and Perotin 1987; Fitzroy and Kraft 1987; Gunn 1984; Jones and Svejnar 1982; and Pryor 1983).

moral hazard, and of not honoring a solemn obligation, and more of a social transgression against one's workmates.[6] If shirking becomes widespread, that is to be interpreted as an indication that the implicit contract is breaking down, that workers are not benefiting sufficiently to organize powerful group pressures against shirkers. As mentioned previously, one of the virtues of implicit contracts is their self-enforcing quality. If either party believes the other is not adhering to its part of the contract, the contract will be terminated as the aggrieved party exercises its option of withdrawal. In an implicit contract world, supervision has only a supporting role and is not the main guarantor of compliance.

The second consequence is that under the reigning property rights arrangements, the time shape of the firm's income stream and, correspondingly, the workers' earnings flow may be distorted in a predictable way. If worker compensation is geared, however indirectly, to current performance, then workers would have an incentive to rob the future to augment the present, to capture income earlier even if, properly discounted, the present value of the resultant stream would be less than could otherwise be obtained. Workers do not usually have claims, under existing property rights dispensations, to income accruing when they are no longer employed. They accordingly are bound to utilize their now-acknowledged tremendous influence on the fortunes of the firm to skew earnings forward in time (and thus enjoy their higher pro rata share) at the expense of a future when they will not be around. They will not concern themselves with what is to them the irrelevant future; they will have an abiding interest in getting all they can while they can. Such disregard of future consequences in favor of the present can be very bad news for the firm and for society, too.

---

6. Sometimes strong arguments are made (Meade 1972 and Miyazaki 1984) that firm size is critical in this respect, since the larger the work group, the less the sense of one's obligation to workmates. Such views should be tempered, however, by recognizing the importance of organizational arrangements as an intervening variable. Decentralized responsibilities and self-directed, small-group work teams can foster a highly developed sense of mutual responsibility. As Fitzroy and Kraft have suggested:

Group incentives imply that individual actions impose externalities on other members of the group, and, provided that interaction is not made too difficult by technology and work organization, the rational response to group incentives is cooperation to "internalize" these externalities. Thus, particularly in team work situations where at least some components of individual effort and performance are difficult to monitor and reward directly, it is possible to mobilize peer-group pressure *against* shirking and encourage "consummate cooperation" with group incentives. Team members are generally better informed about each other's contributions than supervisors not directly involved in joint tasks, and group incentives are a scheme for utilizing this information to increase efficiency. (1986, 115–16)

Perhaps in a more fundamental sense, these results can be viewed more generally as the logical and necessary outcome of revisionist theories of the firm based upon implicit contracting and the employment relationship. Expanding the scope and potential variability of the workers' contribution and making it so sensitively and intimately dependent upon more complicated incentive schemes must influence both the form and extent of workers' rewards. If effort matters so much, firm-specific human capital is so very much at risk, transaction costs are so important, and organizational rent is so eminently tangible and sharable—if in effect, the worker has become a virtual principal—then how, and how much, workers are compensated must be confronted.[7] In a nutshell, as a matter of logic, workers seem to have the equivalent of an equity stake by virtue of this interpretation of their contributions.[8] Devising property rights mechanisms to actualize such claims would seem to be the precondition for efficient resource allocation in both an instantaneous and intertemporal sense.[9] Yet, in practice, one does not observe any headlong rush to offer workers the participative responsibilities and augmented income share that would seem to be the natural accompaniments of their heightened productive contribution. Logic and fact seem sharply at odds. Theory suggests fundamental alteration in income shares and decision-making authority; practice reveals no such dominant trends. This puzzle will be discussed further in a subsequent section of this article.

---

7. Leveraged buy-outs, in which operating managerial groups take over firms by borrowing on the basis of their functional responsibility for the firm's performance, have become commonplace in recent years. Extending this principle to embrace larger numbers of employees should not appear as strange.

8. As equity holders, workers would, of course, be exposed to bearing the firm's losses, too. It would, therefore, be advisable to insulate them, through provision of a reserve fund mechanism, from extreme fluctuations in this regard. Similarly, cumulating equity holdings would mean that both one's human capital and one's financial assets are narrowly concentrated in a single enterprise. Normal diversification considerations would suggest that workers would want to hold alternative financial assets. For those appreciative of irony, a paradox should be noted: implicit contracting as a doctrine stemming from a desire by workers to avoid risk comes full circle to accepting risk as both inevitable and compensable.

9. Perhaps it is useful to remind ourselves that property rights undergo continuous modification in response to changing legal and political conditions. For instance, collective bargaining has been defined as the progressive erosion of managerial prerogative. Change in the firm's internal governance structure should be viewed in a similar evolutionary perspective.

Authority and Legitimacy

Next, issues of authority and power emerge as fundamental matters of dispute once the implications of implicit contracting are followed through; indeed, questions of legitimacy flow directly from the theoretical implications of emphasizing the expanded importance of workers. After all, it should not be strange that responsibility, reward, status, and power should all follow function. When so much depends upon properly motivating workers, it would be incongruous to expect that institutional forms and power-sharing arrangements would not be affected by such a drastic shift in relative emphasis. Indeed, workers also have a strong theoretical claim to an equity share. The fact that equity holders put up capital and thus bear the risk of loss and failure has historically justified their claim, but do not workers bear even more risk? Their firm-specific human capital is very much at stake since, by definition, its usefulness depends upon being maintained in its present employment; if this firm should fail, it is not worth very much elsewhere. Furthermore, workers must also bear the additional internal risk that their claim and position as shareholders might, by virtue of both its novelty and traditional opposition, be in constant jeopardy. Unlike the stake of those holding paper claims, their firm-specific capital is, again by definition, not transferable or exchangeable. Finally, workers have an indisputable claim on the organizational rent; at the limit, they could quit en masse, hire their own machinery and equipment, and as their own firm, appropriate the entire surplus. Realigning property rights is accordingly the natural outcome of the functional recognition of the collective importance and claims of workers and of their contribution to the firm's fortunes. Theirs is an earned right to a larger income share and to greater participation in firm decision making.[10]

But whatever logic implicit contracting and the employment relationship may entail for reshaping the disposition of property rights, managerial and shareholder sensitivity concerning power and prerogatives will ensure opposition to such implied shifts. After all, at stake is not merely a marginal redivision of income but the far more sensitive and fundamental issue of who is boss. That issue must be confronted in situations where, *ex hypothesi*, no objective market or other standard exists by which the parties can measure their position. Firm-specificity

---

10. Such changes represent concrete recognition of what is so often stressed in firms' advertising and public relation efforts: viz., our workers are our most important resource; a company is its people; we owe all our success to our hardworking employees, etc. La Rochefoucauld's maxim seems apposite, "Hypocrisy is the homage that vice pays to virtue."

and organizational rent make each firm, with respect to its collection of workers taken as production teams, unique and sui generis. Certainly individual workers may be replaced from time to time without much impairing the firm's performance, but firm-specific talents and skills and the experience of working together as production teams imply the impossibility of completely replacing, within reasonable time frames, pools of workers. Thus the parties must work out their differences without objective market evaluations as precise guidelines.[11] Compared to their alternative opportunities, their present situation generates huge rents, whose appropriation will be a source of constant struggle.

Both issues of power sharing and the absence of market standards would push the parties to rely very heavily on strategic behavior in an environment where the stakes are very high and the rules of engagement very fluid. Any action by either party will be judged not only by what it appears to be on the surface but also by how it makes sense in a longer-run pattern of move and countermove; and the game is never over since each completed round of strategic moves only sets the stage for the continuation of the process. Nor are there any precise limits to contested areas, since each will try to move the conflict to its favored field. Nor does strategic gaming provide a hospitable ambience for compelling moral imperatives, such as honesty and fairness, since the parties are not likely to agree on how such abstract concepts are to be operationalized in a world of ceaseless struggle. As a distinct form of conflict, strategic behavior comes under the "all's fair in love and war" rubric.

Finally, because strategic behavior can both be so socially disintegrative a process and have such socially wasteful outcomes, the public has a large stake in how the employment relationship evolves. As we have seen, the market cannot be relied upon to generate socially optimal results, and the parties can easily be quite nasty and brutish to each other with consequent dangers for social stability and civility. Because of these externalities, society has an obligation, as we shall discuss, to create a public presence that pushes the parties toward more socially desirable ends.

Implications

As these discussions of various aspects of labor market and on-the-job behavior have illustrated, there is much grist for the analytical mill in

---

11. These observations apply more to labor markets than to product markets, where firms will usually confront other firms. Firms do not have the alternative of completely replacing their labor force en masse without incurring huge efficiency penalties.

exploring where implicit contracting leads and what kind of behavior it covers. The implications range far and wide, and the purpose of this section is to highlight some of these as illustrative of the kinds of changes in thought required. First, those more directly connected with the behavior of agents will be surveyed, with special attention to theoretical implications, and then some public policy issues will be discussed.

Perhaps the most important insight gained from the implicit contracts approach is the necessity to deal with the strategic behavior problem as a pervasive consequence of associational continuity. Strategic behavior implies a pattern of continuous interaction within the context of latent or active struggle; the parties deal and/or duel. From the firm's point of view, its problem is to get workers to utilize their capabilities fully without the firm's giving up too much of either its income share or its decision-making prerogatives. From the workers' standpoint, their problem is to achieve an income share and participative role commensurate with their collective economic contribution, since on an individual basis, each is dispensable. The collective proviso is very operationally significant because of all the well-known difficulties of acting in concert. In this contest, the firm would seem to have numerous advantages. It usually has more resources and options; it initiates most of the action; it has relatively complete freedom with respect to job design, organizational arrangements, and investment policy, and hence can utilize those powerful tools to strengthen its position and even promote control-maintenance at the expense of economic efficiency; it can intentionally segment and stratify the work force as a technique for weakening group cohesion and making collective action difficult; it can co-opt the workers' natural leadership by offering tempting prospects for individual gain at the expense of the larger group; and finally, the legal and political status quo provides it with many advantages in this unequal contest. In sum, whatever the underlying logic for eliciting superior worker performance by a larger income share and meaningful participation, firms have so far been clever and powerful enough to avoid such drastic change without apparently also having to pay a very high price in the form of a great reduction in worker productivity.

The other side of this coin is that workers have been largely unable to translate their theoretically strong claim into the practical currency of a larger say and share.[12] Partly, this reflects the traditional difficulties of

---

12. This is true even for a country, such as Britain, with a strong socialist tradition. For some British evidence of the extent to which workers have not vigorously pressed for expanded participation, see P. Edwards and H. Scullion 1982. It should be added that it is not strange for the spread of unorthodox and unfamiliar ideas to take considerable time.

speaking with a single voice and the blandishments of profitable individual egress; partly, it reflects the lack of intellectual definition of position in a situation where novel action is required — like a sleeping giant, workers are not aware of their potentially enormous powers. Furthermore, the major segments of organized labor have looked to collective bargaining as an instrument for achieving direct and short-run material gains and not as a lever to extract any measure of joint responsibility and participation; a majority of workers are not even under the collective bargaining umbrella.

Strategic gaming is thus pretty much loaded against workers. But implicit contracting suggests that ultimately the disparity between what should be and what is will react negatively on productive potential as a consequence of inadequate incentives. Although tactically, firms will be able to sustain their advantage, the cost in productivity gains foregone will become greater and greater. If workers are not able to overcome the organizational and inertial barriers to bringing actual motivating conditions into line with the implied theoretical standard, their disenchantment will make it harder and harder for firms to elicit superior performance. Indeed, unless public policy intervenes, stalemate and standoff seem the most likely outcomes.

Whatever the future may bring, the value of the implicit contracting approach lies also in the richer and fuller account it provides for otherwise unconnected and truly puzzling phenomena. By strongly asserting the claims for situational dependence, it sensitizes us to the circumstances that generate variety in observed outcomes. Economics is done a disservice when essential and important complexity is assumed away in the rush to obtain a spurious generality of result. As indicated, wage instrumentality and multidimensionality, infinite variety in terms and conditions of employment, sophisticated job-worker matching processes, on-the-job behavior highly dependent upon the pattern and quality of incentives, and the legitimacy of existing structures of property rights are all proper subjects for more thoroughgoing investigation once the concept of implicit contracts (and/or the employment relationship) is accepted. Beyond questions of proper subject matter, the implicit contracting approach also alerts us to the centrality of conflict in defining how the parties interact; and, ineluctably, if we accept the idea of struggle, long-standing issues concerning moral hazard and efficient outcomes must then be reinterpreted within that context.

Indeed, implicit contracting notions are helpful in dispelling the confusion created by two blind alleys, relating to moral hazard and efficient outcomes, that theoreticians are prone to enter. For one, moral hazard, in the sense of resort to unprincipled and unethical behavior, can be interpreted only within a well-defined context. Just as a nation does not apply ordinary standards of morality to its own espionage agents, and just as one person's "freedom fighter" is another's "terrorist," so in the rough-and-tumble between workers and the firm, one cannot arbitrarily impose a higher and universal morality that applies only to a collection of individuals in basic harmony with each other. Formal contractual relations are buttressed by legal compulsions affecting precise undertakings; but implicit contracts depend upon mutual forbearance applied to imprecise understandings. A breach of an implicit contract is not so much dastardly and immoral behavior but rather a sign that forbearance is no longer forthcoming from at least one of the parties.

Interpreting all such breaches as necessarily and prima facie unethical conduct or acts of dishonesty and cheating presumes their precise identification and the prior existence of an agreed moral code, against which they can be objectively measured. But in a world of conflict and differences in interpretation, agreement on plain facts and/or unambiguous moral imperatives is unlikely. This is not to say, as those stressing shirking seem to believe, that human beings will lie, cheat, steal, and generally behave dishonorably according to an intricate calculation concerning whether the expected gains from such actions are likely to exceed their expected costs.[13] Instead it is to suggest that in an implicit contract context, trust and mutual forbearance are both precious and fragile and must be patiently and carefully nurtured rather than taken for granted. Conflicting interests create a fine line between legitimate strategic behavior and tactical maneuver, on the one hand, and morally despicable conduct, on the other. Only high trust between the parties ensures that line will not be crossed. Successful implicit contracting thus symbolizes an ongoing cooperative and forthcoming relationship wherein the parties fashion arrangements permitting each to achieve valued objectives satis-

---

13. The notion of shirking as calculated and deliberate individual maximizing behavior within a utility framework is espoused most notably by Alchian and Demsetz (1972). At least three other grounds for shirking can also be proffered. (1) Shirking as innate laziness: human beings are inherently work avoiders, always preferring leisure to work because of their, respectively, presumptively positive and negative utility. Tendencies toward idleness arise not so much from rational calculation as from the imprinted, innate nature of human beings; hence eternal vigilance against such backsliding is required. (2) Shirking as a competitive gambit: workers shirk to make a point; shirking is symbolic communication, indicating dissatisfaction and addressing itself to changing specific conditions of work. (3) Shirking as a manifestation of the class struggle: shirking is a collective protest against an unjust and exploitative system and seeks its overthrow through one of the few avenues open to workers for pursuing industrial guerrilla warfare.

factorily, despite a conflictual context capable of otherwise eliciting mutual withdrawal and reflexive hostility.

Similarly, the argument that implicit contracting must necessarily yield efficient outcomes, in the sense of attaining the best possible results under the stipulated circumstances, is equally misdirected. The struggle-for-control and interaction aspects of implicit contracting presage the possibility of multiple equilibria, and combined with the impact of associational continuity in insulating the parties from close market discipline, spell the doom of the Panglossian position. Many implicit contract theorists have sought to put an irresistible efficiency spin on their argument by claiming that observed outcomes simply reflect ordinary maximizing behavior under more richly specified circumstances, and hence the stylized facts are indeed the best attainable results, given those conditions, the parties can reach. Such an interpretation, however, fails to recognize the conflict spin element in implicit contracting.

If the parties are so mistrustful of each other that neither accepts the other's legitimacy, then strategic jockeying for advantage and for assertion of dominance largely defines the relationship. Each completed encounter is but the prelude to another round of engagement, and the dominant strategy for both parties will be to protect and advance one's own position in the face of worst-case assumptions about the other. Workers can consciously withhold and withdraw their effort if, in their view, incentive patterns are inadequate; likewise, firms can deliberately, for reasons of authority and control maintenance or cost shaving, adopt inferior and less desirable work arrangements. When implicit contracting fails to resolve conflicts between the incentives workers require and what firms are prepared to offer, then efficient outcomes can be derailed by this incompatibility gap between augmented worker capabilities and unchanged property rights and income-sharing arrangements. The best of all possible worlds is thus not a preordained result; inferior outcomes are all too possible because the parties can move in vicious, as well as virtuous, circles; and the market cannot drive them to a unique and best equilibrium.[14] What implicit contracting unerringly teaches us is that as common sense would suggest, it all depends on the particulars and the setting, and what happens today will not necessarily happen tomorrow. Most important, there may be a significant role for third-party intervention to steer the parties toward better outcomes.

One factor, though, that can mitigate destructive impulses inherent

---

14. C. Schultze (1985), quoting R. Solow, begins his presidential address as follows: "(T)he world may have its reasons for being non-Walrasian," to which it may be added, "and non-Panglossian, too." This assumes that Walras was not inevitably Panglossian.

in the employment relationship is the development of trust between the parties. Enough has been said already to establish the linkage between mutual forbearance and positive interaction, and trust is clearly the lubricant that smoothes the way for the parties to be generous and forthcoming with each other. Bonds of trust must be forged, however, by concrete deeds; the basis for trust lies in whether the actual relationship reinforces the willingness of the parties to afford each other the benefit of doubts and is clearly very much a two-way street.[15] Thus adversity, if it induces good-faith and cooperative efforts at joint resolution, can strengthen rather than undermine implicit contracting. Trust, of course, builds upon itself; each positive experience lays the groundwork for deepening and extending trust, and with such augmentation of trust, the resolution of difficult and divisive issues becomes that much easier to accomplish. Perhaps in rare cases, where the implicit swaps are well and simply defined and their consequences patently apparent and not dependent upon interpreting each other's behavior, trust would not matter. More likely, however, where high trust prevails, the parties can jointly realize the full potential of the inherent gains from associational continuity; absent such trust, inferior outcomes and persistent conflict would logically follow. For achieving joint goals, strangely enough, trust can be an infinitely more compelling force than legal obligation.[16]

The role of public policy should also be quite clear by now. With economic outcomes inherently variable, depending upon the parties' ability to fashion the appropriate internal arrangements, the question arises as to how their choices can be influenced by third-party intervention. In this regard, many precedents exist. We have defined a legal structure for labor relations that establishes a support system for encouraging voluntary collective bargaining; we have created mechanisms for mediating and resolving labor disputes; we have established standards and implementation mechanisms for occupational safety and health; we have used the tax code to encourage employee stock-ownership plans—in all of these actions, one can discern a broad public purpose to encourage and support particular patterns of behavior based on the belief that society's interests are directly at stake and are thereby better served. Providing

---

15. Substantive parity between the parties, or at least the absence of great disparities, in the relevant dimensions of economic strength is likely to be a prerequisite for trust to bloom. Dependency, because it implies one-way flows, corrodes trust.

16. At first glance, mixing conflict and trust may seem incompatible, but on reflection, where long-term association is the context, mutual dependency creates incentives to establish trust as a way of enabling the parties to accomplish their objectives most expeditiously over the long haul. If the parties are stuck with each other, they may as well make the best of it, and that's a lot easier done if trust prevails.

incentives for firms and workers to move in more cooperative and participatory channels would be well within these traditional forms of support.
Such programs could usefully complement efforts at building up trust
and could be instrumental in softening the trauma associated with ongoing institutional evolution.

Indeed, the likelihood of continuing institutional evolution is what
should drive public policy and is itself based upon what kinds of firm-
worker relationships are ultimately compatible with associational continuity. As I have argued, associational continuity and the strengthened
collective position of workers flowing therefrom will be the strongest
influence on the future of the firm. The logic of variable effort, firm-
specific human capital, transaction costs, and organizational rent im-
parts a syndicalist push to the firm's evolution. The insulation that associational continuity provides from direct market competition creates the
space within which the parties contend and the incentives for relying
strongly on strategic gaming as the dominant behavioral mode. The
parties have room to maneuver and duel without the immediate threat of
entry to condition their actions and without an objective standard for
measuring their conflicting claims. In the face of powerful structural
forces and trends that, over the long run, strengthen the workers' position, will not the internal arrangements within the firm have to mirror
this increasingly recognized functional reality?

Challenge: The Mean-Lean Firm and Neoclassical Resurgence

Such intimations might seem to fly in the face of the apparently massive
stability and solidity associated with existing organizational arrangements within the firm. Certainly one cannot discern any managerial
mass flight from the desire to hold tightly onto the levers of power and
authority; nor can one point to the overwhelming superiority of the
modest number of cooperative firms on the scene.[17] Indeed, in what

---

17. Some (A. Alchian and H. Demsetz 1972) view this observation as conclusive
refutation of the implicit contract plus argument on the grounds that if such work arrangements were in fact superior, they would be winning out in the marketplace. Since that is
obviously not so, it must follow that such approaches are misled. A short answer to those
views would be that to think that such far-reaching transformations can take place within a
brief time is naive, especially when they are bitterly resisted by those who might lose as a
result and are in a position to make that resistance highly effective. In any case, the current
interest and experimentation with forms of work organization that move in a participative
direction presage a more rapid pace of change.

may be termed a neoclassical resurgence, many argue that real-world developments within the past decade have become increasingly difficult to square with the logic of implicit contracting and certainly contradict its predictions. In this view, a neoclassical "mean-lean" firm, and not an implicit contracting firm, occupies center stage. Authority and command, not cooperation and persuasion, are dominant governance modes; restructuring and change, not continuity, the order of the day.

In particular, a world of layoffs, shutdowns, pecuniary concessions, intensified high-tech surveillance, unilateral work rule changes, two-tier wage structures, out-sourcing, COLA downgrades, runaway plants, decertification pressures, and the assertion and expansion of managerial prerogative in general bears little resemblance to the precepts of internal governance under implicit contracting. Such mean behavior is presumptively imperative as the market dictates survival terms; it is not to be understood pejoratively as a character defect. Firms have little choice but to take whatever actions stern and unyielding market forces press upon them. Niceties and perquisites that were perhaps tolerated in palmier days have to give way to new competitive realities. Implicit contracting was a fair-weather theory; when exposed to the rigors of more demanding times, it had to fold its tent.

Likewise, although takeovers, mergers, divestment, plant closings, transnational locational shifts, leveraged buy-outs, recapitalizations, personnel reductions, subcontracting, leasing workers, downsizing, and other such forms of corporate restructuring seem antithetical to the organizational implications of associational continuity and firm-specific human capital, they, too, reflect leanness in the service of the market's *Diktat*. Here, too, the market has its way.

Discontinuity and restructuring merely reflect normal adaptation to the pulls and tugs of market forces, as they themselves are shaped by a ceaselessly, and increasingly rapidly, changing world economy. It would indeed be anomalous, and even bizarre, if when all else is in flux, the organization of the firm remains chaste and inviolate. The emergence of the mean-lean firm, driven by a demiurgic market, thus seemingly challenges implicit contracting's importance and even its existence.

At issue is what particular organizational form firms should assume. Implicit contracting is to be judged in that context. Because trust, loyalty, and cooperation cannot be bought and sold on markets as we understand them, associational continuity will be a desideratum where those qualities are essential. The implicit contracting firm comes into being in those circumstances as a consequence of inevitable market deficiency. Where contrary conditions prevail, the firm can operate differently and assume other guises. There is no neoclassical organizational straitjacket to which all firms must conform; if being mean and lean pays off in some circumstances, in others it will be inappropriate.

Several additional factors, some currently prominent and others more enduring, have also contributed to the neoclassical resurgence and challenge to implicit contracting. The conservative drift in the country in recent years provides the appropriate mood music for emphasizing market hegemony and discipline within the firm. Similarly, the generally more difficult times and worse economic conditions offer a convenient excuse for unilaterally imposed measures, tougher attitudes, and restructuring initiatives. The natural and almost irrepressible drive for retention of authority by its possessors also finds ample scope for expression in times of relatively high unemployment and increasing mobility for firms to establish seemingly congenial arrangements elsewhere. Finally, the comfortable fit of traditional theorizing creates a climate for too easily dismissing unconventional alternatives. In combination, all of these factors greatly buttress traditional organizational arrangements.

Turning to more specific theoretico-economic comparisons between implicit contracting and neoclassical approaches, one notes that two interrelated aspects are central: how well do markets work, and what role does motivation play? First with regard to the question of markets, the differences are many and deep. For neoclassicists, the market is swift, inexorable, compelling, and irresistible. Firms are left with no choice and little time; they quickly must dance to the market's tune or face extinction. A single instance of error, inattention, inertia, or other forms of slippage might not bring hair-trigger retribution, but the margin for mistake is very thin. Tough choices are required, failure is severely penalized, and market forces are omnipresent and prepotent. The world in which firms live is neither forgiving nor accommodating; firms are compelled to adjust to its demands as best they can; it is incorrect to believe that cooperation and understanding can always produce happy outcomes. The mean-lean firm is simply the product of market realities.

Implicit contracting sees things quite differently. Market pressures work, in general, more slowly, and firms have more leeway to respond. For better or for worse, firms have some time that can be used constructively or frittered away. Slack can be eliminated; internal reforms can be activated; and, roused by adversity, the firm's resources can be better mobilized and deployed. As argued previously, associational continuity and firm-specific human capital insulate the firm, to a degree, from close market discipline in the sense of requiring instantaneous response and provide the potential space for the firm to react creatively to the challenge of change. For implicit contracting, the market is less a suddenly obliterating and overwhelming force, and more a powerful persuader and catalyst for change. More specifically, implicit contracting stresses the possibilities for internal renewal, especially in the workplace where in a milieu of trust, cooperation, and devolved authority, the latent talents and energies of the entire work force can be focused on the problem at hand. The market does not usually present firms with unexpected and immediate life-or-death situations that require abrupt and destabilizing changes; accordingly, the process aspects suggest a decent interval in which the firm can draw upon the implicit contract to make itself over.

Motivation is the other key area of difference between the two approaches. For the neoclassicists, the money wage, itself adjusted for whatever compensating differentials are present, pretty much does it all; it induces people to do their best at all times. Whatever slippage exists because of monitoring or compliance shortcomings is likely to be small and inconsequential, and, in any case, market discipline would soon make things right. Implicit contracting is much more concerned with the complexities behind motivation. It has serious doubts whether decision makers focus on achieving the best outcomes or instead are very jealous and sensitive concerning authority retention and whether their time perspective is excessively oriented toward the short run and the quick fix. It wonders whether top-down managerial styles — "tell 'em what to do and see that they do it" — can really bring out the full range of worker capabilities and whether a bias toward methodological individualism thereby overlooks the inherent importance of teamwork and group activity. It has little faith that some ultimate market for corporate control will flawlessly ensure that firms do the right and timely thing. Above all, as stressed earlier, implicit contracting's central theme is the interaction of effort variability, firm-specific human capital, transaction costs, and organizational rent aspects — all dependent upon worker volition — in determining firm performance; neoclassicists find the resulting absence of automaticity in outcomes incongenial and unacceptable.

Furthermore, market failure and motivational variability play upon each other. If the market did in fact operate swiftly and perfectly, motivational variability could not persist; the fact that workers can choose performance intensity levels contributes to the inherent variability of market outcomes. For neoclassicists, then, the market works fine, outcomes are mostly predetermined, economic agents can't do very much different since presumptively they are already doing the best they can, and bemoaning these results changes nothing and is just so much crying over spilled milk. It would certainly be nice if, somehow or other, happy outcomes could be achieved through gracious and pleasant means, but implicit contracting is irresponsible in holding out false hopes based on incorrect theory. Implicit contracting rejects this Pollyannish interpretation and insists that it is simply arguing for a more realistic assessment of the market's influence and the firm's options. Of course the market cannot be disregarded, and of course the firm is not free to do anything it wants, but it is foolish to overlook the full range of discretionary choices the market allows and the firm can exercise.

Indeed, at least from an implicit contracting standpoint, the two approaches are not incompatible. Implicit contracting argues for situational dependence, not for exclusivity. Certain conditions conduce toward it, but others do not. Similarly, implicit contracting does not renounce maximizing behavior but argues that under very specific conditions, its expression will be realized in that particular organizational form. Nor does implicit contracting suggest that the application of its organizational remedies guarantees a happy outcome and avoids hard and painful choices. It does envisage a wider range of outcomes when confronting adversity because market leeway and motivational variability expand allocative choice, but that by no means assures success. Finally, implicit contracting underlines the importance of job design. Work organization is not predetermined and fixed; jobs can be structured to stress different organizational arrangements. Rather than accepting the Panglossian position that all has worked out for the best, implicit contracting highlights the possibilities for improving the way work is organized.

But if implicit contracting is thus theoretically respectable, how are the contrary empirical observations to be explained? Although, as discussed previously, the rise of implicit contract notions flowed directly from observation of firm structure and behavior, nevertheless the emergence of the mean-lean firm puts the fat in the fire: of what possible relevance can implicit contracting be if many firms seem to place little value in maintaining organizational continuity? They will, unilaterally and often with little notice, drastically restructure their operations and arrangements and use a suddenly improved bargaining position to press for new working conditions and altered compensation terms. Don't such actions imply the insignificance of implicit contracting? When push comes to shove, or when opportunities present themselves, then traditional managerial prerogatives and techniques are relied upon. So much the worse for implicit contracting; if it can't stand the heat, no wonder that it must leave the kitchen! Being mean and lean is accordingly the right, the normal and natural, condition for the firm.

Nor should such actions be saddled with pejorative connotations. Being mean does not imply repugnant or ethically dubious conduct by the firm. Rather it could signify the absence of vacillation when decisive and quick judgments are required and acting rapidly and surgically, without sentimentality, in doing what has to be done. Likewise, a lean firm could signify the only structural arrangement capable of succeeding when confronted with overwhelming market pressures to get in step with changing conditions; after all, it would be inexcusable for the firm not to change under those circumstances. Put this way, who could object to a firm being mean and lean; has it any choice?

Furthermore, what kind of relationship exists between being mean and being lean? Is being lean as a structural form forced on the firm as a result of market pressures, whereas being mean is more a matter of behavioral choice and style? Proponents of the mean-lean firm would shy away from that distinction since the market determines both responses; attempts to distinguish create the illusion of choice. Mean and lean, however, do usually interact with each other. For instance, downsizing might occasion wrenching and coldly calculated decisions over who and what goes or stays, and increasing worker responsibilities might eliminate supervisory layers. Distinctions between behavioral and structural change will be shaky because structural change will inevitably induce behavioral variations in the firm, and behavioral change will usually set the scene for subsequent restructuring. Mean-lean is thus more than a handy rhyme; it manifests, for its proponents, an organic connection between structure and behavior.

Should the argument for the mean-lean firm, then, be accepted, on the basis of widespread current observation, as the embodiment of wisdom and virtue? Does it reflect the appreciation of necessity, and the fact that implicit contracting is fatally flawed because its emphasis on associational continuity seems to be ill-suited to the structural adjustments and behavioral modifications required by a rapidly changing economy? For several reasons such a conclusion should be resisted.

First, it misjudges implicit contracting's purposes and capabilities. Implicit contracting implies not blind attachment to the status quo; rather it uses continuity as a vehicle for more effective change. An implicit contract does not mean that the firm is frozen into the particular pattern of activity and relations prevailing at some instant of time. Precisely because implicit contracting builds upon the solid pillars of trust and cooperation, it should be able to accomplish resource reallocation tasks more smoothly and with less pain. All parties recognize that change is a constant challenge; when reciprocal obligation and mutual trust lubricate the mechanics of change, greater efficiency and equity will prevail.

An ambience of trust and cooperation also opens up greater possibilities for a longer-run perspective and for not, as a first resort, undertaking those adjustments that preserve benefits for some only at the expense of sacrificing others. Sometimes, of course, the trauma of shut-down, selective termination, undesired relocation or reassignment, compensation reduction, more onerous working conditions, and the like cannot be avoided; but then at least having a voice in determining implementation and knowing that more desirable options could not be found make the situation more bearable. Implicit contracting is aware that life offers no guarantee of only happy choices, but that does not thereby entail the acceptance of inferior options if they can be avoided. Although the oft-heard incantation "we owe it all to our workers" may seem ritualistic and ceremonial, to be trotted out at suitable formal occasions, it nevertheless bespeaks truth. Because implicit contracting can offer, in stipulated circumstances, a more effective way of both responding to the challenge of economic change and of moderating its negative consequences, it should not be dismissed as being hopelessly wedded to the past.

Second, neither should it be taken as axiomatic that being mean and lean is the most efficacious response to market pressures. Becoming mean and lean can be counter-productive for several reasons. It can reflect ingrained and reflexive behavior that often fails to review systematically a more extensive range of options. Moreover, its use as a first resort will inevitably induce a backlash in the form of lowered morale and persistent resentment that can hardly fail to have adverse productivity consequences. Furthermore, firms do not usually take into account the sometimes very great social costs of such an action. Communities whose social viability is undermined; terminated workers, especially older ones, whose skills will atrophy and who cannot find comparable employment; and the heavy toll of disruption in personal and family lives must somehow be reckoned in the balance. Certainly circumstances may make such tragedies unavoidable, and the only option may be to mitigate their severity. But experience indicates that all too often calculation of such social costs is given very short shrift.

Additionally and more specifically, being mean and lean can flow from less than worthy motives; the mean-lean firm can do the wrong things for the wrong reasons. The mean-lean firm may, perhaps instinctively, focus excessively on short-run quick fixes; it may simply be interested in retaining authority and command, even at the expense of forgoing efficiency; if, in an adversarial context, maintaining precedents and not losing face are presumed to be tactical necessities, its actions may be strategically correct but functionally wrong. Again largely as an article of faith, the mean-lean firm may unwisely downgrade the prospects of internal renewal; its hierarchical outlook may inhibit it from tapping the energies and talents of its workers; and, more generally, its simplistic mind-set regarding motivation and organization renders it incapable of appreciating the potentially immense contribution of trust and coopera- tion. Thus, far from being the firm's natural and correct response to evolving market pressures, becoming a mean-lean firm could worsen rather than improve matters.

These contrasting characterizations of the implicit contracting firm and the mean-lean firm suggest no prima facie case, flowing directly from abundant observation, for rejecting implicit contracting. Indeed, a more accurate rendering of the factual situation would conclude that empirical evidence exists for both approaches, and thus judgments con- cerning their respective worth must depend upon further analysis. The choice of the mean-lean approach offers no guarantee of superiority since it could be based on numerous considerations unrelated, and even antithetical, to efficiency. Alternatively, implicit contracting offers the promise of a better response to market pressures, especially where varia- bility in the performance of the human agent is critical. Those who believe that correct theorizing requires the presumption of market per- fection and unidimensional human beings may express surprise at such a conclusion, but the major argument of this article is directed precisely against accepting the universal applicability of such beliefs. Situational contingencies will largely determine the best approach.

One powerful force remains, however, that might accelerate the development of more participative approaches. The world economy has become increasingly knit together in recent decades in ways that quicken and intensify the need for economic adjustment to the inevitable string of shocks and disturbances that accompany its evolution. At the same time, most national economies have, by virtue of the growth in influence of formerly less-organized groups, diminished freedom to adjust by impos- ing disproportionate burdens on the weak and less privileged within their societies. In other words, the world economy dictates that we will have to adjust more rapidly and frequently, and our domestic economies have seen their adjustment capabilities, as traditionally conceived, reduced in power and scope. This condition lends a contemporary urgency to poli- cies that support and encourage the kind of implicit contracting that enhances the internal flexibility and adaptability of firms by extending the domain of participation and cooperation.

Concluding Remarks

Whatever might happen, the evolution of implicit contracting ideas, in those areas where they apply, is transforming the analytical landscape. From a restricted and narrow interpretation, based upon assumed attribute differences between firms and workers, implicit contracting has moved on to embrace all interactions between the parties and has refocused the theory of the firm on effort variability of workers and its implications for incentive patterns and organizational structure. Concern with explaining rigid wages has given way to analysis of who should control the firm; identifying precise swaps of specific quid pro quos has been supplanted by exploring the proper ambience and incentives for high-level worker performance; views of workers as mechanical robots responding to well-defined commands and rewards have yielded to the recognition of the complexities and conflicts involved in eliciting effort; and the easy invocation of moral hazard to account for self-serving deviant behavior has been replaced by the realization that parties ensnared by a web of strategic dependence are not always cooperative and forthcoming with each other. Implicit contracting leads us to a fundamental dilemma: once our view of the production process accepts the workers' enlarged role and contribution, then the institutional arrangements defining the firm must be recast to accommodate this functional realignment. What began as an ambitious attempt to explain certain stylized facts within a traditional analytic framework has burst its bounds to enter a more fluid and undefined world. Inescapably, in that new world, will not institutional form follow, eventually, economic function?

REFERENCES

Alchian, Armen A., and Harold Demsetz. 1972. "Production, Information Costs, and Economic Organization." *American Economic Review* 62:777–95.
Aoki, Masahiko. 1980. "A Model of the Firm as a Stockholder-Employee Cooperative Game." *American Economic Review* 70:600–610.
Azariadis, Costas, and Joseph E. Stiglitz. 1983. "Implicit Contracts and Fixed-Price Equilibria." *Quarterly Journal of Economics* 98:1–22.
Becker, Gary S. 1975. *Human Capital.* 2d ed. New York: National Bureau of Economic Research.
Edwards, P., and H. Scullion. 1982. *The Social Organization of Industrial Conflict.* Oxford: Blackwell.
Estrin, Saul, and Virginie Perotin. 1987. "Producer Cooperatives: The British Experience." *International Review of Applied Economics* 1:152–75.
Fitzroy, Felix R., and Kornelius Kraft. 1986. "Profitability and Profit-Sharing." *Journal of Industrial Economics* 35:113–30.
Fitzroy, Felix R., and Kornelius Kraft. 1987. "Cooperation, Productivity, and Profit Sharing." *Quarterly Journal of Economics* 102:23–36.

Freeman, Richard B., and James Medoff. 1979. "The Two Faces of Unionism." *Public Interest* 57:69–93.

Grossman, S., and O. D. Hart. 1981. "Implicit Contracts, Moral Hazard, and Unemployment." *American Economic Review* 71:301–7.

Gunn, Christopher E. 1984. *Workers' Self-Management in the United States.* Ithaca: Cornell University Press.

Hall, Robert E. 1980. "Employment Fluctuations and Wage Rigidity." *Brookings Papers on Economic Activity* 1:91–123.

Jones, Derek C., and Jan Svejnar. 1982. *Participatory and Self-Managed Firms.* Lexington, Mass.: D. C. Heath.

Leibenstein, Harvey. 1987. *Inside the Firm.* Cambridge, Mass.: Harvard University Press.

Meade, James E. 1972. "The Theory of the Labor-Managed Firm and Profit-Sharing." *Economic Journal* 82:402–28.

Miyazaki, Hajime. 1984. "Work Norms and Involuntary Unemployment." *Quarterly Journal of Economics* 99:297–312.

Pryor, Frederic L. 1983. "The Economics of Production Cooperatives: A Reader's Guide." *Annals of Public and Cooperative Economy* 54:133–72.

Robertson, Dennis H. 1952. *Utility and All That.* London: George Allen & Unwin.

Rosen, Sherwin. 1985. "Implicit Contracts: A Survey." *Journal of Economic Literature* 23:1144–75.

Schultze, Charles L. 1985. "Microeconomic Efficiency and Nominal Wage Stickiness." *American Economic Review* 75:1–15.

Stephen, Frank H. 1984. *The Economic Analysis of Producers' Cooperatives.* New York: St. Martin's Press.

Vanek, Jaroslav. 1970. *The General Theory of Labor-Managed Market Economies.* Ithaca: Cornell University Press.

Vanek, Jaroslav. 1977. *The Labor-Managed Economy.* Ithaca: Cornell University Press.

Weiler, Paul. 1983. "Promises to Keep: Securing Workers' Rights to Self-Organization under the NLRA." *Harvard Law Review* 96:1769–1827.

Williamson, Oliver. 1980. "The Organization of Work: A Comparative Institutional Analysis." *Journal of Economic Behavior and Organization* 1:5–38.

Yellen, Janet L. 1984. "Efficiency Wage Models of Unemployment." *American Economic Review* 74:200–205.

Supply of Incentives and Demand for Motivation: A Microanalysis

Klaus Weiermair

Motivation and Effort as the Emerging Factors of Production

Throughout the industrialized world, business organizations are currently involved in massive exercises of industrial and organizational restructuring. This invariably includes changes in the division of labor and corporate systems of rewards and incentives. A number of reasons are frequently cited for these developments. First, those who believe in corporate Darwinism see this restructuring as the last stage in a corporate evolution that began with the entrepreneurial firm and evolved through the mechanistic corporation to today's dynamic organization (Blake, Avis, and Mouton 1966; Blake and Mouton 1985).

Closely associated with the Darwinist perspective is a second category of theories that view today's process of labor and work organization adjustment as a direct consequence of altered product/market conditions. Heightened competition exists, largely technology driven and also due to a combination of other factors, namely falling trade barriers, lower cost technology transfers, and improved market transparency. This has led to a relative decline in the importance of traditional mass production and export of standardized products by highly developed economies. Instead, comparative advantages for many highly industrialized countries have shifted toward more specialized production characterized by rapid technological change and shorter product cycles (Piore and Sabel 1984; Reich 1983). Increased competition among other high technology producers has, in turn, imposed new demands on worker skills and worker adaptability. Innovation, cooperation, communication, and human capital have increasingly become key factors of production. These skills are less easily monitored and are not motivated by traditional incentives and work organization schemes (Tomer 1987). New, competitively successful product markets such as computers, precision casting, specialty steel, specialty chemicals and bioengineering

127

(Piore and Sabel 1984) all rely "on the development function within teams of sophisticated employee skills, merging the traditionally separate business functions of design, engineering, production and marketing into new flexible systems of production" (Reich 1983, 46). Such approaches are necessary when solving new problems versus routinizing old ones and when highly integrated systems must respond quickly to new opportunities (Davis 1979). These methods rest on people working closely together, since both innovation and cooperation are people skills requiring new forms of work organization and reward systems (Hackman and Oldham 1980).

A third major explanation of the restructuring addresses the issue of changes in production technology — notably information-processing technologies. Both the introduction of CAD/CAM technologies in manufacturing processes and the computerization of office work have resulted in new forms of work organization, work incentives, and monitoring possibilities (Abernathy, Clark and Kantrow 1983; OECD/CERI 1986). The relative success of some jurisdictions, especially Japan and West Germany, in adopting various forms of worker participation and in developing a more flexible and responsive work organization within an environment of cooperative labor relations has led to a renewed and somewhat changed interest in worker motivation as a new and internationally competitive factor of production.[1]

Taken together, the secular shift toward a service economy, the fact that a greater proportion of exports are human-capital-intensive goods, and the more rapid diffusion of information-processing technologies have all created a new context for a "high discretion" workplace (Yankelovich and Immerwahr 1983, 17–18). Not only has growth of discretionary space in workers' jobs meant increases in the amount and importance of discretionary effort but it has also brought the human resource factor to a position of critical strategic importance.

In the past, the economies of many industrialized countries were dominated by low skill levels and low discretion type jobs. They could, therefore, be managed by Tayloristic management practices without producing negative effects upon overall economic performance. In this low-discretion workplace and industrial environment, such intangibles as commitment to work, creativity, and cooperative behavior could be safely ignored. The same factors, however, have become pivotal

---

1. This is probably best exemplified in such works as Peters and Waterman's "In Search of Excellence" or Ouchi's "Theory Z: How American Business Can Meet the Japanese Challenge." For an older and less popularized study on comparative management systems, see Rensis Likert 1967 "The Human Organization — Its Management Value."

resources critical to economic vitality in a high-discretion, postindustrial society. Ability to come to terms with and to adapt to these new realities, sometimes described as problems of "commitment gap" (Yankelovitch and Immerwahr 1983), "distributional compulsion" or "zero sum game mentality" (Hirsch 1976; Olson 1982; Thurow 1980) or simply "poor work ethic" (Bernstein 1980), has become a hallmark of industrial leadership capability. In many ways, the capacity to adapt is comparable to the technological and organizational leadership challenges of firms in their historical antecedent, namely, the first industrial revolution.

Thus, while issues of effort and motivation have remained extremely important in the management literature, particularly as it relates to organizational design and development (Davis and Taylor 1979; Galbraith 1977), mainstream economics has barely scratched the surface of the black box. Given its preference for a theory of markets rather than a theory of the firm, mainstream economics has, in the past, never been particularly concerned with aspects of organizational design (Aoki 1984, 32).

Before charting a useful avenue for the socioeconomic analysis of work organization and work incentives based on X-efficiency theory, the next section first provides an overview of the typical treatment of motivation and work incentives in the economics literature.

Work Effort and Work Incentives in the Economic Theory of the Firm

Work organization and relationships among workers involved in production have become the subject of analysis in a growing number of social science disciplines. The multidisciplinary nature of this field and the previously mentioned importance of secular changes toward new forms of work organization have lately led to a mushrooming literature of interdisciplinary treatises and readers.[2] It would be both impossible and impractical to review all the relevant literature. Hence, we will restrict ourselves to a discussion of key arguments and paradigms as they have appeared in mainstream economic thinking. In this way we hope to be able to build a convincing case for the further development and work organization application of X-efficiency theory (Leibenstein 1976).[3]

---

2. Typical samples of such interdisciplinary readers are Ouchi and Barney (1986) or Putterman (1986). The recent creation of a number of new interdisciplinary journals in behavioral economics, economics and organization, and psychology and economics also attests to the emerging interest in the refinement of the theory of the firm in general and work organization in particular.

3. Readers interested in greater detail are referred to the literature (Putterman 1986).

Industrial psychology typically tests for a relationship between job characteristics, critical psychological states, and outcomes in terms of varying levels of internal work motivation (Hackman and Oldham 1980, 72–98). To the extent that workers do not behave uniformly across and within organizations, motivational phenomena have also attracted the attention of economists. In addition to pure personality determinants, workers are apt to display differences in the degree of motivation and choice (discretion) over levels of work effort, depending on the social and economic conditions and characteristics of the workplace.

Motivation and variability in effort thus become crucial determinants in the production function. What makes their treatment difficult if not intractable is the fact that from a strictly neoclassical perspective, no direct or easily verifiable relationships can be postulated between effort and motivation and production. The problems of specifying a production function with effort or motivation as one of its operators are tantamount to the practical problem of creating a mutually satisfying exchange relationship in production and employment leading to full versus perfunctory cooperation. Mutually satisfying exchange relationships could be viewed in this context as relations perceived as fair among all members of the production organization. Evaluation of fairness must, therefore, precede, both chronologically and logically, the physical exchange of transactions on which market analysis typically centers.

Fairness relates not only to present price, quality, and quantity of an exchange but also to the more or less uncertain conditions of a future exchange relationship, its clarification, and its evaluation in respective transactions. Furthermore, all transactions occur and are facilitated within an institutional framework of historically determined laws and social norms. Thus, the organizational problem could be restated as one of finding appropriate patterns of agreements and institutional arrangements for different types of transactions.

Varying institutional arrangements could be safely regarded as irrelevant if they had no cost consequences for organizing. Orthodox economists typically recognize those transaction cost savings that are associated with any specific institutional arrangement in production and exchange. Instead of analyzing the total factor set causing transaction cost differences, neoclassical analysis has emphasized the contractual properties. An example of this would be the legal framework of exchange as the ultimate determinant of institutional development and thus organizational variety (see, e.g., De Alessi 1983; Pejovich 1972). Analysis of social or institutional change is reduced to an observation regarding the creation and specification of property rights over resources, including human resources. The problem of collective organization is reduced to one of metering joint output in the face of potential shirking among organization members (Alchian and Demsetz 1972).

Property rights theory views the problem of organization as one in which command over resources turns out to be the sole motivating factor. Even if reducing all organizational tasks to problems of shirking or information in team production (De Alessi 1983) were acceptable, no explanation is offered in property rights/transaction costs theory as to what constitutes varying and nontechnical conditions for the ex-ante existence of opportunism and discretion. It is true that if everybody were maximally opportunistic in Williamson's terminology (Williamson and Harris 1975), organizational problems would dovetail into simply devising suitable contracts or, failing the efficiency of courts, suitable private orderings (Williamson 1983). Both employee and employer opportunism, however, appear to vary appreciably across institutions, history, and jurisdictions. Social determination in terms of, for example, reciprocal relations of trust/mistrust (Fox 1974) therefore have to set aside market determinants and contractual arrangements.

In the theoretical terms of transaction costs (Williamson 1979), governance relations are seen as cost-saving techniques to facilitate exchange and cooperative behavior. Hence, in the neoclassical view, they appear to be and are used by management as pure means or instruments for the purpose of organizational control. Both in microcultures and macrocultures (environments), governance relations (for example, in the form of socially prescribed norms of behavior) may, however, represent consumptive ends rather than means. Not only does changing social values into pure means (e.g., becoming purely instrumental) cause qualitative changes in exchange relations but the consequences may also lead to a decline in motivation or increases in distributional compulsion as shown by Hirsch (1976). Whether social norms that facilitate exchange exist and persist and whether they are viewed as pure means or ends should therefore affect both transaction costs and effort motivation irrespective of property rights arrangements.

In property rights theory, as in most neoclassical analysis, management's role is viewed as specifying optimal incentive structures for organization members through varying forms of contracts, profit maximization motives, and environmental constraints in the form of attenuation of property rights (De Alessi 1983). Variations of efficiency cannot, therefore, result from being off the production possibility frontier but arise only ex post from ex-ante estimating errors (e.g., Stigler quoted in De Alessi 1983). Instead of allowing efficiency variations to result directly from or to reside in the decision-making process of the organization itself, neoclassical analysis reasons that variations in production techniques and variety of efficiency stem entirely from differential supplies of entrepreneurial capacity (Oi 1983). A fair amount of both theoretical and empirical evidence regarding the nature of decision making and managerial work finds these assumptions untenable. Instead, a number of authors have successfully centered their analyses on organizational efficiencies and inefficiencies as the dependent variable (e.g., Campbell and Pritchard 1976; Cyert and March 1963; Mintzberg 1973).

The notion of efficiency labor as determined by worker preferences and contractual incentive structures, pervasive in neoclassical thinking, closely parallels the dichotomy between labor power and labor and associated conflicting theories of the firm entertained in Marxian economics in its distinction between worker and efficient labor.[4]

This brief review of neoclassical theory, particularly agency theory and transaction cost approach, and Marxian reflections on work organization and employment relations, suggests one and possibly two critical shortcomings:

1. These theories represent economic models that are based entirely on individuals rather than on organizations and on competitive self-interest among individuals. As such, they can handle self-regarding behavior only in contrast to "other-regarding" behavior (Perrow 1985) and thus deal only with a subset of total behavior at work.
2. Somewhat related to the first point, individuals and organizations are assumed to be perfect profit or utility maximizers, at least in intent if not in practice. This runs counter to a host of theoretical analysis and empirical evidence on organizational change and development, organizational slack, and "satisficing" behavior (Nelson and Winter 1982; Simon 1957).

In other words, in neoclassical analyses of the firm, there is nothing wrong with the pure economic analysis of organizations, but there is everything wrong with its psychology of work behavior, both implied and used. The latter also renders it inapplicable for a game theory analysis of work organization and work incentives. For all of these reasons, we prefer instead to build our arguments on the X-efficiency paradigm, which will be attempted next.

---

4. The analytical proximity of the Marxist and neoclassical interpretation of the radical account of the employment relationship and a demonstration of their similarities can also be found in Goldberg 1980.

Motivation and Working Conditions in an X-Efficiency
Theoretical Framework

The X-efficiency theoretical framework of analysis, developed by Leibenstein (1976, 1979, 1982, 1983, 1984) and applicable to questions of organizational design and development, departs from the psychological assumptions of unidimensional and purely self-interested (psychologically unconstrained) human behavior criticized in the previous section. It adopts, instead, the notion of coexisting superego (ethical) and selfish or calculated interests. According to Leibenstein (1976, 71ff), the interaction and balancing of superego needs and considerations of self-interest yield differing levels of "selective rationality" for both individuals and aggregations of individuals, such as groups and firms. By admitting real other-regarding behavior[5] into the realm of economic analysis, Leibenstein has managed to put the economics discipline on a different and, one might argue, more general psychological foundation of human behavior. Now, the neoclassical case of pure rationality (complete constraint concern calculatedness in Leibenstein's terminology: 1976, 72) becomes a special case along a continuum of possible and differing levels of selective rationality. Among other things, this implies that profit and utility maximization in this paradigm can be executed in varying degrees, in contrast to the neoclassical formulation of absolutes. As could be expected, there has been a wild and at times polemical reaction, particularly from the neoclassical camp in the literature (see e.g., De Alessi 1983; Leibenstein 1983; Stigler 1976). Deviations from pure profit maximization based on bounded rationality and postulated by the Carnegie school as "satisficing behavior" are equally achievable behavioral outcomes under the X-efficiency paradigm (Frantz 1985). The theory of selective rationality as fully described in Leibenstein (1976, 71–94) thus allows variable deviations from profit-maximizing behavior contingent upon group, firm-external, or firm-internal pressures as well as pressures emanating from within the decision maker (personality factors).

In this way individual choice, including the choice of effort, becomes directly related to the underlying conditions determining selective rationality. For example, firm-external pressures in terms of varying degrees of market competition and resulting "constraint concernedness," the context of firm-internal decision making and associated questions of entropy, and horizontal and vertical interpersonal relations (pressures) jointly determine

---

5. This is in contrast to the tautological treatment of other-regarding behavior and altruism in the neoclassical tradition that redefines altruism as an act of selfishness in order to proceed with the normal models of profit and utility maximization (see Becker 1981).

the interpretation and evaluation of jobs, effort levels, and constraint concernedness.[6] In contrast to other approaches that either provide a mere ex-post rationalization of the surviving organizational and institutional variety (property rights and agency theory) or are merely satisfied with advancing ideas and further insights regarding the complexities, imperfections, and limitations of decision making in the pursuit of profit maximization (Carnegie school and transaction cost approach), X-efficiency theory comes up with a general theory of effort choice and effort equilibrium. It thus paves the way toward a general theory of organizational design and behavior.[7] X-efficiency theory no longer shows utility as a strictly negative monotone function of effort but instead posits a concave function incorporating the new psychological foundations. Up to a point, intrinsic motivation or other psychological pressures lead to higher utility, associated with higher levels of effort. Beyond some level of utility, additional effort leads to utility losses. Figure 1 depicts typical effort-utility equilibrium points for individual workers.

In addition to perceived utility levels associated with differing amounts of effort, the worker's ultimate effort equilibrium point also depends on utility costs associated with movements from lower to higher effort-utility combinations (a movement from A to B). Thus, the distance C_0 C_1 measures the utility cost of moving from effort point E_1 to point E_3. Critical to the theory discussed so far as well as to later extensions into analyses of work organization or incentives is the recognition of effort inertia areas (the space E_1 E_2) within the utility cost bound (C_0 C_1) that will not induce changes in work behavior.

The area of inertia, E_1 E_2, shows a range of effort points within which it would not pay for the individual to move to the optimal effort point, E_3. Effort-adjustment costs (contributing to inertia) stem from objective, subjective, real, and perceived costs of moving from one position to another and from settling into a higher effort position. The existence of horizontal (peer group) and vertical (subordinate-superior) influence relationships within organizations and the general interconnectedness of work flows have the effect of either shifting the entire EU function (i.e., management's introduction of policies containing varying sets of sanctions and rewards can shift individual workers' EU function to EU') or redefining the inertial space. In the latter case overlapping EU functions between individual workers and between workers and manage-

---

6. For a more elaborate treatment, see Leibenstein 1976, 71–94, or Leibenstein 1979.
7. For a comparison and evaluation of the X-efficiency perspective in relation to postulates from organizational theory, see Leibenstein and Weiermair 1986.

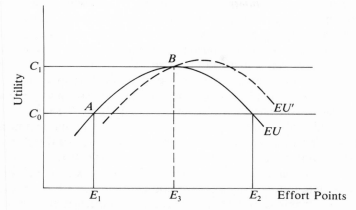

Fig. 1. Effort-utility functions and effort adjustment cost

ment redefine the effort-adjustment cost for the group.[8] Since space limitations prevent us from delving into further details of a theory otherwise rich in potential applications in organization internal decision making, we proceed directly to an analysis of effort choice under comparative forms of work organization.

We can define work organization as an interaction of supply of incentives and demand for motivation. Firm-internal incentives and requisite demands for effort and motivation are analyzed below as a game-theory problem (Leibenstein 1982). In contrast to alternative approaches,[9] this methodology offers the advantage of internal examination of organizational processes and routines and as such also provides insights into the dynamics of organizational adaptation and change. Choice and conflict over varying forms of work organization and level of effort are initially viewed as being uniquely determined by firm-internal forces, an assumption that is later dropped in favor of varying forms and levels of firm-external pressures.

Departing from the now generally accepted assumption that there is appreciable discretion on the part of management in offering diverse packages of working conditions and on the part of workers in offering

8. The reader is again referred to Leibenstein's original work (1976, 188ff). An application of selective rationality and effort equilibrium of the firm under varying human resource policy regimes can be found in Weiermair 1984.

9. See, for example, Williamson 1980 or Alchian and Demsetz 1972 for a transaction cost/property rights theoretical analysis or Hackman and Lawler 1971 for an organizational perspective.

varying amounts of effort,[10] both parties can be said to have considerable control over the supply of effort and working conditions. Managers' and workers' options or strategies could conceivably be represented as continuous or nondimensional. For purposes of exposition, the present analysis employs a three-way classification of strategy in terms of full, partial, and minimal supply of effort on the part of workers and three corresponding levels of supply in satisfying working and workplace conditions on the part of management.[11] Matrix 1 and figure 2 show the three options available to managers and employees: maximum commitment, negotiated (peer-related) standards, and minimum (selfish) standards.

Row numbers in matrix 1 indicate the net payoff, i.e., the total of monetary and nonmonetary benefits in terms of working conditions for three alternate states of work organization associated with three levels of effort. For example, if workers gave maximum effort (row E_1), they would obtain 20, 8, or 3 measured units of net return (wages net of effort-utility cost). Payoffs for management are shown as labor-cost-adjusted levels of productivity. For example, if management were to minimize cost associated with working conditions (column M_3), it would obtain net payoffs of 30, 15, or 5, depending on which of the three effort alternatives workers chose. If management were able to rely on a stable and predictable level of effort, it would always want to minimize cost associated with work organization. Similarly, if workers could count on stable working conditions, it would pay for them to reduce efforts. This is illustrated by the arrows in figure 2 denoting increases of employee and management payoffs as a result of unilateral maximization exercises. The payoff matrix constructed in this way demonstrates the well-known properties of the Prisoner's Dilemma (PD) under conditions of adversarial behavior, a concept written about quite frequently. Under conditions of information and behavior symmetry, moves along given arrows call for countermoves along the other arrow, thus eventually landing both parties in the selfish quadrant with the lowest payoff—the infamous PD trap. In most economic theories on work organization, levels of effort (motivation) and productivity related to the cost of workplace conditions

---

10. Both neoclassical and nonneoclassical writers have by now acknowledged the incomplete nature of labor contracts (exchanges). See, for example, Alchian and Demsetz 1972; Leibenstein 1976; and Williamson, Watcher, and Harris 1975.

11. Dimensions of working conditions typically include training, promotion and career options, interpersonal relations at the workplace, and degrees of worker autonomy. Work efforts can be decomposed according to quality, pace, choice patterns, and length of the activity. In order to simplify, we assume that both alternate working conditions and effort levels can be expressed unidimensionally in terms of productivity-yielding efforts and packages of working conditions creating differing levels of total labor cost.

Management

Employee		Full Commitment M_1	Acceptable Peer Standards M_2	Minimum Cost per Person M_3
Maximum Commitment E_1		20 \ 20	25 \ 8	30 \ 3
Negotiated (peer-related) E_2 Standards		8 \ 25	10 \ 10	15 \ 4
Minimum (selfish) E_3 Standards		3 \ 30	4 \ 15	5 \ 5

Matrix 1

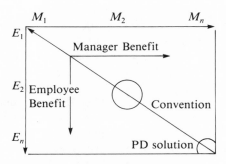

Fig. 2

represent essential ingredients. Our three-way classification scheme for efforts and working conditions could therefore conveniently be translated into a three-way typology of work organization, often denoted as systems *X, Y,* and *Z*.[12] *X, Y,* and *Z* systems of organizational structures, processes, and rewards, including aspects of work organization, have also formed an integral part of recent organization theory (Ouchi 1980). In this typology *X* usually stands for a Taylor type work organization with a strong division of labor, segmented job structures, little training, tight worker control, and a prevalence of extrinsic motivation and benefits. *Y* denotes a more differentiated system of both structured and unstructured jobs containing firm-specific training and leading to more or less well-defined jobs, promotion, and training ladders, which in turn

---

12. For an earlier treatment, see Leibenstein and Weiermair 1986.

are governed by explicit contracts (e.g., collective bargaining provisions) and, to a much lesser degree, by social norms. While extrinsic motivation and rewards dominate, interpersonal horizontal and vertical relations (pressures) nevertheless add intrinsic motivation and rewards to an otherwise purely contractual employment relationship. Finally, the Z type of work organization in its purest form constitutes a clan that is bound together and governed through psychological contracts. There are few job demarcations; workers have considerable autonomy over their jobs; and ample, general cross training is provided to all workers. There is considerable work group homogeneity and little divergence between organizational goals and individual goals. As can be seen from figure 3, the Z type organization represents a Pareto optimal form of work organization.

Clearly, X, Y, and Z are ideal types. In reality, work organizations are likely to represent intermediate systems along a continuum ranging from X to Z. More important than characterizations of management and work organization systems so typical of the behavioral sciences are questions as to the conditions surrounding the creation, stability, and disappearance (destruction) of alternate systems of work and pay. In other words, we might want to know why organizations work along the diagonal of the payoff matrix instead of being either to the left or right of it and why organizations have tendencies to settle at particular points along the diagonal. Discussing these points becomes an analysis of the firm-internal demand and supply of incentives and effort. Before pursuing this direction, one should flag the typical neoclassical solution within this game-theory framework once more. If profit maximization or cost minimization in its purest and unpolluted form is undertaken, management will attempt to move eastward along its payoff arrows—a move that leads, however, to a countermove on the part of workers and ends in an inferior PD solution. Cost minimization and associated controls appear to have a direct and negative effect on effort levels, resulting, in turn, in even tighter work and cost controls. Thus, a process unravels that appears to feed on itself and whose dynamic properties and histories have been amply described in the literature under the heading "distributional compulsion" (Fox 1974; Olson 1982; Thurow 1980). An alternative neoclassical view is to deny effort discretion altogether and assume the existence of efficient control and monitoring devices (Alchian and Demsetz 1972). Whichever view is entertained, the results are the same in that movements in M toward M_n cannot be countered by analogous moves on the part of workers. This is the same as saying that motivation and effort levels among workers are being viewed as nondiscretionary. In this way management can easily establish effort and payoff points to the

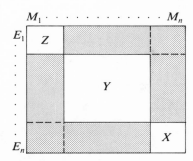

Fig. 3. Management system and effort conventions

right of the diagonal in the *EM* square. Furthermore, these points are unrelated to points on the left-hand side. The uniquely managerial character of such reasoning and the static nature of the implied exchange relationship make this case rather unattractive for further discussion. Instead, we return to Leibenstein's effort-utility functions and their organizational prevalence (Leibenstein and Weiermair 1986). These effort-utility functions are presented in figure 4 and are marked as EU_c, EU_h, and EU_m corresponding to a clan, hierarchy and market type of employment relations (work organization) situation.

The pure market type is sharply sloped (peaked), displaying the lowest achieved effort-utility level, which reflects both the motivational effects from Tayloristic work design and the low-effort discretion encountered in a market transaction mode. The hierarchy curve has a flatter top and lies at a higher level, reflecting increases in both discretion and effort (motivation). The former effects result from the greater versatility of human resource use in internal organization, while the latter effects stem from the added motivational effects of both lateral and vertical relations (pressures). Finally, the clan curve shows some resemblance to the hierarchy curve but has a higher position and a smaller peak. Both derive from the latter's implicit social or psychological contract nature of the employment relationship—the existence and social conditioning of which has been amply described in the literature (Argyris 1960; Macneil 1980; Tomer 1980, 1981). Typical constraint lines are indicated by C_m, C_h, and C_c showing, at the same time the utility cost of effort adjustment to reach maximum levels of utility and the size of the discretionary effort space for each of the three modes of work organization and given costs of effort adjustment. Based on evidence from organization theory, the constraint lines are constructed in such a way that effort-adjustment costs typically rise over the three modes of work orga-

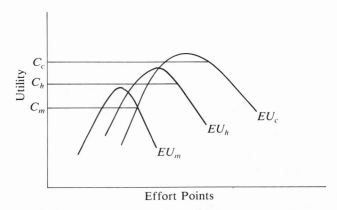

Fig. 4. Effort-utility functions and effort-adjustment cost for different forms of work organization

nization from C_m to C_h and further to C_c. Next, in figure 5 we array the effort-utility functions shown previously in figure 4 and, with the help of a 90-degree clockwise rotation, connect it to the payoff matrix previously displayed in fig. 2.

In this manner, inert areas for each given mode of organization can now be mapped onto convention areas along the diagonal of the payoff matrix. The following observations emerge:

1. Relative to the hierarchical organization and the pure market exchange relationship, clans show much greater areas of effort inertia (discretion). An implication of this, according to X-efficiency theory, is that clans tolerate much greater variability in working conditions and effort levels without leading to symmetrical changes in the nature of the work organization or the employment relationship.
2. Since the width of effort and inertia (effort conventions) are jointly determined by the height of utility costs of effort adjustment and the shape of the effort-utility function, it follows that the very same factors that determine inertia must also be responsible for the development and change of effort conventions and, hence, modes of work organization.

Thus, whatever the chosen form of work organization, increases in effort-adjustment costs widen inertia (in terms of the drawn circles in fig. 5) thereby reducing the likelihood of changes in conventions in either

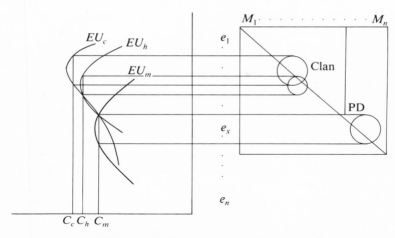

Fig. 5. Effort-utility functions and effort conventions

direction, that is, toward a PD or pure clan solution. Those who favor a transaction cost approach in the explanation of institutional change may at this point interject and claim that this is analogous to stating that variations in conventions or forms of organizations have, in effect, been shown as the result of changing objective costs of alternate governance structures (Williamson 1979, 1980). In Leibenstein's theoretical framework, and for that matter in most of the behavioral literature on work organization, the relevant costs are, however, subjective costs; that is, what individual workers and managers perceive as the costs of effort adjustment are distinct from observable variations in the actual cost of creating, monitoring (policing), and abolishing alternate contractual relations. Organization history and resultant organizational cultures or psychological differences among workers and managers (e.g., with respect to work ethics) can therefore affect perceptions of risks and costs of effort adjustment by as much as if not more than objectively determined technological constraints, information impactedness, or the costs of monitoring the employment contract.

Whether or not changes in the utility cost of effort adjustment lead to changes in the mode of organizations also critically depends on the successive locations of EU_c, EU_h, and EU_m. The further to the right subsequent EU functions cut the declining slope of the lower EU function, the less likely the chance that organization members will perceive of new or alternative forms of work organization. In our example EU_h and EU_c cut EU_m below the constraint line C_m and hence participants of an existing market exchange type relationship (EU_m) would not likely even consider hierarchy or clan as alternative forms of (work) organization. Even if EU_m and EU_h were to cut through C_m in the inert area of EU_m, there is no guarantee that the signal would automatically lead to action. Participants will consider new and changed work conventions or newer forms of work organization only if associated perceptions of lower utility costs of effort adjustment exist (e.g., such as C_h or C_c). Both evolutionary changes and shocks in the external environment of the organization exercise varying degrees of pressures on the organization's members and, as such, can clearly lead to changes in effort conventions and forms of work organization. Given the history of firm-internal structures and processes, and the inertial character of intrafirm exchanges between economic agents, there is every reason to believe that processes of social experimentation are being based on nonmaximizing or at least noncalculating behavior in the narrow sense. Furthermore, this process is "shot through with adverse incentives and maladaptive attributes" (Williamson 1980). Contrary to mainstream economic theorizing, X-efficiency theory is quite comfortable with and can easily deal with these social aspects of organizations, for effort conventions are simply viewed as the development of specific norms, cultures, and routines as a process of "emulating coordinated effort" (Leibenstein 1984, 342).

If our predictions at the beginning of this article regarding production and employment in postindustrial societies were to come true, both higher levels and higher variability of motivation will be required. This requirement will, in turn, suggest the need to supply adequate working conditions and work organization systems. In terms of our game-theory model presented earlier, this means a movement along the diagonal into the left-hand corner of the EM square. While market forces can be expected to help these processes somewhat through shifts of EU functions (due to firm-external pressures), there are obvious limitations. For one, clan type forms of work organizations within firms have few, if any, reference points in the firm-external labor market. Second, the flat-top EU function associated with clan type organizations suggests considerable organizational inertia. These factors taken together point to the relatively more important role of "intrapreneurship" and entrepreneurship in the creation and maintenance of new forms of work organization. Entrepreneurs tend to have different (usually enlarged) alternative sets and thus differently shaped EU functions. Also, their leadership capabilities tend to have a negative effect on perceived risks and cost of effort adjustment. Both facilitate changes in effort conventions toward the upper-left-hand corner of the payoff matrix.

It comes as no great surprise that we are currently witnessing a renaissance of economic theorizing on entrepreneurship as well as a return of Schumpeterian economics. First contours of this debate, which is still being pursued, indicate, however, that entrepreneurship and entrepreneurial processes can hardly be explained by neoclassical market theories or market analogies for firm-internal processes. Once more it appears that a wider frame of socioeconomic analysis, analogous to X-efficiency theory, will be required. This, however, should be the subject of another article.

REFERENCES

Abernathy, William J. 1978. *The Productivity Dilemma*. Baltimore: Johns Hopkins University Press.

Abernathy, William J., Kim B. Clark, and Alan M. Kantrow. 1983. *Industrial Renaissance*. New York: Basic Books.

Alchian, A., and H. Demsetz. 1972. "Production, Information Costs and Economic Organization." *American Economic Review* 62:777-95.

Aoki, Masahiko. 1984. *The Cooperative Game Theory of the Firm*. New York: Oxford University Press.

Argyris, Chris. 1960. *Understanding Organizational Behavior*. Homewood, Ill.: Dorsey Press.

Becker, Gary. 1981. "Altruism in the Family and Selfishness in the Market Place." *Economica* 48:1-15.

Bernstein, Paul. 1980. "The Worst Ethic That Never Was." *Wharton Magazine*.

Blake, Robert R., and Jane Mouton. 1985. *The Managerial Grid III*. Houston: Gulf Publishing Co.

Blake, Robert R., Warren E. Avis, and Jane S. Mouton. 1966. *Corporate Darwinism: An Evolutionary Perspective on Organizing Work in the Dynamic Corporation*. Houston: Gulf Publishing Co.

Bowles, Samuel. 1985. "The Production Process in a Competitive Economy: Walrasian, Neo-Hobbesian, and Marxian Models." *American Economic Review* 75:16-36.

Brandegaard, A. 1983. "Market, Hierarchy and Terminology: Some Implications of Economic Internationalism for Labor." In *Power, Efficiency and Institutions: A Critical Appraisal of the "Markets and Hierarchies" Paradigm*, ed. A. Francis, J. Turk, and P. Willman. London: Heinemann Books.

Campbell, John P., and Robert D. Pritchard. 1976. "Motivation Theory in Industrial and Organizational Psychology." In *Handbook of Industrial and Organizational Psychology*, ed. Marven D. Dunnette. Chicago: Rand McNally.

Coase, R. H. 1932. "The Nature of the Firm." *Economica*, n.s. 4:386-405.

Cyert, Richard, and James March. 1963. *A Behavioral Theory of the Firm*. Englewood Cliffs, N.J.: Prentice Hall.

Davis, Louis E., and James C. Taylor, eds. 1979. *Design of Jobs*. 2d ed. Santa Monica: Good Year.

Davis, Louis E. 1979. "Optimizing Organization – Plant Design: A Complementary Structure for Technical and Social Systems." *Organizational Dynamics* 8:3–15.

Davis, Stanley M. 1983. "Management Models for the Future." *New Management* 1:12–15.

De Alessi, L. 1983. "Property Rights, Transaction Costs and X-Efficiency: An Essay in Economic Theory." *American Economic Review* 73:64–81.

Doeringer, P., and M. Piore. 1971. *Internal Labour Markets and Manpower Analysis.* Lexington, Mass.: Penguin.

Fox, A. 1974. *Beyond Contract: Work, Power and Trust Relations.* London: University of London Press.

Frantz, R. 1985. "X-efficiency Theory and Its Critics." *Quarterly Review of Economics and Business* 25:37–58.

Furobotn, E. G., and S. Pejovich, eds. 1976. *The Economics of Property Rights.* Cambridge: Ballinger.

Galbraith, Jay. 1977. *Organization Design.* Reading, Mass.: Addison Wesley.

Gershuny, Jonathan, and Jan Miles. 1983. *The New Service Economy.* London: Francis Pinter.

Goldberg, Victor. 1980. "Bridges Over Contested Terrain: Explaining the Radical Account of the Employment Relationship." *Journal of Economic Behavior and Organization* 1:249–74.

Hackman, J. R., and G. R. Oldham. 1980. *Work Redesign.* Reading, Mass.: Addison Wesley.

Hill, Christopher T., and James M. Utterback, eds. 1979. *Technological Innovation for a Dynamic Economy.* New York: Pergamon Press.

Hirsch, Fred. 1976. *Social Limits to Growth.* Cambridge, Mass.: Harvard University Press.

Leibenstein, Harvey. 1976a. *Beyond Economic Man: A New Foundation for Microeconomics.* Cambridge, Mass.: Harvard University Press.

Leibenstein, Harvey. 1976b. "On the Basic Proposition of X-efficiency Theory." *American Economic Review* 68:328–34.

Leibenstein, Harvey. 1979. "A Branch of Economics Is Missing: Micro-Micro Theory." *Journal of Economic Literature* 17:477–502.

Leibenstein, Harvey. 1982. "The Prisoner's Dilemma in the Invisible Hand: An Analysis of Intra-firm Productivity." *American Economic Review* 72:92–97.

Leibenstein, Harvey. 1983. "Property Rights and X-efficiency: Comment." *American Economic Review* 73:831–42.

Leibenstein, Harvey. 1984. "On the Economics of Conventions and Institutions: An Exploratory Essay." *Zeitschrift für die Gesamte Staatswissenschaft* 140:74–86.

Leibenstein, Harvey, and Klaus Weiermair. 1986. "X-efficiency, Managerial Discretion and the Nature of Employment Relations: A Game Theoretical Approach." Presented at the Second Symposium on Comparative Management, Berlin, West Germany. Mimeo.

Levitt, Theodore. 1981. "Marketing Intangible Products and Product Intangibles." *Harvard Business Review*, May-June, 94–102.

Likert, Rensis. 1967. *The Human Organization—Its Management Value.* New York: McGraw-Hill.

Luce, Duncan R., and Howard Raiffa. 1957. *Games and Decisions.* New York: Wiley.

MacNeil, Jan R. 1980. *The New Social Contract: An Inquiry into Modern Contractual Relations.* New Haven: Yale University Press.

Mintzberg, Henry. 1973. *The Nature of Managerial Work.* New York: Harper and Row.

Nelson, Richard, and Sidney Winter. 1982. *An Evolutionary Theory of Economic Change.* Cambridge, Mass.: Harvard University Press.

OECD/CERI. 1986. *The Evolution of New Technology, Work and Skills in the Service Sector.* Paris: CERI/OECD.

Oi, Walter. 1983. "Hetrogeneous Firms and the Organization of Production." *Economic Inquiry* 21:147–71.

Olson, Mancur. 1982. *The Rise and Decline of Nations.* New Haven: Yale University Press.

Ouchi, William. 1980. "Markets, Bureaucracies and Clans." *Administrative Science Quarterly* 25:129–41.

Ouchi, W., and J. Barney. 1986. *Organizational Economics: Toward a New Paradigm for Understanding and Studying Organizations.* San Francisco: Jossey Bass.

Pejovich, S. 1972. "Towards a Theory of the Creation and Specification of Property Rights." *Review of Social Economy* 30:309–25.

Perrow, Charles. 1985. *Complex Organizations.* New York: Irvin.

Piore, Michael J., and Charles F. Sabel. 1984. *The Second Industrial Divide: Possibilities for Prosperity.* New York: Basic Books.

Putterman, Louis, ed. 1986. *The Economic Nature of the Firm: A Reader.* Cambridge, Mass.: Harvard University Press.

Reich, Robert R. 1983. "The Next American Frontier." *Atlantic Monthly*, March, 43–58.

Schelling, T. C. 1960. *The Strategy of Conflict.* Cambridge, Mass.: Harvard University Press.

Simon, H. A. 1957. *Models of Man.* New York: Wiley.

Stigler, George J. 1976. "The Xistence of X-efficiency." *American Economic Review* 66:213–16.

Thurow, Lester C. 1980. *The Zero Sum Society.* New York: Basic Books.

Tomer, John F. 1981a. "Organizational Change, Organizational Capital and Economic Growth." *Eastern Economic Journal* 7:1–17.

Tomer, John F. 1981b. "Worker Motivation: A Neglected Element in Micro-Micro Theory." *Journal of Economic Issues* 15:351–62.

Tomer, John F. 1987. *Organizational Capital: The Path to Higher Productivity and Well-Being.* New York: Praeger.

Vroom, V. H., and E. L. Deci, eds. 1976. *Management and Motivation: Selected Readings*. New York: Penguin.

Weiermair, K. 1984. "Heterogeneity in Production and Organizational Design: Comparative Economic Perspectives of Organizational Innovativeness." Presented at EARIE Conference, Fontainbleau, France.

Williamson, O. E. 1975. *Markets and Hierarchies: Analysis and Antitrust Implications*. New York: Free Press.

Williamson, O. E. 1979. "Transaction-Cost Economics: The Governance of Contractual Relations." *Journal of Law and Economics* 22:233–62.

Williamson, O. E. 1980. "The Organization of Work: A Comparative Institutional Assessment." *Journal of Economic Behavior and Organization* 6:5–38.

Williamson, O. E. 1983. "Credible Commitments: Using Hostages to Support Exchange." *American Economic Review* 73:519–40.

Williamson, O. E., M. Wachter, and J. E. Harris. 1975. "Understanding the Employment Relation: The Analysis of Idiosyncratic Exchange." *Bell Journal of Economics* 6:250–78.

Yankelovich, D., and J. Immerwahr. 1983. *Putting the Work Ethic to Work: A New Public Agenda Report on Restoring America's Competitive Vitality*. New York: Public Agenda Foundation.

Commentary

Friedrich Fürstenberg

Comment on the Article by Bruno S. Frey:

Frey's article aims at integrating economic and psychological approaches to behavior within the framework of rational choice. He starts with the observation that individuals tend to overestimate or underestimate objective possibilities. Thus, the differentiation between an objective possibility set and an ipsative possibility set appears to be realistic. Properties of these sets are characterized in terms both of theoretical assumptions and of empirical observations. As a consequence, a certain conceptual ambivalence emerges: "OPS is transpersonal." "OPS is not given but rather is the result of an interpretative process of an actor." This hints at a basic difficulty in explaining rational choice: The so-called objectivity is a hypothetical construct, serving as a measure for individual deviations. Whatever properties may be assigned to objective possibilities, they are not fully recognizable by any actor. Thus, ipsative orientation is a feasible strategy in open-end situations, under the condition of a given goal structure.

The author then differentiates between the deviations in assessing objective possibility that are due to human nature and those which occur by design or intent. One might argue that the latter are a necessary consequence of the former. If actors are bound to overestimate given possibilities, the strategy of deliberately setting up a certain range of possibilities might be rather intelligible. This may be easily demonstrated by taking possible divorce as an example. No statistical evidence of a high divorce rate predetermines the outcome of an individual marriage. Thus, a strategy based upon the assumption of avoidable divorce certainly makes sense, if only "to induce a motivation and work effort" due to increased commitment.

Referring to underestimates of a possibility set, the author deals with coercive processes, determining behavior solely by the objective possibility set. This may be the case in coercion due to natural or quasi-natural constraints. However, coercion often also results from asymmetric power distribution among competing or contracting actors. In that case, calling the given possibility set "objective" may cover the fact that this "objectivity" results from other actors' strategies. It is rather an intersubjective phenomenon.

The author's approach stimulates creative thinking. Further discussion might develop along the following lines:

1. From a logical point of view a decision should be made whether objective and ipsative frames of reference are considered as hypothetical constructs or as empirical facts.
2. If ipsative possibility sets are based upon empirical evidence, the step from description to analysis should be taken.
3. This would imply taking into consideration situational factors: The genesis of an ipsative probability set may be conceived as a reaction to challenges and as an attempt to enable the individual to take strategic action in uncertain situations.
4. As a rule, only an ex-post analysis reveals whether an individual has overrated or underrated given possibilities.
5. Finally, it may be questioned whether probabilities really are initially given or whether they develop in the course of an interaction process. In the latter case, a dynamic view of the issue needs to be adopted.

Comment on the Article by Marvin E. Rozen

The author pleads for implicit contracting as a means to cope with circumstances that generate variability of effort as well as with their consequences. Against the assumption of a simplistic wage-effort bargain, issues of authority and power, among others, generate complicated compensation packages. Certain important work requirements such as trust, loyalty, and voluntary cooperation also require associational continuity beyond ad hoc bargaining.

The author's point of view perhaps could even be supported by taking into consideration the issue of qualification, which is constantly rising in relative importance. Qualification is a special type of effort, directed toward long-term efficiency of work. It cannot be treated as simply a given and tied to a given position. Instead, it emerges continuously from a process of active learning. Where the training of workers is required, implicit contracting about the terms of such efforts and their outcome appears to be necessary, and actually does occur as part of employment relations (career planning, etc.).

Comment on the Article by Klaus Weiermair

The author starts with the observation of a new context for a "high-discretion" workplace in connection with requirements for higher levels and higher variability of motivation. While mainstream economics has been less concerned with organizational design to meet such requirements, the X-efficiency paradigm offers a general framework for coping with the fact that both management and workers have considerable control over the supply of effort and working conditions. As a result, work organization may vary between "Taylor" and "clan" type structures. Situational choices will become a major task of entrepreneurship.

From a sociological point of view there will be few objections to this approach. However, management's and workers' autonomy of choice also appears to be limited by the fact that organizational structures are sociocultural phenomena. Their relative flexibility is conditioned by the relative importance of gainful employment to segments of the labor force, by qualification structures, by prevailing patterns of cooperation and conflict, and so forth. Organizational design related to effort motivation, therefore, operates within the margins for establishing a segmented subculture of the firm. Further research should also be directed toward the conditions for establishing and shaping such margins.

Part 3
The Design and Structuring of Organizations

Norms, Convention, and the Design of Organizations

Friedrich Fürstenberg

Organizations develop in the process of strategically structuring problem situations in which cooperation is required. Their actual shape may be conceived of as depending externally upon the type of problems and internally upon the type of structuring. The following analysis concerns organizations dealing with the problem of utilizing resources economically. Their main feature is efficiency-oriented structuring. While economic analysis focuses upon rational choice in situations related to efficiency, sociological analysis is mainly directed toward situational factors determining the extent and the modes of rationality and choice.

Organizations as Systems of Norm-Oriented Cooperation

In order to achieve efficiency in contingent situations, organizations must take strategic action. The starting point of this contribution is the thesis that such strategic action is centered around establishing norm-oriented cooperation. As Harvey Leibenstein has pointed out, the transformation of given inputs into predetermined outputs is not determined: "Instead, a good deal is left to custom, authority, and whatever motivational techniques are available to management as well as to individual discretion and judgment" (1986, 45). A key problem of organizational design is inherent in the phrase the direction of effort (1976, 95). The problem becomes more easily accessible to scientific investigation if we consider types of organizational structuring as modes of social norm-setting, made necessary by the absence of self-regulating mechanisms. Thus, cooperation as efficiency-directed, coordinated effort, is based upon social norms.

Rensis Likert has shown (1961) that different modes of norm-setting result in more or less coercive or participative cooperation. His characterization of coercive norm-setting as "authoritarian," however, needs further explanation. Authoritarian behavior in the strict sense is very much person based. In modern organizations we find another type of behavior, which we may call bureaucratic, based upon objective functional authority. Therefore, we may define three basic types of norm-oriented cooperation:

1. authoritative control based upon personal power and influence;
2. bureaucratic regulation based upon administrative guidance by experts; and
3. participative bargaining based upon convention or contract.

Industrial organizations first developed in a social climate favoring a conventional setting of efficiency norms (a "fair day's work"), but soon the conventional setting was replaced by authoritative control based upon property rights. Due to continual rationalization, industrial organizations gradually tended to replace personal authority, based upon traditional and charismatic features, with functional authority based upon factual competence. Therefore, there has also been a trend toward replacing traditions and beliefs by intelligible systems of evaluative norms.

As a consequence of external changes in power and market structures, more and more participative elements were introduced. They replaced the prevailing systems of coercive control, and new bargaining structures evolved.

The structures of Western industrial organizations may be characterized as mixtures of these different historically rooted types. Within an institutional framework based upon both convention and regulation, we find expert interference as well as bargaining procedures. Before assessing this situation from a theoretical point of view, we will give a closer and more detailed analysis of the actual establishment and functioning of efficiency norms within organizations.

The Generation and Structure of Efficiency Norms

Technically, there are two basic approaches for setting efficiency norms and for evaluating organizations' members accordingly:

  a. position-oriented ranking of task assignments, resulting in hierarchies of work functions;
  b. person-oriented ranking of task prerequisites and fulfillments, resulting in hierarchies of performance levels.

The evaluation of work functions or clusters of such functions (jobs) is related to the growth and development of studies of work initiated by Frederick Winslow Taylor. Specialists and departments for the analysis of work systems are integrated parts of corporate cultures.

Perhaps the most elaborate normative systems for the evaluation of work functions are job evaluation systems. They were developed in the late thirties and had their peak of application during the early postwar decades. Job evaluation usually comprises the following procedures:

a. Differentiating job requirements, whose major components are knowledge, ability, responsibility, and stress;
b. Making the different dimensions operational; knowledge gained from vocational training thus may be made operational by the length of successful school attendance;
c. Measuring the different dimensions of job requirements, e.g., by constructing scales (high — medium — low);
d. Weighting the different dimensions against each other by distributing the total of attainable scores among the dimensions, e.g., giving knowledge a maximum score of 30 percent, ability 40 percent, and so on;
e. Determining this constructed value of a job for a set of key positions;
f. Ranking the remaining jobs by analogy.

Closer analysis of this procedure shows that there are several normative components. The differentiation of job components follows a preconceived model as does the weighting of the various dimensions.

Therefore, the hope for making the status-related task evaluation objective by means of job evaluation was only partly realized. There is general consensus that such systems certainly serve to standardize and clarify evaluation procedures. However, they do not eliminate the arbitrary elements. Therefore, the results are, by no means, the mere outcome of applying a scientific methodology. Instead, they demonstrate the need for bargaining, and the outcome is usually based upon conflictual consensus by matching differing interests of management and workers.

Other less sophisticated sets of efficiency norms and evaluative procedures related to work functions may be found in the remuneration clauses of collective agreements in industrial establishments. West German trade unions prefer summary job evaluation to analytical methods because the former offers greater margins for negotiations (Berkessel and Humml 1982). Generally, however, the hierarchical ranking of jobs and job contents, as the main basis for differential remuneration, reflects normative preconceptions and decisions. In many such hierarchies we find a bias in favor of male as against female jobs, of skilled as against semiskilled jobs, and of mental as against manual operations. The evaluation of job contents and requirements is structurally determined by valid goals and values.

Perhaps the most obvious application of efficiency norms to the ranking of work functions is the establishment of status hierarchies, especially for executives. Usually, the evaluative functional description of job properties establishes certain personality features as a fundamental prerequisite for any serious job applicant. Thus a rationalized placement policy becomes possible.

The evaluation of individual (or group) performance also has a long tradition. The administration of Imperial Sung China utilized an elaborate evaluation system marked by linking entrance qualifications, as demonstrated in competitive examinations, with merit ranking by superiors. Traditionally, there are two ways of evaluating individual contributions to task fulfillment:

a. the ranking of general individual attributes that are supposed to influence differential performance indirectly. These may be formal education, vocational qualification, experience (e.g., measured by age or length of service);

b. the ranking of actual performance according to more or less elaborate systems of measuring quantitative and/or qualitative output.

Usually, combined sets of relevant efficiency norms are applied. The ranking of individual attributes is fundamental to the practice of job assignment, thereby assigning status within the industrial organization. Although practice differs widely, some common components may be listed. The job candidate is evaluated on personal and occupational background, and some kind of aptitude test (including a most informal placement interview) is used. The underlying efficiency norms (e.g., behavioral standards) have been systematized and formalized to the extent that large industrial organizations usually apply highly bureaucratized procedures when hiring apprentices or even university graduates from hundreds of applicants.

Likewise, the change of job assignments (transfers), especially in case of promotions, is based upon elaborate procedures reflecting norms set by the company's personnel policy and by traditional practice. One major norm, still largely applied either formally or informally, is seniority.

Within U.S. industrial organizations, two types of seniority are to be found: benefit seniority, regulating the distribution of bonuses and fringe benefits, and competitive status seniority, regulating the status distribution and personnel mobility among unionized employees. Such formalized seniority rights may be considered as a kind of property, increasing over time.

In contrast to this pattern, seniority rules in West German industrial organizations are less formal. Rainer Dombois in a recent study (1982) refers to seniority as an informal norm and cites examples among dockworkers. Similarly, Gerhard Bosch and Rainer Lichte (1982) have shown that status distribution among semiskilled workers at a steel tube processing plant was influenced by seniority, thus, regulating the opportunity for learning on the job and for advancing to higher-level jobs.

Other efficiency norms are inherent in merit rating systems and procedures. They are probably most elaborate and most extensively used in Japanese industrial organizations, where all employees are regularly reviewed by their superiors, and where career-related decisions and the distribution of bonus payments are based upon the results (Fürstenberg 1981). In West German industry, a merit rating is usually applied to white-collar workers. Procedures are based upon such criteria as quality and quantity of work completed, work speed, and willingness to work (e.g., overtime). Actual performance, then, is measured by grading within these dimensions, applying ordinal, and in rare cases also interval scales. The arbitrary element is especially obvious in cases where a superior evaluates only the performance of a small group of employees, thus never dealing with the normal distribution of attributes. Therefore, the main criterion guiding such systems is applicability in terms of reasonability and practicability. This, of course, refers to sets of underlying informal and often traditional norms that are difficult to evaluate rationally.

A major component of industrial work culture in the Western world is systems of performance rating based upon the measurement of output. All incentive pay systems are based upon such procedures. The classical example is the setting of piece rates for wage earners. The underlying norm usually is a "normal performance," derived from a set of work studies. Based on an estimated efficiency level of the individual workers, time allowances are made for achieving more or less steeply rising and then leveling pay rates per additional unit produced. Again we find in these systems elements based upon individual experience and arbitrary decisions or preconceptions. The century-long struggle for reasonable application of such norm-setting devices ultimately resulted in rules for joint consultation and decision making by both management and union representatives including the participation of the individual worker (Brown 1973; Fürstenberg 1976; Offe 1970).

Thus, we can observe that efficiency norms, when applied to the evaluation of individual or group performance in industrial organizations always pose the problem of legitimization and acceptance. As a consequence, norm-setting is a highly complex procedure, involving different hierarchical levels of the organization as well as different interest groups trying to match their perspectives and expectations.

Social conflict as an outcome of the application of norms may result from intraorganizational or extraorganizational factors. Internally, the following constellations deserve special consideration:

   a. Ambiguity of efficiency norms, permitting a wide range of interpretations: This is often considered to result from incomplete contracts. In the case of administered norms, this may be due to a failure to make them fully operational. In the absence of clearly defined standards and strict guidelines for their application, differential interpretations may arise, for example, in the case of stress, an underrating or overrating of psychical against physical stress. Such ambiguity sometimes is even considered to be functional as it offers options for strategic action, for a status-related policy by superiors.
   b. Inherent contradictions in systems of efficiency norms: The interrelationship between norms included is a crucial issue. A typical example of contradictions is the mixing of efficiency norms based upon the principle of competition, with norms based upon cooperation. Quite often, an employee is expected to work more efficiently than his colleagues and at the same time to foster mutual aid and trust.
   c. Erratic, arbitrary application of efficiency norms according to a large span of discretion: Such norms usually are not completely adjusted to the situational context. Instead, they cover a wide range of cases. Thus, there is ample space for differential, manipulative practice. Efficiency norms may be utilized for side purposes and their application oscillates with the strategies applied to serve such purposes.
   d. Coincidence of formalized and informal efficiency norms: Industrial organizations generate specific subcultures based upon differential situational challenges and selective mechanisms, both resulting in group formation and informal action systems. Thus, competitive situations may arise, where status assignment is the outcome of partly formal and partly informal evaluation proce-

dures. Within German industry, the coincidence of formal efficiency evaluation and informal seniority ranking often is to be
observed on the shop floor.

e. Inherent differentiating dynamics of norm systems: Any system
of efficiency norms has to meet the challenge of situational
change. There may be some inbuilt inertia, but more often than
not adjustments take place, possibly affecting system components with different intensity. In industrial organizations, such
major challenges are mainly technologically, economically, and
politically induced. An example is the shift in systems of job
evaluation due to automation, meaning that individual jobs
become integrated parts of larger work systems with decreasing
margins for individual influence upon system output.

As industrial organizations need to be considered as open interactive
systems, closely interrelated with their environments, normative conflict
also derives from external factors. These are usually identified as factors
bringing about major challenges due to technological, economic, political, and sociocultural change. But conflicting norms may also be generated by the interference of competitive external efficiency systems. They
may be classified as:

a. market mechanisms,
b. bargaining systems,
c. political decisions,
d. administrative practice,
e. legal awards, and
f. sociocultural norms.

Even if the income dimension of organizational evaluation is more
or less controllable under conditions of highly segmented and administered internal labor markets, external changes in labor demand and supply need to be considered. During recent periods of full employment, it
was hardly possible to hire capable office staff at internally applied
salary rates based upon job evaluation. As a consequence, so-called
personal rates were introduced, including a kind of scarcity bonus for
newly hired staff. Market value and the internally calculated value of
labor no longer matched. Similar discrepancies occur in multinational
corporations between pay rates for local staff and those for expatriates,
even if their official status differs only slightly.

The second type of conflict-generating interference may be observed
when intrafirm wage administration must be matched with a wage system

resulting from industry-wide and regional collective bargaining. In these cases, effective wage rates exceeding the standard rates often are not evenly distributed, so that good and bad rates for similar performance levels may develop.

Governmental influence upon industrial efficiency norms usually is due to political decisions and administrative practice. Important examples are attempts in some Western countries to apply equal employment opportunity policies in order to decrease handicaps of sex or race. The persons concerned are subject to status inconsistency, as some aspects of their positions are upgraded due to external prescriptions. Similarly, legal awards may modify a given status.

Sociocultural norms strongly influence both formal and informal efficiency norms in industrial organizations. But the more the status assignment is rationalized due to the introduction of devices to measure efficiency, the more the ascribed status, reflecting a given sociocultural environment, becomes a residual category. Nevertheless, it may contribute to status inconsistency, for example, in the case of employees of different ethnic origin doing the same kind of work.

The interference of external normative systems or aspects generally results in generating additional efficiency criteria. We then encounter not only the complexity of internal formal and informal efficiency norms but also their partial modification. This is especially obvious in the setting of wage rates. Within the organization, a productivity concept prevails, based upon performance evaluation. It is modified by a market price concept, taking into consideration both internal and external supply and demand relationships. It is further modified by governmental policy aiming at social adequacy.

As a result, we encounter a vast heterogeneity and complexity of constellations in which conflict is likely to occur. But as all performance criteria in industrial organizations are integrated into an efficiency concept, it is necessary to consider possible inconsistencies in this fundament of norm setting.

Efficiency norms applied to human work usually are defined in technical terms and are related to quantitative and/or qualitative input/output ratios. Therefore, they are influenced by any technological changes that affect the ability to:

   a. define efficiency and efficiency standards in operationalized terms;
   b. measure efficiency accordingly, including the provision of accurate data;

c. ascribe efficiency to human effort in terms of efficiency standards;

d. influence efficiency by employee action; and

e. keep evaluation criteria consistent.

Increased mechanization and automation have diminished the chances for employees to interfere directly with work processes. Therefore, their contribution to maintaining and improving efficiency increasingly needs to be measured by using indirect indicators such as the extrafunctional qualities of attention, speed of response, and reliability. The crisis of efficiency norms, due to their vanishing basis in outdated production systems, inevitably results in instability of organizational structure (for examples, see Lutz 1975). In concrete situations, gradually disappearing efficiency criteria are mixed with newly emerging ones, while subjective perception still is guided by traditional frames of reference perpetuated through training systems (e.g., vocational skill). In such situations, the organization appears not only as a fixed set of normative ascriptions or achievements, but also as the outcome of strategic actions to manipulate evaluation. What appears as a fixed norm may well be a fragile bargaining compromise. This leads us to some general and concluding remarks about the theoretical consequences of the empirical findings.

Consequences for a Theory of Institutional Economics

In order to contribute to a theory of optimal allocation of human resources within the firm, we must make a realistic analysis of factors determining and affecting efficiency. It was clearly shown that any concept of organizational efficiency is norm based. The question posed by Harvey Leibenstein, "whether something like conventions or institutions are required *inside* the firm to substitute for the sort of things that markets do outside the firm" (1984, 75), can be answered affirmatively. Structuring is needed in order to cope with a highly contingent problem situation. Such structuring is accomplished by strategic action within a range of discretion. The objective of such strategic action is the establishment of normative control. The limits of this control are set by external and internal contingencies, especially individual and social acceptance.

Facing rather complex situational and motivational challenges, management cannot take refuge in one-dimensional maximizing behavior. In the absence of fixed parameters for such an endeavor, management's first task is to establish such parameters by structuring human behavior into a normative system.

There is a widespread neoclassical assumption that management is able to set such norms, especially efficiency standards, rather autonomously and that acceptance of such norms by the workers is simply a matter of setting the right price for labor. Time and again, however, empirical research has shown the fallacy of such simple assumptions (e.g., Whyte et al. 1955). The setting of efficiency norms and their acceptance are socioculturally conditioned. Some basic types of norms have been analyzed here. In reality, we are facing combinations characteristic of specific situational and motivational challenges. Their basic components are:

1. an institutionalized framework, which is needed to make action calculable;
2. regulative strategies based upon personal or functional authority, the latter leading to expert guidance;
3. bargaining procedures modifying these components by considering the basic interests of persons and groups involved.

As a result, the evolving network of efficiency norms is highly dynamic and is the prerequisite as the outcome of intrafirm cooperation. It also shows a rather high degree of inconsistency.

Are there then any observable principles determining or, at least, influencing efficiency-based allocation of human resources within the firm? The problem is multidimensional, and each dimension is marked by its own rationality or its partial absence. Thus, there may be such different guidelines as economic profitability, technological efficiency, and social acceptance. The setting of efficiency norms, therefore, is a multistep procedure where such different guidelines are successively incorporated and matched.

One important and independent variable, noted by Leibenstein, is the amount and direction of external pressure, or, in other words, the relative autonomy of the actors. Their paradoxical situation is characterized by the fact that some autonomy is needed to set efficiency standards but that it is partially lost by the very act of doing so. This means that any efficiency-based organization is successfully operating within margins of adaptability partially inherent in its very design.

The extent of relative autonomy also influences the attempts to solve a basic dilemma of organizational design: the matching of both economic and social efficiency. The former is fostered mainly by competitive structures, the latter by solidaristic structures. Too much competition endangers social integration, too much solidarity impedes adjustment to market demands.

In Western societies, a high level of managerial autonomy is likely to produce competition-based efficiency norms that potentially neglect socioemotionally based integration. A low level of managerial autonomy tends to establish highly socioemotionally acceptable norms but neglects competitiveness. An acceptable compromise between competitive and solidaristic norm setting may be achieved in situations combining moderate external market pressures with internal power equilibrium. A special case is the persistence of preindustrial cooperative structures and status-bound conventions that, as in the case of Japanese corporations, limit the extent of socially acceptable competition by granting high group standards of performance at the same time.

All these considerations suggest that there is no easy solution to optimizing endeavors. Efficiency-oriented allocation of human resources within the firm does not result from automatic mechanisms. It needs the development and acceptable application of efficiency norms. All efficiency-related concepts are normative constructs. In the complex reality of any organization, their application involves multidimensional structuring. If it is successful in achieving general acceptance, we may call it "institutionalization."

REFERENCES

Berkessel, P., and K. Humml. 1982. "Methoden inhaltlicher Entgelt-differenzierung." *WSI-Mitteilungen*, 552–61.
Bosch, G., and R. Lichte. 1982. "Die Funktionsweise informeller Seniori-tätsrechte." In *Statussicherung im Industriebetrieb*, ed. K. Dohse et al. Frankfurt and New York: Campus.
Brown, William. 1973. *Piecework Bargaining*. London: Heinemann Educational.
Dombois, Rainer. 1982. "Die betriebliche Normenstruktur." In *Statussicherung im Industriebetrieb*, ed. K. Dohse et al. Frankfurt and New York: Campus.
Fürstenberg, Friedrich. 1976. "Der Lohnanreiz im Urteil der Gesellschaftswis-senschaften." *afa-Informationen*, 3–17.
Fürstenberg, Friedrich. 1981. *Erfolgskonzepte der japanischen Unternehmens-führung*. Zürich: Moderne Industrie.
Hartmann, Heinz. 1970. *Funktionale Autorität*. Stuttgart: Enke.
Leibenstein, Harvey. 1976. *Beyond Economic Man: A New Foundation for Microeconomics*. Cambridge, Mass.: Harvard University Press.
Leibenstein, Harvey. 1984. "On the Economics of Conventions and Institutions: An Exploratory Essay." *Zeitschrift für die gesamte Staatswissenschaft* 140:74–86.
Likert, Rensis. 1961. *New Patterns of Management*. New York: McGraw-Hill.

Lutz, Burkart. 1975. *Krise des Lohnanreizes.* Frankfurt: Europäische Verlagsanstalt.

Offe, Carl. 1970. *Leistungsprinzip und industrielle Arbeit.* Frankfurt: Europäische Verlagsanstalt.

Weiermair, Klaus. 1985. "Worker Incentives and Worker Participation: On the Changing Nature of the Employment Relationship." *Journal of Management Studies*, 547–70.

Whyte, William F., et al. 1955. *Money and Motivation.* New York: Harper and Brothers.

The Patterning of Work Meanings That Are Coterminous with Work Outcome Levels for Individuals and Organizations in Japan, West Germany, and the United States

George W. England

Currently, there is widespread recognition that the activity of working and the outcomes flowing from working are of fundamental significance to many if not most individuals in industrial societies. In Japan, West Germany, and the United States (as in most industrial societies), employed people spend about one-third of their waking hours in the activities called working. Additionally, the time one spends in preparing and training for work, seeking work, and planning for changed work situations strongly implies that work-related activities constitute a major use of time in the adult life. Directly connected to this time-utilization feature of working is the fact that the majority of adults in these societies derive the major part of their own economic well-being (and that of their family) from income and fringe benefits generated by their work activities.

Working also provides noneconomic benefits to individuals. Were this not the case, it would seem impossible to understand why 65 percent to 95 percent of individuals in national labor force samples in a variety of countries (including Japan, West Germany, and the United States) state that they would continue to work even if they had enough money to live comfortably for the rest of their lives without working (MOW International Research Team 1987; Vecchio 1980; Warr 1982). This stated preference for working even when financial necessity is presumed not to be a major consideration is undoubtedly related to the broader social and

The author expresses thanks to colleagues from the MOW International Research Team and especially to Professor Jyuji Misumi for use of the Japanese data and Professors Bernhard Wilpert and S. Antonio Ruiz Quintinilla for use of the German data and for great intellectual support. The eight countries in the MOW project are Belgium, Britain, West Germany, Israel, Japan, the Netherlands, the United States, and Yugoslavia.

psychological significance and value that many individuals attach to working.

Working activities and situations also have the potential to generate negative consequences and outcomes for individuals. Working can be experienced as boring, dull, or unchallenging at one end of the spectrum or as excessively overloaded and demanding at the other; it can result in frustration, dissatisfaction, stress, or inadequate person-job fit and may have a negative effect on both mental and physical health. Cooper and Payne (1978, 1980) have recently summarized much of the literature on this subject.

Working, then, would seem to be of general significance to individuals because it occupies a great deal of their time, because it generates economic and sociopsychological benefits and costs, and because it is so interrelated with other important life areas such as family, leisure, religion, and community.

If working is important to individuals for such a variety of reasons, it seems logical that national labor forces would include several major work-meaning patterns that express different rationales of work significance. The interaction between individuals with varied backgrounds and diverse work settings makes it highly unlikely that there is only one major work meaning or work ethic within a country. In other words, we would expect that there are a variety of work ethics within any national labor force and certainly across national labor forces. Recent analyses by myself and my colleagues have supported these expectations by empirically identifying eight major patterns of work meanings that have been demonstrated to be reliable and descriptively valid for the labor forces of several technologically advanced nations, including Japan, West Germany, and the United States (England and Quintinilla 1989; England and Whitely, n.d.). This identification of eight major meaning-of-work patterns provides the framework and the opportunity to study the relationship between membership in meaning-of-working patterns and various work outcomes that are relevant to individuals and/or organizations.

The basic thrust of this article is to determine the nature and extent of these relationships between work-meaning pattern membership and consequences of working in terms of levels of work outcomes. To phrase this as a question: to what degree are work meanings coterminous with work-outcome levels for individuals and organizations in Japan, West Germany, and the United States? To answer this question, one must understand the eight meaning-of-working patterns and their development.

Major Components in the Meaning of Working[1]

This article uses a portion of the data base from a comprehensive Meaning of Working (MOW) study jointly designed and conducted by behavioral scientists from technologically advanced industrial nations. The study was first reported in the scientific literature in 1981 (MOW International Research Team 1981). The primary data collection from nearly 15,000 respondents in eight countries took place in 1981–83, and detailed international comparative results were published in the book, *The Meaning of Working* (MOW International Research Team 1987). The MOW project defined and assessed the meaning of working in terms of three major components.

Work centrality is defined as the degree of general importance that working has in the life of an individual at any given point in time. The work centrality index is a scale that varies in value from two to ten points based on responses to two questions. The first question asked respondents to rate working on a seven-point scale from one of the least to one of the most important things in their life. The second question asked respondents to allocate 100 points among five areas of their lives to reflect their relative importance. The five areas were leisure, community, work, religion, and family.[2]

Work goals were defined as the relative importance of eleven work goals and values sought and preferred by individuals in their working lives. The eleven work goals were:

- A lot of opportunity to learn new things
- Good interpersonal relations (supervisors, coworkers)
- Good opportunity for upgrading or promotion
- Convenient working hours
- A lot of variety
- Interesting work (work that you really like)
- Good job security
- A good match between your job requirements and your abilities and experience
- Good pay

---

1. The following three sections draw extensively on the papers by England and Quintinilla (1989) and by England and Whitely.

2. The method chosen for combining the two indicators for each individual was a simple addition after each indicator was transformed to the ordinal position of work on a scale of 1 to 5 (see chap. 5, MOW International Research Team 1987 for complete details).

- Good physical working conditions (such as light, temperature, cleanliness, low noise level)
- A lot of autonomy (you decide how to do your work)

Work goal indices for each individual were developed to represent each of two dominant work goal dimensions found through factor analysis. These were the economic work goal dimension and the expressive work goal dimension. The economic work goal index is based on the responses of an individual to the importance of good pay and good job security in the individual's life. The expressive work goal index is based on the responses of an individual to the importance of interesting work, autonomy in work, and a good match between the job requirements and the individual's ability and experience. Responses to each set of goal statements were averaged to form the appropriate work goal index.

Societal norms about working. The MOW project focused on two normative views toward working that capture much of the historical and contemporary discussion relevant to the meaning of working. The entitlement norm represents the underlying rights of individuals and the work-related responsibilities of society and organizations toward all individuals. This norm includes the notions that all members of society are entitled to have work if they desire it, that they are entitled to interesting and meaningful work, that they are entitled to retraining when it is needed, and that they have a right to participate in work method decisions. All of these notions are entitlements or rights that come from standards of reasoning about property rights and the psychological contract as applied to the work setting.

The obligation norm represents the underlying duties of all individuals to organizations and to society with respect to working. This norm includes the notions that everyone has a duty to contribute to society by working, that they should save for the future from their work income, and that they should value their work whatever its nature. These notions are obligations or duties that come from standards of reasoning about internalized personal responsibility and social or institutional commitment.

Societal norm indices about working were developed for each individual on the entitlement norm and on the obligation norm. The extent of agreement with each set of normative statements (previously identified) was averaged to provide an index score on each of the two societal norms about working (entitlement index and obligation index).

In focusing on similarities and differences in the meaning of working among three national labor forces, I have made two significant choices. First, only West Germany, Japan, and the United States are included. These three countries were chosen because they are major industrial and technologically advanced nations and because they well represent the range of national diversity on work centrality, work goals, and societal norms about working found in the eight-country study (MOW International Research Team 1987).

Second, the choice has been made to consider a holistic view of the meaning of working to individuals as opposed to a comparison of individuals in countries variable by variable (e.g., looking first at work centrality, then work goals, then societal norms). While both approaches have utility, it seems clear that the totality of meaning assigned to working by a person may be quite incomplete when we examine single dimensions in isolation. Theoretically, at the level of the individual, the major work meaning variables do not operate independently of each other; rather they form some pattern. The development of work-meaning patterns is a move toward this more holistic view, and it is believed that more meaningful comparisons among individuals or aggregations of individuals (i.e., labor forces) can be made by treating the meaning of working holistically.

Work-meaning clusters were developed using the five work-meaning indices previously discussed so that individuals within a cluster were maximally similar to each other in terms of the work-meaning indices while different clusters were maximally different from each other. The specific method used was Ward's hierarchical clustering method (Ward 1963). To represent each of the three countries equally, we drew 980 individuals randomly from each country's national labor force sample, and it was on this combined group of 2,940 individuals that the cluster analysis was conducted. All indices were expressed as standardized T-scores with a mean of 50 and a standard deviation of 10. Considering the optimal ratio between loss of variance (error coefficient) and the number of clusters, the identification of eight work-meaning clusters was the optimal solution (Wishart 1982). Multiple discriminant analysis revealed that relatively high percentages (64 percent to 85 percent with a mean of 74 percent) of respondents were correctly classified into the appropriate work-meaning cluster, using their scores for discriminant functions.

Development and Description of Meaning-of-Working Patterns

The eight meaning-of-working patterns were initially developed by considering the three most salient work-meaning index scores in each of the eight clusters of individuals and interpreting their content. Table 1 provides the basic data for this step. Secondly, demographic and work correlates for the members in each cluster were examined to increase understanding of the eight meaning-of-working patterns further.

The demographic correlates examined are age, gender, and education. The work correlates examined are occupational distributions and organizational role (nonsupervisory, supervisory, or managerial). Table 2 provides a summary of these correlates for each of the eight meaning-of-working patterns. Each work-meaning pattern will be discussed in turn utilizing the relevant data from tables 1 and 2.

Additionally, other MOW project data not shown in tables 1 and 2 will be utilized when they significantly aid pattern interpretation.

Pattern A. Members of Pattern A have the lowest work centrality scores among the eight groups. They have low economic work values and the lowest obligation scores among the eight groups. These workers do not value working very highly nor do they have a normative orientation toward duty to employers and society through working. This is why we label this group the "nonwork-centered, nonduty-oriented workers."[3] These workers have a high leisure orientation (assigning 29 points to leisure as compared to an average of 20 points for all groups) and place

TABLE 1.   Meaning-of-Working Patterns for Combined Labor Force Samples in Japan, West Germany, and the United States (*N* = 2,940)

MOW Pattern	Work Centrality Index	Economic Index	Expressive Index	Obligation Index	Entitlement Index	Percentage of Total Sample
A	39.4	45.1	51.8	37.3	53.5	9.8
B	39.7	50.6	46.3	53.4	50.4	18.4
C	51.2	60.3	39.6	46.7	50.0	15.2
D	51.3	58.7	43.7	62.5	61.3	8.5
E	50.9	46.5	49.0	46.5	32.9	7.1
F	53.8	36.6	53.4	57.7	49.1	10.5
G	57.1	52.8	56.0	50.4	49.0	21.3
H	57.0	38.3	61.3	43.8	51.5	9.2

Note: Boxed numerals indicate the three primary defining scores within each pattern.

3. The labels serve as easy references for each pattern. The reader should be aware, however, that even though empirically correct, these labels represent only a small amount of the information that is available for each pattern.

TABLE 2. Summary of Meaning-of-Working Patterns (A-H) Correlates

Correlates	A	B	C	D	E	F	G	H
Demographic								
Age	Younger workers	Average age distribution	Average age distribution	Relatively high % over age 50	Slightly higher than average age distribution	Highest % over age 50 lowest % under 30	Lowest % in under-30 age group and highest % in 30–50 age group	High % age 30–50 low % over age 50
Gender	Highest % female	Second highest % female	Average sex distribution	Slightly higher than average % male	Average sex distribution	Average sex distribution	Highest % males	Average sex distribution
Education	Average educational distribution	Slightly lower than average % college graduates	Highest % of primary and secondary education	Highest % of primary and secondary education	High % of college graduates	Slightly above-average education level	Average educational distribution	Highest % of college graduates
Work								
Occupational distribution	Clerical and sales jobs are overrepresented	Service, clerical, and production jobs are overrepresented	Production, service, and clerical jobs are overrepresented	Production and clerical jobs are overrepresented	Professionals, sales, and managers overrepresented	Proprietors, sales, and managers overrepresented	Most even occupational distribution of all groups	Professionals and proprietors highly overrepresented
Organizational role	Overrepresentation of nonsupervisory jobs	Overrepresentation of nonsupervisory jobs	Overrepresentation of nonsupervisory jobs	Overrepresentation of supervisory jobs	Overrepresentation of supervisory and managerial jobs	Overrepresentation of supervisory and managerial jobs	Overrepresentation of managerial jobs	Underrepresentation of supervisory jobs

relatively high values on comfort-oriented work goals (convenient hours of work and good working conditions). They highly value interpersonal relations (assigning it 19 points vs. an average for all groups of 16). In defining what characterizes working, they are the highest of all eight groups in saying it is work "if you must do it." Table 2 provides further information about the individuals comprising work-meaning Pattern A. Nearly half (48 percent) of Pattern A members are under age 30 as compared to an average of 30 percent in all groups; females make up 47 percent of the cluster as compared to an overall average of 38 percent. The group has an educational distribution that closely matches that of the total group. Clerical and sales jobs are overrepresented in Pattern A and 71 percent are in nonsupervisory jobs as compared to 61 percent for the total group. Pattern A membership is 9.8 percent of the combined three-country sample.

Pattern B. Pattern B members have very low centrality scores (more than one standard deviation below the overall mean). They also have low expressive work values and above-average obligation scores. We label this group the "nonwork-centered, high duty-oriented workers." These workers have relatively high family, religious, and leisure orientations and are the highest of all eight groups in defining working as an activity that is "not pleasant." Pattern B members have an average age distribution and an above-average female representation (47 percent vs. an average of 38 percent). The educational level distribution of this pattern is near average except for a slightly lower percentage of college graduates than the average. Service, clerical, and production jobs are overrepresented in Pattern B, and the proportion of nonsupervisors is 69 percent compared to an overall average of 61 percent. Pattern B membership is 18.4 percent of the combined three-country sample, and it is the second largest group.

Pattern C. Pattern C workers have about average work centrality scores and relatively low obligation scores. The strongest distinguishing characteristics of this group, however, are their very high economic values and their very low expressive values; in both cases these values differ from the overall average by more than one standard deviation. These workers are highest of all eight groups in defining working in terms of "being told what to do" and as "being physically strenuous." This pattern clearly represents very strong economic orientation to work, and we label this group the "economic workers." Pattern C members have age and sex distributions that are similar to the overall averages. Their educational level is overrepresented in terms of primary and secondary levels of education. Production, service, and clerical jobs are overrepresented in this pattern and 67 percent are in nonsupervisory positions compared to a 61 percent overall average. Pattern C membership is 15.2 percent of the combined three-country sample.

Pattern D. Pattern D workers have about average work centrality scores. The most salient features of the pattern, however, are high economic work values and very high levels of obligation norms and entitlement norms (both of the latter being more than one standard deviation above the overall averages). These workers are the highest of all eight groups in defining working in terms of "obtaining a feeling of belonging." This group clearly represents strong normative obligation and entitlement beliefs about working as well as a strong economic orientation. We label the group the "high rights and duties economic workers." Pattern D members are overrepresented in the over-50 age group (25.1 percent vs. a 20.6 percent overall average). They have a slightly higher-than-average percentage of primary and secondary educational level representation. Clerical and particularly production jobs are overrepresented in the pattern, and there is an overrepresentation of supervisory jobs. Pattern D includes 8.5 percent of the combined three-country sample, and it is the second smallest group.

Pattern E. Pattern E is the smallest of the eight groups (7.1 percent of the total) and is also the most difficult pattern to interpret. Members of this group have average work centrality scores that are rather tightly clustered around the mean. The most salient defining characteristics of the group, however, are relatively low economic values, relatively low obligation norms, and extremely low entitlement norms (more than 1.7 standard deviation below the overall average). This pattern is similar to Pattern A in having all of its major defining characteristics lower than the overall averages. We label the group the "low rights and duties non-economic workers." Members of this pattern are the most status- and prestige-oriented of all groups (assigning it 13.5 points vs. an overall average of 11.1 points). They are the lowest of all eight groups in defining working in terms of "if it contributes to society" (only 24 percent compared to an overall average of 36.1 percent). The group is also high in describing working as "mentally strenuous" and "not pleasant." We believe that this group has a complex work motivation pattern and primarily represents the technocratic and bureaucratic structure of organizations. From table 2, we see that the group has a slightly higher than average age distribution (about one year older), an average sex distribution, and a high proportion of college graduates (35.9 percent vs. an overall average of 22.8 percent). Professional, managerial, and sales jobs are overrepresented in Pattern E, and there is an overrepresentation of supervisory and managerial organizational roles.

Pattern F. Members of Pattern F have a moderately high work centrality level, a very low level of economic values, and a moderate level of expressive values. Their obligation index scores are significantly above the average and are considerably higher than their average level entitlement scores. Pattern F members show a strong company orientation and are highly concerned with the products and services they produce or provide. They are the group that most strongly defines working in terms of "contributing to society." We label this group the "moderately work-centered, noneconomic, duty-oriented workers." Pattern F members are about two years older than the overall average age and are particularly underrepresented in the under-30 age group and overrepresented in the above-50 age group. They have an average sex distribution and slightly higher than the average educational level. Proprietors, sales, and managerial occupations are overrepresented in Pattern F, as are supervisory and managerial roles in their organizations. Pattern F includes 10.5 percent of the three-country combined sample.

Pattern G. Pattern G members have high work centrality scores and relatively high economic and expressive values. Their obligation and entitlement scores are close to average and about equal. Members of Pattern G are the second highest group to define working in terms of "something which adds value" and "being accountable for their work." We label them the "work-centered and balanced-work values workers." Members of Pattern G are underrepresented in the under-30 age group and overrepresented in the 30-to-50 age group by about 7 to 8 percent. They have the highest percentage of males of all eight groups (72.6 percent vs. an overall average of 62 percent) and have a near average educational distribution. Pattern G members have the most even occupational distribution of all groups and never vary by more than 4 percent from the overall sample occupational percentages. The managerial organizational role, however, is slightly overrepresented in Pattern G. Pattern G has the highest percentage membership of all eight groups and accounts for 21.3 percent of the combined three-country sample.

Pattern H. Pattern H workers have high work centrality scores, very low economic values, and very high expressive work values. Their obligation norm score is below average while their entitlement norm score is about average. Pattern H members are highly concerned about the type of tasks they do, the type of occupation in which they work, and the types of products or services they produce or provide. They give the highest endorsement of all eight groups to the statement "working itself is basically interesting and satisfying." They are highly concerned with "contributing to society" through their work and are the highest of all groups to define working as "something which adds value" and in terms of "being accountable for their work." Members of Pattern H seem strongly attached to work and working as they experience it and exhibit several ideal elements of professionalism. We label this group the "work-centered expressive workers." Members of Pattern H are about one year younger than the overall average age but have about a 7 percent over-representation in the 30-to-50 age group. There is an average sex distribution in Pattern H, and it contains the highest percentage of college graduates of all eight groups (39.5 percent vs. an overall average of 22.8 percent). Professional and proprietor occupations are highly overrepresented in Pattern H while production and clerical workers are highly underrepresented. Supervisory jobs are about 7 percent underrepresented while managerial jobs are about 7 percent overrepresented in Pattern H. Pattern H includes 9.2 percent of the combined three-country sample.

Country Differences in MOW Pattern Incidence

To utilize these work-meaning patterns in addressing issues about national differences and similarities among West Germany, Japan, and the United States, one needs to know what proportion of each country's labor force is most closely identified with each of the eight patterns. Table 3 presents this information.

Table 3 shows that all three countries have multiple work-meaning patterns. In each country there are five patterns each of which contains at least 10 percent of the country's labor force. Together these five patterns include the work meanings of more than 80 percent of each country's representative sample. The residual of about 20 percent per country is distributed among three remaining patterns, which include between 4 and 8 percent each. In consequence, it would be theoretically deficient and empirically false to regard any single work ethic as being a valid

TABLE 3. Work-Meaning Pattern Incidence in West Germany, Japan, and the United States (in percentage)

Pattern	West Germany	United States	Japan	Overall Percentage
A. Nonwork-centered, nonduty-oriented workers	13.8%	7.0%	8.8%	9.8%
B. Nonwork-centered, high duty-oriented workers	19.7	23.3	12.0	18.4
C. Economic workers	20.6	14.5	10.4	15.2
D. High rights and duties economic workers	15.3	5.4	4.9	8.5
E. Low rights and duties noneconomic workers	4.0	12.8	4.6	7.1
F. Moderately work-centered, noneconomic, duty-oriented workers	6.3	14.0	11.1	10.5
G. Work-centered and balanced work values workers	14.7	16.8	32.4	21.3
H. Work-centered, expressive workers	5.6	6.2	15.8	9.2

description for the totality (or even for the majority) of any of the three labor forces under study. Three patterns are required in each country to include at least 50 percent of the total labor force. The reality of working life is complex and differentiated, and it must be treated as such.

Additionally, the results show that no pattern is country specific. Had results demonstrated the existence of one specific, idiosyncratic pattern with a majority percentage for Japan only, another one for the United States only, and a third pattern for West Germany only, we would be led to discussion with largely nominal classes like "the Japanese," "American," and "German" work ethics. We could not enlarge our comparative cross-national understanding and would lose the real possibility of pattern distribution comparisons over the countries. Thus, the results indicate that the dimensions identified in the cluster analyses serve well as dimensions for cross-national comparisons of the meaning of working. Looking more closely at the most frequent pattern(s) in each country, we note that the nonwork-centered, high duty-oriented workers (B) are clearly the most frequent in the United States (23.3 percent) and the work-centered and balanced work values workers (G) are most frequent in Japan (32.4 percent). In the total sample these two patterns (B and G) each exceed the next most frequent pattern. However, in West Germany the two largest patterns, economic workers (C) (20.6 percent) and nonwork-centered, high duty-oriented workers (B) (19.7 percent), have nearly identical inclusion percentages.

Looking at the five most frequent patterns per country, we note that the nonwork-centered, high duty-oriented (B), the economic (C), and the work-centered and balanced work values (G) patterns each include more than 10 percent of each labor force as members. Altogether these three patterns account for about 55 percent in each country. The similarity ends, however, when we inspect the relative distributions. While the work-centered and balanced work values pattern (G) includes only 15 percent in Germany and 17 percent in the United States, it comprises 32 percent in Japan, as previously noted. The high rights and duties economic pattern (D) and the nonwork-centered, nonduty-oriented pattern (A) each account for more than 10 percent of the labor force in Germany and less than 10 percent in the United States and Japan. The low rights and duties noneconomic pattern (E) is typical for more than 10 percent of the U.S. labor force and less than 5 percent in Japan and West Germany. The moderately work-centered, noneconomic, duty-oriented pattern (F) has a frequency above 10 percent in the United States and Japan and around 6 percent in Germany. The work-centered, expressive pattern (H) is the second largest group in Japan (15.8 percent) and has a frequency around 6 percent in West Germany and the United States.

These observations indicate clear differences in the distribution of work-meaning patterns among the three countries. This is especially noticeable if we focus on work centrality, economic orientation, and duty orientation. If we categorize the patterns with respect to only these dimensions, patterns A and B share the attribute of being nonwork centered while patterns G and H are work centered. Patterns C and D members have high economic values while patterns B, D, and F members have a strong duty orientation.

Comparing the relative frequencies of work force members with these attributes in the three countries leads to the following conclusions:

- About one-third of the labor force in West Germany and the United States is nonwork centered; this is about 10 percent more than in Japan.
- Nearly every second Japanese worker is work centered, as opposed to only about one out of five in Germany and the United States.
- Over one-third of the German work force has strong economic orientations in comparison to one-fifth in the United States and only one-sixth in Japan.
- West Germany and the United States have slightly over 40 percent high duty-oriented workers, while Japan has slightly less than 30 percent.

The conclusion reached is that while all three countries have significant membership in each of the MOW patterns, there clearly are meaningful differences among the countries in the pattern distributions.

Relationships between Work-Meaning Pattern Membership and Outcomes or Consequences of Working

The preceding development of eight major meaning-of-working patterns that are reliable and descriptively valid for the labor forces in Japan, West Germany, and the United States provides the opportunity to explore the relationship(s) between meaning-of-working pattern membership and outcomes of working. Previous research clearly shows that there are multiple and contrasting work outcomes or consequences of working as was the case with work meanings (see MOW International Research Team 1987, Chap. 12). The basic question is: to what extent are work-meaning patterns coterminous with levels of work outcomes? The term *coterminous* is purposely used to indicate clearly that the nature of the evidence presented does not necessarily imply unidirectional causality.

In the MOW project, data were gathered on three outcomes of working that are demonstrably important from the perspective of the individual. Those outcomes are: (1) the income that individuals receive from their work, (2) the occupational satisfaction of the individual measured in terms of whether or not he or she would choose the same work if they were beginning work again, and (3) the quality of the work in terms of the level of skill utilization, autonomy, responsibility, and variety existing in the present work situation.

In addition, data were available on two outcome measures that imply involvement with work and that have relevance from the perspective of the organization. These were: (1) a commitment to working expressed as whether or not individuals would choose to continue working if the economic necessity for working were removed, and (2) the hours worked per week by the individual, a direct measure of work involvement. As previously indicated, we are concerned about the nature of the patterning of levels of these outcomes with meaning-of-working pattern membership.

Since each of the above five outcomes is expressed in a unique measurement term, a common relative metric was developed for classification of outcomes into levels. This metric assigns a value of 1.0 to the work-meaning pattern that has the highest mean level on a given outcome among the eight patterns. The value assigned to each of the other meaning-of-working patterns for that same outcome is the proportion its mean outcome value is compared to that of the highest pattern. Thus, relative comparisons are made among the eight patterns on each outcome. Using occupational satisfaction as an example, work-meaning pattern H has the highest percentage of membership stating that they would choose the same work if they could begin work again. Pattern H is assigned a value of 1.0 on this outcome. The percentage of the membership in each of the other patterns who would choose the same work again is expressed as a proportion of that of Pattern H and ranges from 66 percent to 92 percent. The same form of metric is employed in identifying outcome values for each one of the five work outcomes. Table 4 shows the relative metric on each outcome for the members of the eight meaning-of-working patterns.

Table 4 clearly shows that values for each of the five outcomes increase across meaning-of-working patterns A to H. The classification of outcome values into low, medium, and high levels also shows that outcome levels and meaning-of-working pattern membership are coterminous to a rather high degree. Meaning-of-working patterns A, B, and C generally occur with low outcome levels. Patterns F, G, and H occur with high outcome levels, while meaning-of-working patterns D and E occur with mixed outcome levels that center at a medium level. The lower part of table 4 (summary of work outcome level distributions across individual countries) shows the similarity of relationships between MOW pattern membership and work outcome values (levels) whether observed on an aggregate sample basis or in terms of each country being treated separately.

These results show that specified ways of viewing work as expressed in meaning-of-working patterns are associated with work outcome levels in Japan, West Germany, and the United States. The nature of these meaning-of-working patterns (work personalities), their wide distribution across all types of labor force categories, and the MOW pattern–work outcome relationships leads me to conclude that Leibenstein is basically correct in positing the presence of worker discretion in determining a worker's effort outlay in much of the world of work (Leibenstein 1976, 1985).

Further, these results indicate that individual effort outlay is a highly complex phenomenon. It is complex in the first place because it results from the interplay between individual worker characteristics and managerial system designs in a given organization within the context of a national culture. It is complex secondly because effort outlay seems to stem from at least three different etiological origins. This latter observation comes from efforts at modeling our results. Effort to do at least satisfactory work

TABLE 4. Work Outcome Values and Levels for MOW Pattern Membership in Japan, West Germany, and the United States

Outcome	A	B	C	D	E	F	G	H
Occupational satisfaction	*.71*	*.66*	*.70*	.84	.84	.92	.87	1.0
Income		*.74*	*.75*	.83	.86	.96	.90	1.0	.90
Quality of work		*.78*	*.80*	*.74*	.78	.97	.93	.92	1.0
Commitment to working		*.79*	*.80*	*.79*	.83	.87	.95	.95	1.0
Hours of work		*.83*	*.86*	.89	.89	.94	.96	.99	1.0

Summary of work outcome level distributions when each country is treated separately (3 countries × 5 outcomes × 8 MOW patterns)	35 Low 10 Medium 0 High			10 Low 12 Medium 8 High			0 Low 13 Medium 32 High	
Average outcome index	.78			.86			.93	

Note: Italic numerals indicate low outcome level; arabic numerals indicate medium outcome level; and boxed numerals indicate high outcome level.

("satisficing" performance motivation) seems to stem largely from having balanced or nonentitlement imbalanced norms about working. Effort to do one's work well (high performance motivation) seems to stem largely from the development of high levels of work centrality in the individual. Effort to do one's work in a manner to satisfy one's major work goals or values is dependent upon what these work goals or values are and the extent to which they can be met in one's work situation. The extent to which this latter type of effort enhances organizational goal attainment is problematical and in our data depends upon one's work goals being expressive *or* expressive and economic combined. Human motivation in the work setting, its determinants, and its consequences must indeed be more thoroughly examined by economic theorists.

REFERENCES

Cooper, C. L., and R. Payne. 1978. *Status at Work*. New York: Wiley.
Cooper, C. L., and R. Payne. 1980. *Current Concerns in Occupational Status*. New York: Wiley.
England, G. W., and S. A. R. Quintinilla. 1989. "The Meaning of Working: Major Work Meaning Patterns in the National Labor Forces of Germany, Japan and the USA." In *Advances in International Comparative Management*, ed. B. Prasad, 77–94. Greenwich, Conn.: JAI Press.
England, G. W., and W. T. Whitely. N.d. "Cross-national Meanings of Working." In *The Meaning of Work*, ed. A. Brief and W. Nord. Lexington, Mass.: Lexington Books. Forthcoming.
Leibenstein, H. 1976. *Beyond Economic Man*. Cambridge, Mass.: Harvard University Press.
Liebenstein, H. 1985. "On Relaxing the Maximization Postulate." *Journal of Behavioral Economics* 14:5–20.
MOW International Research Team. 1981. "The Meaning of Working." In *Management Under Differing Value System: Political, Social and Economical Perspectives in a Changing World*, ed. G. Dlugos and K. Weiermair, 565–630. Berlin and New York: Walter de Gruyter & Co.
MOW International Research Team. 1987. *The Meaning of Working*. London and New York: Academic Press.
Vecchio, R. P. 1980. "The Function and Meaning of Work and the Job: Morse and Weiss (1955) Revisited." *Academy of Management Journal* 23:361–67.
Ward, J. 1963. "Hierarchical Grouping to Optimize an Objective Function." *Journal of American Statistical Association* 58:236–44.
Warr, P. B. 1982. "A National Study of Nonfinancial Employment Commitment." *Journal of Occupational Psychology* 55:297–312.
Wishart, D. 1982. Supplement, CLUSTAN User Manual, 3d ed. Program Library Unit, Edinburgh University.

On the Foundations of Socio-Behavioral Economics: X-Efficiency as Standard, Norm, and Actual Behavior

Kurt Dopfer

This article is an attempt to explore the full theoretical potential of Harvey Leibenstein's concept of X-efficiency. It is assumed that the ambitious task may be pursued best by introducing a clear analytical distinction between X-efficiency as a behavioral *ideal* and X-inefficiency as *actual* behavior.

As for behavioral rules, two basic features can be considered. A first feature refers to the concept of standards. If police authorities of a city suggest that pedestrians and car drivers obey traffic signals, they do so because such signals allow an orderly traffic flow. Similarly, a mathematician will attempt to provide proof that the favored ideal paradigm is superior to any other. There is a certain idea about the correctness of the rules that gives them a rationale justifying their application; thus rules are nonarbitrary in the sense that they claim a rationale for their correctness. The status quo is usually a powerful support (for instance, habit) for any behavioral rule. Economics has a long tradition in formulating optimum conditions or optimum regimes that serve as standards for either ideal economic behavior of agents or ideal economic policies of governments.

Traffic lights and mathematical paradigms, however, are usually not ideal or optimal for their own sake. Within a society, standards usually come in normative guises that demand that they should be applied. This normative element may be explicitly stated, as in the case of traffic lights, or it may be implied, as in the case of a mathematical paradigm. We call a standard that is addressed to agents in the form of an "ought to do" a norm. Thus, a behavioral rule, such as X-efficiency, generally states optimum properties in terms of normative scheme that assures the implementation of that optimum.

Contrasted to ideals, actual behavior is a horse of a different color.

I gratefully acknowledge comments and suggestions by Michael Braulke and Ms. Annegret Irrgang. I assume the responsibility for remaining errors.

Some individuals may cross the street when the light is green, others may cross it when it is red. Similarly, some students may solve a linear differential equation adequately, others may not.

The two examples bring out an important difference with regard to the explanation of actual behavior. Whether an individual crosses the street or not when the light is red depends on whether or not that individual wants to do so. It is a question of will, not of cognition. The situation is different in the case of the solution of a mathematical problem. Concentrated willpower may not compensate sufficiently for a cognitive deficit. Most economic problems in real life may be assumed to require the faculties of both adequate will and adequate cognition. Accepting the two (endogenous) determinants of behavior, one may put forth a basic behavioral assumption axiomatically: actual behavior is differential. Clearly, there are differences in willingness and in cognitive faculties between individuals.

The concept of X-efficiency will be assessed on the basis of the four analytical categories introduced: X-efficiency as standard, X-efficiency as norm, X-efficiency as actual behavior determined by cognitive faculties, and X-efficiency as actual behavior determined by willpower. The first two issues refer to X-efficiency as a determinant of behavior, the second two to X-efficiency as realistic assumptions about actual behavior.

Behavioral Standard and Actual Behavior

We start off with a brief analytical exposition that juxtaposes the homomorphic features of a behavioral rule — a standard or norm — with the differential features encountered in actual behavior. We confine our present analysis to the issue of standard, ignoring at this point the issue of norm (standard implementation). In dealing with actual behavior, one brings into focus the issue of cognitive faculties.

The argument is summarized in figure 1. The uniformity of the ideal behavioral standard is indicated by B_d; the differential characteristics of actual behavior are represented by the descending line B_c. The standard line B_d shows what economic agents might achieve if they had perfect cognitive faculties. (Cognitive faculties or deficiencies may apply to various performance modes, related to calculatedness, decision making under uncertainty, complex problem solving, etc.)

An alternative assumption about actual performance, that is, about deviances from a behavioral standard, is that we could conceivably produce empirical evidence that shows uniformity in actual behavior as well as in the standard. Two positions seem defensible. The conventional

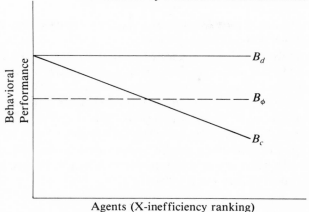

B_d = behavioral standard
B_ϕ = average actual behavior
B_c = actual behavior

Fig. 1.   Uniform standard and differentials in actual behavior

approach would equate ideal behavior with actual behavior; it would state axiomatically that all economic agents maximize. An alternative approach, as suggested by Leibenstein, would assume a general gap between potential and actual outcomes — implicitly suggesting that there is a behavioral standard that defines what ought to be and actual behavior that generally deviates from it.

The Leibenstein position allows for two theoretical options: Deviances in actual behavior may be assumed to be either uniform or differential. It seems that Leibenstein is concerned not with the structure of actual behavior so much as with the more general notion that there are deviances between ideal behavior and actual behavior as such. He devotes considerable analytical effort to show that there are numerous sources of X-inefficiency, but the structure of actual behavior underlying this X-inefficiency is left unspecified. He treats the curve of actual behavior simply as a horizontal line, as suggested by dashed line B_ϕ. The Leibenstein position also implies, more substantially, either that there are no genotypic differentials or that "objective" determinants (e.g., environmental pressures) wipe out representative individual performance characteristics in a population. An alternative application of his approach might rely on a more atomistic interpretation, in that individuals, in fact, have different characteristics and that the resulting differentials are relevant for grasping the meaning of X-efficiency. This is the position taken in the following analysis.

The analytical picture suggested in figure 1 refers to an intrafirm structure. The cognitive faculties are a given datum for a productive entity (say a firm or industry) once the inputs are purchased (that is, once the agents are employed). The $B_d:B_c$ ratio represents what may be called "contractual X-inefficiency." Taking this ratio as given for an intrafirm process, the B_c line represents the optimum X-efficiency for that entity at the prevailing conditions or level of contractual X-inefficiency. The B_d line is, all else being equal, an optimum standard with regard to inputs potentially available on the market.

What Standard Is Appropriate?

Conceptually, actual behavior may be treated either in a hypothetical way or in an empirical way. If the approach is hypothetical, a hypothetical standard must accordingly be applied. But if behavioral assumptions are understood as generalizations about actual behavior, the realism of standards will be of primary theoretical concern. In any empirical version, a behavioral standard represents nonactualized behavior with feasible optimum properties.

Three standards will be discussed in terms of their feasibility. Leibenstein does not introduce a concept of standard, but the following statement suggests that he implicitly applies a behavioral standard:

> Standard neoclassical microeconomics, with its emphasis on equilibrium and its employment of a maximization postulate, may be viewed as the study of optimal conditions. It is the study of those circumstances where everything goes right. But it is equally important to understand deviations from optimality. To use a medical analogy, we have to understand ill health and its causes as well as the conditions for perfect health in order to assist patients who are ill. With respect to such a basic economic actor as the firm, we have to understand why things go wrong, or deviate from optimality, in order to see how improvements can be made at the firm and the economy level. The view taken here is that we are likely to get a little further in this endeavor if we relax the maximizing postulate. This will allow us to examine a basic cause of the "ill health" of firms, namely circumstances under which nonoptimal decisions are made by either individuals or groups when they act inside the firm, or in behalf of the firm. (Leibenstein 1985a, 5)

Leibenstein seems to accept a neoclassical standard, since being healthy may be considered as a realistic state. We are healthy if "everything goes right" and this constitutes a feasible standard. Actual behavior, though, often goes wrong, and "ill health" is rampant. Once we "understand ill health and its causes as well as the conditions for perfect health in order to assist patients who are ill," we can contribute to and restore, less metaphorically now, the neoclassical optimum. In this view, only actual behavior, but not the behavioral ideal, is constrained.

Leibenstein, however, accepts Simon's concept of procedural rationality, which requires that we allow for time and costs in information gathering and problem solving. Perfect rationality, if applied to realistic problem-solving situations, is limited; actual human actions yield not neoclassical maximization but suboptimal results. Accepting neoclassical maximization (NC) as a behavioral standard and Simon's environmentally bounded procedural rationality (B) as actual behavior, we get a first X-inefficiency index, R_1:

$$R_B / R_{NC}.$$

The R_1 index bestows upon the neoclassical maximization procedure an empirical status, since the relational R_B is empirically oriented (relies partly on experimental results). Since Leibenstein is highly critical of hypothetical approaches and presses for empirical substance, he might well be dissatisfied with this index, though the recent quotation suggests that he was satisfied with it as a first approximation. Anyhow, index R_1 is inconsistent conceptually since it mixes hypothetical variables with empirical variables.

A second step — in order to improve the realism of standards — is to replace the hypothetical neoclassical standard by a more realistic standard: a first candidate being bounded rationality itself. We now have an alternative index, R_2:

$$R_A / R_B.$$

In this index, R_A (actual behavior) remains theoretically unspecified. The need for specification does not arise in the neoclassical index, since we have some sort of identity index defined by unity in the ratio R_A / R_S, where R_S stands for behavioral standard. It is possible to evade the theoretical problem stated in index R_2 by treating R_B as identical with actual behavior, as in the neoclassical index. The result would be an identity index of a higher order that equates the standard of bounded rationality with actually applied rationality — leaving unspecified a theoretical rationale for differences between bounded rationality as ideal and actual behavior. Evidently, index R_2 makes sense only if an analytical distinction between ideal and actual behavior is accepted a priori and if actual behavior is assumed to be different from relevant ideal standards for a significant range of behavior.

Having accepted the analytical distinction and its substantive assumptions, one may appropriately assume a close theoretical relationship between ideal and actual behavior. Indeed, the concept would not make much sense if we did not assume, at least implicitly, that the ideal determines actual behavior. In our present analytical context, however, the relevant question is: What ideal standards are actually effective in determining behavior? The realism of determination is expected to yield meaningful theoretical statements about actual behavior.

Such expectations are inconsistent with those derived from a hypothetico-deductive research program. The neoclassical standard relies on maximizing assumptions that belong to the ideal world of economists; the bounded rationality standard adds additional constraints and flirts with an experimental base. Both standard concepts fail to represent a generalization about reality with a standard emerging from actual behavioral interactions. Indeed, any such theoretical interpretation requires some sort of social theory of economic behavior. While the present analytical confines are too narrow to discuss such theory, we might suggest a hypothesis with regard to the emergence of behavioral standards—that, at a later stage, might be given more theoretical substance on the basis of an elaborated sociobehavioral approach.

We suggest that a prevailing best behavior that occurs in a population or institution over a time span sufficient for shaping its activities takes on the rank of a behavioral standard of that population or institution. The presupposition is that in actual institutions, any behavioral standard may be viewed to be the result of behavioral interactions of the institutions to which that standard applies. This rules out the preconception that agents usually apply standards that are provided from outside. Instead, a firm's management is viewed as postulating behavioral standards on the basis of an interpretation of actual behavioral interactions—which means that even if standards are prescribed from outside and do not result directly from behavioral interactions of that group, the proposed standard will still reflect the behavioral interactions of that group. This approach allows us to assess the practical significance of behavioral research. The economist is seen as entering a concrete sociobehavioral context as an adviser, suggesting ideal behavior on the basis of observation, reassessments, and applying a relative choice paradigm. The present approach suggests not that we take a hypothetical ideal as the starting point but instead that we conceive of ideal behavior as a factor that results from a theoretical interpretation of sociobehavioral interactions themselves.

The proposed standard may be seen as a generalization about reality. A critical test of any theoretical claim will, therefore, consist in its empirical validation. Empirical testing in a hypothetico-deductive context is meaningless since the theoretical statements are not understood as representing inductive inferences from reality. The proposed standard is derived from actual behavior, and, therefore, invites empirical observation and measurement. The empiricist perspective permits competing hypotheses. The most plausible behavioral standard of a firm or group may be not the best behavior but rather a prevailing average behavior. We may write behavioral differentials of a group in terms of a performance ordering

$$R_{A_1} < R_{A_2} < \ldots < R_{A_k} < \ldots < R_{A_n} = R_A^*.$$

According to the first hypothesis, the best performance R_{A_n} will stand for the behavioral standard R_A^*; according to the second, the behavioral standard will be located around a medium value, say, R_{A_k}. The fact that various hypotheses are plausible suggests that there is no simple course, say, as a detour via quick axiomatization, to develop meaningful hypotheses for an economic theory aiming at increased realism.

Why Norms Must Enter Economics

The question arises why a standard should influence actual behavior at all. Even if an ideal is stated on paper, there is no inherent necessity that the paper ideal be implemented in reality. The question as to the conditions under which a standard is effective is entirely different from the question of whether that standard exhibits optimum properties. The issue of standard effectiveness addresses the question whether or not individual agents are willing to implement a behavioral ideal. The critical issue at stake is will, not cognitive capacity.

This theoretical orientation implies a dual extension. On the one hand, an adequate analysis of economic man requires integrating aspects of human will. On the other, the notion of a standard requires a restatement in terms of its effectiveness. Moreover, a theoretical rationale is required relating the two restated sets of explanatory variables.

As for a model of man, the voluntarist property is allowed for by propounding that an individual agent typically has not a single but rather a set of behavioral options from which he or she may choose. There is nothing new about this suggestion, of course, since the entire body of neoclassical doctrine relies on the paradigm of relative choice. However, what is new in Leibenstein's suggestion is that the paradigm of relative choice applies also to instrumental options, that is, to rational behavior itself. Conventionally, relative choice is between options of an objective function but not between instrumental possibilities required to implement it; behaviorally, there is only the single-exit solution of maximization. Leibenstein suggests a generalization of the relative choice paradigm by including the instrumental side of behavior.

The dichotomization into objectives ruled by free will, on the one hand, and means of instruments ruled by criteria of rationality alone, ignoring all other variables, on the other, has never been satisfactory either from the point of view of a voluntarist-humanist philosophy or from that of internal consistency of the basic underlying assumptions. The attempt to extend the concept of free will into areas of instrumental behavior should satisfy any mind concerned with individualism and consistency.

Free will is a general concept that may be applied to any behavior or decision-making process. As for the present discussion, the concept has been limited by Leibenstein in its application to rationality in economic behavior. He suggests that when executing a task people select among various degrees of rationality—that is, they apply "selective rationality." Since Leibenstein had introduced Simon's procedural notion of bounded rationality into his analysis earlier, a more appropriate term for his concept may be selective bounded rationality. In the microtheoretical context suggested, an economic agent will select among various degrees of "bounded calculatedness" when performing a task, though the standard addressed to that individual may actually embody a feasible optimum rule, that is, perfect bounded calculatedness. It is essential for the concept of selectiveness that an individual agent is able to perform according to a standard by means of cognition, but that the individual prefers not to do so solely because he or she does not want to do so. It is apparent from Leibenstein's analysis that not wanting cannot simply be relegated to a domain of reformulated objective functions but that it must stay analytically in the realm of instrumental behavior—a point that shall be further elaborated in the subsequent section.

The concepts of boundedness and selectiveness are demonstrated in figure 2. The key explanatory variable is actual behavior, which is a composite outcome of what people can do and what they want to do. The starting point is, as in figure 1, a notion of standard permitting a distinction into the neoclassical (S_{NC}) and the bounded rationality standard (S_B^*). The area above S_B^* constitutes the domain of infeasible behavior since any behavior that is more perfect than perfectly rational under realistic conditions of boundedness is *ex hypothesi* infeasible. Actual

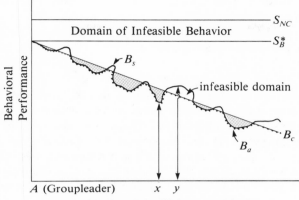

S_{NC} = neoclassical standard
S_B^* = bounded rationality standard
B_s = selective component (free will)
B_c = actual behavior as determined by cognitive differentials
B_a = actual behavior (as can be observed)

Fig. 2. Feasible standard and differentials in actual behavior

behavior resulting from cognitive differentials is represented by the descending straight line B_c. The phenomenon of free will is represented by the fluctuating line B_s. Actual (observable) behavior results as B_a, a superimposition of both lines B_c and B_s. The shaded area encircled by lines B_c (upper boundary) and B_s reflects a lack of willingness. Agent X would cognitively be able to perform better but selects routine or leisure over calculatedness that would represent a more X-efficient course of action. Agent Y, in turn, is a man with good intentions but who suffers from a lack of cognitive capacities. His willingness or motivations aspire to a behavioral standard beyond him cognitively. Bounded rationality is an option that may be selected by an agent as a behavioral standard only within the realm of his or her cognitive faculties, and a standard above constitutes a domain of infeasible courses of desired actions — even if the agent is fully motivated.

The line of actual behavior, B_a, allowing for the compound theoretical rationale of lines B_c and B_s, coincides with the line of selected behaviors if it is within a feasible domain of cognition but is delimited by the upper boundary B_c in the case where behavioral aspirations exceed the cognitive potential. Each agent faces, given identical complexities of an environment, his or her own personal bounded rationality and is free to select among various degrees of bounded rationality within the cognitively feasible domain.

Norms as Effective Standards under Conditions of
Interest Asymmetry

We now turn to the second requirement for a theoretical reorientation: standard effectiveness. We start with our earlier hypothesis that the standard for a group that shows a differential pattern in actual behavior is S_B^*; by assumption, the group leader A applies the best standard, that is, by assumption, perfect bounded rationality. The management of a firm may take this behavioral performance as an ideal standard. Even though the standard results from a real-life context, in terms of actual application, it is restricted to a single, that is, the best agent, excluding all others whose actual performance falls short because of cognitive limitations. Generally, any average standard is bound to be hypothetical for that section of agents whose actual cognitive potential lies below the average value. As indicated earlier, the B_c curve represents the only optimum standard that is feasible.

Up to this point, our analysis has relied heavily on the distinction between the variables of behavioral standard and of actual behavior. We have left unspecified the type of behavioral agencies or hierarchical echelons to which the two sets of variables may apply. Intuitively, we assume that a behavioral standard applies generally to a superior behavioral agency and that actual behavior refers to subordinate ones. Though apparently plausible, this is not necessarily so and, in fact, the point of departure of received microeconomic doctrine does not follow this line of reasoning. Instead, individual agents are assumed to maximize their own utility functions respectively; the behavioral standard, thus, is not separated from an individual's objective function, and there is no conceivable hierarchical asymmetry between objectives and courses of action. The issue of will, therefore, does not enter into the domain of instrumental options but is resolved entirely within the notion of the objective function itself. If an individual agent does not maximize, this will mean that the individual has changed his or her objective function and that it is this change in the objective function that results in apparently suboptimal behavior — that, nevertheless, turns out to be quite rational when reassessed in terms of an adjusted objective function. Thus, the problem of implementation with regard to a behavioral standard cannot occur. As stated earlier, there is no implementation problem since all agents are capable of applying perfect cognitive faculties, and, furthermore, the implementation of a standard is never called into question since all agents are willing to do their best for themselves.

The peculiarity of this approach is that no distinction is made within the application of the analytical unit (objective function cum maximization) between human agents and institutions, such as firms and households. It is assumed that an aggregation of individual maxima will yield, in a symmetric fashion, an overall institutional objective function. Individual agents always maximize, and the behavioral standard — an aggregation of individual maxima — will be met always by definition. A problem, however, arises if the superior agency that sets the standard and the agents who execute it represent different behavioral agencies and, hence, may have conflicting interests. Perfect implementation of behavioral standards can be expected only if the interests of standard setters and executors are identical. It is the implied assumption of this harmony of interest that is questioned by Leibenstein.

Leibenstein starts with the opposite assumption, namely, that typically there are conflicts between the interests of a principal and those of the agents. The agents of a firm, for instance, could meet the requirement set by a standard, but they do not wish to do so since their objective functions differ from the standard. Hence there is a gap between the behavioral performance as postulated by the standard and the behavioral performance as it actually occurs.

In such a situation the problem of standard implementation is posed. An additional element is required to make a standard effective in its application. Generally, we shall call a standard that meets implementation requirements a norm. The critical feature of a norm is that the standard can actually be implemented. In the case of symmetry of interest, a standard is a norm that does not require an additional implementation scheme to be effective. In the case of asymmetry of interest, a standard requires an additional implementation scheme to be effective.

Most social sciences have, unlike conventional economics, recognized both symmetry and asymmetry in human interests. Particularly, the legal sciences have long recognized that behavioral standards require additional schemes for implementation under conditions of interest asymmetries. They suggest drawing a distinction between primary norms and secondary norms. A primary norm constitutes a standard addressed to agents in terms of what they "ought to do." A secondary norm explicitly recognizes an asymmetry of interest and its consequences. Secondary norms specify sanctions for primary norm offenders — as incentives ex ante or punishment ex post. In a symmetric case, we have an objective utility function subject to maximization, and the instrumental primary norm — the self-imposed "ought to do" — demands that an individual apply perfect rationality. An individual may fail to act with perfect rationality and thus fail to maximize his or her utility function. Deviation from the primary norm will result in an individual's welfare loss that may be viewed as a sanction in terms of the secondary norm notion. We run into an analogous circular reasoning since an individual is always in a position to maximize his or her utility if that individual wants to do so and that the nonmaximizing behavior merely expresses a change in that individual's utility function. Indeed, the norm concept would not be meaningful if applied to atomistic agents with individual standards. The case differs if the formulator of a primary norm and the addressee constitute different behavioral agencies. It is now inconceivable that an individual merely changed his or her primary norm, since in any hierarchical and/or asymmetrical context, say in a principal-agent relationship, an individual will not be in a position to do so. Any deviation from a standard now appears as a violation of a primary norm that calls for sanctions as stated in secondary norms.

The character of secondary norm is subsidiary, since it pertains to the relationship between the primary norm and the actual behavior. Secondary norms are designed to close the gap between the primary norm and actual behavior. The relationship between primary and secondary norms, or standard formulation and implementation, is highlighted analytically. As a behavioral standard we have the relational $1/R_s$, and for conforming behavior the condition

$$R_a \cdot 1/R_s = 1.$$

For norm-deviating behavior we have accordingly any relationship

$$R_a \cdot \sigma < 1,$$

where σ stands for standard or primary norm, respectively. The question may be posed whether a behavioral surplus is conceivable — a question that again raises the problem of an appropriate standard. If a primary norm constitutes a standard that may be reached easily since the average cognitive requirements are set low, the potential for overfulfillment will accordingly be high. If a primary norm is oriented toward a superior performance, a positive deviation may be impossible cognitively. The issue of behavioral surplus is relevant since actual behavior may become suboptimal in a situation where standards are low compared to a behavioral potential. If the performance deficit is compensated by voluntary positive norm deviation, a lower standard may be more appropriate since it may serve as a realistic behavioral ideal for a larger portion of population. The relevance and probability of norm overshooting will depend on whether the norm scheme rests primarily on a symmetric or an asymmetric interest base.

Having accepted the asymmetry assumption as plausible for most institutional contexts, one notes that the crucial issue refers to the establishment of adequate secondary norms that permit monitoring of actual behavior to achieve an established primary norm system. Secondary norms may be given the formal structure

$$\eta = \frac{1}{R_a/R_s}.$$

For perfect compliance of actual behavior with a primary norm the condition

$$R_a \sigma \, \eta = 1.$$

$\sigma \, \eta$ represents the relationship between primary and secondary norms. We have for any deviant behavior R_a', a secondary norm η' that corrects or compensates actual behavior; that is, σ and η are inversely proportional.

Further theoretical contemplation on the nature of secondary norms in economics may yield interesting theoretical extensions. Two instances of economic secondary norms will be mentioned. The first is selective pressures due to market competition. The primary norm in this case will be to maximize a firm's objective function (i.e., profits, turnovers, social acceptance, etc.), and the secondary norm will consist of the sanction of a welfare loss or existential threat if the objective functions (assumed to be effective as selective devices) are not met. An interpretation of competitive pressure as a secondary norm permits a reinterpretation of some of the fundamental features of an economic process. A market economy is based on consumer and producer sovereignty. While entrepreneurial behavior is subject to secondary norms, consumer behavior is not subject to a comparable external secondary scheme that forces actual behavior toward its primary norm directions. There is X-inefficiency, hence, by consumers or of the norm implementation system that is addressed to consumers.

The other instance of a secondary norm in economics refers to the microtheoretical domain. Leibenstein has mentioned the empirical findings of Yerkes and Dodson, who propose that behavioral performance is correlated with environmental pressure yielding an inverted U-curve. It is possible to interpret environmental pressure of the Yerkes-Dodson type in terms of secondary norms. However, such interpretation requires the additional assumption that the agents are free to choose between the options of norm-conforming and norm-deviating behavior. The principal theoretical conclusion of the experimental findings, however, do not allow such assumption. The empirical results show that individual behavior varies together with environmental pressures imposed, and the regularity of this statistical pattern indicates that free will to choose among multiple behavioral options is, in principle, ruled out. Since the entire norm concept rests essentially on the notion of selectiveness, the concept of environmental pressure as a behavioral determinant that evades selection must be set apart analytically from the norm concept. It appears that Leibenstein's concept of selective rationality may be inconsistent with his reference to the Yerkes-Dodson model — to the extent his reference conveys a necessary acceptance of deterministic features. Generally, behavioral economists who attempt to find empirical regularities in order to improve the realism of assumptions may run into analogous consistency problems when featuring a model of man that also includes willingness as a relevant behavioral constituent.

Conclusions

It is considered important to distinguish clearly between X-efficiency as a standard and X-efficiency as actual behavior. A standard is viewed as a determinant of actual behavior. Its guiding function is to bring optimum or maximum behavior into focus. Having accepted the ideal character of standards, actual behavior emerges as typically deviant behavior. If the standard, for instance, is X-efficiency, actual behavioral outcomes will indicate that X-inefficiency is rampant.

Various standards have been suggested. As individual standards, neoclassical perfect and Simonian bounded rationality have been suggested as candidates. As sociobehaviorally emerging standards a best-behavior as well as an average-behavior standard have been proposed and suggested as testable hypotheses.

As for actual behavior, structural features have been introduced. The conventional assumption of homomorphic maximization has not been carried over and the notion that an aggregation of individual maxima could ever result in a representative overall behavioral structure has not been accepted. Instead, differences in cognitive faculties and in the willingness of agents of a population have been assumed. This has led us to the feasibility issue. Since perfect rationality is heteromorphic, the question as to the level at which a standard should be set becomes crucial if that standard is designed to serve as feasible guide of behavior. The realism of assumptions with respect to actual behavior has rendered conclusions about the standard issue less apodictic than conclusions based on traditional optimum notions would allow.

It has been further recognized that a feasible standard is not yet an effective standard in terms of its implementation. Leibenstein has drawn attention to conflicts of interest in social entities, such as firms. This has allowed the theoretical pinpointing of the issues of standard effectiveness and implementation. He has proposed distinguishing between two research areas — microtheory and micro-microtheory — which would permit highlighting the distinct theoretical features of each. Any findings from these two areas are not only expected to increase the realism of assumptions and the predictive capacity of microeconomic theory, but also to provide a causative rationale for the existence of X-inefficiency.

The existence of interest asymmetries has required the introduction of an additional element to secure the implementation of a standard. We have defined a standard that meets implementation requirements and hence constitutes an effective standard as a norm. Thus defined, norms have been seen to consist not only of a primary element, behavioral performance as specified by a standard, but also — critically important in the context of interest asymmetries — of a secondary element designed to direct actual behavior toward the standard. It may be concluded that policies designed to increase X-efficiency must take into account aspects of feasibility, the recognition of cognitive differences, as well as aspects of effectiveness, recognizing interest differentials and plain unwillingness of human beings. The complexity that results from dual differentials renders the standard problem, both theoretically and practically, extremely difficult. We suggest as a research program for the future greater reliance on a process understanding of sociobehavioral interactions.

REFERENCES

Albanese, P. J. 1985. "Comments on Amitai Etzioni's Opening the Preferences: A Socio-Economic Research Agenda." *Journal of Behavioral Economics* 14:207–8.
Barke, R. 1985. "Regulation and Cooperation among Firms in Technical Standard-Setting." *Journal of Behavioral Economics* 14:141–54.
Barney, J. B. 1985. "Theory Z, Institutional Economics, and the Theory of Strategy." In *The Management of Productivity and Technology in Manufacturing*, ed. P. R. Kleindorfer, 229–37. New York and London: Plenum Press.
Becker, G. S. 1968. "Crime and Punishment: An Economic Approach." *Journal of Political Economy* 76:169–217.
Boland, L. A. 1983. "The Neoclassical Maximization Hypothesis: Reply." *American Economic Review* 73:828–30.

Bohnet, A., and M. Beck. 1986. "X-Effizienz-Theorie: Darstellung, Kritik, Möglichkeiten der Weiterentwicklung." *Zeitschrift für Wirtschaftspolitik* 35:211–33.

Bruening, L. G. 1987. "I'm Optimal, You're Optimal: An Economist on the Couch." *SABE* (The Official Publication of the Society for the Advancement of Behavioral Economics) 3:1–5.

Buchanan, J. M. 1969. "Is Economics the Science of Choice." In *Roads to Freedom: Essays in Honor of F. A. Hayek*, ed. E. Streissler, 47–64. London: Routledge & Kegan.

De Alessi, L. 1983a. "Property Rights, Transaction Costs, and X-Efficiency: An Essay in Economic Theory." *American Economic Review* 73:64–81.

De Alessi, L. 1983b. "Property Rights and X-Efficiency: Reply." *American Economic Review* 73:843–45.

Dopfer, K. 1976. *Economics in the Future: Towards a New Paradigm*. London and Basingstoke: Macmillan.

Etzioni, A. 1985. "Opening the Preferences: A Socio-Economic Research Agenda." *Journal of Behavioral Economics* 14:183–205.

Frantz, R. 1985. "X-Efficiency Theory and Its Critics." *Quarterly Review of Economics and Business* 25:38–58.

Frantz, R. 1986. "X-Efficiency in Behavioral Economics." In *Handbook of Behavioral Economics*, vol. A, ed. B. Gilad and S. Kaish. Greenwich, Conn.: JAI Press.

Frantz, R. 1988. *X-Efficiency: Theory, Evidence and Applications*. Norwell, Mass.: Kluwer Academic Press.

Frantz, R., and H. Singh. 1988. "Intrafirm (In)Efficiencies: Neoclassical and X-Efficiency Perspectives." *Journal of Economic Issues* 22:856–64.

Frey, B. S. 1983. "The Economic Model of Behavior: Shortcomings and Fruitful Developments." Institute for Empirical Economic Research, University of Zurich, June. Discussion Paper.

Frey, B. S., and K. Foppa. 1986. "Human Behavior: Possibilities Explain Action." *Journal of Economic Psychology* 7:137–60.

Gilad, B., S. Kaish, and P. D. Loeb. 1982. "From Economic Behavior to Behavioral Economics: The Behavioral Uprising in Economics." *Journal of Behavioral Economics* 13:1–24.

Gramm, W. S. 1985. "Behavioral Elements in the Theory of the Firm: An Historical Perspective." *Journal of Behavioral Economics* 14:21–34.

Hayek, F. A. v. 1967. *Studies in Philosophy, Politics and Economics*. London: Routledge & Kegan.

Heiner, R. A. 1983. "The Origin of Predictable Behavior." *American Economic Review* 73:560–94.

Hodgson, G. 1985. "The Rationalist Conception of Action." *Journal of Economic Issues* 19:825–51.

Kramer, E. 1970. "Zum Problem der rechtlichen Motivation." *Oesterreichische Juristenzeitung* 25:564–67.

Leibenstein, H. 1976a. *Beyond Economic Man: A New Foundation for Microeconomics*. Cambridge, Mass.: Harvard University Press.

Leibenstein, H. 1976b. "Micro-Micro Theory, Agent-Agent Trade, and X-Efficiency." In *Economics in the Future: Towards a New Paradigm*, ed. K. Dopfer, 53–68. London and Basingstoke: Macmillan.

Leibenstein, H. 1978. *General X-Efficiency Theory and Economic Development*. New York: Oxford University Press.

Leibenstein, H. 1979. "A Branch of Economics Is Missing: Micro-Micro Theory." *Journal of Economic Literature* 17:477–502.

Leibenstein, H. 1980. *Inflation, Income Distribution and X-Efficiency Theory*. London: Croom Helm.

Leibenstein, H. 1983. "Property Rights and X-Efficiency: Comment." *American Economic Review* 73:831–42.

Leibenstein, H. 1984. "The Japanese Management System: An X-Efficiency-Game Theory Analysis." In *The Economic Analysis of the Japanese Firm*, ed. M. Aoki, 331–57. Amsterdam: North-Holland.

Leibenstein, H. 1985a. "On Relaxing the Maximization Postulate." *Journal of Behavioral Economics* 14:5–20.

Leibenstein, H. 1985b. "Entrepreneurship, Motivation, and X-Efficiency Theory." Cambridge University. Discussion Paper.

Maital, S., and Y. Roll. 1985. "Solving for 'X': Theory & Measurement of Allocative and X-Efficiency." *Journal of Behavioral Economics* 14:99–116.

Simon, H. A. 1955. "A Behavioral Model of Rational Choice." *Quarterly Journal of Economics* 69:99–118.

Simon, H. A. 1957. *Models of Man*. New York and London: Wiley, Chapman and Hall.

Simon, H. A. 1978. "Rationality as Process and as Product of Thought." *American Economic Review* 68:1–6.

Tomer, J. 1987. *Organizational Capital*. New York: Praeger.

Wagner, A. 1988. *Mikroökonomik*. Stuttgart and New York: Gustav Fischer Verlag.

Zamagni, S. 1987. *Micro Economic Theory: An Introduction*. Oxford and New York: Basil Blackwell.

Commentary

Bruno S. Frey

Comment on the Article by Friedrich Fürstenberg

Professor Fürstenberg presents a mass of important factual information on the forms and aspects of various efficiency norms. This information is of great interest for economists who generally have little knowledge about such norms as they used in existing industrial and other organizations.

In the last part of his article, Professor Fürstenberg offers more general thoughts on institutional economics from his particular point of view as an industrial sociologist. He sees a trade-off between "economic efficiency" nurtured by competitive structures, and "social efficiency" nurtured by solidaristic structures. On this basis, the hypothesis is advanced that a high level of managerial autonomy (vis-à-vis the other employees in the firm) leads to competitive efficiency norms, while a low level of managerial autonomy leads to socioemotionally highly accepted norms. It would be interesting to know what theoretical rationale in terms of a behavioral theory is behind this hypothesis. If managerial autonomy is considered from the point of view of competitive pressures from outside the firm, the opposite relationship is to be expected: much autonomy leading to the choice of socioemotionally acceptable norms, low autonomy to efficiency norms. Does this mean that the two kinds of managerial autonomy are simply inversely related?

Comment on the Article by George England

This article collects a vast number of observations for three different countries and therewith makes a fascinating contribution to our knowledge about people's preferences, with regard not only to the meaning of work but also to residual time, leisure. Such large-scale empirical research on individuals' evaluations of their life is rare and certainly represents a disregarded area in economics. Professor England has to be commended for having engaged in this effort.

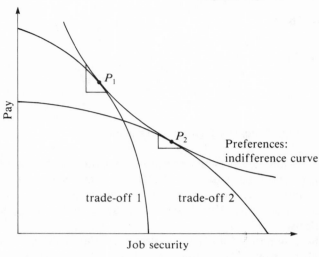

Fig. 1

Professor England endeavors to capture individual preferences empirically. The question then arises whether it is possible to identify such preferences at all without explicitly taking into account the constraints with which the individuals are faced when they respond to the survey questions. After all, everyone is confronted with a restricted opportunity set. Therefore, the answers given by the individuals, in general, reflect the influence of these constraints, and not only of preferences.

An example may illustrate this point. England discusses economic work goals, involving questions about good pay and job security. Economic theory suggests that there is a trade-off between these variables: firms tend to offer either jobs with good pay and low job security or jobs with low pay but high job security. The individual workers are thus constrained in their choice between these two values, as shown in figure 1.

With given preferences regarding good pay and job security, i.e., a constant indifference curve between the two variables, the point chosen switches from P_1 to P_2 when the trade-off changes from position 1 to position 2. Accordingly, the individuals indicate a different marginal evaluation of good pay versus job security in P_2 than in P_1. If trade-offs differ between individuals, over periods, and between countries, the survey results, eliciting the evaluation of the two variables, depend not only on preferences (i.e., on the shape of the individual indifference curves) but equally on the constraints individuals face (i.e., the shape and position of the trade-offs). It follows that the results presented in the article should be interpreted with much care, as the influence of the constraints on the individuals' responses has not explicitly been accounted for.

Comment on the Article by Kurt Dopfer

Professor Dopfer has embarked on a most laudable pursuit, namely to deal with Leibenstein's notion of X-efficiency in depth, and, in particular, to contrast it with neoclassical economics, bounded rationality, and behavioral economics. This is a worthwhile and important task that is undertaken in an original way. Possibly due to this fresh approach, I have not found it easy to follow the arguments, and some parts remain rather unclear to me. In order not to do any injustice to Professor Dopfer, my comments are, therefore, directed to two rather minor points where I disagree with Dopfer's interpretation of the neoclassicists. This point is, perhaps, not without use because it seems to be very important to contrast X-efficiency theory with present-day neoclassical economics and thus, not to fall into the trap of constructing an adversary who is no longer relevant.

Dofper criticizes the neoclassicists' obsession with perfect rationality. This criticism seems to be based on a misunderstanding of neoclassicists, because their adherents would stress that the cost of information and decision making should be weighed against the benefits of deciding more rationally. The example given that in reality an "engineer . . . wants only 98.5 percent accuracy and not 100 percent" is thus quite compatible with the neoclassical position.

Dopfer also claims that neoclassics is based on invariant relationships: The commentator does not see neoclassics in this light; rather he believes the contrary to be true. A stimulus, say a change in the price of a good, has widely differing effects on individual behavior depending on the income, time, and other constraints with which the concerned individuals are faced, as well as on his or her specific preferences. It therefore is unwarranted to criticize neoclassical behavioral theory as following a mechanistic stimulus-response mode.

Part 4
Organizational Adaptation and Change

X-Efficiency, Transaction Costs, and Organizational Change

Claudio U. Ciborra

Since the appearance of the *homo economicus* as an ideal agent who populates the models of economic institutions, attempts have been made to cope with the unrealistic behavioral and psychological assumptions contained in that rather deprived model of the individual.

Among the most recent and ambitious research programs to reconcile economics and everyday life in organizations are X-efficiency theory and transaction costs theory. Both rely on more complex assumptions than neoclassical economics insofar as the psychology and behavior of the agent are concerned. In X-inefficient institutions the agent can be lazy, dominated by emotions, even irrational emotions, and certainly not purely calculative. Transaction costs that pervade economic action stem from the bounded rationality of the agents and from their opportunism, that is, from their potential or actual cheating, shirking, and other types of strategic behavior.

The richer attributes that Williamson and Leibenstein attach to their models of man have a variety of implications for the understanding of the dynamics of economic institutions, ranging from the welfare loss involved in monopoly, to vertical integration, the scope of antitrust, the origin of the hierarchy, the nature of the employment relation, and so forth.

There are limitations, however, to both the Leibenstein and the Williamson approaches, and an inquiry into such limitations will be carried out in this article. We are not interested in a detailed comparison of the advantages and disadvantages of the two theories, or in finding out which is superior (De Alessi 1983). Rather, we draw attention to some aspects of human behavior and decision making that seem to be neglected, or are unsatisfactorily dealt with, in both approaches. Specifically, we focus on the lack of realistic learning skills in the respective models of the individual. By identifying simple traits of human learning, it is possible to show that the agents in X-efficient or transaction costs organizations learn either too much or too little, and that, in any event, they do not show the variety of behavior that human beings display when confronted with new events. Both theories reveal some inconsistencies when a richer set of assumptions is introduced to account for realistic human behavior.

It appears, consequently, that the problem of organizational change cannot be dealt with adequately by either of the two approaches and that industrial mutations, qualitative structural changes, the inner revolutions of economic institutions, in other words, those very processes of "creative destruction" that characterize capitalism (Schumpeter 1950), remain up for grabs despite these two modern explanations of economic institutions.

The analysis begins by defining two types of change, morphostatic and morphogenic. The latter is the product of radical learning events and can be contrasted with the change of a gradual sort stemming from learning by doing. An inquiry into the limits of organizational and individual learning follows to provide a deeper interpretation of organizational inertia. The implications for some of the basic assumptions and results of X-efficiency theory are then critically examined, and the model of the contractual individual that lies at the core of the transaction costs approach is shown to be wanting as well. The concluding remarks suggest areas worthy of further theoretical and practical investigation.

Two Types of Change

In general, one can distinguish between morphostatic and morphogenic organizational changes. The former encompasses two variations: superficial changes that leave things basically the same, or, more importantly, changes that occur as steps of a gradual, developmental sequence, where the possibilities of change are contained within the routines coded into the organization.

This is the evolutionary view of organizational change that pictures agents adjusting incrementally, responding locally to local problems. Incremental patching up allows the organization to learn from its previous actions while retaining control and ability to remedy them.

The learning curve concept and its implicit application at the Ford Motor Company during the second decade of this century is an example of an organization's efforts at morphostatic change: increasing plant size and production volumes led to a variety of improvements and ameliorations in the Model T, the production process, workers' skills, and methods of organization. However, such incremental changes accompanied by a noticeable decrease in production costs did not help management to perceive and avoid the crisis in demand for a car that was available only in black. More flexible and decentralized organizations, namely, General Motors, suddenly gained a large market share by cashing in on the inertia and the specialized investments that kept Ford bound to a specific product, production process, strategy, and mind-set.

The second type of change, morphogenic, is, then, a radical one: it is associated with major innovations and is known to economists as Schumpeterian change (Rosenberg 1982). When organizations need to modify their structures to cope with new environments and strategies, the change may encompass many basic aspects of the organization: authority lines, coordination structures, incentives, behaviors, and decision-making processes. Such change is revolutionary (Miller and Friesen 1984) for it is a major, dramatic, vast, lengthy, costly, and uncertain shift.

Organizational revolutions are not isolated cases. Empirical investigations show that "dramatic change seems to be more closely associated with success than does incremental (i.e., piecemeal and evolutionary) change" (Miller and Friesen 1984).

While morphostatic change occurs almost as a natural side product of an often tacit process of learning by doing, morphogenic change is much more difficult to implement. Specifically, many of the planned changes we attempt to make in organizations seem to fly in the face of naturally occurring changes. We are uncertain about how interpretations of events shape our actions and how we go about the implementation of the planned actions. Such uncertainty is greater when innovation contradicts a well-established way of doing things, ingrained background assumptions, or tacit preconceptions that govern the skilled execution of current routines.

Organizational Flexibility and Learning by Doing

One way of framing the problem of change is to look at the costs attached to disequilibrium transitions facing institutions from the vantage point of the flexibility versus efficiency trade-off. In order to achieve efficiency, what is required is the solution of a fairly structured problem of choice along a known, predetermined production-possibilities frontier. In the case of flexibility, the problem has to be defined before it can be solved by choosing the best alternative: here one tries to extend the frontier by exploiting a possible potential (Klein 1977).

The principal difference between the achievement of efficiency versus flexibility is the higher level of uncertainty and complexity involved in the latter case. To wit, the type of knowledge involved differs significantly: in the case of efficiency, knowledge is largely given, and rational behavior consists of making decisions on the basis of known initial conditions, whereas achieving flexibility requires making tomorrow's decisions without becoming a prisoner of today's knowledge (Winter 1987); indeed, inventions, creation of new knowledge, and learning appear to lie at the core of the phenomena of flexibility (Klein 1977).

This conclusion suggests that the efficiency-flexibility dilemma must be reframed in terms of the production and application of knowledge, that is, the learning processes. As Knight puts it: "To speak of evolution in a cultural (as distinct from biological) setting is necessarily to be concerned with learning and production of new knowledge" ([1921] 1964). Comparing organizations in terms of their flexibility means in this perspective comparing their abilities to create new knowledge, i.e., to learn new practices and skills, and to unlearn old ones (Hedberg 1981).

There are at least as many ways of learning as there are of describing change and flexibility (Fiol and Lyles 1985). Economists seem to indulge primarily in the description of learning processes that are smooth and evolutionary.

Through learning by doing, organizational members accumulate knowledge of an idiosyncratic kind: such knowledge is acquired by osmosis, by close familiarity with machines, procedures, organizational jargon, in coming to know subtleties of behavior of other team members, etc. (Nelson and Winter 1982; Williamson 1975). Learning by using is responsible for gains and innovations that are generated as a result of the use of a product, especially a complex capital good (Rosenberg 1982). Though the locus and agents of learning are different (buyers and users vs. designers and producers; production process vs. products), the focus in both cases is upon those minor improvements that ultimately influence the rate of productivity growth that innovations are capable of generating. But what type of learning takes place in relation to major innovations in technology and organization?

An answer is provided by the evolutionary theory of the firm (Nelson and Winter 1982); here Schumpeterian innovations are seen as the result of complex forms of learning by doing achieved by the modification and recombination of organizational routines that store coordinating information and knowledge underlying effective performance and skill. Organizations live and remember by repeating such routines. Every time an organization has to select an alternative, it will select it from a narrow menu composed of idiosyncratic routines. As a consequence, the individual firm is not characterized by highly flexible adaptation; innovation can emerge only from the puzzles or anomalies relating to prevailing routines.

Nelson and Winter say that the innovative and successful combination of existing routines depends upon two conditions:

1. that the routine be reliable and fully under control: "during trial and error search, familiar routines should behave properly, i.e., not themselves contribute problems, particularly if the problems from that source would complicate the task of detecting and solving problems arising from the novel elements" (1982).
2. that the new application of existing routine be as free as possible of any ambiguity.

Unfortunately, the qualitative account that Nelson and Winter give of the learning processes surrounding major innovations fails to recognize important aspects of learning as performed by human agents rather than by routines. First, learning by human agents can be impaired. For example, search routines may not be triggered at all, for new events are considered threatening. Second, the direct link between search, problem solving, development, and trial of a new routine is not automatic. Third, imitation may not be started at all, even if it is perceived as appropriate. Finally, routines aimed at correcting errors may lead to the repetition of the performances that were considered faulty in the first place: instead of new routines, vicious circles are unwittingly generated (Masuch 1985).

The Notion of Limited Learning

Bounded rationality, i.e., a form of rationality whereby economic behavior is assumed to be "intendedly rational, but only limitedly so" (Simon 1961), is of paramount importance in the study of economic organizations (Alchian and Demsetz 1972; March and Simon 1958; Williamson 1975). One can distinguish two main ramifications of this idea, both stemming from the limited information-processing capabilities of the human brain.

The first reference is to the inability of the decision maker to process all the relevant information when choosing between alternatives. This limits significantly the number of instances where the decision maker can make an optimal choice. "Satisficing" as opposed to maximizing behavior is the consequence of such limitation (Simon 1978).

The second ramification is more complex and often ignored by authors concerned with the implications of bounded rationality. Limited information-processing capabilities require the actor to develop ruthlessly generalized programs or routines that store the answers to previously solved problems and previously committed mistakes. These programs are often tacit, opaque, rigid, and unquestioned until further notice. Their role is double-edged. On the one hand, they permit economizing on decision making and information processing when one is facing an event that requires an action or response: they represent the competence of the decision maker; on the other hand, being generalized, they contain poor representations of external reality, usually precluding attention to the details of the actual situation at hand (Kahneman and Tversky 1974). They are thus responsible for biases in problem solving; cognitive dissonance (Ackerlof and Dickens 1982; Festinger 1957), framing (Tversky and Kahneman 1986), resistance to alternative modes of reasoning (Nisbett and Ross 1980), and ill-structured processes of inference and defensive routines (Argyris 1982).

The distinction between satisficing choices and limits to learning determined by rule-based skills is akin to the principles of Heiner's theory of reliability, whereby agents not only have to rely on limited information but also suffer from a lack of decision-making competence in using observed information, no matter how difficult their decision problem might be. These restrictions affect agents' ongoing experience (Heiner 1988).

"Limited learning," meaning by that term all the cognitive barriers to learning from experience (Brehemer 1980; Einhorn 1980; Frey, in this volume; Kahneman, Slovic, and Tversky 1982) is a second ramification of bounded rationality. Before applying this concept to test X-efficiency and transaction costs theories versus the problem of change, we must briefly examine its impact on economic units.

There are various ways in which learning can be limited, bogged down into vicious circles and eventually result in organizational inertia (Hannan and Freeman 1984). In the following section, we explore limitations at the individual and organizational levels as they are discussed in the psychology and organizational theory literature. At both levels the skilled execution of individual and organizational routines seems to be the source of such limitations.

Cognitive Limits to Individual Learning

Many experiments with individuals and organizations that want to change their behavior consistently show: (a) routines invoked to correct mistakes reproduce the same mistakes, at another level; (b) only learning that maintains the status quo takes place; and (c) introducing any innovation is far from easy, even for an external observer who does not participate in the organization's routines or power games: learning and action seem to be disconnected in the mind of the agent when analyzing and intervening in a situation (Argyris 1982).

What are the origins and cognitive status of limited learning, a factor that, in addition to conflict of interest and/or lack of information, seems so crucial in explaining the costs of changing organizational and individual behavior?

In order to explain the impediments to learning (phenomena of great relevance in dealing with quantum growth of knowledge, flexibility, and dynamic efficiency) one has to hypothesize about a dual structure of cognitive processes. There are interpretive frames, mental constructs that help us to select events in the flow of experience, that actually help us to build experience (Loasby 1985). Experience is not composed merely of a set of responses to events. Which events are perceived as relevant depends upon prevailing frames; they influence the range of alternatives where actual choices are made, set the contexts for decisions, orient preferences and expectations, and condition the invention of new solutions.

The dual structure of cognitive processes challenges the idea of the standard cycle of failure-search-solution, i.e., of the direct, automatic link between more knowledge and improved action. Any search routine, perception of events, or absorption of new knowledge occurs within a given interpretive framework. The framework may impede the recognition of failures or lead to vicious circles, cover-ups, and so forth. The situation is not that agents simply lack information when making a decision and that more information would be enough to improve their maximizing performance; they do not simply perform myopic search routines and stumble upon solutions to problems; rather, they are like scientists continuously engaged in inquiry (Kelly 1955), the inquiry of making sense of everyday life with its major and minor riddles: as scientists they are conditioned by paradigms, of which they may be unaware when acting.

Control and Learning in Hierarchical Organizations

Consider the routines of different hierarchical order in an organization (Argyris 1980b; Leibenstein 1987; Lohumaa and March 1987). At a lower level there are routines for the execution of tasks that require a certain amount of skill. At a higher level one finds routines aimed at controlling the subordinates' performance. These will be rigid, schematic, opaque, and simplified just like the lower ones, for they allow the supervisor to control many subordinates simultaneously.

Note that the two types of knowledge and goals embedded in the routines conflict with each other. Generalized schemata are used to evaluate, monitor, and govern performance of lower-level routines. However, the means-ends chain at the core of the lower routines is not transparent, making control difficult, yet managers are held responsible for control, and subordinates are responsible for performance. The distribution of responsibilities clashes with the distribution of knowledge, and the outcome can be a series of vicious circles, namely:

1. in order to improve control, the top group requires more complete information and more details; as a reaction, the subordinates will feel that they are not trusted and will try to withhold information;
2. defensive routines, such as hiding information and covering up mistakes for fear of control, will multiply, while local and supervisory control systems will interfere with each other and be polluted by opportunistic information.

Whenever a change is required or a new event emerges, the intertwining of higher and lower routines, each executed in a skilled way, will foster responses that are self-sealing and do not disrupt the status quo.

If the change required is only incremental, it may be compatible with the orderly functioning of the hierarchy. As a result, organizational learning, facing puzzles, and solving problems can deal with only those events that are correctable within the existing structures and frames. Errors that are not correctable are those whose discovery is a threat to the individual system of hiding and correcting errors, errors that can be easily camouflaged and whose correction violates existing organizational norms.

The hierarchical distribution of knowledge and the different goals to which agents are subject explain why new events are filtered out. Note, also, how Nelson and Winters's explanation of how innovation is generated by a straightforward recombination of routines is incomplete for it ignores the cognitive mismatch caused by routines arranged hierarchically.

By contrast, innovation and radical change must be the result of learning that arises from inquiry into the norms and standards that sustain existing coordination and control routines: it is learning that is able ultimately to question the organizational and cognitive contexts, or paradigms, where learning by doing takes place.

The Dynamics of X-Efficient Organizations

The notion of limited learning can now be applied to X-efficiency theory to provide a broader understanding of its basic postulates. At the same time, however, it will challenge some of the basic propositions contained in Leibenstein's work.

Consider first the basic postulate concerning the existence of "inert areas," whereby individuals who find themselves in a given position, i.e., a chosen effort point, will not necessarily move to a superior position in the standard utility sense (Leibenstein 1978). The assumption of limited learning justifies this basic principle: there are costs of change and adaptation, due to the nature of the individual's competent execution of routines, i.e., his or her skills. Leibenstein (1987) has recently added a rich account of several other individual and organizational factors that may cause inertia, such as habits, conventions, standard procedures, rules of thumb, etc.

It is interesting to see the interplay between the idea of inert areas with another basic principle of X-efficiency theory, namely selective rationality, when new, significantly different circumstances require the agent to shift away from inert behavior. Inert areas are upper and lower bounds (thresholds) within which any decision maker will not change his or her decision (Leibenstein 1984); such bounds depend on the agent's personality and external pressures. External shocks or crises, or, more generally, stronger environmental pressures, squeeze inert areas and induce the agent to select a behavior closer to the neoclassical standard of maximizing.

This account of how the agent behaves as a consequence of a major change in the environment is problematic, at least, in two ways. First, if one can choose to be lazy or inert, this can be seen as a maximizing behavior where the set of constraints has been enlarged: thus the utility maximization postulate is lurking behind the choice to be lazy (Stigler 1976). In fact the whole concept of selective rationality exposes Leibenstein to the critiques made by the new neoclassical economists (De Alessi 1983).

Limited learning would provide a different treatment of the whole matter. Inert behavior of course can be chosen but often becomes something that is difficult to abandon; it sticks to one's behavior and mind, no matter what his or her will and intentions are. Thus, selective rationality cannot be fully exercised but is limited.

A second, related point is that external shocks or greater pressures do not necessarily lead to a decrease in X-inefficiency. When learning is limited, no change in behavior may take place and thus individuals and organizations may remain inefficient even beyond their desire to adopt new strategies and courses of action. In a way, Leibenstein's account of how organizations and individuals react to external pressures, i.e., the whole dynamic aspect of his theory (1976, 1987) is still very neoclassical. The economic agent embedded in his framework constantly chooses what to do; in particular, the agent may choose to be inert (selective rationality). Instead, in the present account, such choice is limited, and the agent may be unaware of such limitations.

Another way of presenting the difference between the role played by limited learning and Leibenstein's theory is to focus on the motivational aspects behind the attainment of higher levels of efficiency. If higher outputs stem from a different combination of capital and labor and a better choice of techniques, new knowledge will be involved. As Leibenstein (1980) indicates, that knowledge may already have been there in a latent way, as intellectual slack. The problem of eliciting such knowledge and inducing agents to apply it to productive purposes is a matter of motivation and incentives. These are not purely economic but depend upon the firm's unique structure, culture, and atmosphere (Leibenstein 1980). But, once again, no clear idea is given on how to motivate employees, besides saying that consultants have to be hired; and yet, what does motivate management to hire consultants? The answer, once more, is pressure for change imposed by the environment (the market). Higher pressure makes agents more calculating, thus more responsive to economic incentives; also learning from experience is more likely to take place when pressure is high rather than low. It is just a matter of choice, laziness, and inertia: an agent in the X-efficient world can choose whether to learn from experience or not; human inertia is up for grabs for the decision maker; signals to change effort can be selectively ignored; if pressure signals trigger some degree of constraint concern as a response, ultimately the agent can select a degree of response that will reduce pressure. In other words, the model of the individual created by Leibenstein is, or can be, an opportunist, though a torpid one (Williamson 1975).

The limited learning perspective provides a different explanation: inertia, motivation, degree of choice of constraints to action are only partially subject to control by the decision maker, who is often stuck beyond his or her will. Pressure is not enough to unfreeze inertial behavior, as many social psychologists have shown (Lewin 1940) in experimenting with change strategies (Argyris 1985). Pressure actually may be counterproductive to higher learning from experience: it could just worsen existing vicious circles. Leibenstein (1980) acknowledges the phenomenon, mentioning the case of firms whose inert areas are too tight (inflexible), that, therefore, cannot respond successfully to cost-reduction pressures and eventually will not survive and will leave the industry.

Consider, as an example, the case of a large corporation such as AT&T. The rules regulating the telecommunications industry in the United States have changed dramatically from a regulated monopoly (the Bell System) to a regulated oligopoly and free competition in selected sectors. Changes are still unfolding before our eyes, although it is not clear that a decrease of X-inefficiency will eventually appear. AT&T has found enormous difficulties in changing its corporate culture to adapt to the new competitive environment. Its entry into new fields such as computers has so far been disappointing as it lacks skills in marketing in a highly competitive arena. Alliances have been established, such as the one with Olivetti, to allow new know-how to penetrate the traditional organization, but the management of the alliance requires skills and culture that are not germane to the incumbent management organization. Finally, if prices have been declining this has been accompanied by a degradation of service.

This case seems to show that organizations are sluggish beyond their will and that external pressure may be a necessary condition to eliminate, or reduce, X-inefficient conduct, but it is not sufficient. Other factors, commonly labeled "culture," "mentality," and so forth, matter as well, as Leibenstein (1987) insists. However, there is no suggestion in his theory on how to overcome inertia, on how to enact effective learning, or on how to harness culture and atmosphere to achieve higher motivation. No concern is shown for the complex cognitive structure of the agent and all the ramifications of bounded rationality. The concept of limited learning not only captures these aspects but also is being put to work on more general theories of individual behavior and economic organizations (Frey in this volume; Heiner 1983, 1988) and can indicate a means to overcome organizational inertia and establish conditions for effective learning (Argyris 1985).

Limited Learning and Opportunism

How is adaptation or lack of adaptation of economic institutions in the face of radical change explained by the transaction costs approach? In order to answer this question, one must systematically review the learning skills of the contractual individual (Williamson 1985), the building block of that framework, in order to evaluate under what conditions the individual is able to change or, alternatively, to generate organizational inertia.

To begin with, the contractual individual is able to learn by doing and using, that is, to accumulate idiosyncratic, tacit knowledge. Thus, the individual can cope with gradual change, that is, change that takes place within given boundaries and does not deeply affect the structure of the learning system (be it the identity of the individual or the routines of the organization).

If learning of a gradual kind is the only type admitted by the transaction costs approach, the discovery of new behaviors and knowledge, the invention of new organizational forms, the creative application of technological innovations must be left to chance. Random events or sheer luck would be the major sources of innovation, and it is up to the contractual individual, as an entrepreneur, to take advantage of them (Alchian 1950; Nelson and Winter 1982; Williamson 1981). Once the lucky event has occurred, the competitive selection process determines the success of radical innovations, while learning by doing is responsible for their further improvement.

Recall, however, that we build experience, and thus even "random" events and "surprises" are designed, that is, mentally and socially constructed. Perceiving a surprise, i.e., framing an event as a puzzle, requires some sort of preexisting context or cognitive framework, where the event can be cast as something to wonder or worry about. Facing the event requires an orientation, the creation of a goal structure and planning — influenced by preexisting knowledge structures, such as frames or "because of" motives (Minsky 1975; Norman 1983; Piaget 1974; Schank and Abelson 1977; Schutz 1964). The willingness to solve the puzzle may also require a certain degree of openness and vulnerability: to revise one's views and beliefs, especially in the case where puzzles may threaten the status quo. Otherwise, puzzles would simply be ignored within the existing formative context, avoided, or bypassed by invoking the self-defense routines at hand.

The introduction of major organizational innovations is, at the same time, the result of tinkering and breakthroughs, and of random events but also the result of the agents' intention to select fluctuations and anomalies and transform them in a new way of running things through purposeful redesign and radical learning experiences.

Hence, in dealing with radical changes the contractual individual must be able to experience sharp twists in beliefs, views, and behaviors that go beyond incremental learning (Harman 1986). However, such capability introduces strain in the economic agent employed in the transaction costs approach.

In fact, engaging oneself in a major change process can be framed as making a commitment to action that will affect the future behavior of the individual or the organization. The more radical the change, the more complex and stronger the commitment that the contractual individual has to establish with others and within himself or herself.

If I decide to change my behavior, let's say, to quit smoking, I commit myself to a future course of action, or, in other words, I exchange a promise with myself-at-a-later-stage. The more dramatic and painful the deliberation, the more the two selves at different points in time might diverge: myself-at-a-later-stage may be ready to revise early commitments according to the preferences of the moment.

What happens in the mind of the contractual individual in this perspective?

A first possibility is that the individual would not play the game or would behave opportunistically; he or she might not trust other agents or might even cheat them but will rely safely on his or her own self-at-a-later-stage. Opportunism would thus be ubiquitous toward the others, but it would stop at the contours of the persona. Individuals who can act in such a calculative mode are likely to modify their behavior as soon as circumstances change. In the extreme case, "if a person were to be capable of instant rearrangement of his or her own frameworks, it is not clear that he or she could be recognized as an individual. Such a person would be very disconcerting to deal with, even for himself or herself" (Heiner 1983; Loasby 1985): such a person would be a wanton, a homunculus entirely in the grips of the whims and wishes of the moment (Etzioni 1986).

But phenomena such as self-deception, weakness of will, and, more generally, Knight's injunction not to ignore human nature as we know it, would plainly remind us that to trust ourselves-in-the-future may well be as hazardous as trusting a stranger.

The inner commitments to change must then be modeled as an exchange between two or more different contracting agents set at different temporal stations. Between such agents, each actuated only by self-interest, it is pax or pact, war or contract, including "the proclivity to dissimulation and objectionable arts of higgling" (Edgeworth 1881).

If we accept the idea of two or more selves, of which only one is in charge at any given time, rational decisions have to be replaced by models of collective choice, where the selves can be constructed as engaged not in joint optimization but rather in a strategic game (Schelling 1984). If the situation is framed as a bilateral monopoly between the present self and all the selves-in-the-future, then no change is in view; rather there will be inertia, inability to action, and blockages.

The costs of change, or transition costs, would appear to consist of the costs of transacting with oneself, in a small-numbers situation, where no inner arbitrators are present to identify the settlement point on the contract curve.

As an alternative tack, recall the hypothesis of the agent with a two-layered structure of knowledge. Behind observed choices, decisions, commitments, or any opportunistic behavior, there are complex psychological and cultural processes and knowledge structures called metapreferences (Sen 1977), frameworks (Loasby 1985), or heuristic frames (Winter 1987).

The intrapsychic conflict between such frameworks or metaprefer-ences and lower-level preferences can generate self-defensive attitudes, guilt, fear, and stress that may diminish the capacity for learning and action (Etzioni 1986), leading to instances of weakness of will.

Consider now what being a smart opportunist entails: the desire to stay in control of events and people; the aspiration to win and not lose; the need to be rational and calculative and to minimize emotions; the willingness to achieve one's own purposes by any means. Opportunism is a frame, learned by socialization, that governs routinized responses to events, generates expectations that others may behave in the same oppor-tunistic way, takes for granted that institutions must safeguard them-selves against it. In general, being unable to adapt generates fear and enhances the desire to be in control, no matter what. Organizations that possess a structure of incentives and motivation mechanisms that are based on the notion of keeping opportunistic behavior in check presup-pose a systematic lack of trust among their members and reinforce behaviors that are based on lack of trust.

Hence, when adaptation is required, a transaction costs-efficient organization will meet various obstacles:

1. agents may behave opportunistically toward themselves and be blocked by inner conflicts in their decision making;
2. change will not obtain because of defensive routines set up by the agents to protect themselves from the threats of having to modify their metapreferences; moreover, "smart" opportunistic behavior will justify cover-ups, not discussing the undiscussable and other tactics that ultimately lead to the status quo;
3. hierarchical arrangements based on control of shirking will dis-courage exploration of alternatives, responses to new signals coming from the environment, etc. (the counterproductive effects of monitoring on shirking have been illustrated by Leibenstein [1983] in his critique of property rights and transac-tion costs theory).

Only by attacking the causes of limited learning directly, which may entail running against the dictates of opportunism and designing transac-tion costs-inefficient organizations, can one hope to increase individual and organizational effectiveness (Argyris 1985).

Concluding Remarks

In this article the comparison initiated by De Alessi (1983) between X-efficiency and transaction costs theories has been carried out one step further, by considering dynamic aspects such as adaptation to radical changes in the environment. The results of the analysis are mixed.

Adaptation requires learning both of a gradual and radical kind. Learning is, however, limited because of bounded rationality and the way organizations function.

The transaction costs approach and its reliance on the notion of opportunism takes one of the outcomes of limited learning, i.e., self-defensive routines, as a master criterion in interpreting and designing organizations. Such a strategy prevents that approach from explaining radical adaptations, whereby one has to trust oneself and the others. The emphasis on economizing leads to design organization forms that are efficient but low in learning, and, thus, are doomed to failure when external conditions require radical change.

X-efficiency theory is more open and flexible and does not rely on a pure calculative model of the individual. It acknowledges many of the phenomena that disrupt learning and cause inefficiencies. However, its reliance on the link between higher pressure, almost automatic reduction of inert areas, and reestablishment of the neoclassic calculative behavior does not provide a fully autonomous alternative to generalized neoclassical theory based on property rights and transaction costs. X-efficiency is a theory of friction in economic organizations that needs a deeper inquiry into the psychology of economic agents. The notion of limited learning is certainly one of the aspects to be investigated if the theory wants to give realistic accounts of change processes. It follows that inert areas and inertial behavior should not be taken as postulates (Leibenstein 1983) but should become subjects of further study.

REFERENCES

Akerlof, G. A., and W. T. Dickens. 1982. "The Economic Consequences of Cognitive Dissonance." *American Economic Review* 72:307–19.
Argyris, C. 1980. "Some Inner Contradictions in Management Information Systems." In *The Information Systems Environment*, ed. H. Lucas et al. Amsterdam: North Holland.

Argyris, C. 1982. *Reasoning, Learning, and Action*. San Francisco: Jossey-Bass.

Argyris, C. 1985. *Strategy, Change and Defensive Routines*. Boston: Pitman.

Argyris, C. 1986. "Bridging Economics and Psychology: The Case of Economic Theory of the Firm." Harvard University. Mimeo.

Bateson, G. 1972. *Steps to an Ecology of Mind*. New York: Ballantine.

Brehemer, B. 1980. "In One Word: Not from Experience." *Acta Psychologica* 45:223–41.

Coase, R. H. 1937. "The Nature of the Firm." *Economica* 4:386–405.

De Alessi, L. 1983. "Property Rights, Transaction Costs, and X-Efficiency: An Essay in Economic Theory." *American Economic Review* 73:64–81.

Edgeworth, F. Y. 1881. *Mathematical Psychics*. London: Kegan Paul.

Elster, J. 1979. *Ulysses and the Syrens*. Cambridge: Cambridge University Press.

Elster, J. 1985. "Weakness of Will and the Free-Rider Problem." *Economics and Philosophy* 1:231–65.

Etzioni, A. 1986. "The Case for a Multiple-Utility Conception." *Economics and Philosophy* 2:159–83.

Festinger, L. 1957. *A Theory of Cognitive Dissonance*. New York: Harper & Row.

Fiol, C. M., and M. A. Lyles. 1985. "Organizational Learning." *Academy of Management Review* 10:803–13.

Frey, B. S. 1988. "An Ipsative Theory of Human Behavior." In this volume.

Gilad, B., S. Kaish, and P. D. Loeb. 1987. "Cognitive Dissonance and Utility Maximization." *Journal of Economic Behavior and Organization* 8:61–73.

Hannan, M. T., and J. Freeman. 1984. "Structural Inertia and Organizational Change." *American Sociological Review* 29:149–64.

Harman, G. 1986. *Change in View-Principles of Reasoning*. Cambridge, Mass.: MIT Press.

Hedberg, B. 1981. "How Organizations Learn and Unlearn?" In *Handbook of Organizational Design*, ed. P. C. Nystrom and W. H. Starbuck. London: Oxford University Press.

Heiner, R. A. 1983. "The Origin of Predictable Behavior." *American Economic Review* 73:560–95.

Heiner, R. A. 1988. "Imperfect Decisions in Organizations." *Journal of Economic Behavior and Organization* 9:45–88.

Kahneman, D., and A. Tversky. 1973. "On the Psychology of Prediction." *Psychological Review* 80:237–51.

Kelley, H. H. 1972. *Casual Schemata and the Attribution Process*. New York: General Learning Press.

Kelly, G. A. 1955. *A Theory of Personality*. New York: Norton.

Klein, B. H. 1977. *Dynamic Economics*. Cambridge, Mass.: Harvard University Press.

Knight, F. H. [1921] 1964. *Risk, Uncertainty, and Profit*. New York: Harper & Row.

Langlois, R. N., ed. 1985. *Economics as a Process: Essays in the New Institutional Economics*. Cambridge: Cambridge University Press.

Leibenstein, H. 1978. "On the Basic Proposition of X-Efficiency Theory." *American Economic Review* 68:328–34.

Leibenstein, H. 1980. *Beyond Economic Man*. Cambridge, Mass.: Harvard University Press.

Leibenstein, H. 1983. "Property Rights and X-Efficiency: Comment." *American Economic Review* 73:831–42.

Leibenstein, H. 1987. *Inside the Firm*. Cambridge, Mass.: Harvard University Press.

Loasby, B. J. 1985. "Organisation, Competition and the Growth of Knowledge." In *Economics as a Process. See* Langlois 1985.

Louhamaa, P. H., and J. G. March. 1987. "Adaptive Coordination of a Learning Team." *Management Science* 33:107–23.

March, J. G., and H. A. Simon. 1958. *Organizations*. New York: Wiley.

Masuch, M. 1985. "Vicious Circles in Organizations." *Administrative Science Quarterly* 30:14–33.

Miller, D., and P. H. Friesen. 1984. *Organizations: A Quantum View*. Englewood Cliffs, N. J.: Prentice Hall.

Minsky, M. 1975. "A Framework for Representing Knowledge." In *The Psychology of Computer Vision*, ed. P. H. Winston. New York: McGraw-Hill.

Nelson, R. R., and S. G. Winter. 1982. *An Evolutionary Theory of Economic Change*. Cambridge, Mass.: Harvard University Press.

Nisbett, R., and L. Ross. 1980. *Human Inference: Strategies and Shortcomings of Social Judgment*. Englewood Cliffs, N.J.: Prentice Hall.

Norman, D. A. 1983. "Some Observations on Mental Models." In *Mental Models*, ed. D. Gentner and A. L. Stevens. Hillsdale, N.J.: Lawrence-Erlbaum.

Rosenberg, N. 1982. *Inside the Black Box: Technology and Economics*. Cambridge: Cambridge University Press.

Shackle, G. L. S. 1972. *Epistemics and Economics: A Critique of Economic Doctrines*. Cambridge: Cambridge University Press.

Schank, R., and R. P. Abelson. 1977. *Scripts, Plans, Goals and Understanding: An Inquiry into Human Knowledge Structures*. Hillsdale, N.J.: Lawrence Erlbaum.

Schein, E. H. 1985. *Organizational Culture and Leadership*. San Francisco: Jossey-Bass.

Schelling, T. C. 1984. *Choice and Consequence*. Cambridge, Mass.: Harvard University Press.

Schumpeter, J. A. 1950. *Capitalism, Socialism, and Democracy*. New York: Harper and Row.

Sen, A. K. 1977. "Rational Fools: a Critique of the Behavioral Foundations of Economic Theory." *Philosophy and Public Affairs* 6.

Simon, H. A. 1978. "On How to Decide What to Do." *Bell Journal of Economics* 9:494–507.

Starbuck, W. H. 1983. "Organizations as Action Generators." *American Sociological Review* 48:91–102.

Stigler, G. J. 1976. "The Xistence of X-Efficiency." *American Economic Review* 66:213–16.

Sussman, G. J. 1973. "A Computational Model of Skill Acquisition." Ph.D. diss., MIT.

Tversky, A., and D. Kahneman. 1974. "Judgment under Uncertainty: Heuristics and Biases." *Science* 185:1124–31.

Williamson, O. E. 1975. *Markets and Hierarchies: Analysis and Antitrust Implications*. New York: Free Press.

Williamson, O. E. 1985. *The Economic Institutions of Capitalism*. New York: Free Press.

Winter, S. G. 1987. "Knowledge and Competence as Strategic Assets." In *The Competitive Challenge*, ed. D. J. Teece. Cambridge, Mass.: Ballinger.

Commentary

R. C. O. Matthews

The contribution by Ciborra deals with cognitive aspects of the conflict between short-run efficiency and long-run flexibility. The cognitive orientation is emphasized by his references to the history of science, where similar questions arise. However, as he indicates, the behavioral problems in economic change are more complex because they involve changes not only in the intellectual habits of individuals but also in interpersonal relations, to a greater extent than in science. Change is correspondingly more difficult to bring about, since simultaneous adaptations are needed from a number of people.

Ciborra's idea that the degree of opportunism is a dependent variable, affected by existing institutions, not an immutable consequence of human nature, is welcome. Such a conclusion would have been congenial to Marshall. It is more promising than the hypothesis commonly to be found in current literature, according to which, although most people (presumably including the writer) are not crooks, there are always enough crooks around to determine institutions. How to give empirical content to Ciborra's idea in a systematic way is a matter for further study.

It is easy to see how excessive preoccupation with prevention of opportunism may lead to inflexibility and resistance to change. Whether that is the only source of inflexibility, or even the dominant one, as Ciborra seems to suggest, is perhaps more debatable. Counterexamples suggest themselves. The case of inflexible military strategies — winning the last war — is not in any obvious sense the result of overconcern with opportunism. (I suppose a connection could be traced in some instances. Thus the Duke of Wellington defended the purchase of promotion in the army, despite its admitted ill effects on the quality of senior officers, as a means of preventing the emergence of an opportunistic officer corps that might be too independent of established property interests).

Ciborra's article is perhaps more successful in explaining the obstacles to radical change than in explaining why radical changes do sometimes occur nonetheless. One possibility is that they occur only infrequently and under the pressure of a crisis. This suggests a model similar to that of punctuated evolution in biology (as contrasted with traditional smooth Darwinian evolution). Or else radical changes may not be as infrequent as all that but still be exceptional; one thinks of the Schumpe-terian innovator, who is exceptional in that he is capable of introducing radical change without pressure, in contrast to the imitators, who change only under pressure of competition, if then. Ciborra's reference to the struggle between one's two selves, à la Schelling, might suggest a special role for management consultants, who are birds of passage and hence free of such conflicts; in practice, however, their contributions seem more often of the morphostatic kind rather than the morphogenic kind. There remain, finally, new firms and new managements. At the same time, the frequent failure of new managements to achieve their objectives after takeovers shows that successful change, even radical change, requires some accommodation with existing arrangements.

Part 5
Normative Implications of
X-Efficiency in Business Strategy
and Governmental Policies

The Impact of the Income Tax on Work Effort and X-Inefficiency in Enterprises

Armin Bohnet and Martin Beck

The relationship between the taxation of income and the supply of labor is a topic that has given rise to much discussion among both academic economists and politicians. The prime objective for economists is to determine, by means of microanalysis or macroanalysis, what impact variations of the income tax will have upon the number of hours worked.

By application of the traditional neoclassical microeconomic model, most analyses aim at producing hypotheses with regard to the way in which a utility-maximizing worker will adjust the number of hours he works to a new level of income tax.[1] The main conclusion is that it is impossible to predict with certainty either the direction or the size of the adjustment in working hours.[2]

Even on a macroeconomic level, there is little agreement on the effects of the income tax on aggregate labor supply within the economy, as is shown by recent discussion in the *American Economic Review*.[3]

Moreover, in the case of most industrial nations, the traditional microeconomic approach is in practice irrelevant as the number of hours worked is in most cases not a variable that can be determined by employees themselves. It is indeed impossible for the individual employee

---

The authors wish to thank Morris Altman, Roger S. Frantz, Franz Gehrels, Tadeusz Hadrowicz, Friedrich Hinterberger, Klaus Müller, Mark Perlman, Hirofumi Shibata, Wolfgang Wiegard, and the participants and discussants of the Bellagio conference on X-efficiency for valuable comments on earlier drafts of this article. All remaining errors are our own.

1. See Andel 1983, 148; Brown 1983, 1; Häuser 1979, 177; Hausman 1981, 29; and Koch 1984, 30. A short review of more comprehensive approaches can be found in Heilemann and von Löffelholz 1987, 162–65.

2. This also holds for the further development of the standard model. See Heilemann and von Löffelholz 1987, 165.

3. See Bohanan and Van Cott 1986; Gahvari 1986; and Gwartney and Stroup 1983, 1986.

to adjust the number of hours he works and his scope for such decisions is significantly limited by institutional constraints such as wage
agreements.[4]

In short, academic economists are keenly interested in the relationships that exist between income tax and the number of hours worked but
have not yet been able to reach any firm conclusions.

Politicians, on the other hand, are motivated by other interests. In
their eyes, the impact of the income tax upon the motivation of the
taxpayer to work is of particular significance. A good example is the way
in which politicians in the Federal Republic of Germany have used the
slogan "It must be worth working" to gain support for the proposed tax
reform for 1990, which involves a general lowering of marginal tax rates.
The politicians' argument appears to be based on the following chain of
reasoning: lower rates of income tax result in higher motivation of the
taxpayer, which in turn leads to greater effort and ultimately to higher
rates of economic growth.

Unfortunately, a theoretical foundation for such a causal chain does
not exist, because the economists mostly ignore the vital relationships
between income tax and effort.[5] This discrepancy is of particular significance because all over the world income tax reforms are being introduced
or proposed (e.g., the United States, the United Kingdom, West Germany, Austria, Hungary, and even Poland) and justified on the grounds
that they would encourage increased effort.

A critical review of the situation and some variation of the usual
approach in analyzing these problems would, therefore, appear to be
justified.

Leibenstein's X-efficiency approach has been criticized, for instance, by De Alessi for methodological reasons (1983a, 72; and 1983b,
845). De Alessi points out that "generalized neoclassical theory is simpler
and yields a richer, broader range of implications, including all of those
supposedly generated by X-efficiency" (1983b, 845). Therefore X-
efficiency theory would have little value. We, however, believe that analyzing our topic (that is, the relationship between income taxation and
effort) with the aid of X-efficiency theory may make it possible to derive
new, empirically testable hypotheses because effort is an important variable in X-efficiency theory. Moreover, an empirical test of the implica-

---

4. For a recent criticism of the traditional neoclassical labor supply model and an
analysis of the effects of institutional limitations on the labor supply, see Wagner 1987, 139
and 145.

5. The relationships between wages and effort are discussed in Linde 1984.

tions derived in our article will be a test of the validity of the X-efficiency approach as well.

The main purposes of our article can be described as follows: We want

   a. to investigate the relationship between income tax and effort, making use of the X-efficiency concept.
   b. to derive unambiguous and empirically testable hypotheses about the effect of a variation of the income tax on effort and consequently the degree of X-inefficiency. In particular, we assert that under certain conditions an increase in income taxation will lead to lower work effort and a higher degree of X-inefficiency.
   c. to show how this hypothesis can be tested empirically and to present some tentative empirical evidence.

Effort and X-Inefficiency: A Short Outline of the Relationships

According to Leibenstein, an organization is X-inefficient if its output with given inputs is less than the maximum potential output.[6] The current output of a firm depends largely on the effort of its workers within a given period of work. The higher the degree of motivation, the greater will be each worker's effort and individual output. As the work effort expected of the employee is often not defined precisely in employment contracts, some scope may remain for the worker to determine the level of individual effort. Should the worker decide to lower the effort below the level considered by the managers as both desirable and possible, the worker's contribution to the output of the firm will be suboptimal and, in the absence of any mechanism to correct this decision, the enterprise will be X-inefficient. This state of affairs, which, according to Leibenstein, may well prove to be lasting, is undesirable both for the firm's managers, because of the profits they are having to forgo, and for politicians, because the possibilities for production and growth will not be realized.

In the context of our discussion, this raises the question of whether and to what degree tax policy can contribute to a reduction in the level of X-inefficiency.

Insofar as there may be scope for employees to determine their own level of effort, they may be able to respond to changes in the levels of their income tax by adjusting their work effort even if the number of

---

6. See Leibenstein 1976 (p. 95 in particular) and his comments on X-efficiency theory in general; also see Bohnet and Beck 1986; and Leibenstein 1979, 1987.

hours to be worked is institutionally fixed. A priori, it is, therefore, possible that a change in rates of income tax will affect the effort and output of individual workers within a given working period and will thus have an impact on the level of X-inefficiency within firms and, consequently, on the economy as a whole.

If, as we assume here to be the case, politicians aim at achieving X-efficiency, then they must take into consideration the relationships we have outlined when deciding upon the structure of the income tax. One condition for this, however, is that the interdependencies between the taxation of income and X-efficiency should be clarified by the theoretical analysis of academic economists. In particular, it must be determined if and how a change in rates of income tax affects individual effort (Rosen 1980, 173) and, as a result, the degree of X-efficiency of an enterprise. This analysis is carried out in the following sections.

Individual Work Effort and Income Tax: Some Theoretical Observations

Basic Assumptions of the Model

The first question to be answered concerns the way in which the typical worker will adjust his or her effort at work in response to an increase in the rate of income tax. At this stage, our assumptions represent an abstraction from a far more complex reality. In particular, the reaction of the firm's management is not taken into consideration. Nevertheless, this approach would appear to be justified by the following considerations:

- In the form developed by Leibenstein, the model can easily be represented graphically.
- This simple analysis can later be applied to more complex relationships, in which case restrictive assumptions must be abandoned or modified.
- It will be seen that the hypotheses emerging from the simple model do not differ significantly from those resulting from more complex approaches.

The analysis is based on the following assumptions:

A1. The subject of our investigation is a typical worker whose wages are determined not by the number of hours worked but by the effort applied.[7] For the sake of simplicity, it is assumed that there is a linear correlation between a worker's effort and the worker's gross wages.

A2. It is assumed that a proportional income tax is introduced or that an existing proportional income tax is increased by an extra levy that is proportional to income earned.[8]

A3. For the sake of simplicity, it is further assumed that for the worker each DM earned represents one unit of utility.[9]

These relationships are illustrated in figure 1.

The following assumptions are illustrated in figure 2.

A4. We further assume that the worker has some discretion with respect to work effort; within certain limits the worker can decide what effort to apply. A change in the level of effort will, however, be associated with a given level of inertial costs of moving or of transition costs, K, which is a constant. Under these conditions, there will be an increase in effort only if the resulting gain in utility exceeds K.

A5. We assume that the effort-utility function EU is the aggregate of the function $U(E)$, which represents the utility derived from the work itself, and the function $U[Y(E)]$, which represents the utility derived from earnings. In general, therefore, $EU = U(E) + U[Y(E)]$.

A6. Finally, we assume that the function $U(E)$ is "normal" as defined by Leibenstein in the sense that it has the following characteristics:[10]

a. The worker prefers a certain level of effort at work to remaining completely idle; that is, the maximum for the function $U(E)$ is reached at a value $E > 0$.

---

7. Sectors in which earnings are not linked to work effort (e.g., public service) are not included in the analysis. It is clear that a variation in the income tax will have no effect on effort if gross and net income do not depend on real work effort.

8. This assumption is not so unrealistic as it might appear at first sight. Zones of proportional income tax do exist, e.g., in the U.S. and in the Federal Republic of Germany. Moreover, increased social security contributions are similar or identical in their impact to an increase in the income tax, as they are viewed as an extra burden by those affected. As social security contributions in the Federal Republic of Germany are proportional to gross income, they are regarded within the framework of our analysis as a proportional income tax. Our conclusions, therefore, also hold for changes in social security contributions.

9. The usual assumption of falling marginal utility of income is initially replaced by the assumption of constant marginal utility of income. This assumption is later abandoned.

10. See Bohnet and Beck 1986, 216; Leibenstein 1976, 107-8.

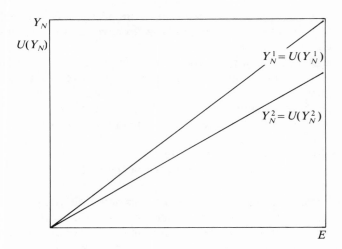

E = effort

Y_N^1 = net income before increase in income tax

Y_N^2 = net income after increase in income tax

$U(Y_N^1)$ = utility of net income before increase in income tax

$U(Y_N^2)$ = utility of net income after increase in income tax

Fig. 1. The relationship among effort, income,
and utility of income

    b. An increase in effort results in an initial increase in utility.
After a certain point, the marginal utility becomes negative
and the utility derived from the work itself declines.

    c. As it approaches its maximum, the function levels off, so
that changes in effort result only in insignificant changes in
utility.

Through the addition of $U(E)$ and $U(Y_N^1)$ or $U(Y_N^2)$, two effort-
utility functions $EU1$ and $EU2$ can be derived that represent the employee's positions when deciding upon the level of effort before and after the
increase in income tax. These two situations have to be compared.

The Situation before the Increase in Income Tax

Before the increase in income tax, there is one level of effort $^1E_{opt}^1$ at
which the worker's utility is maximized. We assume, however, that the
worker does not in fact attain this level because, for example, as the
result of a process of trial and error and unaware of the true course of

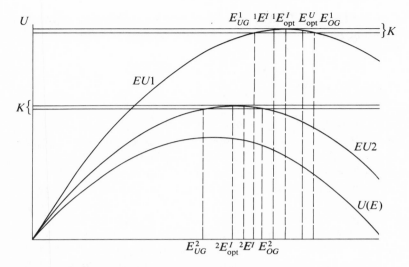

$EU1$ = effort-utility function before increase in income tax
$EU2$ = effort-utility function after increase in income tax
$U(E)$ = utility derived from work itself
E_{UG}^1 = lower bound of inert area before increase in income tax
E_{UG}^2 = lower bound of inert area after increase in income tax
E_{OG}^1 = upper bound of inert area before increase in income tax
E_{OG}^2 = upper bound of inert area after increase in income tax
E_{opt}^U = optimum effort position for employees from management's point of view
$^1E_{opt}^I$ = optimum effort position for employees from their point of view before increase in income tax
$^2E_{opt}^I$ = optimum effort position for employees from their point of view after increase in income tax
$^1E^I$ = employees effort position before increase in income tax
$^2E^I$ = employees effort position after increase in income tax
K = transition costs = inertial costs of moving

Fig. 2. Effort-utility function before and after the raising of a proportional income tax

$EU1$, the worker has decided in favor of the suboptimal effort level $^1E^I$. A later adjustment, however, would not prove worthwhile as any increase in utility would be less than the adjustment costs K. We assume that the individual concerned is situated within the individual's inert area and consequently at a personal point of equilibrium. The inert area encompasses all those levels that, once selected, will not be relinquished. In figure 2 the bounds of the inert area are represented by E_{UG}^1 and E_{OG}^1.

The utilities at levels E_{UG}^1 and E_{OG}^1 are equal and lower than the optimum by the amount represented by the transition costs K. It follows, therefore, that

$$EU1(E_{OG}^1) \; = \; EU1(E_{UG}^1) \; = \; EU1({}^1E_{opt}^I) \, - \, K. \tag{1}$$

Should the effort position lie below E_{UG}^1 or above E_{OG}^1, an increase or decrease in effort becomes worthwhile, as the worker can thus increase utility, even when taking the adjustment costs into consideration. If, however, the worker has decided upon level ${}^1E^I$, he or she will not abandon it, even though the utility at this level is lower than it would be at ${}^1E_{opt}^I$.

${}^1E^I$ will in most cases not coincide with E_{opt}^U, the optimum effort position from the management's point of view. It is much more probable that the worker's effort will be less than that which the firm considers optimal; in other words, the individual output will be too low. If this holds for a large number of workers or all workers, then the firm will be X-inefficient.

The Situation after an Increase in Income Tax

If income tax rates are raised, we must determine if and under what circumstances an employee will decide to vary the effort applied and how this will affect the degree of X-inefficiency.

In general, there will be an adjustment of effort only when the chosen level ${}^1E^I$ lies outside the bounds of the new inert area, which is determined by the effort-utility function after an increase in income tax, $EU2$. We must, therefore, first establish to what extent the two inert areas differ.

Let us first assume that the inert area has not shifted. In this case, there would be no adjustment of effort as the bounds of the old and new inert areas would coincide. Under the assumptions we have made, however, such a result is impossible! Through taxation, increased effort (i.e., increased income) would result in the deduction of increasing absolute amounts of utility. Initially $EU1(E_{OG}^1) = EU1(E_{UG}^1)$, so that for the effort-utility function after an increase in tax levels, it must follow that $EU2(E_{OG}^1) < EU2(E_{UG}^1)$. It is thus clear that E_{OG}^1 and E_{UG}^1 cannot represent the bounds of the new inert area, and there must have been a shift.

It can be shown that this must have been a shift to the left. Let us first observe how the optimal effort position for the individual is affected by the income tax. For this purpose, we must determine the maxima for the functions $EU1$ and $EU2$. Under assumptions A1, A2, A3, and A5,

$$EU1 = U(E) + U(Y_N^1) = U(E) + a \cdot E \qquad (2)$$

and

$$EU2 = U(E) + U(Y_N^2) = U(E) + (1-t) \cdot a \cdot E, \qquad (3)$$

where $0 < t < 1$, t being the average rate of taxation, and $a > 0$, a being a constant parameter.

Through differentiation of equations (2) and (3), we obtain the marginal utility functions for the situations before and after an increase in tax:

$$EU1' = U'(E) + a, \text{ and} \qquad (4)$$

$$EU2' = U'(E) + (1 - t) \cdot a. \qquad (5)$$

The maxima of both functions are determined by the conditions $U'(E) = -a$ respectively $U'(E) = -(1-t) \cdot a$. As $-a < -(1-t) \cdot a$ and on account of assumption A6b, it follows that the new optimum $^2E_{\mathrm{opt}}'$ must be smaller than $^1E_{\mathrm{opt}}'$. The optimum effort position for the individual employee shifts to the left.

We should now like to turn our attention to the effects of an increase in income tax on the lower bounds of the inert area. As $^2E_{\mathrm{opt}}' < {}^1E_{\mathrm{opt}}'$, it follows that $EU1(^2E_{\mathrm{opt}}') < EU1(^1E_{\mathrm{opt}}')$. However, because of the definition of the lower bound of the old inert area, this produces the relationship $EU1(^2E_{\mathrm{opt}}') - EU1(E_{UG}^1) < K$. Since the increase in income tax with increasing E results in constantly growing absolute losses in utility, we have the increased-tax relationship $EU2(^2E_{\mathrm{opt}}') - EU2(E_{UG}^1) < K$.

This means that $E_{UG}^1 \neq E_{UG}^2$; E_{UG}^2 must be smaller than E_{UG}^1 for the condition $EU2(^2E_{\mathrm{opt}}') - EU2(E_{UG}^2) = K$ to be fulfilled. The lower bound of the inert area shifts to the left.

Now let us focus our attention on the upper bound of the inert area. Since with increasing E an increase in income tax will result in increasing absolute losses in utility, $EU2(^1E_{\mathrm{opt}}') - EU2(E_{OG}^1) > K$, from which it follows that $EU2(^2E_{\mathrm{opt}}') - EU2(E_{OG}^1) > K$. Hence E_{OG}^1 cannot be equal to E_{OG}^2. As we are in the decreasing section of the $EU2$ curve, it necessarily follows that E_{OG}^2 must be smaller than E_{OG}^1. In other words, the upper bound of the inert area also shifts to the left!

We have thus shown that under the assumptions we have made, an employee's inert area will shift to the left following an increase in income tax.

Results

We are now in a position to consider some hypotheses with regard to the adjustment in effort and the change in the degree of X-inefficiency induced by a rise in income tax:

1. As the inert area shifts to the left, under no circumstances can there be an increase in work effort.
2. Should the inert area shift so far to the left that $E_{OG}^2 < E_{UG}^1$, the result will in every case be a reduction in effort.
3. If the inert areas overlap so that $E_{OG}^2 > E_{UG}^1$, two reactions are possible:
   a. If $^1E^I > E_{OG}^2$, the employee reduces effort.[11]
   b. If $E_{UG}^1 \leq {}^1E^I \leq E_{OG}^2$, there is no adjustment. The initial effort position lies in both inert areas with the result that the employee cannot improve his or her situation.
4. Ceteris paribus, a reduction in effort will take place earlier,
   a. the larger the increase in income tax,
   b. the lower the transition costs, K, and
   c. the higher the initial effort position, $^1E^I$ (i.e., the farther to the right in the inert area $^1E^I$ lies).
5. In the most favorable case, the degree of X-inefficiency remains constant. If at least a few workers will decide to reduce their efforts, their productivity, consequently, will decline and the degree of X-inefficiency will increase.
6. An increase in X-inefficiency is more likely, the more X-efficient a firm is initially. Relatively X-efficient firms are characterized by a comparatively low K, i.e., narrower inert areas and higher employees' effort positions, so that a reduction in effort is more probable.
7. Hypotheses 1–6 are valid with inverse signs for an income tax reduction.

Generalization of the Simple Model

In the last section, on the basis of very restrictive premises, we have put forward some hypotheses with regard to the effects on effort of an increase in income tax. We now wish to enlarge this simple model by showing that these hypotheses continue to hold if we relax our premises.
    Assumptions A1–A3 are modified as follows:

---

11. This is the case illustrated by figure 2.

A1′. We assume that there is a positive correlation between gross wages and effort, that is, as effort increases, so do gross wages. The linear relationship that we have assumed so far is then just a subcase.

A2′. It is assumed that there is a positive correlation between net and gross income both before and after the increase in income tax, so that marginal tax rates of 100 percent or more do not arise. In addition, the increase in income tax should be general (i.e., for any E^*, $Y_N^1(E^*) > Y_N^2(E^*)$).

A3′. We assume a positive decreasing marginal utility of net income.

We also make one additional assumption:

A7′. For any E,

$$\frac{dU_Y(Y_N^1)}{dE} > \frac{dU_Y(Y_N^2)}{dE} \tag{6}$$

$$[= U_Y''(Y_N^1) > U_Y''(Y_N^2)].$$

First let us see, with these modified premises, what impact an increase in income tax will have on the maximum of the *EU* function. For this purpose we shall modify the *EU* function slightly:

$$EU = U_E(E) + U_Y\{Y_N[Y_B(E)]\},$$

where

U_E = work satisfaction component of effort-utility function
U_Y = income component of effort-utility function
Y_B = gross earnings
Y_N = net earnings
E = effort.

The maximum of the *EU* function depends on E and will be the point where $EU' = 0$, so that it must hold that

$$-U_E' = U_Y' \text{ or } -U_E' = \frac{dU_Y}{dY_N} \cdot \frac{dY_N}{dY_B} \cdot \frac{dY_B}{dE}. \tag{7}$$

As a result of assumptions A1′ – A3′

$$\frac{dU_Y}{dY_N} > 0; \frac{dY_N}{dY_B} > 0; \frac{dY_B}{dE} > 0, \tag{8}$$

and

$$U_Y^r = \frac{dU_Y}{dY_N} \cdot \frac{dY_N}{dY_B} \cdot \frac{dY_B}{dE} > 0. \qquad (9)$$

For the situation before an increase in the income tax ($EU1$) we have the condition

$$-U_E^r = U_Y^r(Y_N^1), \qquad (10)$$

and for the situation after the increase in income tax ($EU2$),

$$-U_E^r = U_Y^r(Y_N^2), \qquad (11)$$

As we are on the decreasing curve of the U_E^r function and on account of assumption A7, it follows that the E value, which is the $EU2$ maximum, must be smaller than the corresponding $EU1$ value. In other words, $^1E_{opt}^I$ is larger than $^2E_{opt}^I$ and the maximum of the effort-utility function also shifts to the left under the new set of assumptions.[12] Figure 3 illustrates this clearly.

In figure 3 U_E^r represents the marginal utility derived from the work itself and U_Y^r that derived from the gross or net earnings resulting from different levels of effort. The respective optimum is attained where the positive marginal utility derived from the income earned equals the marginal cost in terms of effort. As $U_Y^r(Y_N^2)$ is situated below the $U_Y^r(Y_N^1)$ function for all values of E, and U_E^r does not depend on the tax, it follows that $^1E_{opt}^I > {}^2E_{opt}^I$.

Now that we have shown that E_{opt}^I shifts to the left, we must determine what effect an increase in income tax has upon the bounds of the inert area. Assumption A7 postulates that, in the case of increasing effort, a tax increase will result in ever increasing losses of utility. The vertical distance between $EU1$ and $EU2$ increases as effort is increased. Hence, with respect to the shifting of the bounds of the inert area, the arguments advanced in section 3 are also valid here and the inert area must shift to the left. The immediate result is that hypotheses 1–7 are also seen to be valid under the changed premises.

Let us finally consider briefly a special case that is not of great significance for us. Under the modified assumptions the EU function may have no maximum. This can occur if U_Y^r increases constantly, that is, if $U_Y^{''} > 0$. In this degenerate case the employee's maximum utility will be determined by that employee's individual effort frontier. If, however, the

---

12. This holds insofar as the EU function has a maximum at all! The special case $-U_E^r < U_Y^r$ for all values of E is for the moment exluded. We shall reconsider it later.

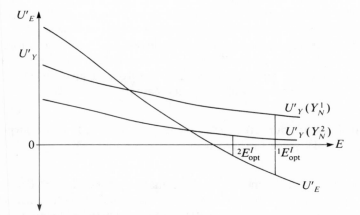

Fig. 3.   The shift of E^I_{opt} due to an increase in income tax

effort is on or near the employee's effort frontier, it is evident that in no case can an increase in income tax result in an increase in effort.

This also means that this special case in no way undermines the hypotheses we have advanced. Furthermore, it would appear to have little relevance even in practice, as it would occur only if the existing progressive income tax and the falling marginal utility of net income were to be overcompensated by a greater than proportional increase in gross effort-related income.[13]

Extensions of the Model

We wish to conclude the theoretical section of this article by outlining possible extensions of our model.

The first extension is the inclusion of management reactions. As we have pointed out, we have arrived at our conclusions on the assumption that the principal in the enterprise, the owner and/or manager, will not react to a variation in effort on the part of employees. This assumption we shall now abandon and consider possible reactions on the part of the firm's management and the consequences thereof with regard to hypotheses 1–7.

The firm's management can react in two possible ways:[14]

---

13. In this case it must at least hold that $(d^2Y_B)/(dE^2) > 0$.

14. Obviously, in practice combinations of the two possible reactions are possible. Here they have been separated for purely analytical reasons.

- It can increase gross earnings per unit of output to compensate for the disincentive created by the increase in income tax.
- It can increase pressure on employees (e.g., through more thorough checks on work effort or higher production targets) so that employees do not reduce their effort at a given level of gross income when income tax is increased.

Let us first turn our attention to the last alternative. For this purpose we wish to make some further assumptions:

A8. The gross income of the managers of the Firm Y_B^L depends on the profit resulting from the firm's activities. It is also subject to income tax and will, therefore, be affected by an increase in the latter.

A9. Labor costs are the only production costs. (This assumption is made only in the interests of simplicity.)

A10. Greater effort on the part of management implies increased pressure on employees and leads to greater effort on their part.

Let us now examine the firm's equilibrium situation before an increase in the income tax. Neither managers nor employees feel any need to change their effort positions although, from the management's point of view, the employees' effort position $^1E^I$ is lower than the optimum position E_{opt}^U. In other words, an increase in profits and, consequently, an increase in the managers' income would be possible if employees were to step up their effort. That the firm's managers do not apply more pressure in order to coax a higher effort from their employees leads us to conclude that such a measure would involve too high a cost in terms of managerial effort. In the initial situation, therefore, the absolute value of the manager's marginal effort is at least as high as the utility of his or her marginal income.

If, however, the employee reduces his or her effort as the result of an increase in income tax, the managers have a greater possibility of increasing their gross income. The marginal sacrifice may be lower than the marginal utility of the extra income to be expected. There will be incentives for management to make an extra effort to encourage employees to be more productive. The employees' effort position ($^2E_{tats}^I$) will then fluctuate between the positions before and after the increase in income tax without any reaction on the part of the managers, and

$$^2E^I < {}^2E^I_{\text{tats}} < {}^1E^I. \tag{12}$$

The position before the increase in income tax will not be attained again, as the extra effort involved for the management to reach $^1E^I$ will be greater than the obtainable marginal utility of the income. The point of equilibrium will be, therefore, somewhere in the middle.

This, however, is not our final conclusion, as we have not yet taken into consideration the following two factors:

- It is possible that there will be no reaction on the part of the firm's managers, who, in spite of the lower effort of their employees, remain within their inert areas and accept a lower income.
- The firm's managers must pay a higher tax on their incomes and, as we have shown in the case of employees, this will tend to result in a reduced effort on the part of the management. In this case the incentives are acting in opposite directions, and it is far from clear whether management's efforts will be lowered, maintained, or increased.

To sum up:

- Managers may respond by lowering, maintaining, or increasing their efforts. Under the assumptions we have made, their reactions cannot be predicted.
- Should there be no reaction on the part of management, hypotheses 1–7 can be maintained. If managers reduce their efforts, this will add to the negative impact of the increase in income tax and hypotheses 1–7 will not be invalidated. If managers step up their efforts, this will militate against, but not compensate for, the negative effects of the increase in income tax.

This leads us to the conclusion that management's reaction will not compensate for, and at best will alleviate and at worst will aggravate, the negative effects of an increase in income tax. Regardless of management's reaction, hypotheses 1–7 retain their validity as does the postulate that an increase in income tax results in greater X-inefficiency.

A similar argument applies in the case where management reacts with an increase in gross wages to a reduction in work effort on the part of employees. We shall consider this case very briefly.

Let us suppose that management maintains its level of effort and increases gross wages to a level where employees' net income after the tax increase for an effort level $^1E^I$ is equal to their net income before the increase. There would then be no incentive for an employee to lower his or her effort. In this case, the management's marginal sacrifice for a given effort level would exceed the marginal utility of its income, which would now be lower because of the higher wage costs. For management, therefore, it is not worth compensating the employees' reduction in net income by raising wages. Wage increases will be rather small and employees' real effort level will lie somewhere between $^2E^I$ and $^1E^I$. In this case hypotheses 1–7 still hold, as the following argument corresponds to that for the first possible reaction.

The second extension of our model is induced by the question: What would the reaction of workers be if they were at, or near, the subsistence level and the income tax were increased?[15] More generally, one can integrate a budget constraint (i.e., a minimum net income that an average worker wishes to receive) into the model.

In our model, net income depends on the level of effort the employee chooses. Let us assume that the minimum net income which a worker i wishes to earn (Y^N_{MIN}) corresponds to the effort level $^1E^I_{\text{MIN}}$ before, and to the level $^2E^I_{\text{MIN}}$ after the increase in income tax. Because of assumption A2′, it is obviously true that $^1E^I_{\text{MIN}} < {}^2E^I_{\text{MIN}}$. In other words: the effort level that must be chosen by the employee to receive the minimum net income Y^N_{MIN} increases, if the income tax is increased.

The worker's ability to reduce his effort is, therefore, restricted by the budget constraint. If the income tax is increased and if $^2E^I_{\text{MIN}} > {}^1E^I$, the employee is forced to raise his or her effort level.

If $^2E^I_{\text{MIN}} \leq {}^1E^I$, the conclusions in our article still hold, though the scope for an effort reduction is diminished, compared to a situation without a budget constraint.

The results can be summarized as follows:

- Integrating a budget constraint into our model yields (theoretically) ambiguous results. In general, the direction of the effort adjustment due to an increase in income tax cannot be predicted with certainty, because it depends on the relationship between $^2E^I_{\text{MIN}}$ and $^1E^I$.

  Whether, in reality, $^2E^I_{\text{MIN}}$ is smaller or greater than $^1E^I$ depends on the shape of the effort-utility function, the degree of the tax variation, and the level of Y^N_{MIN}.
- Nevertheless, in most cases our previous results still seem to be valid because workers with very low wages are not affected by a

---

15. The following revision and enlargement of our article is stimulated by the critique of Morris Altman and Roger S. Frantz.

change in income taxation. At least for industrialized countries with a high standard of living and with few (if any) workers living close to the subsistence level, we assert that workers will react by reducing their effort if the income tax is increased. The situation may be different in LDCs.

• One can expect that an increase in X-inefficiency is greater, the higher the percentage of workers receiving high effort-related wages in the firm or industry. Therefore, if one tries to test our hypotheses empirically, this figure should enter the multiple regression analysis as an independent variable.

Summing Up, Tentative Empirical Evidence, and Prospects

We now wish to sum up briefly the arguments we have presented and make a few final comments with respect to the empirical evidence and to those areas that we regard as particularly promising for future research.

Our main purpose in this article has not been to present a watertight and detailed theory of X-inefficiency and the effects of income tax variations on work effort. Our modest aim has been to draw attention to some relationships that have been largely ignored in the literature, although they are currently of great significance for reasons of taxation policy. We have analyzed these relationships in a simple model based on Leibenstein's analysis of X-efficiency in an attempt to arrive at some hypotheses that can be verified empirically with regard to the impact of a change in the income tax.

The most important conclusions to be drawn both from the simple and from the more complex approach are the following:

1. An increase (decrease) in the income tax results in a reduction (increase) in an employee's work effort and consequently leads to a rise (fall) in the degree of X-inefficiency in firms, sectors, and indeed the economy as a whole.
2. The negative impact on work effort of an increase in the income tax especially affects those enterprises that were relatively X-efficient before the tax increase.
3. It is possible to derive independently testable hypotheses from Leibenstein's X-efficiency theory, the empirical verification of which also constitutes a test of the relevance of Leibenstein's approach.

With regard to future research we feel that on a theoretical level, much could be done to enlarge the model and to work it out in greater detail. For this reason it should be established under what sufficient and necessary conditions our hypotheses still hold. This is tantamount to an attempt to determine the possible worlds to which the model could be applied or, in other words, to what extent it is of empirical relevance. The model should also be brought closer to reality by including and analyzing, for example, problems that may arise through uncertainty, multiple hierarchical levels, or coalitions.

Let us now turn to the empirical aspects of our approach. Of course it is very desirable to test our hypotheses empirically. Two methods can be applied:

- One can ask the workers directly how they would react if the income tax were increased.
- One can try to measure the impact of income tax variations indirectly by estimating changes in the degree of X-inefficiency due to such variations in income tax.

Fortunately, Bertelsmann-Stiftung (1985 and 1987) published two empirical studies dealing with worker motivation in the Federal Republic of Germany, which can be interpreted as applications of the first method. We present here some of the interesting results (See table 1).

- A significant number of workers are not fully satisfied or are dissatisfied with their jobs (48 percent).
- A large number of workers are willing to work harder (39 percent).
- About one-half of the workers are willing to work harder for a higher income (48 percent). Higher income is the most important factor influencing workers' motivation.
- High taxes and social security contributions are the most important factor in reducing workers' motivation.

As is clearly pointed out in the Bertelsmann-Stiftung studies a substantial potential for increasing work effort and total output exists. The most suitable measure to achieve a higher level of workers' motivation is to raise their net income; in principle, this can be achieved by raising gross wages or reducing income tax.

Although the studies just described are not a real empirical test, we believe that the results support our point of view and stress the necessity and value of further theoretical and empirical research on our topic.

TABLE 1. Job Satisfaction, Motivation, and Its Determinants (in percentage)

	Sample 1					Sample 2	
	Total[a]	Unskilled Workers	Skilled Workers	Lower Management	Middle Management	Top Management	Entrepreneur
Job satisfaction							
Fully satisfied	52%	32%	51%	54%	74%	68%	70%
Partly satisfied	40	43	44	40	25	31	28
Not satisfied	8	25	5	6	1	1	2
Willingness to work harder							
Yes	39	34	40	42	40	35	
No	61	66	60	58	60	65	
Willingness to work harder for a higher income	48					33	30
Averages[b]							
"It is not worth working harder because of the high taxes and social security contributions"	3.25	2.95	3.0	3.43	3.77	4.59	3.57

Source of data: Bertelsmann-Stiftung: Sample 1 1987; Sample 2 1985.
Note: Calculations by authors.
[a]Total of sample 1
[b]average based on a choice of 1–7; totally true = 1; totally false = 7

If one tries to apply the second, indirect, method of testing our hypotheses, at least two problems must be solved:

- The degree of X-inefficiency must be measured at the enterprise level before and after the tax increase in at least one sector with effort-related wages.
- The effects of the increase in income tax must be separated from those of other determinants of X-inefficiency.

Although a suitable method, the so-called frontier production function approach is at hand,[16] we are not able to measure the degree of X-inefficiency before and after tax increase on an enterprise level simply because the necessary data for the Federal Republic of Germany (that is, outputs and inputs in physical units) are not available.

The main purpose of the following empirical analysis at an industry level is to demonstrate how the frontier production function approach can be applied in principle to test the theoretical conclusions of our article empirically. Because of a number of limitations in the available data, the empirical results of applying this method to 30 West German manufacturing industries are of limited value.

The empirical analysis is carried out in four steps. In the first step, we calculate the level of X-inefficiency in the West German manufacturing industry for 1972 and 1974 (i.e., for a situation before and after an increase in income tax). Following Todd (1985), we use a deterministic, nonparametric frontier production function approach and utilize data for 30 manufacturing industries, published by the DIW (*Deutsches Institut für Wirtschaftsforschung*),[17] to determine the level of X-inefficiency for these industries. For the sake of simplicity, we assume linear homogeneity for the underlying production function and that one output (i.e., net output volume in DM) is produced with two inputs, labor (number of employees) and capital (gross fixed assets in DM).[18] The results of our calculations are presented in table 2, column 1 and 2.

In the second step, we measure the change in the degree of X-efficiency, which is the variable to be explained. Therefore we calculate the so-called dynamic X-efficiency (DE) for the 30 industries and the period 1972–74 as the ratio:

---

16. For a survey see, e.g., Färe, Grosskopf, and Lovell 1985.

17. See Krengel et al. 1975. Data on a firm level are not available.

18. The observations on output and capital are expressed in terms of the base year 1970.

$$DE7274 = \frac{XE74}{XE72} - 1, \tag{13}$$

where

DE7274 = dynamic X-efficiency in the period 1972–74
XE74 = X-efficiency in 1974
XE72 = X-efficiency in 1972

The period 1972–74 was chosen because there were several increases in income tax and because social security contributions rose from 13.55 percent to 14.60 percent.

If for a particular industry DE7274 has a positive (negative) sign, the degree of X-efficiency relative to the frontier has increased (decreased) over this time period. The results are presented in table 2, column 3.

TABLE 2. Variables

Industry	XE72 1	XE74 2	DE7274 3	SERW 4
Stone, Clay, Sand, etc.	0.5165	0.4490	–0.1308	
Iron and Steel Industries	0.3747	0.4761	0.2708	
Iron and Steel Foundries	0.4622	0.5070	0.0968	
Steel Drawing and Cold Running Mills	0.5720	0.5764	0.0077	
Non-Ferrous Metals Industries	0.3922	0.4277	0.0903	
Chemical Industry	0.5333	0.6135	0.1505	
Oil Refineries	1.0	1.0	0.0	
Rubber and Asbestos	0.5569	0.5416	–0.0275	0.4996
Sawmills and Timber	0.5154	0.5315	0.0331	
Cellulose, Paper, and Board Production	0.3431	0.4066	0.1850	
Steel Construction	1.0	0.9480	–0.0520	
Engineering	0.6657	0.6457	–0.0302	0.3078
Office and Data Processing Machinery	0.7355	0.7093	–0.0357	
Vehicle Building and Repairs	0.5379	0.4856	–0.0973	0.3776
Shipbuilding	0.4795	0.5300	0.1054	
Aircraft and Aerospace	0.9476	1.0	0.0553	
Electrical Equipment	0.7609	0.7703	0.0124	0.3829
Precision Engineering	0.6972	0.7188	0.0309	0.3733
Metal Products	0.7683	0.7505	–0.0231	0.2800
Fine Ceramics	0.6313	0.6392	0.0125	0.4163
Glass Industry	0.7011	0.6855	–0.0233	0.1068
Wood Processing	0.9557	0.8415	–0.1194	0.3386
Musical Instruments, Toys, Games	0.8962	0.7717	–0.1389	0.3058
Paper and Board Processing	0.6592	0.6480	–0.0171	0.1399
Printing	0.7272	0.7052	–0.0302	0.0148
Plastics Manufacturing	0.7934	0.7773	–0.0203	0.1496
Leather	0.7265	0.6249	–0.1536	0.5201
Textiles	0.5127	0.4956	–0.0333	0.3272
Clothing Industry	1.0	0.8898	–0.1101	0.4827
Food, Drink, and Tobacco	0.6161	0.6490	0.0532	0.0482

In this article we have asserted that the level of dynamic X-efficiency should be negatively correlated with the degree of X-efficiency in the starting period (i.e., with XE72) and with an increase in income tax rates. The smaller the percentage of employees paid effort-related wages, the smaller is the impact of an increase in income tax.[19]

Therefore, in the third step, we calculate the ratio

$$\text{SERW} = \frac{\text{NEEW}}{\text{TNE}}, \tag{14}$$

where

NEEW = Number of employees paid by effort-related wages
TNE = Total number of employees
SERW = Share of effort-related wages

as the second independent variable explaining DE. Unfortunately, due to limitations in our data source, it is possible to measure SERW only for 17 industries in 1972 (Dohna-Lauck 1982, 252 and 256). The results are shown in table 2, column 4. DE is expected to be negatively correlated with SERW.

In the fourth and last step, we use a multiple regression approach to determine the influence of XE72 and SERW on DE7274. The results presented in tables 3 and 4 are not very promising. The estimation coefficients for XE72 and SERW have the expected negative sign and are statistically significant at the 90 percent level. But the adjusted R^2 is rather low (.2922).

There may be several reasons for the unsatisfactory empirical results:

- The high level of aggregation may hide differences at the firm level.
- Not all explaining variables are included in the regression analysis.
- SERW may not be the correct measure to determine the influence of income tax changes in the various industries.
- The degree of variations in income tax and social security contributions may be too small to influence human effort in the period considered.

---

19. The impact of high effort-related wages cannot be tested because of the lack of data.

TABLE 3. Empirical results of the Regression Analysis

Independent variable	coefficient	SE	t Value	p Value
CONSTANT	.143748	.070012	2.0532	.0592
XE72	.195313	.092455	−2.1125	.0531
SERW	.15264	.081912	−1.8635	.0835

R^2 (adj. for *d.f.*) = .2922   SE = .050765   MAE = .037686   DurbWat = 1.606

Note: 17 observations fitted, forecast(s) computed for 0 missing value of dependent variable.

TABLE 4. Analysis of Variance for the Full Regression

Source	Sum of Squares	d.f.	Mean Square	f Ratio	p value
Model	.0221732	2	.0110866	4.30204	.0350
Error	.0360788	14	.00257705		
Total (Corr.)	.0582519	16			

R^2 = .380643 R^2 (adj. for *d.f.*) = .292163   SE = .0507647
Durbin-Watson statistic = 1.60626

- Other determinants of the degree of X-inefficiency (e.g., the degree of competition) were not taken into account.
- The chosen period, 1972–74, may not have been normal because of the oil price shock and changes in the exchange rate system.
- Not all factors of production were taken into account. Therefore, the calculated level of X-inefficiency may be wrong.
- The assumptions underlying the frontier production function approach may be too simple.[20]

Nevertheless, we think that the method presented here is principally suitable to test theoretical hypotheses on X-efficiency if better data are at hand.

REFERENCES

Andel, N. 1983. *Finanzwissenschaft*. Tübingen: J. C. B. Mohr (Paul Siebeck).
Bertelsmann-Stiftung; Institut für Wirtschafts- und Gesellschaftspolitik, eds. 1985. *Die Arbeitsmotivation von Führungskräften der deutschen*. Gütersloh: Selbstverlag.

---

20. These restrictive assumptions can be easily relaxed. See Färe, Grosskopf, and Lovell 1985.

Bertelsmann-Stiftung; Institut für Wirtschaft und Gesellschaft Bonn e.V., eds. 1987. *Die Arbeitsmotivation von Arbeitern und Angestellten der deutschen Wirtschaft*. Gütersloh: Verlag Bertelsmann Stiftung.

Bohanon, C. E., and T. N. Van Cott. 1986. "Labor Supply and Tax Rates: Comment." *American Economic Review* 76:277-79.

Bohnet, A., and M. Beck. 1986. "X-Effizienz-Theorie: Darstellung, Kritik, Möglichkeiten der Weiterentwicklung." *Zeitschrift für Wirtschaftspolitik* 35:211-33.

Brown, C. V. 1983. *Taxation and the Incentive to Work*. 2d ed. Oxford: Oxford University Press.

De Alessi, L. 1983a. "Property Rights, Transaction Costs, and X-Efficiency: An Essay in Economic Theory." *American Economic Review* 73:64-81.

De Alessi, L. 1983b. "Property Rights and X-Efficiency: Reply." *American Economic Review* 73:843-45.

Dohna-Lauck, U. 1982. *Die Lohnstruktur von Frauen in der Industrie der Bundesrepublik Deutschland*. Bonn: University of Bonn Press.

Färe, R., S. Grosskopf, and C. A. K. Lovell. 1985. *The Measurement of Efficiency of Production*. Boston: Kluwer Nijhoff Publishing.

Gahvari, F. 1986. "Labor Supply and Tax Rates: Comment." *American Economic Review* 76:280-83.

Gwartney, J., and R. Stroup. 1983. "Labor Supply and Tax Rates: A Correction of the Record." *American Economic Review* 73:446-51.

Gwartney, J., and R. Stroup. 1986. "Labor Supply and Tax Rates: Reply." *American Economic Review* 76:284-85.

Häuser, K. 1979. "Wirkungen der Einkommensteuer auf das individuelle Arbeitsangebot." In *Wirtschaftswissenschaft als Grundlage staatlichen Handelns*, ed. P. Bohley and G. Tolkemitt, 177-89. Tübingen: J. C. B. Mohr (Paul Siebeck).

Hausman, J. A. 1981. "Labor Supply." In *How Taxes Affect Economic Behavior*, ed. H. J. Aaron and J. A. Pechman, 27-83. Washington, D.C.: The Brookings Institution.

Heilemann, U., and H. D. von Löffelholz. 1987. "Zum Einfluß der Besteuerung auf Arbeitsangebot und -nachfrage." *Steuersystem und wirtschaftliche Entwicklung, Beihefte der Konjunkturpolitik* 33:155-76.

Koch, W. A. S. 1984. *Einkommensteuern und Leistungswirkungen*. Berlin: Dunker and Humblot.

Krengel, R., et al. 1975. *Produktionsvolumen und -potential, Produktionsfaktoren der Industrie im Gebiet der Bundesrepublik Deutschland einschließlich Saarland und Berlin (West)*. Statistische Kennziffern, 17. Folge, Neuberechnung 1970-1974. Berlin: Deutsches Institut für Wirtschaftsforshung.

Leibenstein, H. 1976. *Beyond Economic Man: A New Foundation for Microeconomics*. Cambridge, Mass.: Harvard University Press.

Leibenstein, H. 1979. "X-Efficiency: From Concept to Theory." *Challenge* 22:13-22.

Leibenstein, H. 1987. *Inside the Firm: The Inefficiencies of Hierarchy.* Cambridge, Mass.: Harvard University Press.

Linde, R. 1984. *Lohn und Leistung.* Göttingen: Vandenhoeck und Ruprecht.

Rosen, H. S. 1980. "What Is Labor Supply and Do Taxes Affect It?" *American Economic Review, Papers and Proceedings* 70:171–76.

Todd, D. 1985. "Productive Performance in West German Manufacturing Industry 1970–80: A Farrell Frontier Characterisation." *Journal of Industrial Economics* 23:295–316.

Wagner, H. 1987. "Arbeitsangebot, Freizeitarbeit und Folgen einer Rationierung: Kritik und Erweiterung der traditionellen neoklassischen Arbeitsangebotstheorie." *Jahrbücher für Nationalökonomie und Statistik* 203:138–51.

The Charitable Nonprofit Sector:
X-Efficiency, Resource Allocation,
and Organization

R. C. O. Matthews

How far is the X-efficiency concept applicable to charities and other nonprofit bodies? Insofar as it is, in what respects is its application in that sector distinctive? How do alternative nonprofit forms of organization affect X-efficiency? How, reciprocally, do X-efficiency considerations affect the organizational forms that are adopted? How do the efficiency and organization of nonprofit bodies respond to changes in the environment, and to what extent are they subject to change over time as a result of their own evolution? These are the kinds of questions that relate the nonprofit sector to the theme of the Bellagio conference.

The article is arranged as follows. I consider in turn the various types of nonprofit bodies that exist and the scope of the charitable nonprofit sector as I shall define it; the meaning of the concept of efficiency, seen in relation to the motives of charitable donors; the various influences on the efficiency of the sector and their effects; and, finally, the response of the sector to a major change, viz., the growth in the activities of the state.

One point should be mentioned at this stage. Legal considerations loom large in this field. The law referred to in this article is English law. U.S. law is broadly similar, deriving as it does from the same historical origin, the Statute of Charitable Uses of 1601 (*43 Eliz.I.c.4*), the influence of which has proved remarkably long lasting, though U.S. law has come to differ in a number of respects from English law, particularly in regard to public surveillance. Legal provisions in continental Europe have different origins and will not be discussed.

I am grateful for comments and information to participants in the conference and to James Cornford, Frank Hahn, Roger Schofield, and Bob Scribner.

The Charitable Nonprofit Sector: Definition and Categories

The nonprofit sector is extremely heterogeneous. Not all of it falls within the scope of this article, which is concerned with charitable nonprofit organizations (charities). Even among charities, there are some important differences in type. Consideration of those differences already introduces matters relating to efficiency.

The definition of a nonprofit organization is a negative one: "nondistribution" is the essence. In the conventional firm, the residual claimants on the operating surplus are the owners of the equity capital. Hence, on the principle that an efficient incentive structure requires power and responsibility to go together, the firm is typically managed by persons accountable to shareholders (Alchian and Demsetz 1972). But that is not the only possible form of business organization. Another is the producer cooperative, in which the residual claimants are the workers in the firm, or some of them (the partners), and these people or their agents are accordingly the managers. Another possible form is the consumer cooperative. The causes and consequences of the formation of such organizations as producer and consumer cooperatives have been intensively studied in the literature on worker-management relationships and on clubs.

Ostensibly charitable bodies, whose constitutions lay down purposes other than the advancement of their members' interests, may de facto be captured and operated as producer cooperatives: hospitals by doctors, monasteries by monks, universities by professors; or they may have been set up with that intention from the start. In the case of the private nonprofit hospital, which has been the focus of much of the U.S. literature on nonprofit organizations, it has been suggested that a nonprofit but de facto cooperative form has emerged in order to permit a system of separate charging (for physicians' services and for hospital services) that provides a good incentive structure in the face of the difficulty in measuring physicians' output (Pauly and Redisch 1973). Or, again with measurement difficulties in mind, producers may decide that it is in their interests to impose quite bona fide upper limits on their earnings so as to dispel suspicions of opportunism (Easley and O'Hara 1983), especially if they think that competition will probably restrict their earnings anyway.

Organizations that are cooperatives, whether de jure or de facto, are not nondistributive in the broader sense, even if they do not distribute profit to shareholders. In the language of charity law, they are self-help organizations, a disqualification for charitable status. They therefore fall outside the scope of this article.

For present purposes, charities may be defined in terms of their objectives: they are nonprofit bodies whose constitution or trust deed lays down as objectives some maximand other than the interests of the limited class of people who are their members. The ultimate beneficiaries may be the public as a whole (e.g., by conservation of the environment), some part of the public (e.g., one-parent families), or an abstract principle (e.g., the advancement of knowledge, the glorification of God). This definition is broadly similar to the legal one but rather wider in that the law imposes certain restrictions on charitable purposes, even if their altruism is not in doubt — for example, the promotion of games and sport is not included, nor, most important, is the advancement of purposes that are deemed to be political. I shall for brevity refer to the various possible objectives of charities as good causes. They fall under very much the same headings as the standard categories of government expenditure. These are relief of poverty (income maintenance), the central purpose of charity in popular parlance and also its central purpose as seen in the Statute of Charitable Uses; the provision of public goods (research, environment); the correction of other sources of market failure (education); and the provision of merit goods (religion, art).

A nearly equivalent definition would be that a charity is a nonprofit body that receives or has in the past received donations in cash or kind or in unpaid services. This must be true of any charity, since at the least it requires the unpaid services of the people who take the trouble to set it up. There is, moreover, a close connection between nonprofit status and the receipt of gifts. A body that wants to be able to receive donations must normally be run on nonprofit lines, even if it might have preferred to combine altruistic objectives with a modicum of the profit motive, because otherwise no donor can be sure that his gift will be used for the altruistic purpose intended. (To protect against possible lack of bona fides in grant-giving bodies, such bodies are in any case prohibited by the law from making grants to profit-making organizations.)

There are some organizations that fall into a grey area. Since I am not trying in this article to lay down definitions capable of application in a court, I can be relaxed about whether they are to be included or not. They raise some of the same considerations as charities proper. One is the old-fashioned kind of friendly society, which is run on behalf of its members rather than the public but which customarily involves an input of effort on the part of its founders and its most active members out of proportion to any personal benefit they derive. Another is typified by a church supported by voluntary collections from members of its congregation. This is quantitatively a very important category: in the United States, and doubtless in many other countries, too, giving to churches is far larger than any other class of giving (Pifer 1987). Is the money put in the plate to be regarded as an attendance fee or as a donation? The amount given is determined by the contributor, according to means. It can be regarded as similar to a Lindahl price in public finance theory. If it is regarded as just a fee, the question arises why richer-than-average members of the congregation should consent to be discriminated against, since they will not be turned away if they make only a small contribution. It seems only natural, therefore, to regard any contributions above the minimum as donations. Churches are, of course, legally charities, whereas friendly societies are not. The importance of religion in the whole sphere of charity will be referred to again.

Charitable giving does not necessarily require the existence of any organization at all. The donor could make his gift directly to the ultimate beneficiary, as in traditional almsgiving. But it is likely that in a large proportion of cases it will be most efficient for the gift to be made through an intermediary organization because of economies of scale either in transaction costs or, in the case where the gift takes the form of a service rather than cash, in production costs. The intermediary organization then both receives gifts and makes them. Efficiency in direct giving is not X-efficiency in the normal sense; it is more like efficiency in consumption. However, it is affected by many of the same considerations that apply to charitable organizations, and it will be included in the reckoning when we consider the efficiency of the charitable system as a whole.

Charities differ considerably in the way they function. The following distinctions may be noted.

- Operating, i.e., producing a service, versus nonoperating, i.e., grant giving. This is largely a matter of vertical integration; nonoperating charities make grants to operating ones
- Producing or financing the production of public goods versus making grants in cash (doles) or in kind to individuals as ultimate beneficiaries
- In the case of operating charities, fee charging to some or all users versus nonfee charging
- Endowed versus collecting
- Using significant amounts of volunteer labor versus relying on paid staff

Many other lines of distinction may be drawn. Thus a particular field may be occupied by one charity only or by several (horizontal integration). Or the purposes of a charity may be general or specific (lateral integration). Rather different efficiency considerations arise in each case. Some examples will be given presently.

The heterogeneity of charities invalidates simple, all-purpose indicators as measures of efficiency. One such indicator, sometimes used, is the ratio of administrative expenses to turnover. This ratio must tend to be higher for retailing charities, which make grants to individuals, than it is for wholesaling charities, which make grants to other charities.

Efficiency Criteria and Donors' Motivation

As defined by Leibenstein (1978, 17–18), X-efficiency theory in the narrow sense is concerned with the difference between the actual and the maximum possible output per *given* input of resources. General X-efficiency theory is defined to include also deviations between actual and maximum exploitation of opportunities, resulting from the *choice* of inputs; it thus includes allocative efficiency as one component. In the present context, general X-efficiency is the more relevant concept. Indeed opportunities need to be understood in a rather broad sense to take account of the fact that some charities have no output at all in the normal sense. Thus a charity for the relief of poverty achieves only a transfer of purchasing power (moreover, if it uses exclusively volunteer labor, it may also have no input as normally measured). However, such a charity may achieve the transfers more or less successfully, in relation to its purposes, so the concept of efficiency remains relevant.

Leibenstein's discussion of psychology and motivation relates to people as producers. He refers to selective rationality, to the effort requirements of action, to the effort requirements of change, and to principal-agent problems. No distinctive problems arise in applying these concepts to the paid employees of charities. There are likewise many aspects of the efficiency or otherwise of charities that raise no distinctive conceptual problems: whether a nonprofit hospital, say, has good diagnostic arrangements or whether a foundation has a good filing system or whether a collecting charity is good at keeping down the transaction costs of collection.

Certain questions do arise, however, about how the motives of donors of cash and volunteer labor are to be treated in the assessment of efficiency. Should the concept of efficiency take into account the degree to which the outcome satisfies the donors? Or should it take account only of the degree of success in attaining the ostensible purpose of their benefactions? The ostensible purpose of a gift to a charity is that laid down in the charity's constitution, narrowed possibly by conditions attached to the particular gift. In the case of direct almsgiving, the purpose is the welfare of the recipient. However, donors may have self-interested motives as well. Matters are further complicated by the difficulty of modeling satisfactorily the motive for even genuinely charitable giving. The conventional doctrine is that the motive is benevolence toward recipients, i.e., internalization of the utility of others (or of some others or of some aspects of their utility). However, this doctrine leads to paradoxes (Sugden 1982),[1] and it appears to need supplementation, at least, by reference to sense of duty, including the duty not to be a free rider; the charitable motive to that extent makes itself felt as a constraint on maximization rather than as a part of the maximand. Be that as it may, cynics have naturally tried to impute more self-interested motives to donors. These include: desire for fame or honor or gratitude; self-righteousness; deflection of criticism; avoidance of eternal damnation; weakness in the face of bullying by fund-raisers; in the case of businesses, advertisements or the currying of favor with governments; in the case of donations of labor time, the benefit of work experience or the enjoyment of the work itself. Historically, a variety of motives have no doubt played a part, not necessarily always in the same proportion.

If altruism is regarded as a "taste" (Becker 1976), it could be held that the criterion of efficiency is how far a donor's objectives were achieved, whether they were altruistic or self-interested. Giving can be treated just like any other consumer good. If the donor's real object is to gain a knighthood, and the donor succeeds, why not just say the operation is efficient, even though its ostensible purpose came to nothing? It was the donor's money—if the donor chose to spend it that way rather than in buying a yacht, what business is that of anyone else? However, even if we grant that charitable giving is a taste, i.e., part of the maximand, that way of looking at it would seem to me to miss the point. Giving is a taste that has a distinctive feature, viz., positive externalities. It is reasonable, therefore, in judging efficiency to focus on how far the positive externalities are attained and leave the donor's utility out of the reckoning. This is not to deny that the utility to the donor of making a

---

1. The kind of paradox pointed out by Sugden is this. Suppose that being a benevolent person but not a saint, I derive utility both from my own consumption and, to a lesser degree, from the consumption of the beneficiaries of Oxfam; and suppose that the marginal rate of substitution between the two in my utility function is diminishing in the usual way. I maximize my utility by giving £20 a year to Oxfam. Suppose now that all the many other people who previously supported Oxfam stop doing so and instead give the money to me, with no strings attached. For consistency, I should then give all my enormous extra income to Oxfam, so maintaining constant both my own consumption and the consumption of the beneficiaries of Oxfam. This seems such an implausible outcome as to suggest that there is something seriously wrong with the underlying model.

gift, or of making a gift for a particular purpose, may be relevant for broader welfare purposes.

As far as the X-efficiency of the individual charity is concerned, the same conclusion can be reached by another path. We can regard the act of giving as marking a Marshallian short-run/long-run division, a "fundamental transformation" in the sense of Williamson (1985); once the donor has made the gift, the donor must be deemed to be committed to its ostensible purpose, and we can forget about the donor's motives in making it, which, in any event, we can never know for sure.

The question remains by what criterion the value of the positive externalities should be judged. Should the criterion be, in principle, the interests of the potential beneficiaries of the particular good cause laid down in the charity's constitution? Or should it be broader than that and consist of the interests of the potential beneficiaries of all kinds of charitable giving, or even of the population as a whole?

These questions underlie a well-known crux in charity law, discussed already by J. S. Mill in 1869. We lack information about the future. We lack forever information about what will happen when we are dead. How much respect, then, should be paid by trustees and by the law to testators' wishes about the use of their charitable bequests? If circumstances have changed, should trustees still try to stick as closely as possible to the purposes stated in the will that set up the trust, as required by the legal principle of cy pres? Or should they be free to transfer the resources to some entirely different charitable purpose if they think that might be more useful? The issue of principle is not confined to deceased donors. Living donors, too, make gifts to purposes that are based on faulty information or are otherwise ill conceived.

The dilemma suggests that the efficiency of charities can be assessed at two levels: the efficiency of a charity in serving, within the resources available to it, the particular good cause or causes laid down in its constitution; and the goodness of that cause, or those causes, both absolutely and relative to the other causes that might have been pursued. Each of these may be affected by the internal arrangements of individual charities and by the framework of public policy within which they operate. Taken together, they are relevant to relative system efficiency, that is to say, the efficiency of the charitable system as a means of achieving certain goals, relative to the efficiency of alternative systems in the shape of self-help or government action. Charity failure may be considered alongside market failure and government failure.

Assessment of the relative goodness of different good causes inevitably involves subjective elements, since the possible ultimate beneficiaries are too diffuse for their benefits to be measured, let alone weighed against each other. But it would be pendantic to take agnosticism to extremes. Indeed, it is not difficult to think of altruistic purposes of expenditure that, by common consent, would have bad effects rather than good ones (e.g., relieving the poverty of alcoholics by giving them free liquor). At certain periods of history, quite a large proportion of charitable giving has been thought to fall into that class, on the grounds that it distorted the incentives of the poor and developed in them an addiction to handouts. Hence in a famous dispute Beatrice Webb's sarcastic designation of the Charity Organisation Society, which took that view, as the Charity Prevention Society (Webb 1926, Mowat 1961). There is no need to share the views of the Charity Organisation Society in order to grant that some good causes are more good than others.

The next section will be concerned with the various possible sources of inefficiency. Given that inefficiency is bound to be present to some degree, it is a separate question what, if anything, should be done about it by public policy. Mill's problem was one of the property rights of testators, chiefly in relation to their trustees. This is a problem with which the law has to concern itself. Charities are corporate bodies and hence, at the least, the law must make clear the rights and duties of the parties involved, as it does with companies. Testators do not in any case have unrestricted property rights over the use of their estates; they are not allowed to set up noncharitable perpetuities, for example, nor are they allowed, nowadays, to cut their families off with a shilling. In regard to charitable bequests, there is a trade-off. If testators were allowed to dictate the purposes forever, waste would result because of changes in circumstances that they could not have foreseen. On the other hand, if it were known that trustees had a free hand to do what they liked, charitable bequests would be discouraged, presumably with prejudice to the public interest. Hence the case for some second-best middle path.

How far it is desirable for the state to be able to alter the purposes for which charitable funds have been given, whether by deceased donors or by living ones, is another matter altogether. Respect by the state for the expressed wishes of donors and trustees is partly a matter of adherence to whatever general system of property rights prevails. It is also partly a matter of the system of property rights deemed most appropriate in the particular case of charities. In deciding what that system should be, it is admittedly not possible to invoke without qualification the general case for decentralized decision making, namely, that people are the best judges of their own needs, since it is not their own needs that are at issue. However, in the case of giving, too, the arguments for having a pluralistic system are obvious.

Questions about the relative efficiency of charities and of governments are partly of a familiar general kind, lying outside the scope of this article, about the efficiency or otherwise of governments. However, some points specifically relevant to the overlap between state spending and charitable spending will be mentioned later.

Influences on Efficiency

At the micro-microlevel, the efficiency of charities depends on influences that I shall discuss under the following headings: (i) information availability and bounded rationality; (ii) opportunism and incentives to effort; and (iii) entrepreneurship. In addition, the efficiency of individual charities and of the charitable system as a whole is affected by (iv) competition. The operation of these influences may be compared with their operation in the business sector, taking the latter simply as a benchmark, not with any necessary implication that the two institutional arrangements are substitutable. The potential strengths and weaknesses in charities in regard to efficiency affect and are affected by their organization.

Information Availability and Bounded Rationality

Of the various types of good cause, public goods and income maintenance do not have a market price, nor does the meritorious aspect of merit goods. Therefore, the price mechanism does not provide any shortcut information on the value of a charitable operation at the margin in the way that it does for business operations. In its absence, detailed scrutiny of miscellaneous indicators is likely to be needed. This helps to explain certain features of charitable organizations. It also points to unavoidable imperfections in the way the system works.

The need for information, for purposes both of ex-ante evaluation and of ex-post monitoring, is part of the reason why charities have tended to be set up for restricted purposes, for example, for the benefit of residents in a particular place. The restriction makes the information easier to get by direct observation and easier to digest. In the same way, large charitable foundations, even if they do have broadly defined objectives in their constitutions, almost always in practice narrow them and run a limited number of programs or schemes; or, alternatively, they confine themselves to a wholesaling role, leaving the detailed allocation of funds to intermediary recipients.

This kind of consideration has implications for the optimum size of charitable units. Very small units, including direct almsgiving as the limiting case, may be nonoptimal on account of the presence of overhead cost elements in the collection of information. But a relatively small charity may be more efficient for some purposes than a big one because it is better placed to exploit personal knowledge without putting undue strain on bounded rationality.

Such considerations about division of labor in the gathering and processing of information are essentially Hayekian. They operate more strongly than in the Hayekian context of the profit-maximizing firm, inasmuch as the value of the product has to be assessed qualitatively rather than by the common denominator of profit. But a proliferation of small charities provides no check against divergences appearing between the usefulness of expenditure on alternative good causes at the margin. If the prevention of such divergences were given the top priority, the logical outcome might be a monopolistic national charity.

However, that would be open not only to Hayekian objections but also to objections on the motivational side. Divergences in usefulness at the margin are of two types: divergences due purely to lack of information, which donors in principle would be quite happy to see ironed out, and divergences that arise because donors deliberately favor one good cause rather than another. Donors do differ in the good causes they want to promote. They likewise differ in the kind of unpaid labor they want to offer. So the attractions of subscribing money or labor time to an all-purpose national charity would be extremely feeble (very few people make gifts to the state). This restriction on size does not have an analogy in business firms. It helps, moreover, to explain why collecting charities, which have to win the favor of the public, tend to have narrower objectives than endowed foundations set up by a single rich donor.

Some of the consequences of bounded rationality can, as suggested, be mitigated by suitable choice of organizational structure. However, there is good reason to suppose that donors' rationality is not only bounded but also systematically biased in certain respects. It is well attested that donors are disproportionately attracted to purposes that are spectacular — "salient," in the terminology of Downs (1957). For example, blindness is a more spectacular disability than deafness, and charities for the blind are, I believe, a good deal better off in relation to their needs than charities for the deaf. Disaster appeals are another area where saliency and narrow purpose have sometimes combined to yield relative overallocation of charitable funds. A well-known British example was the Aberfan Disaster Fund, which was set up in 1966 after the collapse of a coal tip had buried a school, with heavy loss of life among the children. The public was so moved by the horrifying nature of the disaster that far more money was subscribed than could possibly be used to compensate the inhabitants for their financial losses. The allocation of the remainder became a source of embarrassment and rancor (Chesterman 1979, 339–46).

Another application of the principles of biased rationality and saliency is implicit in the dry comments in David Hume's *History of England* on the remuneration of the clergy, quoted in Smith's *Wealth of Nations*. If the stipends of the clergy, says Hume, instead of being fixed, as in the Church of England, depended on the subscriptions of their congregations, their zeal would be stimulated. On the face of it that would be a desirable outcome.

> But if we consider the matter more closely, we shall find, that this interested diligence of the clergy is what every wise legislator will study to prevent. . . . Each ghostly practitioner, in order to render himself more precious and sacred in the eyes of his retainers, must . . . continually endeavour, by some novelty, to excite the languid devotion of his audience. . . . Every tenet will be adopted that best suits the disorderly affections of the human frame. Customers will be drawn to each conventicle by new industry and address in practising on the passions and credulity of the populace. And in the end the civil magistrate will find . . . that in reality the most decent and advantageous composition, which he can make with the spiritual guides, is to bribe their indolence, by affixing stated salaries to their profession. (Hume 1759, 1:117)

Opportunism and Incentives to Effort

It is common to treat under the same heading opportunism, meaning use of guile in pursuit of one's own interests (Williamson 1985), and the incentives to effort, as determined by rewards and penalities for efficient or inefficient performance. In the charitable sphere, the two work rather differently in some respects. Let us consider the various parties in the charitable chain.

The ultimate beneficiaries, in the case of income-maintenance charities, may, obviously, practice opportunism by exaggerating their needs (the question of effort by them on behalf of the charity does not arise). Moreover, compared with recipients of money (sellers) in the business sector, they are likely to be less subject to the discipline of repeat transactions, provided there are many donors: money has zero asset specificity! Hence public policy customarily discourages beggars as they are likely to take advantage of ill-informed individual donors. It insists instead that claims of potential recipients be made in some way that enables them to be systematically scrutinized. Hence, too, the moral-hazard dilemma in all income-maintenance schemes, whether private or public: how to confine relief to those genuinely in need without weakening the incentive to avoid becoming in need.

At the other end of the chain, donors of cash are not likely to be involved in opportunism. If they are genuinely altruistic, it is not something they would wish to practice. Even if they have ulterior motives, they are not in a good position to practice opportunism. At the same time, effort is not something they are called on to display in their capacity merely as donors, leaving aside possible entrepreneurial roles (see below). However, ulterior motives may influence their choice between alternative good causes and thereby affect efficiency in the broader of the two senses.

Donors of labor time are of crucial importance in small local operating charities and as collectors of contributions for national collecting charities (their input in the United States is estimated as equivalent of 5 percent of the total labor force [Menchik and Weisbrod 1987]). As with donors of cash, they are under no obligation to do what they do, and the question of opportunism hardly arises. They are called on to display effort, however. The efficiency of their inputs is determined only by their personal motivation since they do not receive either rewards or penalties. Voluntary workers do not submit to the same discipline as employees. They can pick and choose what to do. In the words of one charity administrator, "there is no chain of command . . . everything has to be done by goodwill and good relations" (quoted in Murray 1974, 29). This may lead to what looks like inefficiency. To the individual charity, however, restrictions on what volunteers are prepared to do are a datum, just like restrictions on purpose that may be imposed by donors of cash. They therefore do not necessarily constitute a source of X-inefficiency in the narrow sense, though they may certainly be relevant to overall system efficiency.

Employees of charities, including their managers, are in much the same position in respect of the internal working of the organization as employees in those business firms where payment by results is not feasible. Hence arise questions about monitoring, delegation, divisional structure, and so on. These may be quite important questions, but they are not essentially different from those discussed in modern industrial organization literature. In respect of relations to outside donors, however, managers of operating charities are a bit like beggars. Opportunism is facilitated by the lack of objective measures of the value of the operating charity's output — within limits, of course, since really bad performance will be clear enough. Admittedly, the managers will not be able to pocket the proceeds personally, and that is a significant safeguard. But they may gain personal advantages in other ways (security, empire-building). In addition, naturally, they are likely to use at least some elements of guile on behalf of the operating charity itself, if only in not going out of their way to draw attention to its weak points. This is expected of them and is no different from salesmanship in business.

Trustees are comparable to a board of directors, with some differences. To avoid opportunism of the cruder sort, they are normally unpaid or at least subject to tight restrictions on their pay. By the same token, they lack financial incentives to effort. As with other donors of unpaid labor, much depends on their internal motivation. They are not accountable in the way that boards of directors are, in principle, accountable to shareholders or that trustees in noncharitable trusts are to the ultimate beneficiaries of those trusts. It is a distinctive feature of charities that the ultimate beneficiaries are not identifiable by name in advance. They are typically either the general public or else an open-ended class of people no one of whom has an indisputable claim. If one of them were to attempt to bring an action against negligent trustees, he would have little chance of success (even though he would no longer be liable to be whipped for impertinence, as in former days [Chesterman 1979, 22]). This problem was recognized already in Tudor times. The full title of the Statute of Charitable Uses was "An act to redress the misemployment of lands goods and stocks of money heretofore given to charitable uses." The act accordingly established a system by which a public authority could be responsible for the supervision of charitable trusts, on behalf of the unidentifiable beneficiaries. This system, in one form or another, has survived in England to the present time. Hence there emerges the next class of people whose X-efficiency, or lack of it, becomes significant.

The issues regarding the members of the supervisory authority have similarities to the issues discussed in the literature on regulation, with pros and cons of strict monitoring in the light of transaction costs. But whereas regulatory authorities have usually been set up to deal with monopolies, the Charity Commissioners in the United Kingdom have thousands of charities on their books, many of them quite small. The transaction costs are therefore overwhelming. The authorities have inevitably to confine themselves mainly to grosser abuses, to larger charities, and to cases raising general principles.

Entrepreneurship

Entrepreneurship could have been put under the previous heading, but it is important enough to deserve treatment on its own. In the sense of such writers as Kirzner (1973), it is equivalent to Schumpeterian innovation; it means discovering the scope for some new type of activity and carrying it into execution. It may involve establishing a new organization, or it may take place within an existing one. In this it differs from management, which implies an existing organization (governance structure).

There is scope for entrepreneurship in charitable activity, no less than in business. As in business, entrepreneurship calls for energy and drive, as well as imagination, especially if it involves creating a new organization. That being so, it is natural that a large proportion of new charities should be operating charities, founded by zealots for a particular cause, since, as noted earlier, completely generalized altruism provides a much weaker motive for action than enthusiasm for a particular cause.

It has been argued convincingly by James (1986) that zeal in particular causes is most likely to be manifested by people of a strongly religious turn of mind, and, moreover, that this may help to explain differences in the total amount of charitable effort between times and places. Likewise Beveridge found that religious convictions were to the fore in the great majority of his catalogue of Victorian philanthropic pioneers (Beveridge 1948, chap. 5). These are two separate points here. First, religious convictions may inspire entrepreneurial zeal. Second, they may make it effective by creating trust among potential donors. The trust factor applies to operators as well as to entrepreneurs: pace Hume, people may feel trust that priests or nuns will not behave opportunistically. Medical researchers can perhaps be regarded as a modern secular priesthood in this respect.

The foregoing applies particularly to collecting charities. Much of the zeal has to be devoted to the task of collection. Rather different considerations apply to endowed charities, set up by a single ultrarich founder. Large charities of that type include both operating ones and nonoperating ones. Whatever idealistic motives their founders may have, their entrepreneurial zeal is likely to have been needed more in making their fortunes than in giving them away. However, at least they are likely to be people of abnormal energy and enthusiastic about their objectives.

Collecting charities and endowed charities are alike in that after the death of the founder—if not earlier—they pass into the control of a different kind of person. Smaller charities often fizzle out altogether. Larger operating charities have tended to pass into the control of their professional employees, the professors in the universities or the doctors in the hospitals, people who are by no means necessarily opportunistic but who also are not necessarily either entrepreneurial or altruistic. Foundations pass into the control of trustees and managers. Clearly, there is scope here for the charitable equivalent to the clogs-to-clogs phenomenon, long-run effort entropy à la Leibenstein. Supervision by public authorities may prevent the cruder kinds of opportunistic degeneration, such as were allegedly exhibited by the monasteries. But they cannot do much to ensure continuing entrepreneurship. The next question to consider is how far competition provides a safeguard, both in this respect and in respect of other possible malfunctions.

Competition

X-efficiency in the business sector may be achieved as a result of optimization within the firm, a process assisted by competitive market signals. The lack of market signals in the charitable sphere has already been mentioned. In the business sector, efficiency may alternatively be achieved by means of competitive selection among firms, which eliminates those whose X-efficiency is below average, whether as a result of bad management or of chance. In addition, optimization may be carried out more sedulously as a result of the pressure of competition, that is, by the fear of being selected against. The question arises, therefore, how far are charities subject to competition?

Charities do compete in a number of areas, both with each other and for some purposes also with other organizations. They compete:

- for donations by demonstrating the usefulness of their activities and by the arts of salesmanship;
- for volunteer labor time, including that of trustees;
- for staff and other factors of production;
- in investment policy, in the case of endowed charities;
- for the ear of government, insofar as their functions include lobbying.

Charities that give away money, in doles to individuals or in grants to other charities, or supply goods and services at less than cost, do not typically have to compete for beneficiaries. By their nature, they are faced with excess demand. This is the central difference between them and business firms. They are consequently obliged to practice rationing, and they may practice it using a variety of criteria, according to the purposes for which they were set up (Holtmann 1983). This absence of competition for beneficiaries is, however, subject to some qualifications. Charities may compete for:

- visibly meritorious recipients, as a means either of attracting donations to themselves or of advancing the reputation of their officers or trustees or founders;

- consumers of merit goods (church congregations);
- customers, in the case of fee-charging operating charities, either if some though not all of their customers pay full cost or if there are economies of scale, so that an increase in demand enables more people to benefit from the services of the organization at any given level (including zero) of its own income from gifts.

It is obvious, looking at this list, that the discipline of competition is weakest in the case of endowed charities that can afford to do without new donations or volunteer labor. Given that the cy pres principle enables them to alter their objectives if those should become redundant, the only way, apart from state intervention, in which they are liable to fold altogether is as a result of bad investment policy (Boulding 1962). Hence, no doubt, the extraordinary longevity of some charities whose opportunism or X-inefficiency at certain phases of their history has been such as would have sunk any competitive business enterprise. British examples often cited in this connection are the City Livery Companies and the Oxford and Cambridge Colleges in the eighteenth and early nineteenth centuries (Owen 1965).

The potential disadvantages of the endowment system, from the point of view of X-inefficiency, are related to the X-inefficiency commonly believed to occur in the public sector if departmental budgets are not tightly controlled (Leibenstein 1982). They have to be set against the considerable transaction costs of continuous collection, as well as the straightforward operating advantages of having financial reserves. (It was no doubt with those considerations in mind that Wesley Mitchell is said to have been anxious to increase the endowments of the National Bureau of Economic Research but not to the point where it could do without outside project grants.) It may be noted that significant transaction costs are also present in several of the other areas of competition I have enumerated.

Charities and the State

I have so far been talking about charities taken in isolation. I now turn to consider them and their evolution in relation to one aspect of their environment and to changes in it that have been partly but not wholly exogenous.

The overlap between charity and the state, both as sources of finance and as means of operation, has been recognized throughout modern times. The Elizabethan Poor Law, which provided the basis of the English system of income maintenance for more than two centuries, was enacted in the same year as the Statute of Charitable Uses and as part of the same program. There have been large differences in the relative importance of the two between periods and places; there have been large differences, too, in the relative importance of self-help co-operatives (nineteenth century friendly societies, the Japanese firm), which are yet another way of achieving some of the same purposes. The Elizabethan Poor Law itself marked a shift to the public sector, compared with the Middle Ages.[2] In modern times (the last century or so) a further enormous shift has occurred in the same direction, though with some attempts at reversal most recently.

These changes over time have no doubt been due in part to political changes not directly connected with economic causes, notably the advent of universal franchise. The same may be said of observed differences among countries. But economic considerations, including X-efficiency ones, have also entered.

A system of providing for good causes by voluntary donations does not elicit contributions from people who lack benevolence or who have no scruples about being free riders. These people, however, are caught in the net of taxation. Hence, assuming that attitudes in respect of benevolence and free riding are given, taxation will be able to provide for good causes on a larger scale than charity can. Moreover, this need not be incompatible with majority preferences. People may be willing to vote to be forced to contribute more to good causes than they would donate voluntarily because free riding is thereby prevented; they are willing to contribute more as long as everyone else chips in (Sen 1967). There is also the cruder consideration that voters include potential donees as well as potential donors. Only on extreme assumptions would these effects on the total amount raised be fully offset by induced reductions in voluntary giving brought about by people's realization that the state is assuming responsibility and that their post-tax incomes are correspondingly reduced. The increase in funding is achieved, of course, at the cost of coercing minorities and at the cost of taxation causing some distortion of incentives, a consideration presumably not present with voluntary giving, except insofar as high post-tax income creates external pressures to contribute to charity. State support will, naturally, be associated with some difference in the kind of good cause supported, since that will be

---

2. The Catholic countries of Europe followed a different path in this period. They continued to rely on private giving and gave renewed emphasis to the Christian duty of charity. Tremendous entrepreneurship to this end was displayed by St. Vincent de Paul. However, effort entropy manifested itself: after his death the movement lost much of its momentum (Hufton 1974, esp. chap. V).

determined politically instead of by individual choice. And there may be nonpecuniary effects on the welfare of donors, who lose the enjoyment of a sense of noblesse oblige, and, on the other hand, effects, too, on the welfare of recipients, if they feel that receiving charity carries a stigma.

Because the political mechanism permits a higher level of support, the state's share in total support is likely to be affected by the magnitude, relative to national income, of the purposes requiring support. The change in Elizabeth's time can be related to demographic increases in the number of the poor.[3] Thinking of some of the traditional purposes of philanthropy, one notes in more modern times such historical trends as the increase in the proportion of the elderly in the population; the increased duration of education; the increased sophistication and cost of medical care; and the emergence of a new public good, scientific research.

Access to compulsory powers is not the only distinctive attribute of the state. Its other forte, which is associated with its monopoly position, is comprehensiveness. This in principle enables it to equate the return from different types of good cause at the margin. Comprehensiveness calls for evenhandedness, and hence uniformity, and hence it is achieved at the cost of impersonality. It is therefore a natural hypothesis that the trend increase in government involvement owed something to the very long-run trend toward a more impersonal, mobile, market-based economy in which personal knowledge and local loyalties come to count for less (Boulding 1962). The greater continuing strength of voluntary activity in rural communities than in urban ones can be explained in similar terms. An analogous hypothesis is that the particularly strong propensity of Americans to form private voluntary associations, commented on already by de Tocqueville in the 1830s, is a historical reflection of its pioneer origins and/or its ethnic heterogeneity (Pifer 1987; Weisbrod 1987).

Not only is the state well placed to be even handed; it must be evenhanded, because of the open-ended scope for opportunism (corruption) that would otherwise be created by its open-ended powers. This imposes certain restrictions on the kinds of good causes that the state can support and hence may put it at a disadvantage in exploiting the deeper but narrower knowledge of the kind potentially available to private bodies. By contrast, provided that there is a multiplicity of donors, no

---

3. Wrigley (1988, chap. 4) argues that the assumption of responsibility by the state under the Elizabethan Poor Law made an important contribution to England's early start in industrialization, by diminishing dependence on kin and so facilitating the replacement of custom by contract.

one is likely to object much if the purpose of a private benefaction is narrowly restricted in its potential recipients or is experimental or even is at odds with currently prevailing orthodoxy. A great deal of public spending is on purposes that were pioneered, on a smaller scale, in the private nonprofit sector. Indeed, it has been a commonplace in the thinking of foundations that a major part of their role is to seek out new good causes that the state can then take over once their value has been established.

So far in this section I have been speaking of direct support by public spending. The tax privileges of charities add a very important indirect public contribution, linking the two. The privileges have increased over time with the increase in tax rates and with the increasing generosity of the tax exemptions granted.

Purposes of expenditure may be categorized in this context as follows:

1. state supported only, by direct public spending, private contributions being nil or negligible (defense);
2. state supported both by direct public spending and by the tax privileges granted on charitable contributions (education, medical research);
3. state supported only, by the tax privileges granted on charitable contributions (religion);
4. not state supported at all, because not legally charitable, even though nonprofit and in receipt of private gifts (political purposes).

Charities have enjoyed tax privileges from the earliest days (Chesterman 1979, 23 and 58), but the privileges have been increased in recent times, so they cannot be regarded as merely a historical survival. Why does government give them?

One possible rationalization is in terms of the relative tax cost to the government at the margin of direct and indirect support for a cause that it would like to see supported. If donors are willing to contribute more (net) because their contributions are deductible from their taxable incomes, £1 spent by the government in allowing the tax deductibility increases the sum available for the good cause by more than £1 directly spent by the government on it: the government partially matches the private contributions, and further private contributions then partially match the government's. It has been estimated econometrically by Feldstein and collaborators that the elasticity of charitable donations in the

United States with respect to their tax deductibility is high enough for this condition to be satisfied (Boskin and Feldstein 1977).

In the process, however, the government loses control over what the money is spent on. It draws a sharp line between purposes that are legally charitable, all of which get matching grants on the same terms, and purposes that are not legally charitable, none of which gets any such support. The loss of control might seem to be a serious breach of general principles of control of public expenditure and to involve the abandonment of one of government's supposedly strong points as a giver, its ability to equate returns at the margin. An alternative rationalization therefore needs to be sought. One possible such rationalization is in terms of certification. The government may think that people's willingness to put their own money into some cause provides a better guarantee of its usefulness than any public scrutiny could do. Or the purpose may be of the noncomprehensive type that the government is debarred from supporting. Or it may belong to category 3 and be something that the government favors in general terms but feels it cannot involve itself in any choices between alternatives.

It is an attractive idea in some ways that the government should defer to members of the public in their choice of good causes and then back them up. It provides a source of pluralism in an area where information is particularly likely to be defective. The tax-deductibility system does have some peculiar features, however, not all of which are easy to defend. One such feature is that a reduction in rates of income tax, undertaken for some entirely extraneous reason, has the effect of diminishing the amount of government matching to charitable donations.

An alternative form of partnership between the state and charities is for the state to provide the money but leave the actual work to operating charities. This form of partnership developed on an increasingly large scale in the post–World War II period. Government grants paid to private charities, for more or less specifically defined purposes, became in many cases their main source of income. This can be regarded as a way of exploiting the respective comparative advantages of the state and of charities. Some of the sources of these comparative advantages have already been mentioned. Another is that charities are better placed than government to make use of volunteer labor, especially of the more unskilled kind. The demerit of the system is the heavy dependence of charities on a single discretionary donor, making for unclear division of responsibility.

The long-term expansion of direct government finance left charities with only niche roles in certain of their traditional spheres, such as domestic income maintenance, primary education, and medical care (partly offset by the expansion of support for similar activities in the Third World). However, in modern times it appears not to have diminished total charitable activity nor to have jeopardized the supply of voluntary labor. The experience of charities in this respect has been different from that of friendly societies, many of which have disappeared. The niches proved surprisingly numerous, to say nothing of fields of activity unaffected by government spending or actually stimulated by it. Lobbying and advice giving became more important functions. Other gainers included higher education and research, which have come to absorb a share of charitable resources, especially those of the large foundations, to an extent that in retrospect appears remarkable, though readily explicable by the optimistic desire of donors to solve society's problems by research rather than merely palliate their effects. Environmental purposes and the arts were other gainers. The arts were relative latecomers under the charitable umbrella; it has been suggested (Feingold 1987) that private donations for this purpose stem from a rather different historical tradition, patronage rather than philanthropy. In medieval thinking patronage was a virtue but not a duty in the way that philanthropy was, and it was no doubt often used for the self-aggrandizement of the donor, just as in more modern times it has been used as a form of advertisement by companies.

The counterrevolution in attitudes toward government spending in the last decade, insofar as it has actually been carried out, has created difficult problems for charities, not least because they do not know how far it will go. They are reluctant to abandon niches that have proved useful in order to take over the support of activities that the government has deemed no longer worthy of its support. Nor do they want to abandon their traditional experimental role. Given saliency considerations, both charitable organizations and individual donors like to feel that their gifts are actually bringing about net improvements not merely holding the fort (worse still, the most marginal parts of the fort). Some foundations have tried to play a preemptive game, announcing that they will not support activities eligible for government finance; but, though this may reduce their transaction costs, their powers of preemption are small relative to government's. Plainly, if the counterrevolution continues far, large changes in attitudes toward private giving will be needed if the total support for good causes is not to diminish.

Some Conclusions

I hope this article has made plain that the X-efficiency concept can be applied to charities no less than to business firms. The analogies not only are of a general kind but can be drawn also in quite a number of details. But there are also a number of differences.

The relative strength of the forces conducing to X-efficiency in charities, as compared with business, is affected by a number of considerations that do not all pull in the same direction. Information problems are worse in charities, though they can be and are mitigated by suitable choice of organization. Incentives to good performance are also weaker, and so is competition, though it is by no means wholly absent. On the side of opportunism, however, charities have some advantage.

It was suggested that efficiency in charities can be measured at two levels: the efficiency of individual charities in attaining given objectives and the efficiency in the choice of objectives. In regard to the former, the operations of charities have no doubt been subject to the same uptrend over time in total factor productivity as business sector operations and for the same reasons (advances in technical and other knowledge). Whether a similar progressive improvement has taken place in the choice between objectives is more debatable.

Disinterested zeal, inspired by religious or other moral motives, has been important in the establishment of charities. It is important, too, in the maintenance of effort and entrepreneurship in establishing charities. Prevailing moral norms, therefore, affect the efficiency of charities. Obviously they also affect the magnitude of charitable giving. We are perhaps unlikely to return to the attitudes toward giving that left the monasteries in possession of one-third of the land in England by the end of the Middle Ages. However, the impulse to give has remained robust, as has the impulse to donate unpaid labor, though the strength of these impulses has differed among periods and regions. These differences reflect not only moral reasons but also differences in the relative efficiency of charity and of other means of securing the same ends.

The question of zeal raises some troublesome problems about rationality, hence about the allocation of money between alternative uses. These affect both entrepreneurs and donors, as indicated in the passage quoted from Hume. Zeal does not necessarily, or even usually, imply irrational enthusiasm. From the point of view of public policy, however, it has to be recognized that charitable giving will lead to an allocation of resources that may occasionally seem eccentric. This is a price of pluralism.

Charities do not exist in a vacuum. Consideration of one of the most important changes that have taken place over time in their environment, viz., changes in the level of state spending on purposes similar to charitable ones, suggests that, contrary to what might have been expected, charities and the state have stood in some ways in a complementary relationship rather than a competitive one: charities have found it easier to adapt to increases in state spending than to a contraction of state spending.

REFERENCES

Alchian, Armen A., and Harold Demsetz. 1972. "Production, Information Costs, and Economic Organization." *American Economic Review* 62:777–95.
Becker, Gary S. 1976. "Altruism, Egoism, and Genetic Fitness." *Journal of Economic Literature* 14:817–26.
Beveridge, Lord. 1948. *Voluntary Action: A Report on Methods of Social Advance*. London: Allen & Unwin.
Boskin, Michael J., and Martin S. Feldstein. 1977. "Effects of the Charitable Deduction on Contributions by Low Income and Middle Income Households." *Review of Economics and Statistics* 59:351–54.
Boulding, Kenneth E. 1962. "Notes on a Theory of Philanthropy." In *Philanthropy and Social Policy*, 57–72. *See* Dickinson 1962.
Chesterman, Michael. 1979. *Charities, Trusts and Social Welfare*. London: Weindenfeld & Nicolson.
Dickinson, Frank G., ed. 1962. *Philanthropy and Social Policy*. New York: National Bureau of Economic Research.
Downs, Anthony. 1957. *An Economic Theory of Democracy*. New York: Harper & Row.
Easley, David, and Maureen O'Hara. 1983. "The Economic Role of the Nonprofit Firm." *Bell Journal of Economics* 14:531–38.
Feingold, Mordechai. 1987. "Philanthropy, Pomp, and Patronage." *Daedalus* 116:155–78.
Gilchrist, John. 1969. *The Church and Economic Activity in the Middle Ages*. London: Macmillan.
Holtmann, A. G. 1983. "A Theory of Non-profit Firms." *Economica* 50:439–49.
Hufton, Olwen. 1974. *The Poor of Eighteenth Century France 1750–1789*. Oxford: Clarendon Press.
Hume, David. 1759. *The History of England under the House of Tudor*. London: Millar.
James, Estelle. 1986. "The Private Non-profit Provision of Education." *Journal of Comparative Economics* 10:255–76.
Karl, Barry D., and Stanley N. Katz. 1987. "Foundations and Ruling Class Elites." *Daedalus* 116:1–40.
Kirzner, Israel M. 1973. *Competition and Entrepreneurship*. Chicago: University of Chicago Press.
Leibenstein, Harvey. 1978. *General X-Efficiency Theory and Economic Development*. New York: Oxford University Press.

Leibenstein, Harvey. 1982. "Notes on X-Efficiency and Bureaucracy." In *The Grants Economy and Collective Consumption*, ed. Robin C. O. Matthews and G. B. Stafford, 191–211. London: St. Martin.

Menchik, Paul, and Burton A. Weisbrod. 1987. "Volunteer Labor Supply." *Journal of Public Economics* 32:159–83.

Mill, John Stuart. 1869. "Endowments." *Fortnightly Review* n.s. 11:377–90.

Mowat, Charles Loch. 1961. *The Charity Organisation Society 1869–1913: Its Work and Ideas*. London: Methuen.

Murray, G. J. 1974. "The Statistics of Voluntary Organizations in the Personal Social Service Field." In *Reviews of United Kingdom Statistical Sources*, vol. 1, ed. W. F. Maunder. London: Heinemann, for the Royal Statistical Society and the Social Science Research Council.

Owen, David. 1965. *English Philanthropy 1660–1960*. Cambridge, Mass.: Harvard University Press.

Pauly, Mark, and Michael Redisch. 1973. "The Not-for-profit Hospital as a Physicians' Cooperative." *American Economic Review* 63:87–99.

Pifer, Alan. 1987. "Philanthropy, Voluntarism and Changing Times." *Daedalus* 116:119–32.

Sen, Amartya K. 1967. "Isolation, Assurance, and the Social Rate of Discount." *Quarterly Journal of Economics* 81:112–24.

Sugden, Robert. 1982. "On the Economics of Philanthropy." *Economic Journal* 92:341–50.

Webb, Beatrice. 1926. *My Apprenticeship*. London: Longmans, Green.

Weisbrod, Burton A. "Non-profit Organizations." In *The New Palgrave: A Dictionary of Economics*. London: Macmillan.

Williamson, Oliver E. 1985. *The Economic Institutions of Capitalism*. New York: The Free Press.

Wrigley, E. A. 1988. *Continuity, Chance and Change: The Character of the Industrial Revolution in England*. Cambridge: Cambridge University Press.

The Competitive Position of British Industry: Are Nonprice Factors a Problem and Is X-Inefficiency the Cause?

Arthur Francis

This article is partly an exploration of some of the issues related to the competitiveness of a nation's industry — in this case, Britain. Included are a discussion of some conceptual issues and the sketching of a research agenda. Because my reading of Harvey Leibenstein's book *Inside the Firm* (1987) has stimulated me to reassess some of the arguments I had advanced in my own book, Francis 1986, this article is also an exploration from a quasi-sociological perspective of the implications of the concept of X-efficiency for organization theory.

My exploration of British industrial competitiveness reflects my current position as coordinator of a research program set up by the Economic and Social Research Council (ESRC) in the United Kingdom as "The Competitiveness and Regeneration of British Industry." Nearly all of the program's 28 individual research projects focus on issues of competitiveness at the level of the firm. The majority of researchers are academics in British business schools in such fields as business policy, marketing, and organizational behavior. Part of my job has been to "develop an overarching conceptual framework" for the program. Though a sociologist, I had to turn to the economics literature to attempt this task. Thus, the first part of this article relates to work I have done on this topic over the last couple of years — see, for example, Francis 1989. I attempt to introduce into discussions about international competitiveness (and efficiency) the notion of X-inefficiency and to sketch a tentative research agenda to test what seem to be the implicit hypotheses that can be derived from the Leibenstein model.

This article reflects some of my concerns as a sociologist. There is a short discussion of the concept of efficiency and the way sociologists have treated the notion — though most of the time they seem to have ignored the concept entirely. This is followed by a comparison of the Leibenstein approach with one that I began to set out in my book *New*

Technology at Work (1986). There, I attempted to develop a new conceptual framework for handling issues of organizational control synthesizing insights from radical and conventional organizational theories in light of recent contributions from institutional economics, in particular Williamson's *Markets and Hierarchies* (1975) framework.

National Economic Performance: Competitiveness and Efficiency as Competing Explanations

The early 1980s saw much interest in most developed countries about the competitiveness of their own national economies. In the United States, the topic was examined in such publications as the Brookings study by Lawrence (1984) and the President's Commission on Industrial Competitiveness (1985). There was similar concerns within a number of continental European countries about their own competitive performance. Within Britain there was not only a spate of academic analysis at the turn of the decade (for example, Blackaby 1978; Beckerman 1979; and Carter 1981) but also a House of Lords Select Committee Report on Overseas Trade in 1985. A member of this Committee, when introducing the report on television, presented the apocalyptic vision of "Britain being on the slippery slope, held back from the abyss only by the drag anchor of North Sea oil."

Attempts to analyze Britain's poor industrial performance in terms of a lack of competitiveness do not seem very plausible; a much more convincing argument can be put forward that British industry has suffered over the long term from inefficiency. This article attempts to set out this case and then to examine the extent to which the hypothesized inefficiency is either allocational or an example of Leibenstein's X-inefficiency. The distinction between uncompetitiveness and inefficiency may be crucial. My argument is that any one nation can have a low level of X-efficiency but remain competitive at that low level by adjusting its exchange rate downward in line with its relatively decreasing efficiency. There is thus no heightened competitive pressure on the firms in that country and thus there is no added pressure to cause them to reduce their X-inefficiency.

The Concept of Competitiveness

Part of the difficulty in arguing that inefficiency rather than uncompetitiveness is the prime cause of poor economic performance within a nation is the extent to which the term *competitiveness* has been debased. Frequently, "being competitive" seems to connote merely good performance, where the measure of goodness remains implicit and is assumed to have such a widely shared meaning that its measurement is not problematic. Moreover, it seems often to be assumed that the concept can be applied equally appropriately to national performance in international trade as to the salability of tomatoes in a street market.

If, however, competition is, as Samuel Johnson suggested (1755), "the action of endeavouring to gain what another endeavours to gain at the same time," the concept can reasonably be used of products but less easily directly applied to nations. Products can be said to be uncompetitive if they cannot be sold at volumes and prices that yield an acceptable return to the vendor. In the narrowest and most satisfactory sense there can be direct competition between specific products for a particular sale. In a wider sense all products in the marketplace are competing with each other for consumers' disposable income. Competition is a zero-sum game, and an increase in one product's competitiveness is at the expense of a decrease in another's.

When extending the notion of competitiveness to firms and to nations, one must specify the goal for which they are competing. This seems to be done rarely, but the implicit meaning applied to the concept appears usually to be that of competitiveness in product markets. In other words, a firm is competitive if it is producing a portfolio of competitive products (as I have defined it) and a nation is competitive if the sum total of firms operating within its territory are competitive in the same sense (though there is some lack of clarity as to whether commentators are more concerned about the sum total of a nation's firms, including their activities in foreign locations, or about the economic activities taking place within the national territory, whether controlled by national or foreign interests).

At first sight, national competitiveness in this sense might seem best measured in terms of market share, and indeed it seems to be the steep fall in the share in world markets of major economies such as the United States and the United Kingdom in the recent past that has given rise to current concerns about national competitiveness. The House of Lords Report, for example, placed much emphasis on the near halving of the United Kingdom's share of world manufactures from 1964 to 1983. There are a number of major weaknesses with this as a measure of international competitiveness. Indeed, Harrod (1967) described the use of the measure in this context as "surely the most absurd ever perpetrated in a diagnosis." There are two powerful reasons for an individual country's share in world markets to fall that may have nothing to do with the competitiveness of its economy. The first is the internationalization of trade. The second is differential growth rates. One country's share in world markets is likely to fall if trade in general becomes more internationalized, and to this extent individual nations' falling world market shares are to be welcomed. Quoting Harrod again, "the British share of world export has declined, is declining and will continue to decline, hopefully at an accelerated pace" (quoted in Thirwall 1982, 238).

Less to be welcomed is a country's loss of world market share due to relatively slow economic growth. Nevertheless, many factors influence national growth rates, and a reduction in world market share due to slow growth may not be the result of uncompetitiveness. Reasons other than lack of competitiveness for slow growth will be explored.

While policymakers may focus on the spurious measure of world trade shares as a gauge of competitiveness, economists cite the more satisfactory measures of changes in price competitiveness and real efficiency wages. However, it is because these appear to explain so little in terms of comparative national economic performance that economists have fallen back on the notion of nonprice competitiveness. It is this concept that I wish to address in some detail.

With nonprice competitiveness, as with competitiveness generally, the question must be asked about the extent to which any nonprice problem is that of competitiveness or efficiency. A slightly more than cursory examination of the data usually used to support the belief that British goods seem generally to be not very competitive in nonprice terms leaves one unconvinced. The argument and the data are usually applied to the so-called balance-of-payments constraint, and the suggestion is that because of nonprice factors, the income elasticity of demand in the United Kingdom for imports is relatively high and the world income elasticity of demand for British exports is relatively low. However Thirwall's data show that, on the former measure, the United Kingdom ranks lower than West Germany, France, or Italy and the same as the United States (1982, 256). The export demand growth is measured by percentage growth in exports volume. Given that the United Kingdom exports a much higher percentage of GDP than most other countries, it is not surprising that export growth is relatively slow.

Though it may be giving a hostage to fortune, given current trends in the British balance-of-payments position, my conclusion at this stage is that the case for the U.K. having a competitiveness problem is unproved and that evidence usually adduced in support of this case should more correctly be taken as evidence of revealed preference or inefficiency. Falling shares of world markets in general and in manufacturing goods in particular are spurious measures of competitiveness and are not in themselves evidence of welfare losses to a nation's citizens. They should not be the focus of policy concern. Better measures of such welfare are output and productivity. Where a nation is performing badly with regard to the level and rate of growth of output and/or productivity (and Britain has been a prime example of such a nation and still is with regard to absolute levels), it is theoretically possible, and in the case of Britain appears empirically to be the case, that the economy can be competitive in the sense I have defined but relatively inefficient. Provided exchange rates can adjust adequately to reflect the differential economic growth rates that are likely to result from international differences in efficiency, countries can continue to compete effectively at different levels of efficiency. The major issue for the British economy is, therefore, that of its level of efficiency. Issues of competitiveness per se would appear to arise only when exchange rates fail to adjust appropriately.

Types of Inefficiency

If it can be accepted that the issue with regard to the British economy has more to do with low and slow-growing output than with competitiveness, then a number of possible explanations can be advanced. Some are couched in terms of revealed preference and others in terms of relative efficiency. Explanations based on efficiency grounds have more commonly been concerned with allocative efficiency rather than with X-efficiency.

Explanations of the first type are well exemplified by Nossiter (1978) in his panegyric about British society, a book he wrote after spending some years in England as correspondent for the Washington Post. The nub of his argument is expressed in the title of his book: *Britain: A Future that Works*. Britain has a civilized set of values, more concern with enjoying what it has rather than anxiously striving for more—a culture with a strong leisure preference, in fact.

Advancing the same kind of argument, though without the same sympathy for the symptoms, Weiner (1981), in a book more popular than rigorous, advances the view that English culture is particularly antipathetic to business and industry, and thus industry has been starved of investment capacity and human talent. This argument can be viewed as an explanation of the revealed preference argument or as indicating some kind of market failure leading to a shortage of both entrepreneurial expertise and capital. Payne's analysis (1986) of the historical evidence suggests little support for the entrepreneurial shortage thesis. His conclusion is that available entrepreneurial opportunities were used as effectively as might be expected and that explanations for slow growth were more related to the lack of mass-market opportunities. In the absence of a relatively affluent working class, and with a middle class wanting semicustomized products, market opportunities were the type that could be met more by Birmingham workshops than by Detroit mass-production plants. In other words, given the market structure, industry was as efficient as might be expected.

Arguments for low and slow-growing productivity that can be put in terms of allocative inefficiency are, for example, those of Elbaum and Lazonick (1986), who argue that British capitalism in the interwar period was too disorganized. Compared to what they term "managed capitalism" in the United States or Germany, British firms were too small and wasted too much effort in competing against each other rather than in combining and rationalizing to achieve economies of scale in research and development, production, and marketing.

Corelli Barnett's *Audit of War* (1985) advances two complementary arguments. One is similar to Weiner's, that British society is antipathetic to industry; the other offers an implicit allocative inefficiency argument—that an effect of what he terms "New Jerusalemism" was too much expenditure in the postwar period on council houses and hospitals and not enough on capital investment in car factories and other "productive" enterprises. This has similarities to the Bacon and Eltis (1976) argument that high levels of public expenditure in the British postwar period expanded the production of nontraded goods and services at the expense of traded products and thus led to an endemic weakness in the balance of payments.

There is, in addition, a whole series of arguments about poor quality of design, manufacture, and marketing of British goods, as well as poor industrial relations. To the extent that poor management is blamed for these apparent failures, the argument is usually, again, that of either revealed preferences (able people prefer to go into the professions rather than into industry) or allocative inefficiency (e.g., not enough is spent on vocational education and training or on salaries of managers). To the extent that poor industrial relations are seen as a reflection of a class-based oppositional social structure, the explanations are seen to be sociological or political and, therefore, to some extent have in the past fallen outside the province of economic analysis. The effects of such structural characteristics may, however, be amenable to analysis within an X-efficiency framework.

There are, finally, attempts to explain some of the phenomena in terms of government's management of the economy, such as governmental ineptness or the effects of the pursuit of goals other than economic growth—a trade-off between growth and social justice/equity sometimes being proposed.

The Role of X-Inefficiency

None of the attempts thus far at explaining the low and slow-growing output of the British economy involve the explicit notion of X-efficiency despite many studies replicating the observation made by Leibenstein in his earliest work on X-efficiency (1966) that there were a great many instances in which allocative inefficiency accounted for only very small welfare losses.

If X-inefficiency is a factor, what conditions would have to obtain? The argument would have to be that British firms can be particularly X-inefficient. We can test the plausibility of this with reference to Leibenstein's seven basic postulates (1987, 129). These seven postulates at this stage constitute little more than a research agenda. For some of the issues the data are well known and the test can be applied immediately. For some others the data may be well known but not to me.

The first of Leibenstein's postulates is that people both maximize and deviate from maximization in their decision making. He terms this the "max/nonmax" ratio and hypothesizes that where decision makers are under less pressure, there is a lower ratio of max/nonmax decision making. Have people in British firms in the past been under relatively little pressure and therefore had a lower ratio of max/nonmax decision making? The general view would appear to be in favor of this hypothesis. The argument would be that factors such as early industrialization and the role of the empire in providing favorable export markets and cheap imports resulted in high levels of GNP early on. This meant a low level of pressure on firms' decision makers from foreign competition or because of perceptions of higher standards of living elsewhere.

Leibenstein's second postulate is that where there are incomplete employment contracts, effort is open to discretion to some extent. This is true of various conditions of work that are controlled by management. The research question would be whether employment contracts are more incomplete in the U.K. than elsewhere. This is a rich area for exploration, interfacing as it does with work by Williamson (1975, 1985, 1986) on the topic.

The next three postulates concern the effort-reward bargain. Postulate 3 is that effort depends on motivation resulting from both incentives and pressures. Postulate 4 suggests that the marginal utility of effort increases up to some point, then decreases, and beyond some point is negative, but that under teamwork conditions there may be an additional positive marginal utility—what Leibenstein calls the "team approval effect." Postulate 5 is about coordination, noting a value to individuals in behaving as others behave both because to some degree people care about the reaction of others toward them and because more desirable results are achieved through coordinated behavior. Hypotheses about the extent to which firms in the U.K. might in general experience high levels of X-inefficiency arising from these three postulates would presumably be in terms of the industrial relations institutions in Britain and strategies by which management exercises control in the workplace and would be associated with the kind of analysis referred to later in this article.

Postulate 6 deals with "inert areas." Leibenstein postulates that many relationships are such that within certain boundaries inertia exists with respect to the dependent variable (e.g., the mechanisms and relationships that affect the various aspects of the effort-reward bargain). This means that no change in behavior takes place within these bounds when the independent variable (the amount of pressure) changes, especially when the values of the independent variable(s) are embedded in a low-pressure environment. This might well fit the British case. As has already been noted, it is plausible to suggest that the economic environment of the U.K. was in the past low pressure in the Leibenstein sense. One could ally this with hypotheses about British management resources and systems. Inert areas are large if the cost of change is relatively high. Inadequate management would, presumably, both blunt the perception of the need for change and heighten the difficulty of managing effective change. To the extent that industry in Britain has had a problem in recruiting and training a high-caliber management cadre, then one would postulate a large inert area.

Leibenstein's final postulate is of imperfect competition. X-inefficient companies (or nations) are assumed to be sheltered from competition to some degree. The greater the shelter, the less the pressure on the firm. This might be the most important postulate in explaining British inefficiency. Elbaum and Lazonick (1986) draw attention to the widespread interwar phenomenon in the U.K. of competing firms merging with each other to avoid competition—a tendency that seems to have persisted until at least the 1960s. There is considerable evidence of imperfect competition in international trade with protected trade links between Britain and the empire/commonwealth.

I am irresistably tempted to advance the view that part of the improvement in British economic performance post–1979 is due to a reduction in X-inefficiency in which heightened competitive pressures due to the strong pound and high interest rates in 1979 and 1980 increased the max/nonmax ratio for those firms that continued to exist and drove them out of their inert areas. In addition, if one were to mount a serious test of these hypotheses it may be methodologically easier to focus on the post–1979 upsurge in performance and on the postulated reduction in X-inefficiency, rather than on the pre–1979 poor performance and the extent of X-inefficiency in the earlier period.

Nonprice Competitiveness

As noted earlier, it is frequently asserted that British goods have been uncompetitive in nonprice terms. The precise implications of this assertion are rarely spelled out, and the concept has been operationalized in empirical research to mean that the reasons customers give for not buying British goods is not cost but that they compare poorly with competitive exports in several respects. Examples are poor quality, lack of particular functional features, poor styling, delivery delays, and unreliability. This operational definition seems inadequate. Each of these characteristics has its price. Goods that lack them should be priced more cheaply. Why is there not a market-clearing price for such goods? Is it that British manufacturers are myopic in their pricing policy, failing to see that their goods are inferior to others in the market and therefore should be priced lower? Is it that they have inadequate marketing strategies and are targeting the wrong product-market sectors? If they are incapable of producing better products, shouldn't they get out of that market or identify more precisely at which sector of the market they are aiming?

Doubtless there are firms that are myopic or incompetent at planning their product-market strategy and such shortsightedness and incompetence would be facets of the high level of X-inefficiency we have already hypothesized. But something more may be going on.

Though issues of nonprice competitiveness arise whenever firms are attempting to produce differentiated goods, the problem of nonprice lack of competitiveness becomes particularly acute in markets for products that are subject to technical development or aesthetic change.

Products become uncompetitive on nonprice grounds when other products incorporating more advanced features or more attractive aesthetic features are introduced and when the cost of developing those features is less than the value put upon them by the consumer. In the absence of competition, the innovator makes supernormal profits. If, however, competing firms have each made similar innovations, normal profits obtain and the price the consumer is prepared to pay for the old product falls. Companies that have failed to make the innovation therefore suffer falling profits.

It is easy to see, therefore, how a vicious circle may emerge. Those firms that do not invest resources in keeping up with the going rate of technical developments (or aesthetic changes) lose either profits, market share, or a combination of both, and therefore have fewer resources remaining to take part in the next round of innovation.

The question in this context is the extent to which a lack of investment of resources directed to innovation, whether money or effort, is due to X-inefficiency, allocative inefficiency, or revealed preference. If revealed preference, the implication is that market signals are working well. It is sometimes argued (e.g., Samuel Brittan, *Financial Times*, various dates) that there is a low level of investment in research and development and design in Britain because the U.K.'s comparative advantage lies elsewhere, in the services sector, for example. If the question is one of allocative inefficiency, the implication is that more resources should be put in research and development and design activity and that managers and government are somehow making a mistake in not doing so.

If the explanation is that of X-inefficiency, we are back to the question of the extent to which conditions in the United Kingdom lead to nonmax decision making and the other six Leibenstein postulates. The distinction between allocative inefficiency and X-inefficiency appears to be twofold in this case. X-inefficiency may lead to allocative inefficiency as in the case where, for reasons yet to be explored, nonmax decisions are made about the level of investment to be put into research and development. In addition, X-inefficiency may have a direct effect even in situations where investment in research and development is equal to international levels because the utility of effort, etc. is low.

It is this last hypothesis—that there may be high levels of X-inefficiency in the area of innovation within one country compared to other countries—that should receive the highest priority if any empirical tests are to be set up. Its importance is twofold. First, it is now argued by many authorities that competition among goods and firms occurs much more on the basis of innovative features than on the basis of price for standard items. X-inefficiency in innovation is thus more significant than in the production area. Second, national levels of X-inefficiency in the production of standard goods can be reflected in the exchange rate, and thus different national levels of X-efficiency can coexist in equilibrium. This does not seem to be a possibility with X-efficiency in innovation. There does seem to be a vicious circle. A company, or nation, that is X-inefficient at innovating can be competed out of its current product range because exchange rates or output prices cannot be lowered enough to cover the value placed by the consumer on the innovative characteristic. Parts of the British car industry seem to have illustrated this process in the recent past (Ashworth, Kay, and Sharp 1982).

A Note on the Concept of Efficiency in Sociology

Of striking note is the lack of attention paid to the notion of efficiency within organizational sociology. Out of ten texts on organizational behavior or organization theory consulted in preparing this article, only four even index the term *efficiency*. Two of these were passing references. Of the ten, only Salaman (1979) sets out an extended critique of the use of the concept of efficiency in organizational analysis. However, this critique suffers from what seem to be the two usual defects in sociological critiques of efficiency — a lack of precise definition of the concept and an inadequate treatment of the associated concept of power.

Efficiency seems usually to be defined by sociologists only in terms of outputs. Salaman (1979) and Willman (1986), for example, both imply that efficiency is to be measured only by the success of the product or the firm in the marketplace. Neither makes reference to the need to compare outputs with inputs.

Part of the reason for this lack of a systematic treatment of efficiency is because the sociologist's focus of interest in organizations is different from that of the economist. As Salaman remarks,

> Weber was an early originator of the genuinely sociological approach to organisations which sees organisational structure not as the outcome of the search for efficiency but in terms of priorities, problems and interests based in the society outside the organisation. (1979, 12)

To the extent that sociologists do concern themselves with efficiency, the sociological critique of economists' assertions about efficient forms of organization is usually to ask "efficiency for whom or what?" The implicit (never explicit) assumption is that there is inadequate measurement on the input side of the efficiency calculation. The implication is that there may be a number of different ways of organizing the labor process that have different physical and psychic costs to workers. These costs are not reflected in the price labor is able to charge for its work, so that methods of organization that might be more efficient to management (because they achieve greater output for a given labor cost in terms of wages and salaries paid) are less attractive to workers because the greater output is obtained at the cost of greater labor intensity or psychic dissatisfaction. At the heart of the sociological critique is, therefore, the belief that labor markets are not perfect. If labor markets were working well, forms of work organization that incurred greater costs to the worker would be associated with higher wages.

To the extent that X-inefficiency arises only under the conditions noted by Leibenstein (1976, 45), the sociological critique has some bearing. To the extent that reducing X-inefficiency can be seen as increasing worker effort without a commensurate increase in worker reward, then, efficiency from the worker's viewpoint is not increased. The apparent increase in efficiency arises only because prices are an adequate measure of all relevant inputs and outputs only when markets are working adequately. When markets have failed, labor costs do not measure all relevant labor inputs, nor do output prices measure all relevant output characteristics. Under these circumstances there may be a difference between managerial or capitalist measures of efficiency change and worker assessments of efficiency change.

The second major difference between economists and sociologists appears to be the extent to which each is prepared to assume that markets are working efficiently, sociologists tending to incline more to the view that power is being exercised by one party to the transaction over the other. Although the concept of power within sociology is the subject of endless debate, there is widespread agreement that it includes the main elements incorporated in Weber's classic definition, viz., that it is the property of a relationship rather than an individual and that it relates to "the capability of an actor to achieve his or her will, even at the expense of that of others who might resist him" (Giddens 1979, 69). In other words the interests of one party prevail at the expense of the interests of the other. If one assumes that markets are inefficient, this means that parties may be making choices about outcomes that reflect their own interests rather than that inefficient choices are being made. The sociological view is plausible to the extent that inefficiency is seen to be widespread.

There may of course be a difference between a case in which output is increased by working harder as compared to a situation in which output is increased by working more intelligently. The former may reflect differences in interests. It is likely that the latter may (also) reflect problems in information and technology transfer.

The puzzle is why economists seem so unwilling to acknowledge the widespread existence of the exercise of power. One conception or definition of power within sociology is the resource-dependent model, which characterizes one party to the transaction, A, as having power over the other party, B, if A controls resources that B wants but cannot easily get elsewhere. This seems exactly equivalent to economists' understanding of monopoly. There does not, therefore, appear to be a problem at the conceptual level. The issue then becomes one of why sociologists seem to see monopolies where economists do not, and notions of social class and social closure are of importance in this context. If translated into the language of economics, the sociological view would be that social groups conduct transactions on the basis of a multitude of signals, not just on the basis of prices set by the market.

Entrepreneurs, Work Organization, and Intrafirm Effort Decisions

This difference in perspective between economists and sociologists is illustrated to an extent in the differing understanding of the role of entrepreneurs in Leibenstein (1987) and Francis (1986). Both books precede their discussion of entrepreneurship by using the idea of the effort-reward curve to explore the nature of the employment relationship. They reach complementary conclusions though Leibenstein's treatment is by far the more sophisticated, and there is much in his approach that could be incorporated in Francis (1986). However, the intention of my approach was to develop a conceptual framework that would allow analysis of the extent to which different forms of work organization were not just more or less efficient but also more or less exploitative. One of the results was to suggest a range of hypothetical roles for the entrepreneur that goes beyond that set out in Leibenstein (1987, 118–19). Whereas Leibenstein suggests that the distinguishing feature of entrepreneurs is their "special business skills and motivational capacities," I (Francis 1986, 126–28) suggest six possible functions performed by the entrepreneur in organizing labor. I distinguish between cases in which the business skills and motivational capacities are used only to enhance efficiency and those in which the entrepreneur's "skills and motivational capacities" also lead him or her to exert power over others. Only in the first of the six cases that follow is efficiency alone an explanation of the role of the entrepreneur. Each of the other five cases involves at least one group's interests being overridden.

Case 1. *The entrepreneur as cognoscente.* Marglin (1984) suggests that the entrepreneur in the late eighteenth century in the textile industry brought to the industry new skills in organizing production within a managerial hierarchy and that the skill and effort involved in producing this new form of organization produced extra output. Marglin argues that these skills and knowledge of organization and management are technically public goods but that the cognoscenti were able to exercise some monopoly control over them and thus were able to charge a rent for this knowledge and skill. McGuiness (1983) also suggests this interpretation of the entrepreneurial role but recognizes that the entrepreneur's skills may be private goods and thus it may be legitimate to rent them out. He also suggests that, in some cases, workers may gain more than they may lose in moving into an employment relationship with an entrepreneur. If this is the typical contribution made by an entrepreneur, one would expect to find this role performed in a number of enterprises, including voluntary or professional organizations where the workers hire the entrepreneur (and call him or her an administrator) rather than vice versa.

Case 2. *The entrepreneur as hero of the unskilled.* There are, however, a clutch of functions that the organizational entrepreneur may perform that are more ambiguous in the desirability of their effects. These functions correspond to the various labor-controlling managerial strategies already discussed. Each involves the entrepreneur in adding managerial work to, or subtracting mental work from, the manual work of the workers. However, the intentions of the entrepreneur, the process of adding the mental work, the evaluation of the outcome by skilled and unskilled workers, and the question of whether laborers would ever conceive it to be in their interests to hire an entrepreneur to carry out this work for them are different in each of the three cases now to be discussed.

The first of these cases is the entrepreneur as the visible hand implementing the Babbage strategy (1963, 175–76) of dividing the work to be executed into different processes, each requiring different degrees of skill or force. To the extent that this strategy reduces labor costs, there is a rent to be earned by an entrepreneur here. This is not always a strategy that operators will resist. If there is ample work for the highly skilled, even after some of the less skilled aspects of their tasks are taken from them, and there are less skilled people seeking work who are given new work opportunities by the implementation of this strategy, then reorganizing work along these Babbage lines might under these circumstances be generally welcomed. Obvious examples are professionals, such as doctors, lawyers, and engineers who might choose to employ paramedicals, clerks, technicians, and even machines to do certain relatively routine aspects of their jobs. It is possible that in a significant number of instances those given these fragmented tasks from the professional table are rather grateful for them, and so the new arrangement may be in everyone's best interests. The radical critique would, of course, be that the subordinate semiprofessions were suffering from false consciousness and also from a false view of their own capabilities. The preferable alternative, from the radical perspective, would presumably be one in which all those involved in performing these collections of activities would be trained to the same level, and the esoteric and routine elements in the jobs would be shared equally.

Case 3. *The entrepreneur as trustbuster.* Another version of this entrepreneurial act would be that of carrying out the strategy described by Stone (1973) of fragmenting jobs simply to break up the existing monopoly of a traditional craft organization over a particular occupation. It is difficult to imagine labor employing someone with entrepreneurial skills to carry out this task for them, though it is possible to imagine a situation where other occupational groups in an enterprise might welcome an entrepreneur breaking the monopoly of one occupational group over a set of tasks.

Case 4. *The entrepreneur as monopolizer of mental tasks.* It is unlikely that labor would be willingly involved in this category of entrepreneurial action. This is the Marglin (1984) interpretation of the entrepreneurial role. Not only does the entrepreneur make a contribution in installing a new form of organization — one that splits manual elements and mental elements of the tasks — but the entrepreneur then goes on to appropriate the public good of this managerial knowledge and gain a rent from the monopoly hold over it. The entrepreneur's profits thus accrue at least as much from the power obtained from the monopoly as from the reduced costs of labor from the Babbage-type effects of fragmenting the task.

Case 5. *The entrepreneur as broker between labor and capital.* The presence of an entrepreneur in the labor process may be explained in some measure and in some instances by that entrepreneur's access to capital and/or product markets. If such access results simply from entrepreneurial initiative or reasonably freely available management training and the development of a specialized competence about the technicalities of how capital and product markets work, then it might be regarded by workers as reasonable that someone should earn a rent from this entrepreneurial activity.

Case 6. *The entrepreneur as capitalist.* The radical argument, however, would be that one's class position in a society is extremely influential in giving access to capital — and control over the means of production through control over the means of marketing the product. In this view, then, the entrepreneur's access to capital and his control over product markets should more correctly be seen as resulting from the exercise of power and privilege rather than of skill (Francis 1986, 126–28).

The reason for this list is to suggest that explanations of forms of organization need to incorporate a discussion of both efficiency and power. The suggestion is that there are some functions performed by the entrepreneur that appear to be justified on efficiency grounds and that would be welcomed under certain conditions even by members of a producer cooperative. Other functions seem to involve the exercise of power and are likely to result from capital imposing its will on labor.

We thus offer the conclusion that only some of the differences in output between higher-performing and lower-performing firms may be caused by the latter having a higher level of X-inefficiency (which an entrepreneur might be able to reduce because of his or her skills and capacities). There also may be differences between the firms in the preferences and interests of members or in the extent to which those with high-performance preferences can exercise power to shift upward the output performance.

In circumstances where these last two conditions apply, an agenda for future research could take one of two forms. Either we should concern ourselves with developing concepts and measures for distinguishing the relative effects of power and X-inefficiency on organizational performance, or we should attempt to analyze the extent to which social and economic structures allow individuals to make choices between alternative arrangements. If, for example, an organization is producing a low level of output and an entrepreneur moves in with the intention of increasing it, how much choice do individuals within that organization have about how they should change their behavior? Is there a choice about staying in the organization or quitting, and what is the range of options if the latter choice is made? What range of organizations exists within any one population with regard to the different levels of work effort (and reward) offered? Studying the process of change may be more informative than a static analysis.

Either research agenda requires the active collaboration of economists and sociologists, and it is hoped that the amiable interchange of views between these disciplines at the Bellagio conference will produce fruit in the form of funded research proposals on this theme.

REFERENCES

Ashworth, M. H., J. A. Kay, and T. A. E. Sharp. 1982. "Differentials in Car Prices in UK and Belgium." IFS Report. London: Institute for Fiscal Studies.
Babbage, C. 1963. On the Economy of Machinery and Manufactures. London, 1832. Reprint. Fairfield, N.J.: Kelley.
Bacon, R., and W. Eltis. 1976. Britain's Economic Problem: Too Few Producers. London: Macmillan.
Barnett, C. 1986. Audit of War. London: Macmillan.
Beckerman, W., ed. 1979. Slow Growth in Britain: Causes and Consequences. Oxford: Clarendon Press.

Blackaby, F., ed. 1978. *De-industrialisation*. London: Heinemann.

Carter, C., ed. 1981. *Industrial Policy and Innovation*. London: Heinemann.

Elbaum, B., and W. Lazonick. 1986. *The Decline of the British Economy*. Oxford: Clarendon Press.

Francis, A. 1986. *New Technology at Work*. Oxford: Clarendon Press.

Francis, A. 1989. "The Concept of Competitiveness." In *The Competitiveness of European Industry*, ed. A. Francis and M. Tharakan. Beckenham: Croom Helm.

Giddens, A. 1979. *Central Problems in Social Theory*. London: Macmillan.

Harrod, R. 1967. "Assessing the Trade Returns." *Economic Journal* 77:499–511.

HMSO. 1985. *Report from the Select Committee of the House of Lords on Overseas Trade*. London: HMSO.

Lawrence, R. Z. 1984. *Can America Compete*. Washington, D.C.: Brookings.

Leibenstein, H. 1966. "Allocative Efficiency vs. 'X-efficiency.' " *American Economic Review* 56:392–415.

Leibenstein, H. 1976. *Beyond Economic Man: A New Foundation for Microeconomics*. Cambridge, Mass.: Harvard University Press.

Leibenstein, H. 1987. *Inside the Firm*. Cambridge, Mass.: Harvard University Press.

McGuiness, T. 1983. "Markets and Hierarchies: A Suitable Framework for an Evaluation of Organizational Change." In *Power, Efficiency and Institutions*, ed. A. Francis, J. Turk, and P. Willman. London: Heinemann.

Marglin, S. 1984. "Knowledge and Power." In *Firms, Organization and Labour*, ed. F. H. Stephen. London: Macmillan.

Nossiter, B. D. 1978. *Britain: A Future That Works*. London: Andre Deutsche.

Payne, P. 1986. "Entrepreneurship and British Economic Decline." University of Aberdeen, Department of Economic History. Working Paper.

Salaman, G. 1979. *Work Organizations: Resistance and Control*. London: Longman.

Stone, K. 1973. "The Origins of Job Structure in the Steel Industry." *Radical America* 7:19–64.

Thirwall, A. P. 1982. *Balance-of-Payments Theory and the United Kingdom Experience*. London: Macmillan.

USGPO. 1985. "Global Competition, The New Reality." Report of the President's Commission on Industrial Competitiveness, vol. 2. Washington, D.C.

Weiner, M. 1981. *English Culture and the Decline of the Industrial Spirit*. London: Cambridge University Press.

Williamson, O. E. 1975. *Markets and Hierarchies*. New York: Free Press.

Williamson, O. E. 1985. *The Economic Institutions of Capitalism*. New York: Free Press.

Williamson, O. E. 1986. *Economic Organization: Firms, Markets and Policy Control*. Brighton: Wheatsheaf.

Willman, P. 1986. *Technological Change, Collective Bargaining and Industrial Efficiency*. Oxford: Clarendon Press.

Institutions, X-Efficiency, Transaction Costs, and Socioeconomic Development

Erik Thorbecke

In the last two decades some important methodological contributions have been made toward a better understanding of the impact of institutional factors on the process of socioeconomic development. These contributions have significantly enriched the explanatory power and realism of the neoclassical theory and alternative paradigms.[1]

There are many strands in the literature on institutions that need to be woven together to provide a better and more integrated picture of the relationship between institutions and socioeconomic performance in terms of both efficiency and equity. Many, if not most, contributions are based on and applied to developed industrialized societies. The aim of this article is to attempt at least a partial integration and adaptation of various institutional paradigms as they relate more specifically to socioeconomic performance in developing, rather than developed, countries. Given the large size and diversity of the literature in this area, the present effort is selective by necessity. As befits the major theme of the Bellagio conference, the X-efficiency concept is given a central place in the present treatment in terms of the actual and potential insights it offers in linking institutional factors and socioeconomic performance.

This article is divided into the following sections. The first section compares and contrasts the X-efficiency theory with the transaction costs approach.[2] Even though these two alternative approaches have much in

---

1. In a recent paper, de Janvry and Sadoulet (1988) have argued, "There have been significant convergence in economics between classics and neo-classics, where the first have contributed the understanding of structure and the preoccupations with institutions and the state and the second the rigor of rational choice microfoundations and of analytical tools." Incidentally, neo-Marxist contributions are included under the classics in their treatment.

2. Bardhan 1988 in an excellent review of alternative approaches to development economics distinguishes among three major approaches, which he classifies somewhat

common, it can be argued that each one has its raison d'être in answering somewhat different sets of questions. It will be seen that this view is contrary to that espoused by some modern neoclassicists who hold that X-efficiency is entirely subsumed under the transaction costs approach.

The next section looks at various definitions of and approaches to institutions and explores their relationship with various aspects of socioeconomic development. Here, again, an attempt is made to determine the extent to which the X-efficiency paradigm might contribute to the design of certain institutional forms such as contracts and conventions so as to improve the total efficiency of firms and perhaps enhance social efficiency and improve income distribution at the macroeconomic level. In this same section, we shall touch, as well, on the concepts of organizational and institutional efficiency and, in a more general sense, on the impact of alternative institutional arrangements on performance.

The following section is devoted to a brief and selective examination of collective actions as they help explain the physiology and the dynamics of socioeconomic systems in developing countries. Finally, the role of the state in the development process is scrutinized. Different conceptions and theories of the state are explored.

X-Efficiency and Transaction Costs

Leibenstein's X-efficiency concept was initiated as a reaction to perceived limitations of the neoclassical framework. Very succinctly, X-inefficiency is defined as the difference between maximal allocative efficiency and the actually observed efficiency. Leibenstein himself uses the following diagram to illustrate X-inefficiency. The two isoquants in figure 1 represent the same level of output (say, 100 units). If the capital and labor inputs were used in the optimal fashion, output Q'_{100} could be produced with K_{min} and L_{min}. However, it is observed that the firm uses K_a and L_a to produce the same level of output. Leibenstein refers to the difference between maximal effectiveness of the utilization of inputs and the actual effectiveness as the degree of X-inefficiency. Thus, a measure

---

loosely as neoclassical, Marxist, and structuralist-institutionalist. He argues convincingly that the differences between the sophisticated versions of these approaches are narrower than generally perceived. All three of these approaches, in their modern versions, have relied on the transaction costs concept—to a greater or lesser degree. Since this article proposes to compare and contrast transaction costs with X-efficiency, I have grouped together, somewhat gratuitously, the neoclassical school and the structuralist-institutionalist approach under the heading of modern neoclassicists.

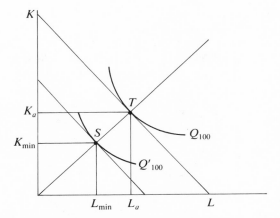

Fig. 1.   A measure of X-inefficiency

of X-inefficiency would be the additional amounts of capital and labor required to produce the output Q_{100}. According to Leibenstein,

> The concept reflects the idea that it is one thing to allocate inputs to economic units such as firms, but it is something else to use these inputs efficiently. Hence, X-efficiency measures the degree of ineffectiveness in the utilization of the inputs. (Leibenstein 1980, 27)

Incidentally, Leibenstein assumes that all firms face the same relative prices so that the two-budget (price) lines in figure 1 are parallel. However, within the setting of developing countries, characterized by segmented markets, some producers may be facing very different relative prices from others. For instance, small farmers or informal sector enterprises in the urban areas with little land or assets (collaterals) can borrow only in the informal credit market at higher interest rates than those faced by larger farms and modern enterprises. This situation is illustrated in figure 2. The higher cost of capital means that for some producers the price line rotates downward around point L yielding a new equilibrium at point V. In this instance, there is a loss of output of two units ($Q_{100} - Q_{98}$) reflecting the price distortions prevailing in the economy. Even though producers have allocated their resources efficiently, given the prices they face, there is a societal cost in terms of foregone output associated with these price distortions. Translating this situation into Leibenstein's conceptual framework

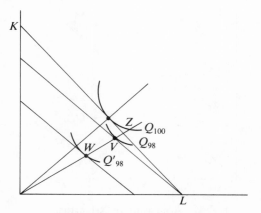

Fig. 2. X-inefficiency and price inefficiency

would suggest that X-inefficiency here would be equal to VW while ZV would reflect price inefficiency.[3]

The major postulates and axioms underlying the X-efficiency theory are the following: (1) the individual rather than the household or the firm is the basic unit of analysis; (2) an individual's response to opportunities for gains and to constraints that can impose losses depends on his personality and on the setting in which the individual operates. This means that the individual is guided by selective rationality rather than maximizing behavior; (3) inert areas are asserted to exist because an individual "will not necessarily move to a superior position in the standard utility sense because of the initial costs of moving" (Leibenstein 1978, 329); (4) contracts are incomplete and, in particular, the effort level is not specified in labor contracts; (5) effort is a discretionary variable with individuals being able to decide on the level and intensity of effort; and, finally, (6) principals

---

3. M. J. Farrell (1957) proposes a breakdown of economic efficiency into two components, price efficiency and technical efficiency. In some respects his technical efficiency concept bears a resemblance to X-efficiency. However, Leibenstein is quite explicit in wanting to distinguish X-efficiency from technical efficiency as indicated, for example, by the following:

X-efficiency is not the same as what is frequently referred to as technical efficiency, since X-efficiency may arise for reasons outside the knowledge or capability of managers attempting to do the managing. . . . In other words, it is not only a matter of techniques of management, or anything else "technical" in carrying out decisions, that is involved in X-efficiency. (Leibenstein 1980, 27)

and agents may have different interests.[4] In a number of works, Leibenstein has argued that combinations of these postulates yield the X-efficiency theory.

On the basis of a very thorough and critical evaluation of X-efficiency, De Alessi has concluded that the latter construct should be dismissed as inferior to the modern neoclassical theory incorporating transaction costs. The following quote is most revealing:

> On purely methodological grounds, the X-efficiency construct may be dismissed by the rule of Occam's razor as a step backwards in the development of economic theory. Whereas generalized neo-classical theory offers fewer, more general axioms yielding a richer, more powerful set of testable implications, X-efficiency offers instead a deductive system with more axioms that seek to be more descriptive yet yield fewer, less clearly specified implications. Indeed, it is difficult to escape the conclusion that Leibenstein is merely trying to offer a more descriptively "realistic" set of actions. This is a methodological route that, for good reasons, may be expected to lead to a dead end. (De Alessi, 1983)

This is a strong indictment that, as you might imagine, I do not share. Even though one can accept and be swayed by a number of De Alessi's well-reasoned arguments, I will subsequently argue that the X-efficiency doctrine can, in fact, be differentiated from the transaction costs approach through its focus on the decision-making process and procedures. However, before this can be done, the essence of the transaction costs approach needs to be reviewed.

In its simplest form, transaction costs represent the aggregation of a number of costs that are generally not included in the concept of production costs, such as information costs, negotiation costs, monitoring costs, coordination costs, and enforcement costs. Matthews defines transaction costs as follows:

> The fundamental idea of transaction costs is that they consist of the cost of arranging the contract *ex ante* and monitoring and enforcing it *ex post*, as opposed to production costs, which are the costs of executing the contract. To a large extent transaction costs are costs of relations between people and people, and production costs are costs of relations between people and things. (1986, 906)

---

4. L. De Alessi (1983) undertakes a critical and detailed evaluation of these axioms and postulates.

In this sense, transaction costs are the costs of getting the different parties to a particular transaction together. Because the socioeconomic system is full of frictions and markets operate imperfectly, each party to a transaction is likely to have the incentive to practice opportunism at the expense of the other party. The classic example is the market for used cars. Asymmetrical information among buyers and sellers of used cars can lead to market collapse and failure as Akerlof (1970) has elegantly shown in his article on the market for lemons. Transactions can occur among firms, between firms and individuals, as well as among different agents within a single firm through explicit or implicit contracts among the individual agents in the firm. Various forms of such contracts entailing different transaction costs are discussed in the next section.

One basic principle of transaction costs economics is that through the actual or potential competition among alternative forms of transactions and contracts, the forms that survive the test of competition are those that minimize total transaction costs for a given level of production costs. It will be seen subsequently that, in fact, it may be more accurate to characterize the modern neoclassical school as implying that the sum of production and transaction costs needs to be minimized. In many instances, a trade-off may exist between these two types of costs.[5]

In a nutshell, Leibenstein contends that the body of microeconomic theory does not explore in any critical way what goes on inside a firm. In his words,

> the enterprise of economic theory is a black box, as it were. We do not look inside. How decisions are made in terms of details and procedures is not part of the problem area of microeconomic theory. The theory is concerned with firm behavior and not with behavior inside the firm. To make the theory work we indicate what the black box does by specifying its objective by such statements as maximizing profits, or maximizing a utility function. . . . It is people, and especially people within organizations, that carry out decisions and put them into effect. (1986, 4)

How far Leibenstein goes in opening up this black box, in identifying the behavioral mechanisms inherent to the organization and in providing operational guidance to reduce X-inefficiency are questions that are subsequently addressed. It is clear that the prevailing socioeconcomic and institutional environment in terms of such elements as systems of property

---

5. For a good discussion of the transaction costs approach in the context of economic development, see Nugent 1986, on which part of this discussion is based.

rights and laws, cultural values and norms, and the importance and pervasiveness of the family play a major role in influencing the behavior of the different transactors (individuals, firms, or even the state) and affect thereby transaction costs. Thus, this last concept is offered as an explanation for the pervasiveness of economic activities taking place within families in both rural and urban areas of developing countries. The farm household and the informal sector enterprise, within which production and consumption decisions are jointly made, are prototypical forms of enterprises in poor countries. So are, on a much larger scale, family enterprises combining modern industrial production and banking activities such as the Group in Latin America. In each instance, the choice of these specific forms can be explained by a desire on the part of the agent to minimize transaction costs. Opportunistic behavior can be much more easily detected and penalized within the family than when other households are involved.

Do transaction costs represent the unavoidable frictional (transactional) inefficiency that exists in the real world characterized by imperfect information, uncertainty, and imperfect markets? If so, as claimed by the modern neoclassical theory, are transactions costs not equivalent to X-inefficiency? Furthermore, is the former concept not more operational and rigorous in explaining observed behavior? Before answering these questions, one must analyze more deeply and concretely how applicable and useful these constructs are both in a positive (descriptive) sense and in a normative sense, particularly as they relate to the socioeconomic and institutional setting of developing countries. This analysis is undertaken in the next two sections dealing, respectively, with (a) institutions and socioeconomic development, and (b) collective actions and the role of the state.

Institutions, Transaction Costs, X-efficiency, and Socioeconomic Development

In this section we explore very selectively the contributions of the new institutional economics (particularly the transaction costs approach) and X-efficiency to a better understanding of institutional arrangements in developing countries, and, more generally, the physiology and process of economic development.

First of all, we have to define what is meant by institutions. The literature on institutions is very extensive and diversified. A plethora of different approaches and definitions — often along disciplinary lines — is characteristic of this concept. For the present purposes, we can start with Matthews's (1986) typology, which identifies four approaches to institutions, before modifying and extending this typology slightly.

The first approach identifies alternative economic institutions with alternative systems of property rights. In the setting of a developing country, property rights systems may be fluid, less formalized, and based more on customs than in more developed countries. In addition, the link between property rights and the prevailing asset distribution (particularly the distribution of land) is a crucial one in poor countries. In one sense the property rights reflect and help maintain the asset distribution while, at the same time, any change in the prevailing asset distribution will almost certainly require, and be contingent on, changes in existing property rights.

The second approach looks at institutions as a set of conventions or norms of economic behavior. Conventions, in contrast with laws, can be thought to substitute internal for external pressure and discipline. In this sense, they many be more effective than laws since they entail a much lower transaction cost. The third approach to institutions is embodied in the types of contract in use, which can be explicit or implicit, formal or informal. Contracts regulate the great bulk of economic activities. The fourth approach, as Matthews points out, is really a subdivision of the previous one but is essential in its own right. It relates to institutions "in the sense of what kind of contracts are in use about authority, about who decides what" (1986, 904). To the extent that most contracts have a certain degree of open-endedness, the question at hand is: How do conflicts get resolved and who decides ultimately? The greater inequality in the distribution of assets and income in developing countries, as compared to the industrialized countries, implies that greater disparities of power are likely to exist among actors so that the authority system may have a key impact on socioeconomic development, particularly equity.

There are two additional institutional concepts that need to be specified before proceeding with the analysis. Organizations—be they firms, state enterprises, universities, public agencies—can be thought of as embodying a set of institutions at the microlevel. They are subject to the prevailing macro rules in having to operate within the legal and property rights system in force, and having to abide by the implicit and explicit contracts they have entered into. Furthermore, individual behavior within organizations is guided by existing conventions.

At the macrolevel a *socioeconomic system* consists of a set of organizations. One can think of this as the architecture of socioeconomic systems, to use the term coined by Sah and Stiglitz. In their words,

the architecture . . . describes how the constituent decision-making units are arranged together in a system, how the decision-making authority and ability is distributed within a system, who gathers what information, and who communicates what with whom. (1986, 716)

The internal structure, or architecture, of a socioeconomic system affects its performance.[6]

We can now use these six aspects of institutions to explore very briefly (1) the extent to which and how they are incorporated into the X-efficiency and transaction costs approaches, respectively; and (2) the explanatory power of the latter in relating these institutional dimensions to efficiency and equity in a positive and a prescriptive sense.[7]

The central proposition of the neoclassical framework with regard to property rights is that property assignments (i.e., the distribution of ownership rights) have no substantive allocative implications. If rights to resources are fully assigned and privately held, then, regardless of the initial assignment, they will be reallocated to the highest-valued use according to the Coase theorem (1960). There are two problems with this view that are particularly acute in traditional societies, (a) many property rights are only incompletely assigned, or not assigned and therefore not clearly transferable; and (b) the initial asset distribution influences the political and economic power of agents and the form and enforcement of contracts resulting in "non-neutrality of property assignments" (Bowles and Gintis 1988).

Although the transaction costs approach has had some limited success in explaining the allocation process in instances where property rights are not fully assigned and other imperfections have prevailed, within the setting of Western societies, the simplistic recipe of full privatization as a way to minimize transaction costs in developing countries should be viewed with considerable skepticism. This point is well argued by Nugent (1986) and Runge (1986) who show that incomplete property rights and the collective use of scarce resources such as water and land within the social context, rules, and constraints typical of developing countries need imply neither inefficiency nor an invitation to the tragedy of the common variety.[8]

---

6. Since at the microlevel an organization, as defined, combines a set of institutions or institutional factors, the socioeconomic system, as the aggregation of all organizations, incorporates all institutions.

7. Since the focus of both approaches has been primarily, if not exclusively, on efficiency, evaluating their implications for equity (income distribution) has to be done indirectly.

8. The X-efficiency concept does not appear to be related to property rights directly. However, the indirect effects of the latter on X-efficiency through the degree of external and internal pressure on the firm are discussed subsequently.

The heart of the X-efficiency doctrine is contained in the nexus of conventions, contracts, and organizations—mainly the area where these three institutional dimensions overlap. The black box is "what goes on inside firms" (Leibenstein 1986, 2); it consists of the decision-making process and the behavior of agents within firms and organizations and the impact of intrafirm conventions and contracts (implicit and explicit) on X-efficiency.[9] In a positive sense, X-inefficiency measures the actual loss in total efficiency resulting from conventions, habits, decisions, and processes of implementation that are nonoptimal and that are an inherent part of organizational life (Leibenstein 1980, 27–28). But, more importantly, in a normative and prescriptive sense, X-efficiency represents the potential gains from changing conventions and rules of the game within the firm.

The causative scheme that is postulated is that the environment applies a certain amount of pressure on the agents that affects their choice of technology (defined as a translation of inputs into outputs) and, thereby, the cost per unit of output. The key concepts that lie behind the decision-making process are pressure and effort, with the level of effort related to the amount of pressure exerted through a lexicographic calculation procedure that has, as its limiting case, maximization. The decision process that is followed varies depending on the level of pressure, as a step function. At the lowest pressure range, decisions are made on the basis of habits; beyond a certain threshold level of pressure, there is a discrete jump to the next decision mechanism based on conventions, followed by work ethics, partial calculation, and full calculation (presumably analogous to maximization) (Leibenstein 1986, sec. III). In short, it is assumed that decisions are made in terms of a lexicographic ordering with an individual shifting from one category to the next as pressure rises.

Since contracts between the firm and employees are incomplete, with a payment side specified but the effort level unspecified, or only partially specified, the two parties face a Prisoner's Dilemma problem. A contributing factor to this dilemma is that even if both the firm and employees stand to gain from a higher effort level, the impact of any one

---

9. The following quotation is revealing of Leibenstein's position:

> The connection between the organizational analysis and institutions is through the concept of intra-firm conventions. Conventions, as used here, are essentially recognized ways of doing things within the firm, while institutions are conventions that go beyond the boundaries of the firm. (1986, 9)

Leibenstein takes the latter as given and concentrates almost exclusively on the former.

employee's increased effort on output is marginal so that the employee tends to become a free rider.

How can this adversarial relation be resolved? First, through greater external (e.g., market) pressure and internal pressure on the organization through the adoption of new conventions and rules of the game within the enterprise that encourage a higher effort level and induce employees and managers to climb the decision ladder substituting superior decision rules for looser ones (e.g., replacing habits by conventions). Second, a Pareto-improved solution for this adversarial relation can be found through a cooperative outcome based on group rationality. This could be achieved, for example, through the involvement of a third (neutral) party and might take the form of binding arbitration or even letting the state or a state agency decide.

I would submit that it is this emphasis on the physiology and mechanism of the decision process that is the distinguishing characteristic of the X-efficiency approach when contrasted with the transaction costs approach. In order to improve its operational usefulness, which is presently limited, much more research of an integrative nature combining social psychology, organizational behavior, economics, and other disciplines is clearly required. The societal payoff could be high, although the increasing trend toward (sub) disciplinary compartmentalization of knowledge makes this a high-risk proposition for individual researchers to undertake. It should be noted that a reduction in X-inefficiency per se does not necessarily contribute to the macroequity objective. However, one can conceive of conventions being designed, particularly within state enterprises, that might contribute to both efficiency and equity objectives.[10]

The main contribution of the modern neoclassical theory has been in explaining the raison d'être of different contracts, and to a lesser extent, conventions, typical of the setting of developing societies. Simply put, they owe their existence to the fact that they minimize transaction costs. Thus, the emphasis has been much more on rationalizing existing arrangements than on unraveling the mechanisms underlying the decision process itself. The transaction costs approach has been particularly successful in providing a strong rationale for the pervasiveness of the following types of contracts: (1) sharecropping; (2) interlinked factor market contracts and interlocking transactions; and (3) intrafamily

---

10. Unfortunately, it is easier to think of conventions that entail a tradeoff between these objectives. For instance, reallocating a given budget for state enterprises by increasing salaries of civil servants and reducing their number could increase efficiency but at the cost of employment.

insurance contracts. To the extent that share contracts allow economies of scope (in supervising, in monitoring labor effort, and in limiting the possibilities of output underreporting and asset misuse — all of these simultaneously), they may be an optimal form of contract in that they minimize transaction costs. Likewise, interlinking (e.g., combining labor and credit contracts centered on the hired agricultural worker from within the village) may reduce transaction costs as compared to an unlinked contract by (a) breaking the differences in access to the credit market among the different agents, and (b) saving on information costs, in addition to saving on supervision costs.

Finally, one important reason for the resilience of the family as a form of organization in rural societies is because it provides cheap insurance to its members. As Nugent (1985) has shown, given (a) the dispersion of rural household, (b) the difficulties of assigning premiums that would be appropriate to the individual farmer, and (c) the likelihood that realized risk might be increased by the existence of insurance, adverse selection and moral hazard problems are likely to be far more serious in poor rural areas. Within the household, opportunistic behavior is easy to detect, thereby reducing the cost of family-supplied insurance. For the same and other reasons the extended household provides a much more efficient way of dealing with disability, old age, and loss of life risks than might be available on alternative commercial terms.

Most, if not all, of these contracts owe their existence to the initial uneven distribution of assets. For instance, if land were evenly distributed and farmers had equal access to credit, sharecropping and interlocking transactions would disappear.[11] Thus, whereas transaction costs explain in a positive sense why certain forms of contracts prevail, this doctrine ignores the normative implications of these contracts on income distribution.

Akerlof (1984) has made major contributions to explaining the pervasiveness of certain conventions in traditional societies. In particular, the persistence of economically unprofitable social customs (e.g., the rigid link between castes and occupations) is explained by the higher individual cost relative to the benefit of breaking these customs (for instance, through a loss of reputation). Individuals would rather be free riders, as is discussed in the next section. The existence of class loyalty and cognitive dissonance (through adjusting one's belief to one's constraints) is, likewise, explained in terms of economic welfare maximization.

Providing a rationale for the persistence of conventions that may be

---

11. For a good discussion of these issues, see Bardhan 1988.

desirable neither on efficiency nor on equity grounds may be a first and necessary step in the design of new conventions conducive to the attainment of a higher level of socioeconomic welfare.

One possible lesson that can be drawn from a comparison of the transaction costs approach and the X-efficiency approach is that they appear to be largely complementary when it comes to their treatment of contracts and conventions. The transactions costs approach provides a rigorous rationale for the occurrence of contracts and conventions while X-efficiency emphasizes the decision-making process underlying them. This suggests that a greater degree of integration between these two approaches could be potentially fruitful in the identification and design of conventions and contracts more conducive to socioeconomic development. We return to this issue in the next section.

Some important recent contributions have been made by modern neoclassicists to the socioeconomic system. Two of these contributions are reviewed here briefly. The first one is by Yang (1988), who builds a relatively simple model consisting of four different alternative market structures ranging from complete autarky (with every individual being self-sufficient) without firms to complete division of labor with firms. He proceeds to solve for the equilibrium price and output levels that minimize the sum of production and transaction costs for each of these market structures. This yields what he calls "organizational efficiency." Next, he solves the model for the market structure that minimizes production and transaction costs for the whole system, resulting in what he coins "institutional efficiency." The optimal market structure is seen to depend on production, utility, and transaction function parameters of the initial system. The following quotation is enlightening:

> For traditional production functions, employers just put labor and other factors into "production functions" and obtain output from such black boxes. What is the internal organization of the black box, what implications does the internal organization have for the traditional theory of equilibrium, and why does an economy evolve from autarky without firms to one with the developed division of labor within firms and among the firms? The model in this paper allow us to open the black box and to answer these questions. (1988, 28)

Thus, Yang attempts to open not only the black box of the firm à la Leibenstein but also the institutional black box. At least, potentially, three types of government distortions can be evaluated within this model: (1) the distortions of resource allocation for given levels of division of labor and institutional arrangements (the major concern of traditional microeconomics); (2) the distortions of organizational structure; and (3) the distortions of institutional arrangements.

The second contribution worth noting here is that of Sah and Stiglitz (1986). They explore the "architecture of the economic system." In particular, they evaluate the implications of two different organizational arrangements, polyarchies and hierarchies. A polyarchy is defined as a system in which there are several decision makers who can undertake projects independently of one another, while decision-making authority is more concentrated in a hierarchy where only a few individuals can undertake projects. These two architectures can be thought to reflect a market-oriented economy and a bureaucracy-oriented economy, respectively. By postulating different decision processes being followed by these two types of organizational forms, one can draw certain inferences regarding their comparative performance with regard to such issues as the screening of good and bad projects, the transmission of information, and the consequences of different types of human errors.

In particular, this approach may prove to be valuable in suggesting the optimal degree of centralization and decentralization in a socioeconomic system given the objective function that, at least in principle, could be expressed as a function of both efficiency and equity. Exploring the impact of different organizational architectures on the performance of the system reminds me of the earlier work of Tinbergen on the "theory of the optimal regime." A blending of these approaches might prove to be very fruitful.

Collective Action and the Role of the State

In its simplest form, the theory of collective action is based on the application of transaction costs to explain the likelihood of success or failure by a given set of individuals in undertaking activities that may benefit them collectively. In particular, failure to change institutions in such cases derives primarily from the free-rider problem. As Nugent states,

> Even if society as a whole might benefit from institutional change, no one person in the group may be willing to violate the existing social rule because of the ill repute that such an individual could expect to earn for violating the social rule. (1986)

This helps explain the fossilization of certain conventions such as the persistence of caste-specific occupations, for instance.

Of course, there are cases where collective action by one or more groups that would have resulted in net societal welfare improvements (but not Pareto improvements) is blocked by other groups that would have stood to lose potentially from it — an issue to which we will return subsequently.

The success of collective action depends on the ability to suppress or at least weaken the free-rider problem. As Olson (1965, 1982) has shown, the possibility of collective action is said to be the greater (a) the smaller the group, (b) the more homogeneous the group, (c) the longer the group has been in existence, (d) the more differentiated the goals of different members of the group, (e) the greater the sensitivity of the group to threatened loss arising from inaction, (f) the closer the social and physical proximity among group members, and (g) the more unequal the distribution of wealth or power among group members.

A quick perusal of these characteristics can be seen to provide a rationale for the urban bias and, more specifically, the large and significant difference, in developing countries, in the relative influence on policymaking exerted by industrialists and civil servants as compared to farmers. This outcome is likely even if the state were to assume a passive role.

In the more likely case that the state is not neutral and associates itself with, or represents certain classes (at the limit the state might actually be captured by these classes), the state will tilt institutions and rules in favor of its clients through such policies as the granting of licenses and monopoly rights, protecting certain sectors, and price and subsidy measures. These actions yield "contrived rents" but are, in fact, artificial transfers by the government to these privileged groups.

The question that needs to be asked in the context of this article is not so much what the collective action-cum-transaction costs theory and X-efficiency contribute to an understanding of existing institutional arrangements, in a positive economics sense, but rather what they can contribute potentially, in a normative sense, to the design of institutions enhancing overall socioeconomic welfare.

An answer to this question depends on one's perception of the role of the state in the process of development, that is, which theory of the state is adopted. At one extreme we have the Tinbergen view of the neutral state with its own social welfare function that in a democracy can be assumed to reflect some consensus of national interest. The role of the state is to choose the set of policy instruments, structural changes, and reforms that maximizes that function. The state stands above the political arena and arbitrates among the various groups and lobbies in a fair and representative way. At the other extreme we find the view espoused by many political scientists and public-choice theorists that the political process is a marketplace and that the regime in power represents the interests of the ruling group(s) (often an alliance) and implements that group's ideology. In some cases, the state can be captured by a group or class as under a totalitarian dictatorship.

A somewhat more realistic portrayal of the state would be somewhere within the above spectrum. On the one hand, the regime may reflect the underlying political power balance and act to serve the interests of the ruling groups in the short run. On the other hand, the state may be at least partially guided by a more enlightened and long-run vision of the national interest. In this sense, the state may be somewhat schizophrenic.[12] Neither the idealized version of (1) the state as a somewhat abstract entity reflecting the national interest and acting as the ultimate arbitrator among conflicting groups to find the common good, nor, alternatively, (2) the state as captive of a lobby are constructs that lend themselves to exploring new institutional arrangements conducive to improved social welfare — even if they sometimes occur. The state is likely to be both (a) a power broker trying to reconcile the divergent objectives of various groups in the design of a long-run development strategy, and (b) an actor on the political and economic scene, siding in the short run with civil servants and other groups with their own vested interests.

Within this model, how useful are the collective action and X-efficiency frameworks in suggesting desired (not just Pareto-improving but also equity-improving) institutional changes? One immediate limitation of the modern neoclassical approach — which, I would claim, does not apply to the same degree to X-efficiency — is that it tends to take as its reference point (benchmark) an idealized first-best world. The prevailing environment and conditions in a typical developing country economy are likely to be full of imperfections — far worse than a second-best approximation. The goal should be to move that economy from its existing state to a somewhat less imperfect state through the design of appropriate policies and institutional arrangements.[13]

In X-efficiency theory — emphasizing the decision-making process within the organization — two recipes suggest themselves. First, conventions and rules of the game within the firm could be designed to increase the level of internal pressure to elicit high-intensity effort levels by man-

---

12. It is unlikely that there is only one universally valid theory of the state. A given regime in time and space might conform best to one of the above characterizations, while another regime might fit another model better.

13. Consistent with the dictum "perfection is the enemy of the good."

agers and workers.[14] At least to some extent, it might be possible to appeal to extra-rational motivation of an ideological nature. There are many examples of developing countries' regimes that have successfully disseminated ideologies in the public sector that significantly enhanced the commitment of civil servants (Indonesia is a good example through its "eight paths to equity" philosophy).[15] By understanding the decision-making process, in its sociological and psychological aspects, one might uncover intraorganization conventions that significantly improve the performance of the agents. Whether these conventions can be introduced independently of ideological packaging is a somewhat open question!

Second, X-efficiency can help guide the firm out of a Prisoner's Dilemma by identifying appropriate cooperative solutions through reliance on a neutral and friendly third party (an arbitrator or even the state at the limit) or proper incentives built into the system to resolve conflicts between parties. Conceivably a learning process could be built in through which agents could reach a superior cooperative outcome.

The collective action doctrine could be most useful in identifying ways of encouraging and promoting group actions (and alliances) contributing to sustained development. (In this sense it is complementary to X-efficiency, where potential prescriptive usefulness is at the enterprise level.) Here again, the state can play a role in mediating conflicts among groups and over time. Two examples might illustrate this point.

First, it has become increasingly recognized that, in the long run, the interest of the state and the various groups constituting it are best served by assigning a priority role to agriculture during early phases of the development process instead of discriminating against it from the beginning in favor of the industrial sector and the urban population. However, in the short and medium run, these latter groups want to squeeze and tax the agricultural sector to obtain the necessary capital resources to industrialize and build an urban infrastructure; they also desire cheap food. This creates a trade-off between long-run economic and political benefits and short-run costs, should the state adopt an enlightened policy of agricultural development. The state will have to convince the urban groups and its own civil servants that the short-run losses of not taxing agriculture too heavily in the early phases should be more than compensated by gains in subsequent periods. Even though this trade-off is an exceedingly difficult one, a comparative study of six poor countries over

---

14. The more competitive markets are, the more external pressure is exerted on the firm, according to Leibenstein. In this respect he aligns himself with the neoclassicists.

15. Of course, the wrong kind of ideology can have opposite results on efficiency and equity.

a twenty-year period, concluded that institutions have a key role to play in resolving this conflict. Specific examples of desirable institutions have been identified (see Lecaillon et al. 1987).

The second example relates to the widespread structural adjustment programs in debtor countries. These programs emphasize liberalization and privatization. Generally, a removal of distortions is a necessary condition to restoring balance of payments and budgetary equilibrium and the resumption of economic growth. Even though the long-run benefits of stabilization and adjustment measures are clear, they entail short-run costs for special groups — ranging from poor households that may lose some (food) subsidies to industrialists producing import-substitute goods. The state and, incidentally, the donors have to work out schemes to compensate, at least partially, the short-run losers in anticipation of long-term gains. How to guide this process is one domain where collective action doctrine can be useful in suggesting which obstacles should be removed to forge the desired alliances.

In conclusion, there is a natural complementarity between the X-efficiency approach and the collective action-cum-transaction costs approach, with the first concentrating on the decision-making process within the firm and ways of increasing internal pressure while the second approach focuses more on the means of increasing external pressure.

REFERENCES

Akerlof, G. A. 1970. "The Market for 'Lemons': Qualitative Uncertainty and the Market Mechanism." *Quarterly Journal of Economics* 84:488–500.
Akerlof, G. A. 1984. *An Economic Theorist's Book of Tales*. Cambridge: Cambridge University Press.
Bardhan, P. 1988. "Alternative Approaches to Development Economics: An Evaluation." Department of Economics, University of California, Berkeley. Mimeo.
Bowles, S., and H. Gintis. 1988. "Contested Exchange: Political Economy and Modern Economic Theory." *American Economic Review* 78:145–50.
Coase, R. H. 1960. "The Problem of Social Costs." *Journal of Law and Economics* 3:1–44.
De Alessi, L. 1983. "Property Rights and Transaction Costs." *American Economic Review* 73:64–81.
de Janvry, A., and E. Sadoulet. 1988. "The Political Economy of Agricultural Policies: Convergence of Analytics, Divergence of Implications." Department of Agricultural and Resource Economics, University of California, Berkeley. Mimeo.
Farrell, M. J. 1957. "The Measurement of Productive Efficiency." *Journal of the Royal Statistical Society*, Ser. A, 120:253–82.

Lecaillon, J., C. Morrisson, H. Schneider, and E. Thorbecke. 1987. *Economic Policies and Agricultural Performance of Low-Income Countries.* Paris: OECD Development Center.

Leibenstein, H. 1978. "On the Basic Proposition of X-efficiency Theory." *American Economic Review, Papers and Proceedings* 68:328–32.

Leibenstein, H. 1980. *Inflation, Income Distribution and X-efficiency Theory.* London: Croom Helm.

Leibenstein, H. 1986. "Organizational Economics and Institutions as Missing Elements in Economic Development Analysis." Presented at a conference on The Role of Institutions in Economic Development, Cornell University, November.

Matthews, R. C. O. 1986. "The Economics of Institutions and the Sources of Growth." *Economic Journal* 96:903–18.

Nugent, J. 1985. "The Old-Age Security Motive for Fertility." *Population and Development Review* 11:75–97.

Nugent, J. B. 1986. "Applications of the Theory of Transaction Costs and Collective Action to Development Problems and Policy." Prepared for a conference on The Role of Institutions in Economic Development, Cornell University, November.

Olson, M. 1965. *The Logic of Collective Action.* Cambridge, Mass.: Harvard University Press.

Olson, M. 1982. *The Rise and Decline of Nations: Economic Growth, Stagflation and Social Rigidities.* New Haven: Yale University Press.

Runge, C. F. 1986. "Common Property and Collective Action in Economic Development." *World Development.*

Sah, R. K., and J. E. Stiglitz. 1986. "The Architecture of Economic Systems: Hierarchies and Polyarchies." *American Economic Review* 76:716–27.

Yang, X. 1988. "An Approach to Modelling Institutional Development." Economic Growth Center, Yale University Center Discussion Paper no. 550, January.

Commentary

Klaus Weiermair and J. H. Hatch

Comment by Klaus Weiermair on the Articles by Bohnet and Beck, Matthews, and Thorbecke

The article by Bohnet and Beck picks up a classical or traditional question in economics, namely, the impact of a tax change on labor supply, and investigates it from the perspective of X-efficiency theory. Points of interest are qualitative changes in labor supply and effort levels. This implies using effort-utility functions à la Leibenstein, to which the authors faithfully ascribe. The exercise of imposing a tax change is executed in a diligent and exacting way. My only question is: What would have happened had we assumed a different functional form for effort utility and a different size shift? In other words, what would have helped me appreciably in interpreting the results would have been a more thorough discussion on the determinants for both the position and shape of the EU function.

Professor Matthews's article on "The Charitable Nonprofit Sector: X-efficiency, Resource Allocation, and Organization," written in a witty and insightful style, is a very full account of what typically goes on in charitable organizations. Moving from a very detailed discussion as to the types and categories of charitable organizations, Professor Matthews goes on to discuss efficiency and the motivational basis of those involved in the process of donating. He does so by giving a full account of the relevant literature, X-efficiency related and otherwise. What is particularly useful is the fact that from the outset he distinguishes between the efficiency in attaining given objectives and the efficiency in the choice of objectives. The latter should be of some interest to this group as it is this point that is usually omitted by orthodox economists who quickly relegate it to the domain of psychology or sociology. Yet we have learned that there may be a large scope for the entrepreneur in the charitable non-profit sector, and that raises a number of additional questions. Notably: What kind of entrepreneurs do you need? Where? For what kind of activities? How do you trade-off entrepreneurial and intrapreneurial talent for professional management and voluntary labor? This seems to be a big issue. In Canada, for example, nonprofit charitable organizations are presently undergoing what may be termed a generation change, which may very well constitute a change in entrepreneurship.

Francis's article concentrates on the application of X-efficiency conditions to whole industries if not to the United Kingdom as a nation. The author distinguishes between competitiveness and efficiency and later argues that Britain's decline as an industrial nation has been due to inefficiency, particularly X-inefficiency, rather than a lack of competitiveness. Finally, the article gives a full account of the sources, functions, and work organization effects of entrepreneurship, which all have implications for efficiency although these are not always spelled out. The article shows, very nicely, the relevance of X-efficiency theory but falls somewhat short in elaborating on the actual differences between British industrial organization and industrial relations on one extreme and those of the Japanese on the other. In other words: Why should effort-utility functions differ between nations or industries and what determines their nature? Also, Francis's distinction between competitiveness and efficiency is not entirely self-evident. If we take competitiveness as having a price and a nonprice dimension, both are driven ultimately by efficiency considerations, although the latter relates to quality concerns (aesthetic and technical sophistication of product, service, etc.). Perhaps Professor Francis could have elaborated a bit more on this aspect.

The article by Professor Thorbecke is a very fine effort indeed in connecting the two competing paradigms of X-efficiency and transaction costs theory within the framework of economic development and institutional change. Most useful is the contrast made between Leibenstein and Williamson that pointed out that X-efficiency theory is about the decision-making process and agency behavior as well as the impact of intrafirm conventions and contracts upon X-efficiency (physiology and mechanism of the decision process), while transaction costs theoretical treatments are more apt at rationalizing existing institutional arrangements.

Similarly, I share Professor Thorbecke's concern in finding ways to extend X-efficiency to a theory of organizational and institutional design, which is missing both as a positive and normative tool in Leibenstein's work. There is some work being done in this area; Tomer's book (1987) on organizational capital and some of my work may be suitable in this regard. In other words, I missed a treatment of the relative importance and relative influence of norms, habits, conventions, standards, and other behavioral aspects in shaping institutional or organizational change.

REFERENCE

Tomer, John F. 1987. *Organizational Capital: The Path to Higher Productivity and Well-Being*. New York: Praeger.

Comment by J. H. Hatch on the Article by Matthews

Professor Matthews addresses a somewhat neglected area of organization theory and in the spirit of the conference attempts to integrate X-efficiency into it. In discussing nonprofit-seeking charities, he very usefully differentiates between the broader social question as to the desirability of a good cause, and the efficiency with which its stated aims are achieved. These two aspects of efficiency are theoretically separable but in practice are likely to be confused, particularly in situations where output is ambiguous and intangible and where objectives may be obscure and difficult to define. In these circumstances, can we usefully introduce the concept of X-efficiency? I believe that the answer is yes, but with qualifications.

The concept of X-efficiency is elusive and ill defined at the best of times, and this may be the more so in the muddied world of charities. It is my belief that the strongest conclusion of X-efficiency theory is that costs are a function of competitive pressures and to be useful this clearly presupposes that competitive pressures are measurable. The difficulty with nonprofit charities is that competition is not usually well defined in the conventional sense. As Professor Matthews points out, charities do compete in factor markets and sometimes but less commonly in final goods markets. In the latter, however, as he points out, they usually face excess demand, so that competition in this area does not necessarily provide the discipline of failure to sell. In this sense we cannot expect competitive pressures to feed back into resource use and efficiency in the way that they may do in profit-seeking sectors of the economy. Thus the relationship between competition and costs may be muted, though not entirely absent.

In a broader sense, however, X-efficiency as a relationship between motivation in all its forms and achievement is very relevant for these organizations. Indeed, in the absence of explicit money rewards, the role of more complex motivational forces becomes paramount. It may be no coincidence that X-efficiency has proved relatively unattractive to mainstream economists who tend to assume away all nonprofit motives. Charities that clearly involve nonprofit motives may well be more amenable to analysis using the more subtle tools of X-efficiency theory.

Professor Matthews has shown that X-efficiency theory can be applied to nonprofit organizations. I believe that it may be the very richness of the X-efficiency concept that has made it somewhat unacceptable to the conventional wisdom of economics. However, one cannot analyze nonprofit charities and similar organizations using neoclassical economic tools alone.

Comment by J. H. Hatch on the Article by Francis

Being a mere economist who knows little of sociology, I shall comment only on the first part of Mr. Francis's paper. In it he addresses a time-honored question, the apparent failure of British industry in international markets in recent decades. He largely rejects the view that this is the result of uncompetitiveness, using Samuel Johnson's 1755 definition of competition as his benchmark. Rather, the author sees the problem as lying in inefficiency and naturally turns to X-inefficiency as a possible candidate. He admits that this article represents "an attempt to sketch a tentative research agenda to test . . . the implicit hypotheses that can be derived from the Leibenstein model."

He proceeds to consider Leibenstein's seven postulates. The problem is that there are effectively no data on any of the postulates, plausible as some of them are. We are left with an agenda for several doctorates but no convincing arguments. In addition, the most plausible candidate is the presence of imperfect competition, which in this case presumably means lack of competitive pressures. Tantalizingly, Mr. Francis largely fails to explain the mechanisms by which exchange rate and interest rate changes rapidly heightened competitive pressures in 1979 and 1980. In addition, it seems that despite earlier comments, he believes competitive pressures are in fact the main source of X-efficiency. Certainly, as I myself have argued, the most useful and testable hypothesis regarding X-efficiency is that which relates it to competitive pressures. We might note that these can take many forms, and it is by no means clear what the policy implications of the argument are. Interestingly the author identifies what seem to amount to dynamic X-inefficiencies. The failure of British firms to innovate is seen as something of a vicious circle, where low sales and profits, presumably in international markets, lead to an inadequate resource base for the next round of innovation. One is reminded of Jack Downie's innovation and transfer mechanism theory of the Competitive Process, but it is not clear that this is a form of X-inefficiency.

Overall the case remains unproved, though one must admit that this may reflect the inherent untestability of X-efficiency concepts as they now stand. It would be attractive to attribute Britain's relative economic failure substantially to X-inefficiency, but before we can do this we must refine the concept and, what is a related issue, collect relevant data. This is, as Mr. Francis says, a research agenda and a good one!

Comment by J. H. Hatch on the Article by Thorbecke

Professor Thorbecke in his own words, "compares and contrasts the X-efficiency theory with the transaction costs approach." The latter approach, though used by those of other persuasions, can be seen as the nub of the conventional neoclassical approach to the performance of economic institutions. Professor Thorbecke rapidly comes up against the central problem that X-efficiency is difficult to define and may be inherently not comparable with neoclassical concepts. As I have suggested in my own contribution to the conference, it may truly represent a paradigm change, so that it may be somewhat fruitless to attempt to marry X-efficiency with neoclassical concepts. Both Professor Thorbecke and I have come up against the same fundamental problem.

Professor Thorbecke also attempts to define the X-efficiency concept. This is not difficult to do in narrow technical terms, but it is difficult to place in the taxonomy of traditional efficiency concepts. For example, is X-efficiency simply a subset of, or maybe even synonymous with, technical efficiency? On the face of it, it would appear to be a subset, but as the article points out, Leibenstein has argued strongly that technical efficiency and X-efficiency are different (see n. 3). The problem is that this seems to create a new black box, this time within the individual rather than within the firm. This may explain Leibenstein's preoccupation with psychological factors and his coining of the phrase "micro-microeconomics." We might note that, by contrast, transaction costs are in the words of Matthews, as quoted by Thorbecke, "costs of relations between people and people." Despite this, Professor Thorbecke reiterates, without complete conviction, the rhetorical neoclassical question: Are transactions costs not equivalent to X-inefficiency? His answer, almost reluctantly, seems to be that there is considerable similarity in the two approaches.

I believe that this is correct but that it ignores one particular feature of X-efficiency theory. As outlined by Leibenstein, some, at least, of the sources of X-inefficiency are of the nature of uncorrected externalities, but uncorrected externalities within organizations rather than between them. The classic example is the case of teams of workers, employed and contracted by the firm, but whose performance is significantly influenced by their workmates' behavior. Certainly this implies transaction costs, but it goes beyond this in that it identifies significant nonmarket relations that nevertheless impinge on production costs. Perhaps in this sense this source of X-efficiency can be seen a subset of transaction costs, but one that is distinctive enough to warrant separate analysis and nomenclature. This dichotomy is captured in Thorbecke's conclusion, which emphasizes that X-efficiency essentially provides insights into the inner workings of firms and institutions, while transaction costs analysis tends to concentrate on interinstitutional relationships, albeit those that have not led to simple market solutions. Thus transaction costs are strictly a neoclassical concept whereas X-efficiency may be, and one must emphasize *may be*, a new way of looking at institutions and their role in the economic system.

Part 6
Measurement Problems

Interfirm, Interregional, and International Differences in Labor Productivity: Variations in the Levels of X-Inefficiency as a Function of Differential Labor Costs

Morris Altman

Economists have traditionally attempted to explain labor productivity differences between firms, regions, and nations by focusing upon differences in capital-labor ratios, differences in the quality of labor and capital, and differences in the quality and quantity of investments in human capital.[1] Richard R. Nelson (1968, 1219–20, 1229–32, 1238–44; 1984, 408) broke with this tradition by arguing that differences in the technologies employed by firms at a given point in time should be incorporated into the analysis. Harvey Liebenstein (1980, 270; 1987, chap. 4) argues that productivity differences between firms in the same industry and between countries at a similar stage of development can be explained to a large extent by the differences in motivational systems embodied by firms and countries. Differences in motivational systems affect the degree of X-inefficiency and thus the level of productivity in firms and countries.[2] Relative differences in wage rates and differential rates of change in wage rates are traditionally treated as variables that can affect labor productivity only by inducing changes in capital-labor ratios. In such a case, wage rates affect labor productivity differentials in the conventional way; through their impact upon factor inputs. Leibenstein, however, has suggested that increases in the price of labor can have an additional effect upon labor productivity. By increasing the pressure on the firm—higher wages increase unit costs—the higher

---

I thank Roger Frantz and Louise Lamontagne for their many helpful comments and suggestions.

1. The conventional analysis also attempts to incorporate variables such as unions, tax policy, and government regulation. For an excellent compilation of the traditional approach see Kendrick 1984. Refer to Salter 1969 for an analysis of differences in labor productivity due to the different vintages of best-practice equipment used between plants.

2. That different management techniques can significantly affect labor productivity is clearly demonstrated by Kilby (1962, 303–10; 1971, 29–35). One should note that Leibenstein (1966) gives great weight to the former article in his initial formulation of X-efficiency theory.

wages induce the firm to reduce X-inefficiency and thereby increase labor productivity.[3] Finally, Robert Solow (1986, 41–44) has explicitly introduced wage rates into the production function in an attempt to explain wage stickiness in the face of diminished demand for output.[4] According to Solow, wage rates affect labor productivity by affecting the supply of labor effort per unit of time.

In this article, I outline those conditions under which it becomes possible for differentials in wage rates and in their rates of growth to explain labor productivity differentials in terms of their impact upon X-inefficiency.[5] I attempt to demonstrate that relatively low wages can be one factor that contributes to the existence of X-inefficiency. Moreover, bringing in wages as an independent variable with respect to the generation of X-inefficiency enables me to demonstrate the possible significance of X-inefficiency even under conditions of perfect competition in the product

---

3. Leibenstein (1981, 104) writes: "It is frequently stated that if the cost of some input, say labor, increases, the cost of the output must increase accordingly. But this does not necessarily follow. If there is a rise in the cost of some input but at the same time the pressure on management to be more effective increases, resulting in more effective effort choices, then this may engender a reduction of X-inefficiency and a decrease in costs." See also Freeman and Medoff 1984, 12, 15, 95, 101, 105, 163–70, 178–79. Elsewhere, Leibenstein and others argue that wages can affect productivity by affecting the caloric intake of workers. This argument applies to individuals earning subsistence earnings. For a summary of this perspective see Altman 1988, n. 7. For a summary of other arguments relating labor productivity to wages, see Akerlof and Yellen 1986, 1–21.

4. Solow argues that labor productivity is positively related, to some degree, and, it would appear, mechanically, to wage rates. Firms set the wage rate, which minimizes cost per unit of labor effort. Thus, firms tend not to reduce wages as output falls if this reduces labor effort per unit of time and, thereby, increases the "efficiency wage." The argument made in this article incorporates Robert Solow's important contribution. However, one important proposition made below is that when the economic agents of the firm are not characterized by compatible objective functions, the wage rate that yields maximum labor productivity is not necessarily the wage rate set by the firm. Rather, it might very well be the wage rate imposed on the firm (more precisely, on the firm hierarchy) by workers or by legislation. Thus, although labor productivity is, in part, determined by the wage rate through its effect on workers' effort supply, it is not the increased wage rate, per se, that induces the increase of effort supply from workers.

5. For an empirically oriented examination of this question, see Altman 1986. See also Shen who hypothesizes that in developing countries changes in input productivity are dominated by changes in X-inefficiency, whereas in developed countries changes in input productivity are dominated by changes in factor proportions. He argues (1984, 99, 104) that changes in the wage level, as one moves from developing to developed countries, is one variable that can explain changing productivity between these two groups of countries. In this article the connection between wages and X-inefficiency is made explicit and conceptionally developed in terms of the more general problem of relative wage differences. The model presented here can serve to illuminate certain of Shen's empirical findings. I thank Roger Frantz for informing me of Shen's article.

market. This last argument serves to strengthen Leibenstein's general X-efficiency paradigm wherein X-inefficiency is significant only under conditions of product market imperfections, such as monopoly, oligopoly, tariffs, or subsidies (1966, 408–10; 1973, 772–75; 1979, 488, 490, 492; 1983, 841).

To the extent that wage differentials and wage increases affect the degree of X-inefficiency, it can be shown that relatively high wages need not cause increases in unit costs or reductions in profits and, thereby, reductions in potential savings. Indeed, relatively high wages can be shown to induce greater economic efficiency and hence contribute to improving the potential material well-being of society. Thus, it can be shown that high wages need not be associated with slower growth and higher unemployment as is the case in conventional economics. However, a basic premise underlying the arguments in this article is that X-inefficiency exists in the typical economy. Therefore, this article begins by stipulating those conditions that would cause X-inefficiency to exist both with and without imperfect product markets. The basic postulates of this argument build upon, although they do not at all times follow, the general tenets of Harvey Leibenstein's argument.[6]

The Existence of X-Inefficiency

To argue, as does Leibenstein, that X-inefficiency pervades an economy dominated by imperfect product markets has proved to be contentious, to say the least, to conventional economic theorists. But to argue that X-inefficiency might be significant even given perfect product markets and all of the pressures for efficiency that these entail would seem to be an even more contentious and untenable proposition. However, if one concedes that the necessary conditions for the existence of X-inefficiency are reasonable, then it follows, as I shall show, that X-inefficiency can also be significant within economies with market structures of differing degrees of perfection.

X-efficient production is defined as a level of output consistent with a firm operating at that point on its production isoquant that is tangent to its factor price line. Only in this case would the firm be minimizing the economic unit costs of production. Thus, as shown in figure 1, only isoquant Q_o' in association with isocost line 2' is consistent with X-efficiency. For if the firm is operating at point a of isoquant Q_o' with relative factor prices represented by isocost line 2″, the firm is using too labor intensive a technology for unit costs to be minimized. This definition of X-efficiency

---

6. See Frantz 1985 for an excellent critical discussion and review of the theoretical and empirical literature on X-efficiency theory.

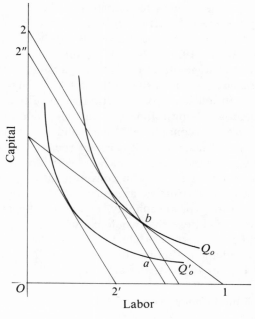

Fig. 1

is the most general one possible and is consistent with the traditional textbook ideal of economic efficiency (Leibenstein 1969, 600; 1978, 18; Blois 1974, 685–86). The technically efficient isoquant can be assumed to incorporate any transaction costs that result from technical considerations, such as the limited capacity of individuals to process unlimited amounts of information. Such costs are a function of existing information technology. This view, of course, would be consistent with Herbert Simon's view of economic man (1959, 259–73; 1978, 8–9, 12–14). Also, the technically efficient isoquant can be assumed to incorporate any monitoring and metering costs generated by the need to coordinate production from an engineering perspective (Alchian and Demsetz 1972). The technically efficient isoquant, however, would not incorporate costs that result from the social setting of a firm. General X-efficiency theory, in effect, assumes that cost minimization can exist only in a world where all firm members (be they workers, managers, or owners) have identical objective functions. If the members of the firm possess different and opposing objective functions, conflict ensues that, in turn, generates additional transaction, and, monitoring and metering costs over and above those that would exist in a cooperative social milieu. Also, as I will demonstrate, a relatively less cooperative environment will cause less than X-efficient levels of effort to be supplied to the firm by firm members. This results in unit costs being necessarily greater than unit costs are when all economic agents are characterized by identical objective functions. The difference in unit costs for an identical firm producing in a noncooperative social milieu as compared to a cooperative social milieu is one measure of general X-inefficiency. Therefore, X-inefficiency represents actual costs that are higher than they need be and, that are, thus, avoidable costs of production. The isoquant that is augmented by socially related production costs and by less effort per unit of time (and, therefore, by less output per unit of labor time) is illustrated by an isoquant to the right of the technically efficient one, such as Q_o as compared to Q'_o in figure 1, where Q_o and Q'_o represent the same level of output.

This view of economic efficiency is rejected by conventional theorists such as George Stigler (1976, 214–16) and Louis De Alessi (1983, 76) since they maintain that economic efficiency simply means cost and output results that are consistent with constrained cost-minimizing and profit-maximizing behavior. Thus, by definition, all behavior becomes minimizing or maximizing once we specify the prevailing constraints. It follows, therefore, that costs are being minimized at all times. According to such a view, there can be no unique minimum unit cost since minimum costs can vary as constraints change. This perspective is, as Leibenstein (1973, 210; 1987, appendix) points out, one that makes neoclassical microtheory into a tautology. One cannot use the X-efficiency definition of efficiency in this general form to determine what is or is not efficient production since production is always by definition efficient. Nevertheless, for the purposes of this article, for which an operational definition of economic efficiency is essential, the general definition of X-efficiency, as I have defined it, is used as a theoretical standard for determining what cost-minimizing or efficient production should be. X-inefficiency, in this case, represents any deviation from this ideal. In other words, unit costs are truly minimized only if a firm is producing along a production isoquant that does not incorporate socially induced costs of production and that represents the maximum output produced per unit of input.

For a firm to produce maximum output, given factor inputs and transaction and monitoring costs (be they technically or technically and socially determined), assumes that labor effort per hour of labor input is at some maximum level. Conventional microeconomics assumes that each hour of labor contributes a unique level of labor effort consistent with the maximum possible effort contribution, although the maximum is never clearly defined. Moreover, it is implicitly assumed that this maximum level of effort supply is consistent with the worker's utility maximization. According to Leibenstein (1969, 602–3; 1979, 484–86, 498; 1980, 96–102;

1983, 833), it would be more realistic to assume that firm members, such as workers and managers, have some discretion over the amount of labor effort that they supply to the firm since, typically, firm contracts are somewhat incomplete. Thus, each firm member has some choice over what Leibenstein refers to as the activity, pace, quality, and time (APQT) bundle and thereby over the effort bundle supplied to the firm. Moreover, Leibenstein (1969, 603; 1978, 12, 27–30; 1979, 481, 488–89, 493; 1982, 92–97; 1983, 835) argues that we must examine the firm in terms of its component human agents as opposed to the approach of conventional economic theory, which treats the firm as a monolithic entity with one homogeneous objective function. Leibenstein also argues that firms' members are typically characterized by different and, more often than not, conflicting objective functions. Thus, what might serve to increase the utility of one economic agent might reduce the utility of another. Leibenstein considers the existence of discretion over the input of labor effort and conflicting objective functions among firm members critical to the existence of X-inefficiency.

In this article, I make the simplifying assumption that there are only two representative types of firm members: workers, on the one hand, and management and owners, on the other, both of whom possess different objective functions. The latter group constitutes the firm hierarchy. As a simplifying assumption I presume that the objective function among workers themselves is homogeneous as well as that within the firm hierarchy.[7] In this two-group model, it is possible that the labor effort demanded from workers by the owners/managers in order to maximize firm output can exceed the labor effort that workers desire to contribute to the process of production. Such conflicting objective functions can contribute to the existence of X-inefficiency, although Leibenstein argues that some X-inefficiency can exist even if the objective functions of the two groups are identical. If all firm members possess identical objective functions, there will be no X-inefficiency, but only if one assumes, along with neoclassical theory, that firm members desire to contribute a maximum amount of labor effort per unit of labor time to the production process. This is illustrated in figure 2, by a worker's effort-utility function (which indicates the relationship between effort supply and utility) that is perfectly inelastic at Ob of effort supply per unit of time, where Ob of effort supply is consistent with X-efficient production.

---

7. Leibenstein argues that one should also take into account the differing and, possibly, conflicting objective functions among workers and among and between owners and managers. This additional level of complexity, although significant in itself, can be abstracted from for the purposes of this article.

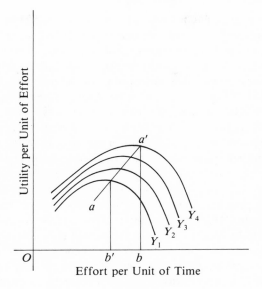

Fig. 2

This, however, need not be the case. Leibenstein (1969, 605) argues that given the degree of internal and external pressure on a firm member, effort supply per unit of time is a function of the utility yielded by the effort supplied. Leibenstein assumes diminishing returns to effort-related utility (see fig. 2). At a certain effort point, such as a', of effort-utility function Y_4 in figure 2, the marginal utility of effort is zero, and therefore the utility from the supply of effort is maximized. Thus, Ob of effort supply is consistent with utility maximization on the part of the firm members and, in this case, also with the X-efficient supply of effort. If, however, firm members are characterized by effort-utility functions such as Y_3, Y_2, or Y_1, the utility maximizing effort supply would be consistent with a supply of effort less than Ob, and hence with an X-inefficient supply of effort. There is no reason to believe that Y_4 is representative of the typical effort-utility function of a firm member. Leibenstein, of course, assumes that this would rarely, if ever, be the case.

I assume, along with Leibenstein, that firm members prefer to supply more effort rather than less effort up to some point. I also assume that, ceteris paribus, the effort level that would maximize utility would be much below the X-efficient level Ob, such as Ob' of effort-utility function Y_1. I further assume that increasing income per unit of time yields increasing utility to the firm members and that this utility increases at a diminishing rate. Assume, moreover, that increasing income incorporates all positive incentives to firm members and that the effect of increasing income per unit of time is to induce firm members to supply more effort at the utility-maximizing point of the effort-utility function. The increased utility generated by the increase in income compensates for the disutility generated by supplying effort in excess of Ob'. This can be illustrated by a shift of the firm members' effort-utility function upward such that the utility-maximizing effort supply associated with the higher income is always greater than that associated with the lower income, up to the point where the marginal utility of income increases can no longer compensate the firm members for the marginal disutility of supplying more effort per unit of time.[8] In figure 2, more effort can be induced by increasing income (including other positive incentives) up to Ob of effort or the X-efficient effort supply. At this point, the supply of effort per unit of time would be perfectly inelastic to further increases in income per unit. The aa' curve (which I refer to as the income-effort curve) indicates the relationship between income increases and the supply of effort per unit of time. Note that according to the assumptions made, Ob of effort would not be put forth unless the income earned per unit of effort (and the positive incentives income is a proxy for) is sufficient to compensate the firm members for the disutility associated with effort supply $b'b$. Thus, at low levels of income, it is unlikely that X-efficient levels of effort would be supplied by the firm members. But it is also possible for firm members to be willing to supply low levels of effort even at high incomes, depending upon the elasticities of their effort-utility and income-effort functions.[9]

---

8. The effort-utility curves need not be drawn such that the increase in income incentives yields a higher utility-maximizing level of both effort and utility. These curves can be drawn so that the increase in income incentives yields only a higher utility-maximizing level of effort while the level of utility does not change.

9. It should be noted that this presentation does not follow Leibenstein. However, the general thrust of the argument is similar to his. See, for example, Leibenstein 1987, chap. 5. In his comments on this article, Roger Frantz argues that my presentation of X-efficiency theory is incompatible with Leibenstein's since I use conventional concepts such as maximizing and minimizing. Frantz maintains that such concepts preclude the existence of X-inefficiency. However, although Leibenstein does argue that for his purposes, dropping maximization and minimization from one's analytic tool box is best, he does not contend that these concepts are necessarily incompatible with X-inefficiency. Indeed, Leibenstein (1985, 12–13) is largely concerned that these conventional concepts should not be used in a tautological fashion. In this article, X-inefficiency is shown to exist even if economic agents are characterized by objective functions that are dominated by maximizing-minimizing arguments as long as maximization-minimization is not used tautologically. If, in fact, economic agents are largely partially maximizers-minimizers, as Leibenstein would have it, then the case for the existence of X-inefficiency becomes even stronger (See also Leibenstein 1986).

The firm members with identical behavioral functions can also be motivated to increase their effort input through external pressures. The effect of pressure upon effort supply is illustrated in figure 3. The *aa'* curve is transposed from figure 2 and a set of income-effort curves is placed to the left of *aa'*. These income-effort curves are constructed from effort-utility curves situated to the left of those in figure 2 (not shown). Increasing external pressure shifts the effort-utility curve toward *aa'*. However, the increased pressure does not affect the location of the sets of effort-utility curves from which the initial income-effort curves to the left of *aa'* are constructed. Therefore, the new effort-utility curves result in firm members supplying more than utility-maximizing supplies of effort. But as Leibenstein (1987, 18–20, chap. 8) argues, referring to the Yerkes-Dodson Law relating "performance" to stress, pressure or stress will affect performance positively only up to a limit. Thereafter, one would expect performance (effort in this case) to diminish. The effect of pressure on effort supply can be illustrated by the following example. Assume that competing firms are identical except that the firm members of one set of firms possess effort-utility functions to the left of those of the firm members in the other set of firms. The utility-maximizing effort supply in the former set of firms is, therefore, relatively lower than that in the latter set of firms for any given income (incentives) per unit of time. The X-efficient firms' members are characterized by income-effort curve *aa'* whereas the X-inefficient firms' members are characterized by income-effort curve *bb'*, which is assumed to be derived from a set of effort-utility functions to the left of those in figure 2. Assume further that lower effort levels are associated with lower levels of output, which, in turn, result in higher unit costs.[10] In this case, the firms with firm members who are characterized by a stronger work ethic will produce at relatively lower unit costs. Given perfect competition on the product market, the members of those firms with the higher unit costs must increase their effort input so as to lower unit costs or, alternatively, experience the economic termination of their relatively high unit cost and relatively more X-inefficient firms. Therefore, external pressures can force firms to produce relatively more X-efficiently as relatively high cost producers are forced to compete with relatively low cost producers. Thus, if a firm's survival is threatened by low cost producers, such external pressure can shift firm members' income-effort curve toward *aa'*. Of course, if the increased pressure finally meets with an inelastic effort supply, the firm will go bankrupt, ceteris paribus. In fact, Leibenstein

---

10. A lower supply of effort per unit of time decreases the average product per unit of labor, which, given the price of labor, increases the cost per unit of output.

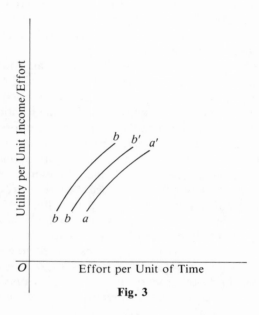

Fig. 3

(1966, 408–10; 1979, 488, 490, 492; 1973, 772–75; 1983, 841) argues that X-inefficiency becomes significant only when imperfect product markets exist since these reduce the extent and degree of external pressures. Nevertheless, even relatively low cost producers can themselves be producing X-inefficiently, given specific effort-utility functions. Therefore, external pressures can eliminate X-inefficiency only if there are enough firms within a product market with firm members whose utility-maximizing effort bundle coincides with the X-efficient effort input, such as Ob' in figure 2. And the degree of relative X-efficiency and, therefore, of relatively X-efficient supplies of effort is determined by the firms and their economic agents that supply the most effort per unit of labor time, ceteris paribus.

It is possible to detail conditions whereby firm members would be willing to supply X-efficient levels of effort without any pressure. Such a scenario assumes unique effort-utility and income-effort functions. Specifically, in a world of workers and owner/managers, a work environment must be constructed wherein cooperation and trust predominate among the firm members, and workers are induced by the firm hierarchy to contribute what approaches X-efficient levels of effort (Leibenstein

1987, 157–78, chap. 4; Dore 1973, 140–62, 229, 240, 264, 277, 347–49; Takeuchi 1985, 18–28).[11] In this case, the X-efficient effort supply is one that is consistent with an ideal, yet achievable, work environment. One must assume that owner/managers have objective functions that are consistent with constructing, implementing, and enforcing the incentive system that would induce maximum effort levels on the part of workers. The owner/managers must be willing to invest the quantity of their own effort necessary to induce X-efficient levels of effort supply from workers (this assumes that workers can be characterized by effort-utility functions that lie below Y_4 in fig. 2). Moreover, owner/managers must be willing to invest the time and effort to coordinate and monitor production from an engineering point of view. In order for the firm hierarchy to encourage maximum output, the disutility incurred by the firm hierarchy in expending the effort to induce workers to work harder and in coordinating and monitoring production must not deter the firm hierarchy from investing the necessary amount of effort into the production process. The disutility incurred by the firm hierarchy can be balanced by the utility that the owner/managers gain in making the firm more X-efficient. This increase in utility can be the result of increasing the income to the firm hierarchy or of reducing unit costs and, thereby, making the firm competitive. In this case, one assumes that owner/managers possess effort-utility functions below Y_4 in figure 2 and, therefore, they themselves require positive incentives to induce X-efficient levels of effort. Moreover, one should note that owner/managers would increase income (incentives) to workers so as to induce more effort from them only up to the point that the marginal value product of the increased effort supply by workers is equal to or greater than their increased compensation. Otherwise, the owner/managers would be better off paying workers less.

On the other hand, the firm hierarchy can be assumed to have no preference for leisure and therefore suffer no disutility in expending more effort in the production process up to the X-efficient level. In this case, the firm hierarchy would be characterized by the effort-utility function Y_4. Such a firm hierarchy is representative of the type of entrepreneur consistent with conventional neoclassical microeconomics. This firm hierarchy is a true profit maximizer in that it attempts to produce that level of output consistent with the equality of marginal cost and

---

11. For a somewhat contrasting view of the Japanese experience, see Shimada 1985, 42–66.

marginal revenue.[12] Under this assumption, X-efficiency will be generated by the firm hierarchy if the effort-utility functions of the firm's employees are also consistent with such a goal—if workers can be induced to supply *Ob* of effort. However, if the entrepreneur (the owners and managers in this article) has a preference for leisure and thus prefers to spend less as opposed to more effort per unit of time, there can be no guarantee that the firm hierarchy will invest the effort necessary to generate X-efficient production even if one assumes that workers are willing to supply the necessary effort under the appropriate firm incentive structure. In other words, the firm hierarchy would possess an effort-utility function to the left of *aa'* in figure 3. But even owner/managers with a strong leisure preference and a strong aversion to effort can be induced to construct an environment conducive to X-efficient production if the competitive pressures on the product market are severe enough. However, in this case, this firm hierarchy would no longer be maximizing utility. Moreover, for some firms to be pressured into producing more X-efficiently, there must exist other firms in the same product market that are relatively X-efficient and that are therefore characterized by owner/managers with a relatively weak leisure preference and a relatively weak aversion to effort.

I have thus far assumed that X-efficient production is possible if workers are willing to provide X-efficient levels of effort given the appropriate positive incentives and if the firm hierarchy is willing to invest the time and effort necessary to generate such incentives and to supply the necessary coordination and monitoring to the firm. However, X-efficiency becomes less likely if, as in accordance with general X-efficiency theory, one assumes that workers and the firm hierarchy are characterized by significantly different behavioral functions. Assume that workers do not trust the firm hierarchy and that, as a result, they are not willing to supply X-efficient levels of effort per unit of labor time. For simplicity assume that workers desire to minimize effort per unit of labor time for any given wage rate. Therefore, increasing the wage rate alone will not induce more effort supply. Workers would be characterized by utility-income curves far to the left of *aa'* in figure 3, which, in the extreme, would be perfectly inelastic. The firm hierarchy would be obliged to coerce labor to work harder by pressuring workers and aug-

---

12. Scitovsky (1943–44, 57–60) argues that for true profit maximization to take place, the entrepreneur must be characterized by a very special psychology, such that the entrepreneur will expend all the necessary effort required to maximize profits. The only way that the entrepreneur will maximize his or her satisfaction will be by maximizing profits. See also Leibenstein (1987, 119).

menting the monitoring of labor. But such negative incentives have their limits and, also, owners/managers would need to be investing more effort than they would have to if labor were more cooperative. Of course, the effort levels of workers cannot be so low that unit costs increase to the point that a firm's survival is threatened. Nevertheless, low effort levels are consistent with firm survival if workers in most firms are characterized by similar behavioral functions. Again, for the sake of simplicity, let us also assume that the firm hierarchy desires to produce X-efficiently (this objective, of course, runs counter to that of the workers). However, the owners/managers desire that this objective be realized at a minimum of effort supply on the part of the members of the firm hierarchy. Moreover, assume that the owners/managers prefer to avoid stress and conflict with their workers as this generates disutility.

Under these assumptions, workers cannot be induced to be more X-efficient by positive incentives, and the firm hierarchy does not believe that such incentives can be effective. In this case, the firm hierarchy attempts to minimize unit costs by minimizing income per unit of time to workers (plus any other cost-related incentives to labor) and by pressuring workers to increase their effort supply per unit of time. To this end the firm hierarchy can be expected to invest in additional monitoring and supervisory activities (which, by definition, exceed such investments in a cooperative work environment). If the firm hierarchy is not intent upon avoiding stress or conflict with labor or upon avoiding increased effort on the part of its members, the firm hierarchy will increase expenditures on monitoring and supervision, and so forth, up to the point where the related increases in costs just equal the related increases in labor productivity. The firm hierarchy, in this case, is characterized by an effort-utility function similar to Y_4 and/or a utility-income function such as aa' in figures 2 and 3, respectively. Given that internal pressures can have only a limited effect on increasing the effort supply of labor (the Yerkes-Dodson Law), one would expect that owners/managers' investment in pressure-related activities would have only a limited effect on increasing labor productivity. The end result of workers and the firm hierarchy possessing conflicting objective functions would be for labor income and labor productivity to be much lower than they would be in a cooperative work milieu. Unit costs would, of course, be higher than under a cooperative regime but only if labor productivity falls proportionately more than wages do. It is therefore possible for unit costs to be identical in a cooperative and a noncooperative environment. But profits would tend to be lower under a noncooperative regime (assuming for simplicity that all nonlabor income is equal to profits) since the relatively low labor productivity and the relatively higher costs of monitoring, supervising, and related activities generate lower nonlabor income. This line of reasoning assumes that unit prices cannot be increased so as to compensate for the decrease in total profits and that wages cannot be further reduced to any significant degree.[13]

Workers and the firm hierarchy would attempt to pursue the above suboptimal material objectives if each group has learned from experience that when one party chooses the cooperative option the other party would probably exploit this cooperation so as to maximize its own material well-being and utility. This leaves the cooperating party with the lowest possible level of income and utility. On the other hand, each group must believe that by choosing an antagonistic mode of behavior the worst outcome would be an improvement over the outcome expected if the cooperative option is chosen. This is the latent Prisoner's Dilemma solution to the productivity question, given the predominance of an antagonistic work environment (Leibenstein 1987, chap. 3). Such a dismal scenario can be avoided if peer pressure or the tradition of the firm's labor-management relations induces workers to exert more than their utility-maximizing effort supply and, similarly, induces owners/managers to introduce more positive incentives. The peer group solution lies, in terms of X-efficiency, somewhere between the optimal productivity results of cooperative behavior and the dreary results of antagonistic behavior. Leibenstein (1982, 94–96; 1987, chap. 7) argues that the peer group solution would be the more typical outcome. The effect of peer group pressures is to shift the workers' utility-effort curve to the right toward aa' (but still below aa') in figure 3. In effect, workers are not maximizing their utility by working harder, but, rather, workers are avoiding the disutility expected to be incurred if they violated peer group standards for effort supply. Thus, the disutility of breaking with peer group standards must exceed the utility gained by working with less zeal if workers are to be induced to follow their peers' standards. This places workers in what Leibenstein refers to as their "inert" area: where the expected utility of changing one's effort position is less than the expected loss in utility (Leibenstein 1969, 607; 1978, 34; 1979, 486; 1980, 112).

The owners/managers would also be operating within inert areas if

---

13. Assume that labor costs are the only costs and that these are $9.00 per hour of labor time. Assume also that there is only one worker who can produce a maximum of 10 units per hour. Finally, assume that normal profits equal 11 percent of unit costs. The unit price must be equal to $1.00 when labor produces 10 units per hour. In this case, total profits equal $1.00. If labor productivity falls by 50 percent and wages fall by the same percentage, unit costs remain at $0.90 and the unit price remains at $1.00. But total profits will equal only $0.50 unless prices can be increased.

one assumes that they desire to avoid stress. Given a noncooperative work environment, any attempt by the firm hierarchy to increase workers' effort supply would increase the tension between workers and owners/managers and thus increase the level of stress experienced by the owners/managers and thereby increase their disutility (Leibenstein 1969, 609–10). If this increase in disutility exceeds the expected increase in utility from increasing the workers' labor productivity, then the firm hierarchy would not contribute as much effort supply to the process of production as it would in the absence of stress concern (which Leibenstein refers to more generally as constraint concern). In this case, owners/managers would be operating within their inert area and below their true utility-maximizing supply of effort. This would result in labor productivity being even lower than in a situation where the hierarchy's constraint on further investment in pressure-related activities is only the related economic costs and benefits of such activities. The firm's productivity performance would be even worse if, ceteris paribus, owners/managers prefer to exert less effort rather than more effort. In this case, the effort-utility function of the firm hierarchy is to the left of *aa'* in figure 3. The effect of stress concern would be to keep the owners/managers from arriving at the utility-maximizing effort point of the utility-effort curve. Labor productivity can be maximized in the context of an antagonistic work environment only if the economic cost of pressure-related activities relative to related benefits are the only constraints on the ability of the firm hierarchy to squeeze more labor effort per unit of time from the firm's employees.

Given that effort is a discretionary variable, I have presented four key and sometimes overlapping causes of X-inefficiency. The first is related to whether the effort-utility and income-effort functions of firm members yield a utility-maximizing supply of effort per unit of time that is less than the X-efficient supply. Second, given these effort functions, an atmosphere of mistrust and antagonism between workers and the firm hierarchy can result in a latent Prisoner's Dilemma solution to the productivity question. Third, the level of labor productivity is prevented from falling to its lowest possible level (apart from peer pressures) by introducing investments in pressure-related activities. However, such productivity-increasing investments also increase the unit costs to the firm as compared to what they would be if firm members possess similar behavioral constraints thereby not obliging the firm to execute these additional socially generated investments. Fourth, if owners/managers desire to avoid stress-related activities they would not invest as much in pressure-related activities as they would otherwise, thus allowing the effort supply from employees to be less than it would otherwise be. This increases the X-inefficiency of the firm above what it would be if only the economic cost of pressure-related activities constrained the behavior of owners/managers.

Given these causes of X-inefficiency, the level of X-inefficiency can be affected by the extent of competitive pressures on the product market. These pressures will not affect the costs of pressure-related monitoring and other costs if these pressures do not affect the degree of noncooperation between firm members. But such pressures can affect the utility yielded to owners/managers and even to workers by increasing their respective effort supplies. These competitive pressures can also reduce the disutility to owners/managers of pressuring workers to be more efficient and, thereby, can push the firm hierarchy out of its inert area. Also, these pressures can simply force firm members to exert more effort even if this yields net disutility (the effort-utility curve is shifted to the right). Thus, the more severe the competitive pressures on the product market, the more likely it becomes that the firm hierarchy will minimize X-inefficiency, even given conflicting behavioral functions between workers and owners/managers. Moreover, it becomes more probable that workers would be willing to supply more effort per unit of time even given the noncooperative work environment. This would further reduce the degree of X-inefficiency. However, competitive product market pressures can serve to reduce the extent of X-inefficiency but only if there exist enough firms whose members are characterized by behavioral constraints that allow for relatively X-efficient supplies of effort. In this sense, the extent to which X-inefficiency exists in a specific product market is a function of the economic performance of the marginal X-efficient firms and, therefore, of the supply of effort contributed by the economic agents of the marginally most X-efficient firms. On the other hand, reductions in the degree of competitive pressures increase the shelters to the relatively X-inefficient firms and permit the relatively high unit-cost firms to survive in spite of the existence of relatively low unit-cost firms in the same product market. Moreover, the increase in shelters induces firm members, who have been pressured to supply levels of effort that yield a loss in utility, to supply less effort. This process, which Leibenstein (1978, 33–35; 1979, 489) refers to as effort entropy, results in increasing the level of X-inefficiency, and it can be illustrated by inward shifts of the utility-income curve toward its original utility-maximizing position.

Wage Differentials and X-Inefficiency

From my discussion of the cooperative and Prisoner's Dilemma solutions to the productivity question, one notes that income and/or the other related positive economic incentives (for which income or the wage rate is a proxy) decrease as one moves from the cooperative to the Prisoner's Dilemma solution. Thus, as labor productivity falls, so do wages. It was also shown that, for this reason, unit costs need not increase as the firm becomes increasingly X-inefficient (see n. 13 on p. 336). Relatively low wages can, therefore, shelter the relatively X-inefficient firms from the relatively X-efficient firms. I will argue that, for this reason, even in the face of perfectly competitive product markets, X-inefficiency can be of significance. Moreover, I will show that wage differentials and changes in these differentials can cause differences and changes in the differences in the degree of X-inefficiency between firms, regions, and nations through their effect on the shelters provided to X-inefficient firms. To isolate the significance of differentials in real labor compensation for differentials in X-inefficiency, I assume for simplicity, perfect competition on the product markets. Thus, from the product markets there is maximum external pressure to reduce X-inefficiency to negligible proportions. I also assume that all factor markets are perfectly competitive except for the labor market. Finally, I make the simplifying assumption that wage payments per unit of time are labor's only source of economic compensation. By assuming that real wages differ between firms producing identical products across localities, regions, or nations, I isolate the potential impact that wages can have upon X-inefficiency.

Wage differentials can affect X-inefficiency by sheltering X-inefficient firms, on the one hand, and by being a source of internal pressure, on the other. This becomes evident once X-inefficiency is examined in relative terms. Compare one plant (A) to the other plants (B) in a particular product market where all plants are identical and produce identical products at the same unit cost of $10.00 which equals the equilibrium market price. This unit cost includes a normal profit per unit of output of $1.00 such that total profits equal 10 percent of total costs. Assume that, initially, all plants are producing with the same degree of X-inefficiency. Assume further that each plant is producing a full capacity output of 1,000 units per week, employing 100 workers, each working the same span of time; and that wages constitute the only cost of production. If wages increase by 10 percent in plant (A), the unit cost of production increases by $0.90 to $10.90. Plant (A) cannot respond to the increase in wages by increasing unit prices given the assumption of perfectly competitive product markets. But plant (A) can respond by reducing plant X-inefficiency to the point that output per worker increases sufficiently to maintain unit costs at $10.00 and total profits at 10 percent of total costs. In this case, labor productivity must be increased by 10 percent to 11 units. This results in total profits increasing from $1,000 to $1,100. If, however, one assumes that total profits can fall as a percentage of total costs as long as they remain at the same level ($1,000) as they were when wages were lower, then labor productivity need increase by only 9 percent.[14] Thus, higher wages need not result in falling profits and, thereby, in falling potential savings. The plant hierarchy is forced to reduce X-inefficiency as plant survival is threatened. Owners/managers are, therefore, pushed out of their inert area and invest more in pressure-related activities and expend more effort in the production process although this generates increasing levels of stress and, thus, increased disutility. Moreover, workers might be more willing to supply more effort per unit of time if they believe that their plant's survival is threatened by their higher wages. On the other hand, the low-wage (B) plants face no pressure to reduce X-inefficiency as their unit costs remain at a competitive level given their relatively low wage rates. Thus, the low wage rates serve to shelter the relatively X-inefficient units of production.

In this example, differences in wage rates are associated with differences in labor productivity. In the low-wage plants the average product of labor is 10 units, whereas in the high-wage plants it is 11 units. Thus, as wages increase in one plant relative to another, labor productivity increases in one plant relative to another. This causal relationship can only hold, however, if and only if X-inefficiency exists. Clearly, if there is no X-inefficiency to begin with, the relative increase in wage rates can result only in lower profits and eventually higher unit prices in the high-wage plant, which, under competitive circumstances, must result in the economic demise of the high wage plant. Even given the existence of X-inefficiency, the ability of owners/managers to respond to increasing wages is constrained by the extent of the X-inefficiency. Assume, in the example given, that X-inefficiency can be reduced no more in plant (A), further increases in wages will result in lower profits and, eventually, in higher unit prices. A further qualification to this argument is that wage increases pressure the firm hierarchy into reducing plant X-inefficiency only when the firm hierarchy is no longer able to reduce profits further in order to compensate for the increased costs of production. Reduced profits can serve as an alternative to increasing labor productivity if one can assume that the firm hierarchy can accept a lower rate of profit or

---

14. When wages are increased by 10 percent, total labor costs rise from $9,000 to $9,900. If profits are to remain at 10 percent of total costs, the value of output must be $11,000. In this case, there must be 1,100 units of output produced if the unit price is to remain at $10.00. Note that after adjustments, total profits are now $1,100 compared to $1,000 when lower wages prevailed. If profits need be only $1,000, then total output must be increased to only 1,090 units ($10,900/$10.00) and, therefore, labor productivity must rise by only 9 percent.

lower total profits. Thus, to the extent that the disutility of increasing labor productivity exceeds that of a reduction in profits, the firm hierarchy can be expected to refrain from reducing X-inefficiency. Nevertheless, there is a limit beyond which profits cannot fall. At the extreme the limit would be zero. But, more realistically, the limit lies above zero due to considerations such as the desired income of owners/managers, a lower-bound price of shares to discourage takeover bids, and required internal funds for investment. When this limit is reached, X-inefficiency must be reduced. Ultimately, therefore, there remains a positive relationship between relative wage increases and relative increases in labor productivity.

The effect a relative increase in wages can have upon X-inefficiency also depends upon the significance of wage costs to total costs. Obviously, as wages represent an increasingly smaller portion of total unit costs. Therefore, if wage costs constitute a negligible portion of total unit costs, relative increases in wages will have a relatively negligible impact upon unit costs. Consequently, there would be less pressure on the owners/managers of the higher-wage plant to reduce X-inefficiency. For example, assume that wages no longer represent $9.00 of plant (A)'s initial unit costs. Assume that capital and material costs constitute $8.00 of unit costs while profits and wages contribute $1.00 each to unit costs. In this case, if wages double, the total wage bill rises to $200. Total costs (inclusive of profits) rise from $10,000 to $10,200. For unit costs to remain at $10.00, total output would have to be increased from 1,000 to 1,020 units or by only 2 percent as opposed to the 10 percent increase required if wages contribute $9.00 to unit costs. Thus, pressure to reduce X-inefficiency increases as plants become more labor intensive. Nevertheless, under competitive conditions, even capital- and material-intensive plants would be pressured to reduce X-inefficiency so as to keep unit costs from rising and profits from falling.

If one introduces nonwage shelters from competitive pressure into the argument, the results presented here should not change. If one starts from an equilibrium position where wages per unit of output are the same in all plants and where plant (A) is assumed to be somewhat sheltered from competitive pressures by product differentiation, for example, X-inefficiency in plant (A) can exceed that of the (B) plants in equilibrium and, thus, unit costs in plant (A) can be somewhat higher that in the (B) plants. The introduction of higher wages in plant (A) will, however, cause its unit costs to rise ceteris paribus, such that its market will be lost to the (B) plants. Thus, the plant hierarchy in plant (A) will be pressured to reduce the level of X-inefficiency in the plant so as to bring the unit costs of plant (A) into line with the existing state of competitive pressures. Therefore, given the particular structure of shelters in a particular product market, relative wage increases or the existence of wage differences between plants can be a cause of changing differentials and the existence of differentials in X-inefficiency between plants.

Nevertheless, it is important to recognize that to the extent that firms, regions, or nations can institute or increase nonwage shelters, this relieves the pressure on the owners/managers of the relatively high-wage plants to reduce X-inefficiency. In this sense nonwage shelters and low wages serve as substitutes. Both reduce the pressure on X-inefficient firms to become more X-efficient. Moreover, reducing wages would be attractive to owners/managers when the plant environment is an antagonistic one since the higher wages force the owners/managers to invest what are for them excessive amounts of effort and time in the production process so as to reduce X-inefficiency. By reducing wages, the firm hierarchy can afford increases in X-inefficiency and thus allow itself to reduce its own contribution of time and effort to the production process. Also, the stress level of the firm hierarchy would be reduced as less pressure would have to be placed on workers since less effort per worker would, under conditions of lower wages, be consistent with the economic viability of the firm. This would reduce the disutility to the owners/ managers. Even if total profits fall in the process, this would pose no problem to the firm hierarchy if the disutility of lower profits is less than the utility gained from the reduction in time, effort, and stress.[15]

Given the creation of nonwage shelters, higher prices can compensate for increasing unit costs as opposed to increases in labor productivity. Thus, up to some point (determined by the extent and significance of nonwage shelters) relatively high-wage plants can be as X-inefficient as relatively low-wage plants. And to the extent that nonwage shelters can be instituted as relative wages increase, the increase in wages need not cause reductions in X-inefficiency. At this point, it is important to note that governments have a greater capacity to institute nonwage shelters than firm hierarchies. Governments can create and raise tariffs and grant subsidies. Thus, governments have a greater potential to neutralize the pressures to reduce X-inefficiency placed on the shoulders of the plant

---

15. Leibenstein writes: "It is important to consider that there exists a set of effort/ wage-cost combinations that imply the same profit level. Clearly the firm seeking to maximize profits would be quite happy with a lower, rather than higher, effort/wage-cost combination, so as to avoid some of the resistance to the high effort levels obtained by monitoring and sanctions. In other words, at very high effort levels there is a disutility to the hierarchy to obtaining that effort, and it is easier to live with a lower effort/wage-cost combination" (1987, 104).

hierarchy by the increasing wages. Moreover, governments can institute policies that keep wages from rising. This, of course, would also reduce the pressure on plant hierarchies to make their plants more X-efficient. Thus, by introducing nonwage shelters and by keeping wages low, governments would be contributing to relatively high levels of X-inefficiency in their nation.

The thrust of the argument presented thus far is that following from the assumption of identical plants, labor productivity across plants will be the same given the same degree of X-inefficiency across plants. The introduction of wage differentials between otherwise identical plants results in interplant differences in X-inefficiency. In this manner interplant differences in labor productivity are introduced through interplant differences in X-inefficiency. One would expect labor productivity to increase or to be greater in plants where wages are relatively high. The negative impact of wage increases or wage differences upon X-inefficiency is cushioned by the willingness of owners/managers to absorb higher unit costs by lowering profits and by the ability of the higher-wage firm or governments to introduce or increase nonwage shelters. However, the following proposition should hold true: given the a priori existence of X-inefficiency, ceteris paribus, relative increases in wages should result in relative increases in labor productivity, and wage differentials should result in differentials in labor productivity in favor of the high-wage plants. Alternatively, relative decreases in wages result in relative decreases in labor productivity by inducing increases in the relative levels of X-inefficiency (firm members reduce their effort supplies to levels that yield more utility—an example of effort entropy). Thus, relative decreases in wages result in productivity differentials moving in favor of the high-wage plants.

The argument made for one plant relative to another can be generalized to plants across regions and nations. At the most basic level, simply assume that all plants are everywhere identical (inclusive of the production of the same output) except with respect to labor compensation. However, matters become complicated once one assumes that all plants producing the same output are identical but that each region produces a different array of products, with the production process of each product represented by a different production function. In this case, there would be differences in labor productivity between regions as a result of the different array of products produced in the different regions and, therefore, by interregional differences in production processes. Nevertheless, one would still expect that interplant differences in wages in plants producing the *same* output would be characterized by differences in labor productivity and that relative increases in wages between such plants would result in changes in relative labor productivity due to the effect of wages on X-inefficiency. Therefore, conceptually one must distinguish between differences and changes in labor productivity due to the impact of the wage variable on *identical* plants located in *different* regions or nations and those that are a function of interregional and international differences or variations in product mix. Given the relative interregional distribution of product mixes, one would expect a relative increase in wages between regions to result in a relative increase in labor productivity in the high-wage regions, as long as within the regions being compared some of the outputs being produced are the same.

On the other hand, interregional differences in labor productivity need not arise even if interregional wage differences result in relative differences in X-inefficiency in those identical plants producing the same output in regions being compared. Such a scenario arises if in the high-wage region, there exists a product mix that is characterized by a relatively lower average capital-labor ratio than in the low-wage region. Ceteris paribus, this generates a relatively lower average labor productivity in the high-wage region that can negate the relatively higher labor productivity per product sector in the high-wage region generated by the relatively higher level of X-efficiency. In this case, although wage differences have no effect upon the average interregional differences in labor productivity, in fact such productivity differences should be found, interregionally, between those plants producing the same output. Therefore, the high-wage regions would still be characterized by relatively less X-inefficiency.

One might assume an alternative and perhaps more plausible scenario whereby the higher-wage region is characterized by a product mix that yields a relatively high average capital-labor ratio and, thereby, ceteris paribus, a relatively higher average labor productivity. In this case, one must distinguish between that portion of the higher labor productivity that is due to the product mix and that portion that is a result of the effect of higher wages upon the degree of X-inefficiency in those plants in the high-wage region that are producing the same output as identical plants in the low-wage region.

The argument thus far presented has assumed that only identical plants can produce the same output. I have, therefore, abstracted from the impact that wage differences or a relative change in wages might have upon the capital-labor ratio adopted in plants producing the same output but experiencing different relative factor prices. Thus, I have abstracted from the productivity differences between the high- and low-wage plants that are due to different capital-labor ratios as opposed to different levels of X-inefficiency.[16] The object of this exercise in simplification was to isolate the relationship between wages and X-inefficiency. Nevertheless, even when relative wage increases significantly affect a plant's capital-labor ratio and, therefore, its labor productivity, the same wage increases can also be expected to affect labor productivity through pressuring the firm hierarchy to reduce the plant's X-inefficiency. Therefore, labor productivity will be affected both by changes in a plant's capital-labor ratio and, at the same time, by changes in its level of X-inefficiency. This argument is illustrated in figure 1. Assume that all plants are operating along isoquant Q_o at iscocost line 1. Further assume that wages increase in plant (A) such that the isocost line shifts inward to isocost line 2'. Total expenditures (costs) represented by isocost lines 1 and 2' are identical. Thus, for Q_o of output to be produced at the old capital-labor ratio, where isocost line 1 is tangential to isoquant Q_o at point b and where the new isocost line 2 passes through point b, costs per unit of output must increase. If factor proportions are adjusted (and they can be given a smooth and convex isoquant) such that the new isocost line is now tangential to isoquant Q_o, total costs per unit of output will fall (given by the inward shift of isocost line 2 to isocost line 2"). However, unit costs at isocost line 2" are still greater than for the lower-wage plants working with isocost line 1. To maintain unit costs at a competitive level the plant hierarchy of the high-cost (high-wage) firms must manage a lower level of X-inefficiency. The plant would then be operating along the more X-efficient isoquant Q_o'. Thus, to maintain unit costs at competitive levels, the high-wage plant must experience reductions in X-inefficiency unless, of course, one assumes the introduction of a new technology particular to the high-wage plant. Simple changes in factor proportions will not suffice. Therefore, my argument that higher wages contribute to relative reductions in X-inefficiency is not affected by the introduction of factor substitution.

My argument is more straightforward for plants characterized by isoquants similar to *XI* in figure 4. This isoquant contains only two feasible input combinations. Thus, increases in wages relative to the price of capital need not result in an increased capital-labor ratio. For example, an increase in the price of labor, resulting in a movement from

---

16. Although Sutcliff (1971, chap. 5) finds that there exist different capital-labor ratios for the same industry, he argues that these are typically few in number and may very well reflect the different products being produced within a specific industrial product classification. This suggests that the production isoquant for plants producing similar output are far from being smooth. Rather, the isoquant would, at best, be characterized by a few alternative capital-labor ratios.

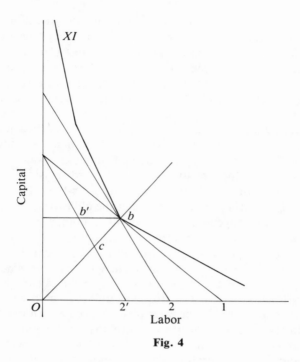

Fig. 4

isocost line 1 to isocost line 2, does not affect the capital-labor ratio, indicated by point b of isoquant XI. In this case, the increased cost of labor results in increased unit costs. The increase in costs is illustrated by isocost line 1 pivoting inward to isocost line 2′—where both isocost lines represent the same level of expenditure—as factor prices change. Thus, isocost line 2 represents increasing expenditures to produce a given level of output as factor prices increase. However, if the high-wage plant is operating X-inefficiently, unit costs can be reduced by reducing the level of X-inefficiency. Indeed, only at the more X-efficient point (c) (where the output at point c is equal to the output at XI) will unit costs be the same for the high-wage plant and for the low-wage plant that is operating relatively X-inefficiently at point b on isoquant XI. If, however, the plant operates X-inefficiently at point b due to overstaffing, point b' can be considered as a relatively X-efficient factor mix. This implies a higher capital-labor ratio for the high-wage plant due to the reduction in X-inefficiency brought on by higher relative wages. In this case, the higher capital-labor ratio is not a cause of increased labor productivity; rather it is the increased labor productivity stemming from the reduction in X-inefficiency that is the cause of the higher capital-labor ratio in the high-wage plant. If one assumes that the mix of capital and labor given by point *b* is the only technically optimal one given relative factor prices, then the reduction in X-inefficiency simply results in an increase in total factor productivity (including labor productivity) in the high-wage plants, with the same combination of factor inputs in the high- and low-wage plants.

Conclusions

An important conclusion of this article is that X-inefficiency can exist in spite of the existence of perfectly competitive product markets. Insofar as wage differentials persist between workers of identical plants, X-inefficiency can be expected to exist in relatively low-wage plants, particularly when workers and the firm hierarchy are characterized by conflicting behavioral functions. Thus, X-efficiency theory need not be restricted to situations where product market imperfections predominate. And these imperfections need not be the ultimate or even the most significant determinants of X-inefficiency.

By focusing on the relationship between relative wages and X-inefficiency, this article focuses upon the possibility that labor productivity can be enhanced by making plants more efficient apart from making operations more capital intensive or introducing new technology. Increasing wages in one plant relative to another, by increasing relative unit costs and prices and/or reducing profits, pressures firm members — the firm hierarchy in particular but also workers — to provide more effort into the process of production so as to reduce the extent of X-inefficiency. On the other hand, relatively low wages reduce the pressure on owners/managers to keep their plants relatively X-efficient.

From this follows another important result. Given the existence of X-inefficiency, relatively higher wages need not cause unit costs to increase, nor need higher wages cause profits to fall. Therefore, relatively higher wages need not be a cause for a decline in savings and thus for a reduction in the ability of firms to invest and, more generally, of regions or nations to grow.[17] Since higher wages need not be a cause of higher unit costs or of lower profits, they need not harm the competitive position of firms, regions, or nations. Moreover, given the existence of X-inefficiency, higher wages can be materially beneficial to society by contributing to its increasing X-efficiency. Alternatively, low-wage policies are a viable option to owner/managers who desire that their plants remain competitive but who do not want to invest the time and effort or

---

17. For further theoretical and empirical details on this point, see Altman 1988.

incur the stress necessary to keep their plants competitive at relatively higher wages. To the extent that low wages prevail, workers lose, but so does society at large, since the economy, through its firms, remains relatively X-inefficient.

I have not attempted to present a case that wage differentials are the key to understanding all or even most labor productivity differentials through their impact upon X-inefficiency. I have attempted only to indicate the conditions under which wage differentials can affect differentials in labor productivity by affecting differentials in X-inefficiency. The overall significance of the connection between wages, X-inefficiency, and labor productivity must, however, remain an empirical question. Nevertheless, I hope that I have demonstrated that this connection can be at least of some importance and, under certain circumstances, of great significance. However, it was Harvey Leiberstein who, by demonstrating the likelihood of the existence of X-inefficiency, opened the door to the introduction of wage differentials and changes in such differentials as potential causes of interfirm, interregional, and international differences in X-inefficiency and, thus, in labor productivity. Therefore, Leibenstein has established the basis for what might appear to many to be the paradoxical hypothesis that relatively high wages can benefit not only workers but also society at large by forcing increases in the material wealth of nations, not only through the increase of traditional factor inputs or the introduction of new technology, but also by increasing the quantity and quality of effort per unit of time. However, relatively high wages need not be viewed only as a means of forcing increased X-efficiency. Rather, in a relatively cooperative firm environment higher wages are part of a package of incentives designed to induce X-efficiency through forms of cooperation between labor and the firm hierarchy.

REFERENCES

Akerlof, George A., and Janet L. Yellen. 1986a."Introduction." In *Efficiency Wage Models of the Labor Market,* 1–21. *See* Akerlof and Yellen 1986b.
Akerlof, George A., and Janet L. Yellen, eds. 1986b. *Efficiency Wage Models of the Labor Market.* New York: Cambridge University Press.
Alchian, Armen A., and Harold Demsetz. 1972. "Production, Information Costs, and Economic Organization." *American Economic Review* 62:777–95.
Altman, Morris. 1986. " 'X-Efficiency' and Differential Labor Productivity Growth: Case Study of Quebec and Ontario, 1870–1910." Presented at the Eastern Economics Association Meetings, Philadelphia.

Altman, Morris. 1988. "Economic Development with High Wages: An Historical Perspective." *Explorations in Economic History* 25:198–224.

Blois, K.J. 1974. "Some Comments on the Theory of Inert Areas and the Definition of X-Efficiency." *Quarterly Journal of Economics* 88:681–86.

De Alessi, Louis. 1983. "Property Rights, Transaction Costs, and X-Efficiency: An Essay in Economic Theory." *American Economic Review* 73:64–81.

Dore, Ronald. 1973. *British Factor–Japanese Factory: The Origins of National Diversity in Industrial Relations.* Berkeley and Los Angeles: University of California Press.

Frantz, Roger S. 1985. "X-Efficiency Theory: A Review of the Literature, 1966–1983." San Diego State University. Mimeo.

Freeman, Richard B., and James L. Medoff. 1984. *What Do Unions Do?* New York: Basic Books.

Kendrick, John W., ed. 1984. *International Comparisons of Productivity and Causes of the Slowdown.* Washington and London: American Enterprise Institute/Ballinger.

Kilby, Peter. 1962. "Organization and Productivity in Backward Economies." *Quarterly Journal of Economics* 76:303–10.

Kilby, Peter. 1971. "Hunting the Heffalump." In *Entrepreneurship and Economic Development*, ed. Peter Kilby, 1–40. New York: Free Press.

Leibenstein, Harvey. 1966. "Allocative vs. 'X-Efficiency.'" *American Economic Review* 56:392–415.

Leibenstein, Harvey. 1969. "Organizational or Frictional Equilibria, X-Efficiency, and the Rate of Innovation." *Quarterly Journal of Economics* 83:600–623.

Leibenstein, Harvey. 1973. "Competition and X-Efficiency: Reply." *Journal of Political Economy* 81:765–77.

Leibenstein, Harvey. 1978. *General X-Efficiency Theory and Economic Development.* New York: Oxford University Press.

Leibenstein, Harvey. 1979. "A Branch of Economics Is Missing: Micro-Micro Theory." *Journal of Economic Literature* 17:477–502.

Leibenstein, Harvey. 1980. *Beyond Economic Man: A New Foundation for Microeconomics.* Cambridge, Mass.: Harvard University Press.

Leibenstein, Harvey. 1981. "Microeconomics and X-Efficiency Theory: If There Is No Crisis, There Ought to Be." In *The Crisis in Economic Theory*, ed. Daniel Bell and Irving Kristol, 97–122. New York: Basic Books.

Leibenstein, Harvey. 1982. "The Prisoner's Dilemma in the Invisible Hand: An Analysis of Intrafirm Productivity." *American Economic Review* 72:92–97.

Leibenstein, Harvey. 1983. "Property Rights and Efficiency: Comment." *American Economic Review* 73:831–42.

Leibenstein, Harvey. 1985. "On Relaxing the Maximization Hypothesis." *Journal of Behavioral Economics* 14:5–20.

Leibenstein, Harvey. 1986. "Leibenstein on the Maximization Postulate: Comments and Responses to Contributors." *Journal of Behavioral Economics* 15:57–63.

Leibenstein, Harvey. 1987. *Inside the Firm: The Inefficiencies of Hierarchy.* Cambridge, Mass.: Harvard University Press.

Nelson, Richard R. 1968. "A 'Diffusion' Model of International Productivity Differences in Manufacturing Industry." *American Economic Review* 58: 1219–48.

Nelson, Richard R. 1984. "Where Are We in the Discussion? Retrospect and Prospect." In *International Comparisons of Productivity*, 397–409. *See* Kendrick 1984.

Salter, W. E. G. 1969. *Productivity and Technical Change.* 2d ed. London: Cambridge University Press.

Scitovsky, Tibor. 1943–44. "A Note on Profit Maximization and Its Implications." *Review of Economic Studies* 11:57–60.

Shen, T. Y. 1984. "The Estimation of X-Efficiency in Eighteen Countries." *Review of Economics and Statistics* 66:98–104.

Shimada, Haruo. 1985. "The Perceptions and the Realities of Japanese Industrial Relations." In *The Management Challenge*, 44–66. *See* Thurow 1985.

Simon, Herbert A. 1959. "Theories of Decision Making in Economics and Behavioral Science." *American Economic Review* 49:252–83.

Simon, Herbert A. 1978. "Rationality as Process and as Product of Thought." *American Economic Review* 68:1–15.

Solow, Robert M. 1986. "Another Possible Source of Wage Stickiness." In *Efficiency Wage Models of the Labor Market*, 41–44. *See* Akerlof and Yellen 1986.

Stigler, George J. 1976. "The Xistence of X-Efficiency." *American Economic Review* 66:213–16.

Sutcliffe, R. B. 1971. *Industry and Underdevelopment.* London: Addison-Wesley.

Takeuchi, Hiroshi. 1985. "Motivation and Production." In *The Management Challenge,* 18–28. *See* Thurow 1985.

Thurow, Lester C., ed. 1985. *The Management Challenge: Japanese Views.* Cambridge, Mass.: MIT Press.

On the Measurement of the Relative Efficiency of a Set of Decision-Making Units

Wade D. Cook, Ya'akov Roll, and Alex Kazakov

The X-inefficiency hypothesis of Liebenstein (1966) is that organizations typically do not optimize as proposed by classical economic doctrine but rather may exhibit some degree of inefficiency. While it may be difficult to pinpoint the reasons for apparent inefficiencies, such may, nevertheless, be present, and the first important step toward explaining may be to attempt measuring the degree of inefficiency.

The early work of Farrell (1957) was directed toward measurement of such inefficiencies; he introduced the concept of an efficient frontier as an alternative to the usual least squares production function. The latter tries to capture average performance while the former is aimed at characterizing best performance.

The Data Envelopment Analysis (DEA) method for measuring the relative efficiency of a set of similar Decision Making Units (DMUs) was originally presented by Charnes, Cooper, and Rhodes (1978). Built on the earlier work of Farrell, the DEA model is based on an engineering-like approach, comparing a set of outputs to a set of inputs, common to all DMUs. The model determines, for each DMU, a set of virtual multipliers or factor weights such that the ratio of weighted outputs to weighted inputs for that DMU is maximized. This ratio becomes the DMU's relative efficiency measure.

The DEA model was developed specifically for efficiency measurement of nonprofit organizations, which are characterized by a combination of qualitative factors for which no established standards exist. Hence it creates a relative rather than absolute efficiency measure. In this article we discuss the applicability of the DEA approach to the assessment of the relative efficiency of highway maintenance patrols in Ontario. Because noneconomic factors such as environmental impacts and safety-related measures are involved, the DEA methodology

---

Supported under NSERC Grant #A8966 and Ontario Ministry of Transportation Contract #26108.

would appear to be an appropriate measurement tool for this environment.

Maintenance Patrol Operations and the Problem of Efficiency

Maintenance Patrols

Most of the routine maintenance activities on Ontario's highways are the responsibility of the 244 patrols scattered throughout the province. Each such patrol is responsible for some fixed number of lane kilometers of highway and the activities associated with that portion of the network. Some 100-plus different categories of operations/activities exist and are grouped under the headings: surface, shoulder, right-of-way, median, and winter operations.

Surface and shoulder operations include, for example, all forms of manual and machine patching and crack sealing. Right-of-way and median operations involve vegetation control, signs, lighting, guardrails, etc. Winter operations pertain primarily to snow removal, salting, and winter safety activities. To a great extent, the work of patrol crews is safety related.

Any operations that cannot be handled by crews are carried out by private contractors. The degree of privatization varies greatly from one patrol to another. The present system for monitoring patrol activities within the Ontario Ministry of Transportation is the Maintenance Management System (MMS). This is a computerized record-keeping system that essentially keeps track of total work accomplished by type of operation, patrol, and highway class. This system is similar to those in other Canadian provinces and in states in the United States.

While various statistics (such as median operations accomplished, by highway class) are maintained, there is presently no formal process for evaluating patrol activities. An area of importance to the ministry has to do with the efficiency with which maintenance operations are carried out in various parts of the province. Since observed accomplishments influence budgetary decisions, a better understanding of efficiency will give management a yardstick for measuring what accomplishments can be expected within a given budget limit. In this context, important questions arise:

- Why do observed accomplishments differ from one jurisdiction to another? What should be considered as standard?
- Are observed differences an indication of patrols' efficiencies,

or are they a function of environmental, traffic, or other considerations?

- What is the influence of the proportion of privatized work on a patrol's efficiency?
- How should the efficiency of a patrol be judged, given the afore-mentioned considerations?

In the sections to follow, a framework for addressing these issues is discussed.

The Concept of Efficiency and Methods of Measurement

The productivity or efficiency level of any Decision Making Unit (DMU), (e.g., a factory, government department, maintenance patrol) is a measure of the extent to which that DMU makes the best possible use of a given set of *inputs* (resources, etc.) to produce some set of *outputs*. In this context, "best possible use" loosely means getting the most out of available resources within a given set of circumstances.

In an industrial setting, efficiency or productivity is usually approached from an engineering perspective. This approach is based upon production standards. The productivity of a DMU, then, is the ratio of standard or required inputs (needed to create the current level of output) to the actual inputs used.

Other measures of efficiency/productivity often found in organizations are based on financial information. Profitability measures, such as return on investment, provide a form of performance indicator. In a nonprofit environment, one might, e.g., compare what the cost could be if jobs were done privately to the actual costs under the current setting.

An alternative to these absolute measures of efficiency is a measure that evaluates a DMU relative to some comparison group. Such an approach is not only realistic but may be the only one applicable in many nonprofit environments. This is the approach on which Data Envelopment Analysis (DEA) is based. It is capable of handling noneconomic factors, such as the number of accidents, maintenance dollars (an economic factor), cars per day, average age of pavement, etc., and allows for measurement of such factors on different scales. Such an approach seems particularly suited to the maintenance area, since factors such as traffic intensity, safety parameters, and average age of pavements are an important part of the picture.

The purpose of the present study was to test whether, indeed, DEA suits the specific environment in which highway maintenance patrols operate, and whether this approach produces the desired outcomes.

Criteria for Efficiency Evaluation

In designing an efficiency-measuring and -monitoring system, certain criteria were specified by the user.

1. The model should be widely discriminating in that patrols should be separable into as many rank classes as possible.
2. The model should aid in pointing to reasons for apparent inefficiencies. Moreover, the model should aid in verifying (or disproving) current popular beliefs/hypotheses regarding certain phenomena believed strongly to influence maintenance effectiveness. It is, e.g., commonly felt that the percentage of commercial vehicles strongly influences maintenance needs and effectiveness.
3. The model should be sensitive to the particular circumstances prevailing in a patrol (e.g., high vs. low traffic, severe vs. mild environment) rather than relying on a common set of standards.
4. The model should attempt to classify patrols through such considerations of circumstances, hence creating groupings of like things.

In the section to follow the applicability of the DEA model to the maintenance patrol problem is discussed in light of these criteria.

A DEA Model for Evaluating Maintenance Patrol Efficiency

The Basic Model

Given a set of J Decision Making Units, the model determines for each DMU_0, the best set of input weights

$$\{\nu_{i0}\}_{i=1}^{I}$$

and output weights

$$\{\mu_{r0}\}_{r=1}^{R}$$

such that the ratio of total weighted outputs to total weighted inputs is maximized. This is done subject to the constraints that the corresponding ratio for each DMU$_j$ (including the one in question) does not exceed 1 and that the weights μ_{r0} and ν_{i0} fall within some set of reasonable bounds (see Roll et al. [1988]). The ratio e_0 is the relative efficiency rating for DMU$_0$.

Let the following notation be adopted:

Y_{rj} = value of output factor r for DMU j,

X_{ij} = value of input factor i for DMU j,

$\mu_{r0}, \nu_{i0}, M_{r0}, N_{i0}$ = weights for the corresponding factor,

$Q1_r, Q2_r, P1_i, P2_i,$ = bounds imposed on weights,

T = transformation factor.

In mathematical terms, the DEA model involves solving the J fractional programming problems:

Max $\left\{ e_0 = \dfrac{\sum_r \mu_{r0} Y_{r0}}{\sum_i \nu_{i0} X_{i0}} \right\}$

Subject to: $\dfrac{\sum_r \mu_{r0} Y_{rj}}{\sum_i \nu_{i0} X_{ij}} \leq 1$, for all DMUs $j = 1, 2, \ldots, J.$ (1)

$Q2_r \leq \mu_{r0} \leq Q1_r \forall r = 1, 2, \ldots, R$

$P2_i \leq \nu_{i0} \leq P1_i \forall i = 1, 2, \ldots, I$

By making the transformation $T = 1/\sum_i \nu_{i0} X_{i0}$ and defining

$M_{r0} = \mu_{r0} T$ and $N_{i0} = \nu_{i0} T,$

it is easily shown that (1) is equivalent to the linear programming model:

Max $\sum_r M_{r0} Y_{r0}$

Subject to:

$$\sum_i N_{i0} X_{i0} = 1$$

$$\sum_r M_{r0} Y_{rj} - \sum_i N_{i0} X_{ij} \leq 0, \forall j$$

$$M_{r0} - Q1_r T \leq 0, \forall r. \qquad (2)$$

$$-M_{r0} + Q2_r T \leq 0, \forall r$$

$$N_{i0} - P1_i T \leq 0 \ \forall i$$

$$-N_{i0} + P2_i T \leq 0 \ \forall i,$$

Interpretation of Optimization Method

In order to demonstrate the DEA method for measuring relative efficiency, consider the following simple example of seven patrols in which a single output Y (e.g., number of lane kilometers serviced by the patrol) is observed, and two inputs are used. Take the two inputs to be $X_1 =$ number of hundreds of thousands of dollars of maintenance budget, and $X_2 =$ average road conditions as assessed by Pavement Condition Rating (PCR). Further simplify matters by assuming that all patrols service the same number of lane kilometers (Y does not differ from patrol to patrol). Let the respective inputs for this group of patrols be as follows:

Patrol	A	B	C	D	E	F	G
X_1 ($00,000)	3	5	8	12	6	8	10
X_2 (PCR)	.90	.70	.55	.50	.84	.80	.60

A picture of these seven sets of inputs is shown in figure 1. It can be seen that different patrols use different combinations of X_1 and X_2, and that some patrols use fewer inputs than others (for rendering the same output Y). By joining the points representing patrols A, B, C, and D, it becomes clear that these four patrols dominate the entire group in the sense that no other patrols use better combinations of inputs. Thus, patrols A, B, C, and D can be thought of as forming an efficient frontier.

Any patrol on the frontier is regarded as efficient in a relative sense and is defined as having an efficiency rating of 1.0. The patrols behind the frontier are inefficient relative to those forming the frontier. Thus the frontier envelops the points representing all patrols (hence the name *Data Envelopment Analysis*).

The efficiencies of patrols E, F, and G can be measured relative to the efficient frontier. Consider, for example, patrol E, which is dominated by patrol B. It has inputs in the same proportions as B, but larger by 20 percent. We say, then, that the relative efficiency of patrol E is $100/120 = 83$ percent. Graphically this is represented by the ratio of distances OB to OE on figure 1. Patrol F is similarly dominated, although by a combination of B and C. The efficiency of F is obtained from the ratio OK/OF in figure 1. Patrols B and C constitute the peer group or comparison group against which the efficiency of patrol F is measured. Patrol B is the peer group for patrol E.

In the simple example with only a single output and two inputs, one can measure efficiency directly from a graphical representation like the one in figure 1. This kind of representation does not highlight the weights

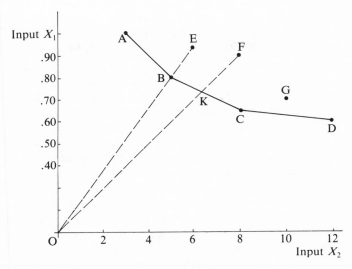

Fig. 1. Efficient frontier

given to factors in determining efficiencies (the weights are embedded in the scales of the two axes of the graph). In the more complex case of multiple outputs and inputs, the measures of efficiency cannot be arrived at in as simple a manner. In the general case it is necessary to solve an optimization problem, using mathematical programming techniques, in order to obtain efficiency ratings for the various units, their peer groups, and the weights accorded to the different input and output factors.

In other words, the model determines, for each DMU_0, the best set of input weights $\{\nu_{io}\}$ and output weights $\{\mu_{ro}\}$ such that the ratio of total outputs to total inputs is maximized. This is done subject to the constraints that the corresponding ratio for each DMU (including the one in question) does not exceed 1.0 (i.e., the highest efficiency score for any DMU is 100 percent) and that the weights μ_{r0} and ν_{i0} fall within some set of reasonable bounds. The ratio e_0 is the relative efficiency rating for DMU_0.

In the production setting, the factor weights are generally the prices associated with inputs and outputs. If, e.g., different classes of labor represent the inputs, and if it is desirable to construct a single labor productivity ratio, the weights on the different inputs would simply be the differential labor rates. Thus, dollars become the common basis of comparison of inputs.

This approach for determining weights for each DMU can be justified by arguing that since noneconomic factors are present, there is no correct set of weights that apply to all patrols. The importance, for example, of environmental factors to patrols in the northern regions may be a different matter than it is to patrols in the south. Thus, rather than having to try to assign some set of common weights to inputs and outputs, the model itself chooses weights that are appropriate for each patrol. In choosing weights for any patrol, the DEA model tries to present the patrol's position in the most favorable light. In this setting, then, if a patrol can be shown to be efficient (has a ratio of 1) by some reasonable set of weights, then such will turn out to be the case. Therefore, a patrol will be declared inefficient only if it is dominated by other patrols or combinations of other patrols. DEA should, thus, be viewed as a technique for identifying inefficiency.

In the process of assigning weights to input and output factors, one may study the relative importance of each factor in terms of its influence on a patrol's standing. By including or excluding factors or by applying various levels of disaggregation, one can evaluate the significance of various factors. For example, maintenance dollars can be considered either as a single input or as two subinputs such as *privatized* versus *inhouse* work. In this manner, the impact of privatization policies can be examined.

Selection of Factors: Considerations and Difficulties

The process of selecting factors in a DEA model should concentrate on finding effects of maintenance activities together with a set of explanatory or causal factors that enable one to create these effects. Outputs should, therefore, measure the effectiveness of what patrols do in carrying out their mandate. Potential candidates would be number of vehicles served, accidents (or reduction thereof), quality of pavements, etc. Inputs are of two types. First, there are controllable factors such as the size of the budget and the percentage of work done under private contract. Second, factors not under the control of the patrol or district include such things as environmental measures (e.g., inches of snowfall), average age of pavements, etc. The latter factors describe the circumstances within which a patrol is forced to operate, and may, therefore, have a strong influence on the way in which outputs can be affected.

The choice of factors (outputs and inputs) must, of course, be guided by another very important consideration, namely data availability. There are, for example, limitations on the extent to which effects of maintenance can be observed. We do not have, for example, observed pavement condition ratings on each section of highway *immediately before and after* surface maintenance operations. Thus, it is difficult to separate out that portion of year-to-year rating changes that is due to maintenance efforts. As another example, in the area of traffic, it is true that data are readily available on the number of vehicles, but data are not available for the wear on vehicles associated with various roughness levels of the pavement. Thus, it is possible to measure service to the public in terms of AADT (Annual Average Daily Traffic) but not in terms of user cost. Therefore, to a great extent, existing data sources tend to dictate what can and cannot serve as inputs and outputs.

Having chosen those factors that are to be used to describe cause and effect in relation to patrol activities, the issue of quantification arises. While it is true that the DEA structure does not require that factors be reducible to a common unit, it is necessary to quantify each on some scale. If, for example, safety is a principal consideration in regard to maintenance effort, some reasonable method of capturing safety (say, skid resistance, number of accidents, number of fatal accidents, etc.) must be found. Severity of the environment is likely an important determinant of the extent to which patrol efforts can be effective. Yet, there is no obvious single measure of environmental impact. Again, quantification is a pressing issue in the selection of factors.

The grouping of various indicators into overall or composite factors also influences the final structure of the DEA model. While technically the model could handle many different indicators of the same factor (thus avoiding the grouping problem), it is highly desirable to arrive at a small number of inputs and outputs. If, for example, we desire as an output "size of system serviced," it becomes necessary to describe on a single scale such measures as the number of lane kilometers of paved surface, the amount of paved versus gravel shoulders, the number of hectares of right-of-way, etc. Environmental indicators, such as the number of inches of snowfall and the number of freeze and thaw cycles, should be combined into some composite factor.

Despite these various issues and reservations, the DEA approach appears to be the most viable method for evaluating patrol efficiency. Moreover, it is these very issues that reinforce the need for a tool as flexible and encompassing as the DEA constructs. In that regard, we now turn to a description of the pilot application of this tool to the highway maintenance area.

Testing DEA: A Pilot Study

The basis of the pilot study was a set of 14 patrols from a single district in Ontario. Two inputs and two outputs were selected for test purposes. On the output side, the first factor is a composite measure of various size-of-the-system indicators. This Assignment Size Factor (ASF) combines values relating to the various components — surface, shoulder, right-of-way and median, and winter operations. Account has been taken of the different surface and shoulder types, and weights have been applied corresponding to the levels of expenditure on the various items in the most recent fiscal period. The other output factor is the Average Traffic Serviced (ATS) indicator. This indicator combines AADT and road length.

On the input side, one economic and one noneconomic factor were used. These were (1) Total Expenditure (TEX) and (2) Average Pavement condition Rating (APR).

Table 1 provides the complete list of factor values for the 14 patrols.

As described earlier, the DEA model involves solving a linear programming problem for each patrol under consideration. In the case at hand, 14 such problems were solved. Appendix 1 provides a sample solution of one such problem. The efficiency rating for this specific patrol is given by the objective function value = .613. The weights assigned to the two outputs are M_1 = .000861 and M_2 = .010759. Those corresponding to the inputs are N_1 = .001077 and N_2 = .003126.

Unbounded model. In the first round of analyses of the patrols, the linear programming model (2) was run without upper and lower bounds on M_1, M_2, and N_1, N_2. Table 2 shows the results of this set of runs.

The table displays for each patrol or DMU the efficiency rating (e), and weights M_1, M_2, N_1, and N_2. It is noted that those patrols showing an

TABLE 1. Summary of Factor Values

Patrol	Assignment Size	Average Traffic Serviced	Total Expenditure	Average Pavement Rating
1	696	39	751	67
2	616	26	611	70
3	456	17	538	70
4	616	31	584	75
5	560	16	665	70
6	446	16	445	75
7	517	26	554	76
8	492	18	457	72
9	558	23	582	74
10	407	18	556	64
11	402	33	590	78
12	350	88	1,074	75
13	581	64	1,072	74
14	413	24	696	80

efficiency rating of 1 are classified as efficient and lie on the efficient frontier. Those with ratings less than 1 are considered as inefficient. The rating of 0.803 for patrol number 3, for example, is interpreted as meaning that technically this DMU is only about 80 percent as efficient as it could be.

The column labeled "DMUs in facet" gives the peer groups. In the case of DMU number 3, e.g., the relevant peer group consists of patrols numbers 4 and 8. Specifically, in evaluating its efficiency standing, number 3 should compare itself to efficient patrols number 4 and 8 (each of which has a rating of 1 or 100 percent). It is these two patrols that number 3 is most similar to and should strive to emulate.

More generally, the efficient frontier consists of facets created by the efficient patrols numbers 1, 4, 8, 12, and 13. It is the combinations or facets of these patrols against which all others are evaluated. The efficient pair 1, 4, e.g., forms the peer group for inefficient patrols numbers 2, 5, 9, and 10. Efficient patrol number 12 must be added to this group (to give 1, 4, 12) to obtain the peer group for patrols numbers 11 and 14.

Bounded model. In the unbounded case we have described, the sets of weights obtained for the 14 patrols are widely varying. It is noted, for example, that $M_2 = .00001$ for DMU number 1 but $M_2 = .017883$ for DMU number 11. Technically speaking, patrol number 11 is permitted to attach a much greater weight or importance to the second output than that given by patrol number 3. There is rather general agreement that while flexibility in the sets of weights is a desirable feature (to allow for the different circumstances of the patrols as discussed earlier), such flexi-

TABLE 2. Outcomes with the Unbounded Model

DMU	Efficiency Rating	Weights ($\times 10^6$)				DMUs in Facet (peer group)	Slacks			
		M_1	M_2	N_1	N_2		S_1	S_2	R_1	R_2
1	1	1,436	10	913	4,690	1	—	—	—	
2	0.999	1,621	10	1,030	5,292	1, 4	—	6.141	—	—
3	0.803	1,760	10	1,688	1,312	4, 8	—	5.578	—	—
4	1	1,623	10	1,557	1,210	4	—	—	—	—
5	0.860	1,535	10	976	5,013	1, 4	—	13.969	—	—
6	0.931	2,087	10	2,246	10	8	—	0.317	—	4.553
7	0.885	1,585	2,501	1,804	10	4, 8	—	—	—	4.258
8	1	2,032	10	2,187	10	8	—	—	—	—
9	0.913	1,635	10	1,039	5,339	1, 4	—	5.173	—	—
10	0.724	1,778	10	1,130	5,806	1, 4	—	3.205	—	—
11	0.874	708	17,883	1,697	10	1, 4, 12	—	—	—	13.365
12	1	389	9,815	930	10	12	—	—	—	
13	1	808	8,291	90	12,208	13	—	—	—	—
14	0.619	742	13,041	1,114	2,805	1, 4, 12	—	—	—	—

bility should fall within some reasonable limits. Thus, some bounds were imposed on the range over which the M_r and N_i weights would be allowed to move.

Table 3 presents the outcomes from the bounded version of the 14 linear programming runs. The bounds imposed on the factor weights are specified in the bottom of Table 3. Generally, the efficiency ratings did not change drastically, although in a pure definitional sense only three of the patrols (numbers 1, 4, and 8) are now efficient. Patrols numbers 12 and 13, which previously, with complete freedom to choose weights, formed part of the efficient frontier, are now behind the frontier with ratings at approximately 0.91 and 0.88, respectively. Of course, under this new scenario, there are fewer different peer groups. The set 1, 4 is now the peer group for the five inefficient patrols numbers 2, 5, 9, 10, 14.

It is noted that all efficiency ratings are at or lower than their previous (unbounded) levels. This is due to the restricted freedom of movement of the weights in the bounded case.

Extensions and Directions for Further Analysis

Common Set of Weights

An important feature of the DEA approach, but in some respects a bothersome one, is its derivation of a different set of weights M_r, N_i for each patrol. One can view this as a mechanism for highlighting the strengths of each patrol and at the same time taking account of the special circumstances in which the patrol operates. However, it may be expedient to assess, quantitatively, the portion of a DMU's efficiency that is supposedly explained by these circumstances.

While the concept of a completely common set of weights (CSW) in the nonprofit sector (e.g., maintenance patrols) may not be fully justified, it is worth examining the phenomenon. In this regard, a procedure was developed for deriving such a set. The approach essentially amounts to closing the gap between the upper and lower limits on the weights used in the bounded analysis discussed in the previous subsection. The efficiency ratings emerging from this analysis are given later in a summary table (see table 5).

Disaggregation of Factors and Patrol Grouping

Disaggregation can be accomplished in one of two ways. The factor itself (say, ATS) can be augmented or replaced by, say, two separate factors, e.g., ATS plus the percentage of commercial vehicles. Alternatively, the issue of the percentage of trucks can be dealt with by splitting the set of all patrols into two or more groups according to the percentage of commercial vehicles. One could, e.g., do an analysis of those patrols where the percentage of commercial vehicles (average on all pavements in the patrol) is above 15 percent and a separate analysis for those patrols where the percentage is below 15 percent.

As an example of the second form of disaggregation, the factor representing the percentage of work carried out by private contractors was investigated. Group A consists of those patrols in which the percentage of work privatized was 20 percent or more. Group B consists of patrols corresponding to the less than 20 percent privatized work. Table 4 presents the results. It is noted that the relative efficiency of any patrol will be at least as high under the disaggregated analysis as under the analysis when all patrols are included. This is logical, since when, say, group A is subjected to a separate evaluation, any given patrol, such as patrol number 3, is being compared to fewer other patrols (eight others) than is the case in the original analysis (13 others).

In this particular evaluation, efficiencies seemed to have changed very little. Thus, it would seem that the effect of the percentage of privatization is not very significant. In cases where the peer group for a

TABLE 3. Outcomes with the Bounded Model

DMU	Efficiency Rating	Weights ($\times 10^6$) M_1	M_2	N_1	N_2	DMUs in Facet (peer group)	Slacks S_1	S_2	R_1	R_2
1	1	1,833	500	1,183	6,000	1	—	—	—	—
2	0.995	1,833	500	1,189	6,000	1, 4	—	6.070	—	(0.506)
3	0.800	2,180	500	2,070	1,336	4, 8	(1.313)	5.513	—	—
4	1	2,100	500	2,070	1,337	4	—	—	—	—
5	0.854	1,833	500	1,189	6,000	1, 4	—	13.802	—	(1.150)
6	0.929	2,100	500	2,233	300	8	(0.719)	291	—	4.576
7	0.884	2,100	6,093	2,500	300	4	(0.355)	—	(0.213)	4.261
8	1	2,180	2,704	2,320	300	8	—	—	—	—
9	0.910	1,833	500	1,190	6,000	1, 4	—	5.115	—	0.426
10	0.722	1,834	500	1,190	6,000	1, 4	—	3.168	—	(0.264)
11	0.803	800	10,000	1,336	300	4	97.570	(7.859)	—	1.790
12	0.913	800	10,000	900	4,043	1	361.709	(48.120)	213.145	
13	0.876	800	10,000	900	4,044	1	90.895	(26.351)	211.989	
14	0.614	800	10,000	1,001	2,936	1, 4	18.713	(1.497)	—	—
Upper bounds		2,100	10,000	2,500	6,000					
Lower bounds		800	500	900	300					

patrol remains the same, no change in the efficiency rating will occur. For example, in both analyses patrol number 7 has patrol number 4 as its peer group. Thus number 7 receives the same rating under both evaluations. Patrol number 3, on the other hand, has 4, 8 as the peer group originally and a rating of $e = 0.80$. Under the disaggregation, patrol number 3 (in group A) has 2, 6 as the peer group, and a rating of $e = 0.82$.

The outcomes listed in table 5 can be used to segregate the analyzed set of patrols into several efficiency classes. The first class contains patrols that come out consistently with high efficiency ratings in any kind of analysis attempted. Patrols numbers 1, 2, 4, and 8 of the sample of 14 belong to this class. The second class (patrols numbers 5, 6, 7, 9, 11) is made up of those patrols with intermediate relative efficiency ratings, while patrols numbers 3, 10, and 14 belong to a third class having consistently low scores. A final class (patrols numbers 12 and 13) comprises the units for which outcomes vary significantly with different kinds of analysis. Such patrols should be examined closely for specific factors affecting their performance.

Efficiency Gap Analysis

The observed inefficiency $(1 - e)$ of any patrol can possibly be explained or rationalized as consisting of different types of efficiency gaps. Figure

TABLE 4. Outcomes when DMUs Are Grouped by Percentage of Privatization

Group	DMU	Efficiency	M_1	M_2	N_1	N_2	DMUs in Facet (peer group)	S_1	S_2	R_1	R_2
A	1	1	2,100	2,011	1,515	6,000	1	—	—	—	—
	2	1	2,100	2,012	1,516	6,000	2	—	—	—	—
	3	0.820	2,100	500	1,760	3,305	2, 6	(0.302)	1.268	—	—
	5	0.850	1,926	500	1,276	6,000	1, 2	—	9.898	—	(0.825)
	6	0.929	2,100	500	2,233	300	8	(0.719)	291	—	4.546
	8	1	2,100	500	2,237	300	8	—	—	—	—
	10	0.732	1,829	10,000	2,020	2,124	1, 2, 8	—	—	—	
	13	0.874	800	10,000	900	4,044	1	90.895	(26.351)	(211.989)	
	14	0.646	800	10,000	1,234	300	1	3.754	(0.647)	—	11.570
B	4	1	2,100	500	1,471	6,000	4	—	—	—	—
	7	0.880	2,100	6,093	2,500	300	4	(0.355)	—	(0.213)	(4.261)
	9	0.910	1,558	500	900	6,000	4	—	5.081	909	(0.560)
	11	0.803	800	10,000	1,336	300	4	97.570	(7.859)	—	1.790
	12	0.933	800	10,000	900	3,697	4	224.497	(59.089)	456.987	
Upper bounds			2,100	10,000	2,500	6,000					
Lower bounds			800	800	900	300					

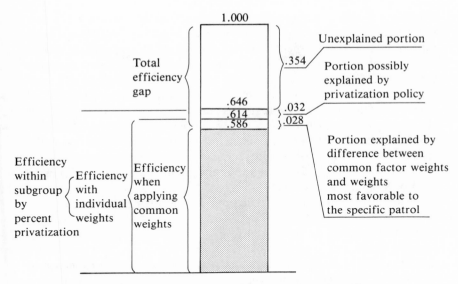

Fig. 2.   Efficiency picture for patrol number 14

2 presents a possible analysis of such gaps. Briefly, if one takes the efficiency *e* arising from the common set of weights (for patrol number 14 the CSW rating is *e* = 0.586), the resulting total efficiency gap is given by 1 − 0.586 = 0.414. Part of this gap consists of the 0.028 portion (0.614

TABLE 5.   **Efficiency Ratings**

Patrol	Unbounded Runs	Common Weights	Bounded Runs		
			Individual Weights		
			All Patrols	Group A	Group B
1	1	0.947	1	1	
2	0.999	0.955	0.996	1	
3	0.803	0.774	0.800	0.820	
4	1	1	1		1
5	0.860	0.780	0.854	0.857	
6	0.931	0.862	0.929	0.929	
7	0.885	0.873	0.884		0.884
8	1	0.943	1	1	
9	0.913	0.889	0.910		0.911
10	0.724	0.697	0.722	0.732	
11	0.874	0.696	0.803		0.803
12	1	0.518	0.913		0.933
13	1	0.653	0.874	0.874	
14	0.619	0.586	0.614	0.646	

– 0.586 = 0.028) due to the improvement in number 14's standing when it is evaluated in terms of its own set of weights. One can perhaps rationalize this improvement by reasoning that special circumstances surrounding number 14's environment are not given proper consideration when the CSW rating is used.

An even further improvement in the rating to $e = 0.646$ is achieved when patrol number 14 is evaluated as part of the patrols of group A that all have a similar privatization policy. This portion (0.646 – 0.614 = 0.032) of the total efficiency gap is, therefore, possibly explainable by the type of privatization policy used.

The remaining 0.354 of the gap is unexplained insofar as the present level of analysis is concerned.

Similar analyses can be carried out for all other patrols.

Conclusions

The pilot study demonstrated the benefits of using DEA for measuring the relative efficiency of highway maintenance patrols. These benefits include the following.

Multiple inputs and outputs. The DEA method accommodates multiple inputs and outputs. Of particular importance is the fact that noneconomic factors can be included in the analysis. Weights on these factors are calibrated within the model in a manner that takes account of the particular circumstances of each patrol and hence presents each patrol in the most favorable light.

Rank orders patrols. The model provides a rank ordering of the patrols in terms of their efficiency ratings. As a management tool, this gives an overall measure of the relative standing of the patrols, as well as an indication of the possible reasons behind any given patrol's inefficiency. It was shown that even in the small set of patrols in the pilot study, considerable differences in efficiency were encountered. Thus, the proposed approach seems to have good discriminating power.

Controlled weights. The DEA approach is very flexible in the sense that the user can impose restrictions on the weights to be assigned to inputs and outputs. For example, if safety is considered to be the predominant output factor, the model can be controlled so that the weight on this factor is higher than the weights assigned to other outputs. Also, a set of common factor weights can be arrived at, fitting the entire group of patrols handled. This CSW may be used for efficiency gap analyses.

Classifying patrols. By carrying out evaluations through several different models (all versions of the DEA approach), one can classify patrols into clearly efficient, clearly inefficient, and middle-of-the-road units. Through this process of peer group identification, three major groups emerge. The first group consists of those patrols that rate high under various weighting schemes. The second group is the set that consistently rates low under different sets of weights. Finally, there is the unstable third set whose ratings fluctuate widely depending on the values used to weight inputs and outputs.

Peer group comparisons. In the process of establishing an efficiency rating for a given patrol i_0, one identifies a small subset of efficient patrols. It is this peer group against which i_0 is evaluated. In a sense, members of this peer group use inputs and produce outputs in proportions that are comparable to those of i_0; however, they are more efficient in their operation. This kind of comparison to demonstrate better performance may make it easier to explain the outcomes of those patrols with low efficiencies.

Analysis of the impact of circumstances in which patrols operate. The DEA analysis can be carried out in many different settings. Patrols in the north, for example, can be analyzed in isolation; patrols with high-volume roads can be separated for individual analysis, etc. Thus, the special circumstances of subgroups of patrols can be pinpointed and a specific DEA analysis targeted at those circumstances.

Uses existing data. An important feature of the DEA approach is that it is based upon existing maintenance and highway inventory data. No costly data collection procedures are required other than those already in place.

The large number of units carrying out similar tasks under generally comparable circumstances renders the approach of measuring relative efficiencies particularly attractive. It provides an effective management tool for controlling patrol performance and highlights specific areas where more in-depth engineering studies should be carried out.

REFERENCES

Charnes, A., W. W. Cooper, and E. Rhodes. 1978. "Measuring the Efficiency of Decision Making Units." *European Journal of Operation Research* 2:429–44.

Farrell, M. J. 1957. "The Measurement of Productive Efficiency." *Journal of the Royal Statistical Society*, ser. A, 3:253–290.

Leibenstein, H. 1966. "Allocative Efficiency vs 'X-Efficiency.' " *American Economic Review* 56:392–415.

Roll, Y., W. D. Cook, and B. Golany. 1988. "Factor Weights in Data Envelopment Analysis." Faculty of Administrative Studies, York University, Toronto. Working Paper.

APPENDIX 1

MAX   413 M1 + 24 M2
SUBJECT TO
   2)   696 N1 + 80 N2 =   1

LP OPTIMUM FOUND AT STEP   1

OBJECTIVE FUNCTION VALUE

   1)   0.613666832

VARIABLE	VALUE	REDUCED COST
M1	0.000861	0.000000
M2	0.010759	0.000000
N1	0.001077	0.000000
N2	0.003126	0.000000
T	1.075853	0.000000

ROW	SLACK	DUAL PRICES
2)	0.000000	0.613667
3)	0.000000	0.195551
4)	0.067252	0.000000
5)	0.223135	0.000000
6)	0.000000	0.479886
7)	0.281218	0.000000
8)	0.157930	0.000000
9)	0.109803	0.000000
10)	0.100372	0.000000
11)	0.130707	0.000000
12)	0.255186	0.000000
13)	0.178512	0.000000
14)	0.143652	0.000000
15)	0.197758	0.000000
16)	0.386333	0.000000
17)	1.398609	0.000000
18)	0.000000	0.018713
19)	0.000000	0.001497
20)	10.220608	0.000000
21)	1.612191	0.000000
22)	0.109174	0.000000
23)	3.328871	0.000000
24)	2.803494	0.000000

NO. ITERATIONS = 1

Commentary

R. C. O. Matthews

The article by Cook, Roll, and Kazakov on highway maintenance is a sophisticated attempt at measurement of X-inefficiency. It is of practical value particularly because it relates to areas where performance is not directly subject to the discipline of competition.

Some behavioral questions are raised by the highway maintenance study. The technique used here is the comparison of different producers. It is not surprising that such a comparison shows a dispersion in performance. Indeed it would be surprising if it did not. Dispersion in productivity is always found in census-of-production type data — just as dispersion in performance is always found between students in a class. What degree of dispersion should be regarded as normal and acceptable? An interesting feature of the technique used by the authors is that it focuses on the laggards not on the stars. Yet presumably there should be some stars, the ones especially favored by the chances of history, personnel, or whatever. If producing units that are especially well endowed in some such way do not turn in an outstanding performance, they may be as inefficient relative to their potential as the visible laggards.

Attempts to bring laggards up to the average standard is a management technique currently much in use. Once the laggards have been identified, the question remains what should be done about them. In the case of a multiplant or multiproduct manufacturer, loss makers may in the last resort be closed down. That option is not available in the present instance — the highways have to be maintained everywhere. So presumably the next step is to look more closely into the circumstances of the laggards and try to find out what the trouble is. In that sense study along the present lines is a valuable first step in the task of management, but only a first step.

Part 7
Summary and the Outlook for
X-Efficiency Theory

X-Efficiency: Past, Present, and Future

Roger S. Frantz

In this summary article I will try to provide an overview of the history of X-efficiency (XE) theory and some suggestions for future research. I will do this by discussing four broadly defined areas: (1) the development and historical context of the theory, (2) some of the salient features of the theory, (3) the critical concept of nonmaximization, and (4) suggestions for future research.

Developing the Concept

Professor Leibenstein once began a seminar on the possibility of non-maximizing behavior by stating that one of his assumptions was that members of the seminar were intellectually curious. Because no one wanted to be identified as being noncurious, all the members acted as if they were! Professor Leibenstein was thus able to present his formal remarks without much interruption. Intellectual curiosity is a helpful personality trait when considering an unorthodox idea; it is also one of Professor Leibenstein's traits that led him to develop the concept and theory of X-efficiency. The concept of X-efficiency may be said to have begun in the early 1960s with Professor Leibenstein's observation that one of his graduate students was underutilized. He wondered whether other resources, human or otherwise, are also underutilized. Thus began a research project which led not only to the development of X-efficiency theory but also to the more complete utilization of that graduate student.

Previously published data on firms in several countries were gathered by that now-more-fully-utilized graduate student and reported by Leibenstein in his seminal article on XE theory (Leibenstein 1966). These data indicated that firms were not producing on either production or cost functions. Some of the data indicated that these firms were able to make relatively minor changes in organizational factors such as the layout of the plant, the handling of waste products, and the manner in which they paid their employees that resulted in relatively large gains in output and reductions in costs. To emphasize one point, the increases in output and the reductions in costs were not the effect of changes in input prices, economies of scale, learning by doing, or changes in technology. Other data showed that (nearly) identical plants, some of which were within miles of each other, had very different cost structures. These reported events should not be considered as isolated.[1]

The data indicated that these firms were neither maximizing their output for a given amount of inputs nor minimizing their costs. The data also indicated that some factors other than traditionally defined inputs influence output and costs. What we can now state in retrospect is that these data may also have pointed to the existence of a free lunch. Professor Leibenstein's response to these data was twofold. He investigated the firm from the cost side and inquired into the welfare effects of monopoly power.

The work on the theory of the firm that ensued represents one strand in what has been a rich history in economic thought. According to Alfred Marshall, the "mecca of the economist" is "economic biology": a study of the evolution of the organism known as the economic system. For this one needs to inject as much realism into one's work as possible. Marshall was concerned with realism; he was also concerned with providing a theory of long-run competitive equilibrium, and he knew that the growth of the size of firms made it necessary to accept the existence of economies of scale. How could he explain the growth of firms without conceding that this meant an end to competition? How could he provide a theory of long-run equilibrium without having to assume that all firms were in equilibrium, an assumption that would greatly reduce the realism of his work? He combined a desire to develop theory with a desire for realism by inventing the "representative firm." Marshall was now able to speak about long-run equilibrium under conditions of increasing returns without having to assume that all firms are in equilibrium. The cost of this bit of realism, however, was that he could avoid a detailed study of any single firm. The representative firm was thus a "black box."

It became apparent that perfect competition was the exception rather than the rule. Several theories then emerged that recognized this and were simultaneously able to reconcile increasing returns with competitive equilibrium. These theories of imperfect competition (Joan

---

1. There is a thriving consulting industry in the United States in which consultants continue to make recommendations similar to those reported by Leibenstein (1966). Why firms don't recognize these low-cost (apart from the high consulting fees) changes has been explained with the analogy that "fish are the last ones to know that they are in water." The point is that the obvious is not always obvious, or something like that!

Robinson) and monopolistic competition (Edward Chamberlin) were based on the concept of product differentiation and a firm that held monopoly power in its own product market. These facts had not gone unnoticed by Marshall. Nevertheless, it was others — among them Chamberlin, Robinson, Sraffa, and Harrod — who worked out the theory.

These theories — as well as theories of monopoly, duopoly, and oligopoly — were perhaps more realistic. However, each of these theories of a market structure also treats the firm as a black box by relying on the assumptions of profit maximization and/or cost minimization. Leibenstein was not concerned with advancing the theory of the (representative) firm under various market structures. He wasn't concerned with market structures per se or about the representative firm. His primary interest was with that sample of firms that were apparently not producing on either their production or cost functions. The representative cost-minimizing firm became the object of study rather than an assumption.

Leibenstein, of course, was not the only one studying what was going on within the black box. Others questioned the assumption of profit maximization as the exclusive goal of the firm while assuming that the firm was minimizing its costs. In contrast, Leibenstein questioned the assumption of cost minimization while allowing the firm to set its output at the profit-maximizing level. These other writers included William Baumol (1959), Robin Marris (1963, 1964), and Oliver Williamson (1964), with Tibor Scitovsky (1943) preceding the group by more than 20 years. Others before them had also questioned the assumption of profit maximization without working out their ideas in what we call a formal model, including Marshall himself (1923), Berle and Means (1932), Keynes (1935), and Hicks (1935). Contemporaries of Leibenstein who also questioned the profit-maximizing assumption were Barnard (1962), Cole (1959), and Gordon (1961).

Scitovsky's paper, although appearing over 20 years before Leibenstein's original treatment of XE theory, was original in its approach and served as a paradigm for the others. Scitovsky's model has the manager with a utility function containing income and leisure as its arguments. Scitovsky showed that profit maximization and utility maximization are compatible with each other only under the condition that the marginal rate of substitution of leisure for profits is zero. While entrepreneurs are said to be representative of persons whose work effort is as described, Scitovsky warns that it may not even be true about the representative entrepreneur. Profit maximization may not be descriptive of the real world, but, according to Scitovsky, it vastly simplifies economic analysis.

William Baumol postulated that for the typical oligopolist, the objective is to maximize sales (total revenue) subject to the firm earning some minimum level of profits. Baumol reports that in his experience only once had the president of a major corporation been quoted in the press as stating that he wanted to make his company the most profitable, not the largest, firm in the industry. Baumol comments that this man had previously been an academic economist.

For Robin Marris, managers maximize utility, which is a function of the growth of the firm and their own security. The neoclassical assumption of homogeneous workers and teams leads to the prediction that any management team working in any firm of a given size, with a given labor force, technology, and goodwill should generate the same profits. This is the assumption that the production function is completely known. Among other things, it assumes that familiarity and experience with the firm are not important determinants of productivity. Marris rejected this in favor of the assumption that these elements affect productivity and profits. Thus, because the firm's growth increases the ratio of new to total members, growth reduces average tenure and hence average efficiency. Similarly to Leibenstein, Marris recognized that effort and not time on the job is the critical determinant of productivity. Similarly to Leibenstein in his work on the Prisoner's Dilemma, Marris recognized that effort has a social component as well as a private component.

Oliver Williamson incorporated nonmonetary values into his model of motivation and behavior with an "expense-preference function." Williamson assumes that managers operate the firm so as to maximize their own utility, which is a function of staff, emoluments, and discretionary profits. Managers attempt to maximize this utility function subject to a profits constraint. In contrast to the conventional wisdom that managers are indifferent toward all types of costs or expenses—a dollar is a dollar—the attitude of managers to costs is asymmetric. That is, some types of expenses are preferred over other types. In the category of preferred expenses are those that yield utility to the manager but that cannot be assumed to have a positive impact on the manager's productivity. Managers would thus be able to maximize their own utility simultaneously with the firm's profits if and only if the marginal rate of substitution of profits for staff is zero, implying that the marginal utility for staff is zero. This means that staff is valued only because of its contribution to profits and not because it yields any utility to management. In Williamson's "expense-preference" model, the first is dismissed and the second is unlikely. As with Scitovsky, Baumol, and Marris, Williamson's firm differs from Leibenstein's in that Williamson's is managed by maximizers.

Leibenstein's approach was not to add another variable to a maximizer's objective (utility) function in order to explain nonprofit maximizing behavior. Instead he attempted to forge a more behavioral approach, one that focused less on the analytics of utility functions and more on alternative human motivations and behavior patterns. This approach was not due to his interest in explaining above-minimum costs. Clearly, Scitovsky, Baumol, Marris, and Williamson could have cast their models in terms of the higher than necessary costs incurred because managers were not profit maximizers. Tullock (1967), who observed higher than necessary costs among firms, cited Leibenstein's seminal article on X-efficiency in his own paper on what has become the more orthodox approach to above-minimum costs: rent-seeking. Part of the reason for Leibenstein's unorthodox approach can be explained by a statement that Professor Leibenstein once made. He was commenting on seminars in economic development that he regularly attended at Berkeley when he said that what was apparent was that the formal models presented during the seminars were very different from the experiences that the participants were having while in residence in less developed countries, experiences that were discussed after the seminars. Certain parts of neoclassical theory were clearly troubling him, and the data that he collected and analyzed reinforced his belief that something was missing from orthodox explanations of firm behavior.

Leibenstein thus took the approach that these higher costs were a form of inefficiency, a nonallocative inefficiency. The inefficiency was clearly nonallocative because it was intrafirm, not an inefficiency of the market caused by market power. To be more specific, the inefficiency that Leibenstein saw in the data was different from the allocative-market inefficiency reported by Harberger (1954). The source of this inefficiency was thus unknown. Therefore, it was X-inefficiency.

Salient Features of the Theory

What theoretical conditions support the existence of these nonallocative inefficiencies? That is, why are given inputs not transformed into predetermined outputs? In his seminal article on X-efficiency Leibenstein (1966) discussed four factors or assumptions of the theory. First, labor contracts are incomplete. This gives workers a certain amount of discretion and makes their performance dependent upon motivation. Second, the production function is not completely specified or known. The process of production always contains an experimental element to it such that the firm does not always know in advance the quantity of the output that will be received from given inputs and input ratios. Thus, given inputs will usually be associated with a variety of output rates. Third, not all inputs are marketed and/or are equally accessible to all buyers. For example, management knowledge is not often known and traded in a well-organized market. The motivations of management, at the same time, may be the decisive factor in a firm finding other inputs at the right price, i.e., finances. Fourth, firms may imitate each other rather than compete. Under this circumstance there is no reason to believe that the firm will necessarily produce on its production and cost functions.

In other articles on X-efficiency Leibenstein has used a larger set of assumptions than the one give here, and he has listed a different number of assumptions in different articles. Justified or not, he has been criticized for this tendency. There is another, more important point about the assumptions that underlie X-efficiency theory. Each one of Leibenstein's assumptions can be given a strict neoclassical interpretation and used in a model of cost-minimizing firms and fully rational individuals.[2] For example, labor contracts are incomplete and/or the production function is not fully known because of transaction costs; not all inputs are marketed because of imperfect information; firms imitate because it lowers their all-important research and development costs. Leibenstein's assumptions can, therefore, be used in a model that does not contain any X-inefficiency but rather describes equilibrium solutions under various constraints.[3] I believe that this tendency among his critics has been a source of motivation to Leibenstein, because it has kept him aware that the X in X-efficiency has implications that transcend economic theory. For example, Leibenstein's use of the incomplete labor contracts assumption is that this incompleteness gives an individual the freedom to choose what activities to perform and how to perform them. The individual has the freedom to behave in what would be called in everyday life a rational manner or to slip into counterproductive, habitual, and yet unsatisfying behavior patterns. When an individual does engage in counterproductive behavior he is contributing to X-inefficiency. The tendency for certain economists to emphasize the more orthodox equilibrium under constraints approach served only to focus in Leibenstein's mind the alternative that individuals are free to choose and that the X factor is somehow related to this freedom. Furthermore, an individual has the ability and

---

2. See De Alessi (1983) for an illustration of this.

3. Leibenstein himself, in an attempt to answer his critics who said that XE theory was not consistent with neoclassical theory, showed how it could be. This involves, for example, discussing "inert areas" as depending upon the costs and benefits of change. The reader can see this clearly in several of his works. See, for example, Leibenstein 1969, 1975, 1976. He later realized that this was a mistake. For example, he dropped the pretense that inert areas were the outcome of a cost-benefit calculation and instead attributed them to human psychology. On this point, see his foreword in Frantz 1988.

the freedom to behave in various ways rather than being genetically or otherwise forced to be the fully rational "economic man" of economic theory.

In developing the theory Leibenstein used several concepts in a way that gave them a behavioral or stochastic dimension. Three primary examples of this are his use of the concepts of effort, pressure, and rationality. For example, effort has four components: the activities chosen by the individual in order to complete some task, the pace at which the individual works, the quality or care with which the individual works, and the time or "stop-go" pattern used. Individuals are assumed to have some discretion over each of these patterns, and hence effort is the outcome of many decisions made daily by each individual. Effort can thus range from very high to very low, with the important point that it is not necessarily going to be at the cost-minimizing level. In other words, noncost-minimizing levels of effort are possible. Furthermore, because it is possible to observe these choices, it is possible to observe effort levels. Therefore, one could subject a hypothesis about effort to scientific scrutiny, that is, are effort levels in firm A cost-minimizing or are they not?

The term *pressure* is used in a similar way; pressure is assumed to be a variable that can range from very high to very low. Leibenstein differentiated, in principle, internal from external pressure. Internal pressure is what an individual feels from some inner prodding, be it religious, moral, or cultural, that motivates the individual to perform with a level of effort that contributes to cost minimization. External pressure is discussed as a function of market competition and intrafirm relations with peers and supervisors. Leibenstein focused on external pressure, especially that created by market competition, because he felt that internal pressure had too much of a psychological component whereas external pressure was more the domain of the economist. That is, he knew that internal pressures were important but that they were probably one X too many!

Rationality is presented as capable of being manifest to various degrees, from fully rational to completely irrational. While the latter is not expected, the former is the limiting case, the world in which neoclassical theory is completely adequate. The closest I ever saw Professor Leibenstein come to losing his temper was at the suggestion that he was opposed to neoclassical economics, that he was not a neoclassical economist. This was in the early 1980s. The point is that Leibenstein believes that neoclassical theory is useful for answering some questions but not all questions. Accordingly, its usefulness is strongest when markets are competitive and individuals are fully rational.

For Leibenstein, rationality like effort has behavioral components.

Thus, the question is: What behaviors or decision-making procedures would lead to fully rational decisions? His answer was that fully rational decisions are most likely to be decisions that are based on several factors, including a realistic assessment of the environment; they reflect learning from the past and are not knee-jerk. In fact, his complete list is very similar to the list of characteristics of the personality type that the American psychologist Abraham Maslow refers to as the "self-actualizing" personality. Working in complete independence of Maslow, Leibenstein's X-efficient personality construct greatly resembles Maslow's self-actualizing personality. As with effort, it is possible to observe the degree to which individual decision making corresponds to factors such as realism and learning and is reflexive or knee-jerk in nature.[4]

What is it that leads a person to make fully rational or less than fully rational decisions? This leads us back to pressure. The environment creates external pressure through the effects of intrafirm, interpersonal relations, and market competition (or the lack of it). The personality creates its own pressure because of the demands of the superego and the id. (Although these are terms taken from Freudian psychology, Leibenstein was not at all interested in incorporating Freudian theory into economics.) The superego is described by Leibenstein as that part of us that naturally adheres to standards, that strives for the maximum, the part of us that is calculating and aggressive and focuses on details. On the other hand, the id is the selectively rational part of us that contains our "animal spirits," that chooses to "kick back," to act unconstrained. The two sides are active within us with the degree of rationality depending upon the outcome of this "internal conflict." In incorporating these concepts Leibenstein made an early, if overlooked, contribution to the economic literature of the two selves.[5]

To illustrate the relationship between pressure and X-(in)efficiency, Leibenstein (1986, 1987) has adapted the Yerkes-Dodson law developed by experimental psychologists in 1908. This law, first written about by Robert Yerkes and John Dodson (1908), showed a relationship between the strength of a stimulus and learning (among mice). Leibenstein's adaptation is to discuss a possible relationship between pressure and performance. His hypothesis is that this relationship is represented as a quadratic equation. That is, an individual subjected to relatively low or relatively high levels of pressure will not do as well as possible. On the other hand, there is a medium (optimal) level of pressure under which an

---

4. See Frantz 1980, 1988 for a discussion of the relation between the writings of Maslow and Leibenstein.

5. A brief review of some of this literature can be found in Etzioni 1988.

individual performs best or maximizes. The word *maximization* is thus used in a way that at least allows for the possibility of nonmaximization. Nonmaximization need not be observed. However, it is considered a possible outcome of human behavior.

Concepts such as effort, pressure, and rationality were all used to conceptualize the possibility of nonmaximizing behavior, and hence the possibility of X-inefficiency. It was not Leibenstein's intention to do anything with these concepts. It was enough to present them in a way that resembled their everyday usage and to show that they imply the potential existence of nonallocative, X-(in)efficiency. I believe that he felt that the more sophisticated the model the greater the likelihood of becoming engaged in a war of words and models that meant "losing the forest in the trees." His primary interest in this regard was to develop an alternative framework for looking at human behavior in order to be able to reason about the possible existence of nonallocative (in)efficiency. Doing that was task enough.

Just as Marshall's desire for realism led him to develop the "representative firm," so Leibenstein's desire for realism led him to use the Prisoner's Dilemma framework in explaining intrafirm productivity (Leibenstein 1976, 1982a, 1987). Marshall's representative firm allowed him to work out the details of long-run equilibrium without requiring the unrealistic assumption that all firms are in equilibrium.

In Leibenstein's Prisoner's Dilemma framework, the "selfish-maximizing," cost-minimizing firm and the "selfish-maximizing," effort-minimizing employees are shown to produce the Prisoner's Dilemma solution. Leibenstein then shows that an effort convention such as "a fair day's work for a fair day's pay" is Pareto-superior to the Prisoner's Dilemma — "business as usual" — solution. Effort conventions are also often observed in the real world. They are also shown to be inferior to the Pareto-optimal cooperative "do unto others" solution. However, effort conventions are "stable" solutions to coordination problems for firms. While the selfish-maximizing solution is avoided, the Pareto-optimal solution is prevented. Within this effort convention the degree of X-efficiency may be expected to vary. Therefore, not all employees need be X-inefficient. The convention, however, is a stable solution that includes some X-inefficiency.

Maximization and Nonmaximization

Having developed (the pressure-effort-performance) X-efficiency theory, having seen approximately 60 empirical studies consistent with the implications of the theory published, and having listened to critics dredging up a seemingly endless number of reasons why X-efficiency can't exist, Leibenstein turned his attention more and more to building a case of why nonmaximization can exist and hence why X-inefficiency can exist (Leibenstein 1986, 1987). Given the enormous history of the concept of maximization within economics and the extent to which this has resulted in the language of economics expressing and implying maximization, this was going to be a formidable task. (A similar case is the response to Amitai Etzioni's 1988 attempts to show that decisions made with pleasure in mind and decisions based on moral considerations are not identical.)

To argue the potential existence of nonmaximization requires that maximization be given some procedural or behavioral meaning. Thus, maximization may mean choosing the best available option, doing as well as possible, taking advantage of all opportunities for net gain. Maximization is thus the result of an optimal decision or series of decisions.

Can a decision be sloppy? Can an individual choose poorly? If individuals have a taste for being sloppy or choosing poorly, then the answer is no. If individuals are assumed to be maximizing their utility given their own personal set of constraints, some of which are known only to themselves and in any case are not specified, again the answer is no. Stated in another way, the language of economics belittles any attempt at introducing nonmaximization. On the other hand, there is a commonly understood sense that some decisions are sloppy, poorly conceived, yielding poor results. If so, then nonmaximization is likely to exist.

Do decisions or behaviors carried out according to habit, conventions, rules of thumb, and/or standard operating procedures necessarily display the amount of calculation that produces maximization? Are decisions based on emulation, religious conviction, and/or morality always of a maximizing variety? The argument is not that maximization doesn't exist; the argument is that human decisions may reflect elements of both maximization and nonmaximization (if not at the same time, then at different times under different circumstances). If individuals have free will, then nonmaximization is part of what it means to be human. That is, I have it within myself to be sloppy, to act out of the force of habit, to make poor decisions. The development of X-efficiency theory led to the issues of the nature of human action, issues of free will, issues of the use and abuse of language.

To study those who deny the possibility of nonmaximization and hence the existence of X-inefficiency is to appreciate that Leibenstein's work has inadvertently pointed out a significant shortcoming of neoclassical economics (or at least the version represented by the critics). His critics have not been able to prove their case. That is, they have not been able to prove that X-inefficiency doesn't exist. His critics have been forced to rely on tautologies and/or specify their models in an ex-post manner.[6] Why?

To say that an individual makes an optimizing decision given constraints is not a very helpful statement in the sense that some reasons can always be supplied to explain behavior. If we wish to assert that human behavior is optimal for a given set of constraints, then we must be committed to discovering these constraints. When we analyze (real) market transactions, we are on relatively solid ground, that is, we understand that people respond to market prices given the income and technology constraints and allowing much of the remainder of the world to be controlled under the ceteris paribus assumption. This ceteris paribus assumption is appropriate because we are interested in analyzing market behavior, that is, reactions to prices. However, when our interest is in nonmarket behavior, then the critical constraints facing the individual become the world surrounding that individual. Since these constraints are the critical ones, we cannot set aside the world and the individual's interaction with it through the ceteris paribus assumption.

These constraints come within the boundaries of many other disciplines. It would seem, therefore, that the process of economic models specifying the constraints facing human behavior is in a very early stage. Therefore, it does not seem efficient to limit our models to those in which human behavior is assumed to be only market behavior, that is, aggressive and tightly calculating.

One effect of including the possibility of both maximizing and non-maximizing behavior is that X-efficiency has the potential of being a more powerful research design than neoclassical theory.[7] We can specify two hypotheses about individual behavior: (1) that individuals are (always) maximizers, and (2) that individuals are not (always) maximizers. There are also two actual types of behavior that individuals engage in: they may maximize, or they may not. Thus there are two types of errors that can be made: type one and type two. A type one error in this context means that an individual is hypothesized not to maximize when, in fact, he does maximize. A type two error means that the individual is hypothesized to maximize when, in fact, he does not maximize. Neoclassical theory, by ignoring the possibility of nonmaximizing behavior, sets type one errors equal to zero (by assumption). Accordingly, the neoclas-

---

6. Leibenstein's (1982b) "bull's eye painting economics" is an amusing story illustrating this shortcoming of certain versions of neoclassical economics.

7. This was initially suggested by my colleague Harinder Singh. An account of the use of type one and two errors appears in Singh and Frantz 1988 and Frantz 1988.

sical framework makes the probability of a type two error to be very high. In fact, within this context neoclassical theory represents a vigorous pursuit of type two errors. That is, there is a conscious effort to show that what may appear at first glance to be nonmaximizing behavior is, in fact, maximizing behavior if all relevant factors are taken into account. Some of these factors are summarized using the terms *utility*, *rent-seeking*, *risk aversion*, and *property rights*.

By contrast with the neoclassical framework, XE theory acknowledges the possibility of both maximizing and nonmaximizing behavior, and thus, acknowledges the possibility of both type one and type two errors. As a research design, XE theory is better able to recognize the trade-off between these errors and to attempt to keep both within manageable limits so that empirical tests can be accomplished. Thus neoclassical theory, by assuming that all behavior is maximizing behavior, limits itself to type two errors, that is, why all behavior (maximizing and seemingly non-maximizing) is actually maximizing.

On the other hand, XE theory represents a more comprehensive research design because by acknowledging the possibility of nonmaximizing behavior, it exhausts all eventualities.

Areas for Future Research

Beginning in 1967 with the publication of Shelton's article in the *American Economic Review* (Shelton 1967), approximately 60 articles were published and subsequently reviewed by Frantz (1988). In the vast majority of these articles, the authors themselves claimed that the evidence was consistent with the implications of X-efficiency theory. However, others have pointed out that the evidence in these articles is also consistent with one or more versions of neoclassical theory. Some of these arguments were cast in strictly ex-post, tautological terms and hence could not be falsified. Other arguments could be checked against the data, and some were. These arguments were shown not to be consistent with the data (Frantz and Singh 1988; Frantz, in this volume).

In recent years, however, a different trend seems to be emerging. One illustrative example concerns the journal *Public Choice*. During the 1970s and early to mid-1980s a typical, critical reaction to X-efficiency theory was twofold: first, that (fully) rational individuals cannot be X-inefficient, and second, that the evidence supporting X-efficiency is actually consistent with neoclassical theory. This was stated as if that meant, by definition, that X-inefficiency could not exist. However, beginning in the late 1980s the journal *Public Choice* published three articles (Crew and Rowley 1988; Formby, Keeler, and Thistle 1988; Frantz and Naughton, forthcoming) in which the authors stated that the evidence is consistent with both theories and that some way of distinguishing these theories is required. Although the approaches and suggestions offered in these two articles differ from each other, the important point is that a new acceptance of the theory seems to be emerging.

How are the theories to be differentiated from each other? One approach is to measure the various constraints impinging upon the firm. Leibenstein has spoken about external (environmental) and internal (personality and intrafirm) constraints. Economists of all persuasions are likely to acknowledge that internal constraints are important, yet they exclude them from their models because of measurement issues and a desire to avoid the Pandora's box that such constraints represent. Avoiding internal constraints, however, leads to a specification or missing variables problem. In any study some variables must be measured and others controlled for, that is, not measured. In terms of an effective research design or strategy, it may be more appropriate to control for the external, more easily measurable constraints, and grapple with the internal constraints that are more difficult to measure. One advantage of this approach is that it increases the probability that appropriate controls are being implemented. Second, it forces the researchers to grapple with the difficult measurement issues raised by the inclusion of the internal constraints. While this approach is very challenging, the potential rewards are high, that is, success allows one the ability to carry out more complete, and much needed, tests on the causes of interfirm productivity differences, intrafirm productivity, and the existence of X-inefficiency. For example, it is very difficult to distinguish increases in X-inefficiency from increases in transaction costs. Identifying external and internal constraints may point the way to a distinction. With few exceptions (Bradley and Gelb 1981; Shapiro and Muller 1977; and perhaps Gillis 1982), studies showing X-inefficiency have also focused on external constraints while offering explanations that include internal constraints. (External constraints are easier to measure!) Case studies using an interdisciplinary team of scholars would be useful for this task.

Another area for future research is to define clearly and to work out the implications of nonmaximizing behavior. Assuming that both parties to an exchange are fully rational leads to the conclusion that all voluntary (market) exchanges improve the welfare of both parties. On the other hand, what are the implications if one of the parties is less than fully rational? How would this inclusion of X-inefficiency change both economic theory and its policy prescriptions? This is a question that Leibenstein began to grapple with but that has been left virtually untapped. For example, what would be the implications if employees are more subject to making suboptimal decisions than are the managers? A second example is the effect of an exchange between, say, a fully rational manufacturer and consumers who are prone to nonmaximizing decisions. In general, the concept of suboptimal decisions could lead us to change our perspective on any contractual relations. Perhaps some suboptimal decisions are unavoidable; others are avoidable. It would clearly be useful to be able to identify both types, as it would be to identify when individuals are rational but not maximizing. The existence of systematic errors is one possibility.[8]

Likewise, preventing XE theory from becoming tautological requires operational definitions of both maximum efficiency and/or output and pressure. Is the amount of pressure felt by the individual unique to that individual or is pressure part of a social construction of reality? Experimental economics could contribute to our knowledge of pressure and its effects on decision making and X-inefficiency. Does maximum efficiency and/or full rationality mean working as a sprinter? Not necessarily. Individuals can be walkers but should at least be careful where they walk. Individuals have a wide range of potential behaviors at their disposal, and part of Leibenstein's reasoning about nonmaximizing behavior is this fact of human flexibility. If individuals can move from a nonmaximizing to a maximizing mode, then the economist's Holy Grail—the free lunch—may actually exist. To find X-inefficiency is to find the grail. The concept of nonallocative (in)efficiency is so foreign to economics that these questions, as well as the measurement of X-inefficiency itself, is very difficult. At the end of the conference, participants were still searching for a definitive definition of X-(in)efficiency as well as its causes.

A related area for research is the relationship between X-efficiency and the existence of human freedom (free will). That is, must we all be maximizers or do we have the capacity to express a wider range of behaviors? A nonmechanistic view of human behavior is implicit in X-efficiency theory. A related, perhaps more fundamental question is whether increases in organizational X-efficiency are always desirable if they reduce human freedom.

A more general framework in this regard is X-inefficiency as an externality. For example, if labor and management cannot create an environment conducive to high effort—X-efficiency—then this reduces both firm productivity and national economic growth. Does public policy point to government as the agent for sustaining high-effort conducive labor-management relations? Is government intervention in the economy

---

8. This is discussed in Frey 1988.

one policy implication of XE theory? Is privatization another? What are the policy implications of the theory?

What brought the conference participants together was both a degree of dissatisfaction with the ability of (any of the versions of) neoclassical economics to answer questions of interest and an admiration for Harvey Leibenstein. The issue was neither XE theory nor neoclassical theory. The issue was to take from each theory the area where it has a comparative advantage in increasing our understanding of the world. Determining this comparative advantage requires testing each theory against a world of facts. The research questions posed in this last section are only a few of the many questions derived from XE theory.

REFERENCES

Barnard, C. 1962. *The Functions of the Executive*. Cambridge: Harvard University Press.

Baumol, W. 1959. "The Revenue Maximization Hypothesis." In *Business Behavior, Value, and Growth*, 45–53. New York: Macmillan.

Berle, A., and G. Means. 1932. *The Modern Corporation and Private Property*. New York: Macmillan.

Bradley, K., and A. Gelb. 1981. "Motivation and Control in the Mondragon Experiment." *British Journal of Industrial Relations* 19:211–31.

Cole, A. 1959. *Business Enterprise in Its Social Setting*. Cambridge: Harvard University Press.

Crew, M., and Paul Kleindorfer. 1985. "Governance Structures for Natural Monopoly: A Comparative Institutional Perspective." *Journal of Behavioral Economics* 14:117–40.

Crew, M., and C. Rowley. 1988. "Toward a Public-Choice Theory of Monopoly Regulation." *Public Choice* 57:49–67.

De Alessi, L. 1983. "Property Rights, Transaction Costs, and X-Efficiency: An Essay in Economic Theory." *American Economic Review* 73:64–81.

Etzioni, A. 1988. *The Moral Dimension*. New York: Free Press.

Formby, J., J. Keeler, and P. Thistle. 1988. "X-Efficiency, Rent-Seeking, and Social Costs." *Public Choice* 57:115–26.

Frantz, R. 1980. "On the Existence of X-Efficiency." *Journal of Post Keynesian Economics* 4:509–27.

Frantz, R. 1985. "X-Efficiency Theory and Its Critics." *Quarterly Review of Economic Business* 25:38–58.

Frantz, R. 1988. *X-Efficiency: Theory, Evidence, and Applications*. Norwell, Mass.: Kluwer.

Frantz, R., and M. Naughton. 1989. "A Note on the Disinterest in Deregulation." *Journal of Regulatory Economics* 1:175–81.

Frantz, R., and M. Naughton. Forthcoming. "X-Efficiency, Rent-Seeking, and Social Cost: A Comment." *Public Choice*.

Frantz, R., and H. Singh. 1988. "Intrafirm (In)Efficiencies: Neoclassical and X-Efficiency Perspectives." *Journal of Economic Issues* 22:856–64.

Frey, B. 1988. "Ipsative and Objective Limits to Human Behavior." *Journal of Behavioral Economics* 17:229–48.

Gillis, M. 1982. "Allocative and X-Efficiency in State Owed Mining Enterprises: Comparisons Between Bolivia and Indonesia." *Journal of Comparative Economics* 6:1–23.

Gordon, R. A. 1961. *Business Leadership in the Large Corporation*. Berkeley: University of California Press.

Harberger, A. 1954. "Using the Resources at Hand More Effectively." *American Economic Review* 59:134–47.

Hicks, J. R. 1935. "Annual Survey of Economic Theory: The Theory of Monopoly." *Econometrica* 3:1–20.

Keynes, J. M. 1935. *Essays in Persuasion*. London: Macmillan.

Leibenstein, H. 1966. "Allocative Efficiency vs. 'X-Efficiency.' " *American Economic Review* 56:392–415.

Leibenstein, H. 1969. "Organizational and Frictional Equilibria: X-Efficiency and the Rate of Innovation." *Quarterly Journal of Economics* 83:600–623.

Leibenstein, H. 1975. "Aspects of the X-Efficiency Theory of the Firm." *Bell Journal of Economics* 6:580–606.

Leibenstein, H. 1976. *Beyond Economic Man*. Cambridge, Mass.: Harvard University Press.

Leibenstein, H. 1982a. "The Prisoner's Dilemma in the Invisible Hand: An Analysis of Intrafirm Productivity." *American Economic Review* 72:92–97.

Leibenstein, H. 1982b. "On Bull's-Eye Painting Economics." *Journal of Post Keynesian Economics* 4:460–65.

Leibenstein, H. 1983. "Property Rights Theory and X-Efficiency Theory: A Comment." *American Economic Review* 73:831–42.

Leibenstein, H. 1986. "On Relaxing the Maximization Postulate." *Journal of Behavioral Economics* 15:2–16.

Leibenstein, H. 1987. *Inside the Firm: The Inefficiency of Hierarchy*. Cambridge, Mass.: Harvard University Press.

Marris, R. 1963. "A Model of the Managerial Enterprise." *Quarterly Journal of Economics* 77:185–209.

Marris, R. 1964. *The Economic Theory of Managerial Capitalism*. New York: Free Press.

Marshall, A. 1923. *Industry and Trade*. London: Macmillan.

Rozen, M. 1985. "Maximizing Behavior: Reconciling Neoclassical and X-Efficiency Approaches." *Journal of Economic Issues* 19:661–85.

Scitovsky, T. 1943. "A Note on Profit Maximization and Its Implications." *Review of Economic Studies* 11:57–60.

Shapiro, K., and J. Muller. 1977. "Sources of Technical Efficiency: The Roles of Modernization and Information." *Economic Development and Cultural Change* 25:293–310.

Shelton, J. 1967. "Allocative Efficiency versus 'X-Efficiency': Comment." *American Economic Review* 57:1252-58.

Singh, H., and R. Frantz. 1988. "Maximization Postulate: Type 1 and Type 2 Errors." *Journal of Post Keynesian Economics* 11:100-107.

Tullock, G. 1967. "The Welfare Costs of Tariffs, Monopolies, and Theft." *Western Economic Journal* 5:224-32.

Williamson, O. 1964. *The Economics of Discretionary Behavior: Management Objectives in a Theory of the Firm.* Englewood Cliffs, N. J.: Prentice-Hall.

Yerkes, R., and J. Dodson. 1908. "The Relation of Strength of Stimulus to Rapidity of Habit Formation." *Journal of Comparative Neurology* 18:459-82.

Index

Abelson, R., 216
Abernathy, William J., 128
Adler, Stanley, 78
Agency theory, 132
Agricultural contracts in developing
    countries, 305-6
Akerlof, George A., 78-79, 210, 300,
    306, 324
Alchian, Armen A., 105, 113, 116,
    131, 135-37, 209, 216, 254, 326
Alderfer, Clayton, 82
Allingham, Michael G., 74
Allocative inefficiency, 43-44, 286
Altman, Morris, 3, 324, 347
Altruism and motivation of donors,
    257-59, 264, 315
American Cancer Society, 78
Andel, N., 227
Aoki, Masahiko, 97, 129
APQT, 18, 328
Argyris, Chris, 139, 210-11, 214-15,
    218
Ashworth, M. H., 286
AT&T, 214-15
Atkinson, Anthony G., 74
Austrian economics, 12n, 20-22
Avis, Warren E., 127
Azariadis, Costas, 97

Babbage, C., 290
Bacon, R., 282
Balance of payments, 280-81
Bardhan, P., 295-96, 306
Barnard, C., 375
Barnett, Corelli, 282
Barney, J., 129
Baumol, William J., 27-28, 32,
    375-77

Beck, Martin, 229, 231, 315
Becker, Gary S., 72, 74, 79, 82, 97,
    133, 258
Beckerman, W., 278
Behavior of agents: actual, 182-84,
    188-89, 193-95; deviating, 192;
    instrumental, 188; standards of,
    182, 184-88, 190, 194-95
Benefits of work, noneconomic,
    165-66
Berkessel, P., 155
Berle, A., 375
Bernstein, Paul, 129
Beveridge, Lord, 266
Bianchi, Susan M., 79
Bierman, Harold, 82
Blackaby, F., 278
Blake, Robert R., 127
Blois, K. J., 326
Boes, Dieter, 74
Bohanon, C. E., 227
Bohm-Bawerk, Eugen V., 20
Bohnet, Armin, 3, 229, 231, 315
Borgida, Eugene, 78
Bosch, Gerhard, 157
Boskin, Michael J., 271, 272
Boulding, Kenneth E., 268, 270
Bowles, S., 303
Bradley, K., 385
Brehemer, B., 83, 210
Brittan, Samuel, 286
Brown, C. V., 227
Brown, William, 158

Campbell, John, 132
Cantillon, Richard, 20
Carlsson, Bo, 38, 57
Carter, C., 278

Chamberlin, Edward H., 19, 375
Charities, 3, 253–75; definition of, 254; efficiency of, 259–68, 315, 317; entrepreneurial, 265–68; functions of, 256–57; tax privilege of, 271–72; types of, 254–56; and X-efficiency, 317–18. *See also* Altruism.
Charnes, A., 351
Chesterman, Michael, 262–63, 265, 271
Ciborra, Claudio, 3, 223–24
Clark, J. M., 20
Clark, Kim B., 128
Coase, R. H., 39, 303
Coercive processes, 86–89
Cole, A., 375
Comanor, W. S., 39
Commons, John R., 21
Competition: and contestability, 32; and external pressures, 331, 338–39; imperfect product market, 338; perfect, and X-inefficiency, 324–25, 347–48
Competitive pressures, 338
Consumer choice, 13; and experimental, 13; and Veblen, 13
Contestability theory, 27–28, 31–38, 39–40, 64–66; and costs, 32–37
Contracts, incomplete, 8, 10, 15, 17, 18
Conventions, 21, 302, 306–7. *See also* Norms
Cook, Wade D., 369
Cooper, C. L., 166
Cooper, W. W., 351
Coursey, D., 35
Crain, M., 46, 53
Crandall, Rick, 78
Crew, M., 51, 52, 384–85
Cyert, Richard, 20, 132

Das Adam Smith Problem, 18, 21
Data Envelopment Analysis (DEA), 351, 354; and extensions of the model, 362–64; model, 354–59

Davis, Louis E., 128–29
De Alessi, L., 53–56, 130, 131, 133, 205, 213, 219, 228, 299, 327, 378
Decision-making units, 17; and measurement of efficiency, 351–67
Decision-making processes within firms and organizations, 304
de Finetti, Bruno, 75
de Janvry, A., 295n
Demographic transition, 11
Demography, 13–14
Demsetz, Harold, 105, 113, 116, 131, 135–36, 138, 209, 254, 326
Dickens, William T., 78–79, 210
DiLorenzo, T., 53
Discretion, 8, 10. *See also* Work effort
Dodson, John, 380
Dombois, Rainer, 157
Dopfer, Kurt, 2, 201
Dore, Ronald, 333
Downs, Anthony, 262

Easley, David, 254
Economies of scale, 29
Edgeworth, F. Y., 217
Edwards, P., 111
Efficiency: and role of power, 288; sociological use of, 287–89
Efficiency frontier, 351
Efficiency gap analysis, 364–66
Efficiency measures, 353
Effort supply, 127, 130, 133, 323–35, 337; and production, 130. *See also* Effort-utility; Income tax increase; Motivation
Effort-utility, 134–43, 329–35
Eichenberger, Reiner E., 74
Einhorn, Hillel J., 83, 210
Elbaum, B., 282, 284
Elster, Jon, 86–87
Eltis, W., 282
Employment relationship. *See* Worker behavior on the job
England, George W., 2, 166–67, 199–200

Entrepreneurs, 132, 143, 289–92, 315–16
Estrin, Saul, 106
Etzioni, A., 217–18, 380, 382

Fabricant, Solomon, 14n
Fare, R., 246, 249
Farrell, M. J., 298, 351
Feingold, Mordechai, 273
Feldstein, Martin S., 271–72
Festinger, L., 210
Fiol, C. M., 208
Firm. *See* Theory of the firm
Firm characteristics: implicit contracting and, 118–24; mean-lean, 116–18, 121–24
Firm hierarchy, 211–12, 333–36
Fischoff, Baruch, 75
Fitzroy, Felix R., 106–7
Foppa, Klaus, 71
Formby, J., 384–85
Forsund, F., 52
Fox, A., 131, 137
Francis, Arthur, 277–78, 289, 291, 316, 318–19
Frankfurt, Harry G., 87
Frantz, Roger, 2, 3, 27, 53, 64, 67, 133, 324–25, 330, 378, 380, 383–85
Freeman, J., 210
Freeman, Richard B., 98, 324
Free-rider, 308
Frey, Bruno S., 2, 71, 74, 84, 147–48, 210, 215, 386
Friesen, H., 207
Fürstenberg, Frederick, 2, 157–58, 199

Gahvari, F., 227
Galbraith, Jay, 129
Galenson, Walter, 14
Game theory and inefficiency, 17, 132
Gelb, A., 385
Giddens, A., 288
Gillis, M., 385
Gintis, H., 303

Golany, B., 369
Goldberg, Victor, 132
Gordon, R. A., 375
Goudriaan, Rene, 84
Gregory, R., 58
Grosskopf, S., 246, 249
Grossman, S., 97
Growth rate of the United Kingdom, 279–80, 281–82; and X-inefficiency, 283–86
Gunn, Christopher E., 106
Gwartney, J., 227

Hackman, J. R., 128, 130, 135
Haefner, D., 76
Hall, Robert E., 97
Hannan, M. T., 210
Harberger, A., 43
Harris, J. E., 131, 136
Harrod, R. F., 279, 375
Hart, O. D., 98
Hatch, John, 63–64, 66
Hauser, K., 227
Hausman, J. A., 227
Hedberg, B., 208
Heilemann, U., 227
Heiner, R. A., 215, 217
Hicks, J. R., 375
Hicks-Samuelson-Solow neoclassical economics, 18
Highway maintenance patrols, 351–67; pilot study of, 359–66
Hirsch, Fred, 129, 131
Hirschman, Albert O., 79, 87
Hobbes, Thomas, 20–21
Hogarth, Robin M., 74–75, 83
Holtmann, A., 56–57, 267
Hufton, Olwen, 269
Hume, David, 263
Humml, K., 155

Immerwahr, J., 128–29
Implicit contracting, 118–24, 148; definition of, 96; types of, 97–99, 102–3. *See also* Worker behavior on the job

Income maintenance, state role in, 268–73

Income tax increase: effect on work effort–effort supply after tax increase, 234–36; effect on work effort–effort supply before tax increase, 232–34; management reaction, 239–42; model, 230–32, 236–39; worker reaction to, 239–42

Inefficiency: and intrafirm behavior, 58–59; nonallocative aspects of, 11, 43

Inert areas, 8, 17–18, 134, 140, 212–14, 231, 233–36, 238, 336–37

Innovation, 208–9, 286, 318

Institutions in developing countries, 295–312; aspects of, 302–3, 316; and X-efficiency, 296–99, 300, 304–5, 311, 316

Internal pressures, 335

International competitive position of the United Kingdom, 3, 277–92, 318; market share of, 279–80; and X-efficiency, 316

Ipsative possibility set. See Subjectivism

Isaac, R. M., 35

James, D., 58

James, Estelle, 266

Job evaluation, 155–56

Job satisfaction, 244–45

Job-worker matching, 103–5

Johnson, Samuel, 279

Jones, Derek C., 106

Kagelas, S. S., 76

Kahneman, Daniel, 74–75, 210

Kalman, Peter J., 19

Kantrow, Alan M., 128

Katz, Arnold M., 78

Kay, J. A., 286

Keeler, J., 384–85

Kelly, G. A., 211

Kendrick, John W., 323

Keyes, Ralph, 78

Keynes, J. M., 375

Kilby, Peter, 323

Kirscht, J., 76

Kirzner, Israel M., 265

Klein, B. H., 207–8

Knight, F. H., 208

Koch, W. A. S., 227

Kraft, Kornelius, 106–7

Kunreuther, Howard, 78

Labor productivity differentials: as demonstration of X-inefficiency, 323–48; interregional, 344; wage rate, 38–41, 47, 323–25

Labor supply. See Effort supply; Effort-utility

Langer, Ellen, 78

Lawrence, R. Z., 278

Lazonick, W., 282, 284

Learning, varieties of: by doing, 207; by using, 208; innovational, 208, 212, 216; limited, individual, 209–10; organizational, 212–13

Lecaillon, J. C., 311–12

Leibenstein, Harvey, 39, 54–55, 79, 97, 129, 133–37, 139, 142, 153, 161, 179, 183–85, 191, 193–94, 205, 211, 213–15, 219, 229, 231, 257, 268, 283, 288–89, 296–300, 303, 311, 318–19, 323–24, 336–38, 342, 351, 373–83, 385–87; and demography, 11–12; and precursors of X-efficiency theory, 17–22, 63, 65; and X-efficiency, 1–2, 3, 7–11, 15–17

Levin, H., 49

Lewicki, Roy W., 76

Lichte, Rainer, 157

Likert, Rensis, 128, 153

Linde, R., 228

Loasby, B. J., 211, 217

Locke, John, 52

Louhamaa, H., 211

Lovell, C., 52, 246, 249

Lutz, Burkart, 161

Lyles, M. A., 208

MacCrimmon, Kenneth R., 75
McGuiness, T., 289–90
McKenzie, Richard, 74
MacNeil, Jan R., 139
Maitel, Shiomo, 30, 87
Management theory: and X-efficiency, 17; and organizational entropy, 17
Managerial pattern of control, 154, 199
March, James G., 2, 20, 28, 74, 78, 82, 132, 209, 211
Marglin, S., 289, 291
Margolis, Howard, 87
Marris, Robin, 375–77
Marshall, Alfred, 13, 18–19, 374–75, 381
Martin, J., 49
Maslow, Abraham, 380
Masuch, M., 209
Matthews, R. C. O., 3, 299, 301–2, 315, 317–18
Maximizing behavior, 8, 11, 20, 185
Meade, James E., 106–7
Means, G., 375
Medoff, James L., 98, 324
Menchik, Paul, 264
Menger, Carl, 20–21
Merit rating, 157
Microeconomic theory, 1, 11–12
Micro-microanalysis, 17
Mill, John Stuart, 259
Miller, D., 207
Minimax, 20
Minsky, M., 216
Mintzberg, Henry, 132
Mitchell, Wesley Clair, 11 n.1, 20
Miyazaki, Hajime, 107
Morgenstern, Oskar, 12 n.1, 20–21
Morrison, H., 311–12
Morrison, S. A., 35
Motivation, 119, 127, 130, 134
Mouton, Jane S., 127
Mowet, Charles Loch, 260

MOW International Research Team, 165, 167, 169, 177
Muller, J., 385
Mundell, R., 43
Murray, G. J., 264

Naughton, M., 384–85
Nelson, Richard R., 132, 208–9, 216, 323
Neoclassical theory, 1, 12; and demand, 28; and X-efficiency, 17–18
Newell, A., 75
Ng, Y. K., 39, 48
Nisbett, Richard E., 78, 210
Nonmaximizing maximizing behavior, 381–86
Nonprice uncompetitiveness, 285–86
Nonprofit sector: definition of, 3, 254; and highway maintenance patrols, 351. *See also* Charities
Nonwage shelters from competition, 341–43
Norman, D. A., 216
Norms: efficiency, 154–63, 194; entitlement, 167; social, 153, 167; social conflict, 158–60. *See also* Behavior of agents
Nossiter, B. D., 281
Notestein, Frank, 12
Nugent, J., 300, 303, 306, 308

Objective function of owners and workers, 328, 334–37; differing, 327–28, 334–37; identical, 326; and principals and agents, 191
OECD/CERI, 128
Offe, Carl, 158
O'Hara, Maureen, 254
Oi, Walter, 132
Oldham, G. R., 128, 130
Olson, Mancur, 129, 137, 309
Opportunism, 205, 216–18, 223, 263–65
Organization, Marxian view of work, 132

Organizational change: evolutionary, 208; radical, 206-7, 216-17, 223-24
Organizational control vs. learning, 211-12
Organizational efficiency, 130-32, 137-42
Organizational flexibility vs. efficiency, 207-9, 223
Organization structuring, 153-63
Ouchi, William, 129, 130 n.2
Owen, David, 268

Panzar, J. C., 27
Pareto, Vilfredo, 21
Parish, R., 39, 48
Pascoe, G., 57
Pasour, E., Jr., 50
Pauly, Mark, 254
Payne, John W., 83
Payne, R., 166, 282
Peel, D., 49
Peer group, 336
Pejovich, S., 130
Penrose, E., 33
Perfect and imperfect competition theory, 374-75
Performance testing, 157-58
Perlman, Mark, 2, 21, 63, 65-66
Perotin, Virginie, 106
Perrow, Charles, 132
Pifer, Alan, 255, 270
Piore, Michael J., 127-28
Pommerehne, Werner W., 84
President's Commission on Industrial Competitiveness, 278
Pressure, 379-80
Primeaux, W., 35, 57
Prisoner's Dilemma, 8-10, 11, 136, 304, 311, 335, 338-39, 381
Pritchard, Robert D., 132
Production functions, 14-15, 130; Cobb-Douglas, 14n
Property rights, 131, 302-3
Pryor, Frederic L., 106

Psychology and economics. See Subjectivism
Putterman, Louis, 129

Quintinilla, A. R., 166-67

Rationality, 11, 20, 133, 185, 188-90, 379-80
Reder, Melvin, 74
Redisch, Michael, 254
Reed, Harvey, 78
Reich, Robert R., 127-28
Rent-seeking, 377
Rethans, A., 76
Reynolds, R. J., 34
Rhodes, E., 351
Robertson, D. H., 96
Robertson, L. S., 78
Robinson, Joan, 13, 19, 374-75
Roll, Y., 30, 369
Rosen, Sherwin, 98, 230
Rosenberg, N., 207-8
Rosenstock, I. M., 76
Ross, L., 210
Rowley, C., 284-85
Rozen, Marvin, 2, 147-48
Runge, C. F., 303

Sabel, Charles F., 127-28
Sadoulet, E., 295
Sah, R. K., 302-3, 308
Salaman, G., 287
Salter, W. E. G., 323
Sandmo, Agnar, 74
Satisficing behavior, 82, 133, 209-10
Savage, Leonard J., 75
Say, J. B., 20
Schank, R., 216
Schap, David, 45
Schelling, Thomas C., 87
Schmidt, P., 52
Schmoelders, Guenther, 82
Schneider, H., 311-12
Schoemaker, Paul J., 74-75, 89
Schultze, C., 98, 114

Schumpeter, Joseph A., 20, 32–33, 206
Schwartz, M., 34
Schwartzman, D., 30
Scitovsky, Tibor, 52, 334, 375–77
Scullion, H., 111
Sen, Amartya K., 86, 217, 269
Seniority, 156–57
Shackle, G. L. S., 20
Shapira, Zur, 74, 78, 82
Shapiro, K., 385
Sharp, T. A. E., 286
Shefrin, H. M., 87
Shelton, J., 56, 384
Shen, T. Y., 324
Shepherd, W., 34, 56
Shimada, Haruo, 333
Simon, Herbert A., 16, 73, 75, 82, 132, 185, 209, 326
Singh, Harinder, 383–84
Slovic, Paul, 74–75, 210
Smith, V. L., 35
Social contract, 20
Solow, R., 114, 324
Spain, Daphne, 79
Sraffa, Piero, 19, 375
Standards. *See* Norms
State, role of, in developing countries, 308–12
Stephen, Frank H., 106
Stigler, George J., 16, 27, 48, 50, 72, 131, 133, 213, 327
Stiglitz, Joseph E., 74, 97, 302–3, 308
Stone, K., 291
Strickland, Lloyd, 78
Strotz, Robert H., 87
Stroup, R., 227
Subjectivisim: ipsative and objective possibility sets, 71–89, 147–48
Sugden, Robert, 258
Sutcliffe, R. B., 345
Svejnar, Jan, 106
Svenson, O., 76

Takeuchi, Hiroshi, 332–33
Taylor, James C., 129
Thaler, Richard H., 87
Theory of the firm, 129–32, 374–76; implicit contracting, 118–24; mean-lean, 116–18, 120–23; restructuring, 127–29
Thirwall, A. P., 279
Thistle, P., 384–85
Thorbecke, Erik, 3, 311–12, 315–16, 319–20
Thurow, Lester C., 129, 137
Todd, D., 246
Tomer, John F., 127, 139
Transaction costs, 130–32, 205, 215–19, 296, 299–301, 303, 305–6, 310–11, 316, 319–20
Tullock, Gordon, 45, 74, 377
Tversky, Amos, 74–75, 210

Uncertainty, 20
Utility maximization with uncertainty, 72, 74, 59–81, 82–89

Van Cott, T. N., 227
Vanek, Jaroslav, 106
Van Raaij, Fred W., 78
Varian, Hal, 1
Vecchio, R., 165
von Loeffelholz, J. D., 227
von Neumann, John, 20
von Weiser, Friedrich, 20

Wage functions, 99–102
Wages, relative increase in, 31, 343–44, 347
Wagner, H., 228
Walras, Leon, 21
Ward, J., 169
Warr, B., 165
Watcher, M., 136
Webb, Beatrice, 260
Weck-Hannemann, Hannelore, 84
Wehrung, Donald A., 75
Weiler, Paul, 103

Weiermair, Klaus, 2, 134–35, 137, 139
Weiner, M., 281
Weinstein, Neil D., 76–77
Weisbrod, Burton A., 264, 270
Weiss, L., 57
Whitely, W. T., 166–67
Whyte, William F., 162
Williamson, Oliver E., 55, 98, 131,
    135–36, 141, 205, 208–9, 214–16,
    259, 263, 278, 283, 375–77
Willig, R. D., 27
Willman, P., 287
Winston, C., 35
Winston, Gordon C., 86
Winter, Sidney G., 132, 208–9,
    216–17
Wishart, D., 169
Work effort: effect on tax on,
    232–36, 315; model based on X-
    efficiency, 229–32, 236–39
Worker behavior on the job, 105–8;
    strategic behavior, 110–16
Work goals, 167–69, 199–201
Work patterns; components of,

169–70; and country differences
    (West Germany, Japan, U.S.),
    173–77; meanings of, 165–80, 199;
    sample of, 169
Work satisfaction, 177–80, 240–45
World trade, U.K. share of, 279–80
Wrigley, E. A., 270

X-Efficiency: areas for research,
    385–87; and contestability, 36–38,
    39–40, 64–66; criticisms of, 45–57,
    64, 67; economies of size and scale,
    29–31; history of economic
    thought, 17–22, 63, 65–66; sum-
    mary, 7–11, 377–88; and West
    German manufacturing, 246–49

Yang, X., 307
Yankelovich, D., 128–29
Yellen, Janet L., 97, 324
Yerkes-Dodson Law, 331, 335, 380
Yerkes, Robert, 380

Zardkoohi, A., 46, 53